Language and the law

LANGUAGE IN SOCIAL LIFE SERIES

Series Editor: Professor Christopher N. Candlin

Language and the law

Edited by John Gibbons

LONGMAN

LONDON AND NEW YORK

Longman Group UK Limited,
Longman House, Burnt Mill,
Harlow, Essex CM20 2JE, England
and Associated Companies throughout the world.

Published in the United States of America
by Longman Publishing, New York

© Longman Group UK Limited 1994

First published 1994

ISBN 0–582–229766 CSD
ISBN 0–582–10145–X PPR

British Library Cataloguing-in-Publication Data

A catalogue record for this book is available from the British Library

Library of Congress Cataloging in Publication Data

Language and the law / edited by John Gibbons.
     p.   cm. – (Language in social life series)
    Includes bibliographical references and index.
    ISBN 0-582-22976-6 (cased). – ISBN 0–582–10145–X (paper)
    1. Law–Language. 2. Legal composition. 3. Psycholinguistics.
4. Language–Philosophy. I. Gibbons, John, 1946- . II. Series.
K213.L35   1994   93–5621
340'.014–dc20   CIP

Typeset by 8 in 10/12pt Palatino
Produced by Longman Singapore Publishers (Pte) Ltd.
Printed in Singapore

Contents

v

List of Contributors

Professor **Rebecca White Berch**, Solicitor General, State of Arizona, and Arizona State University, USA
Dr **Vijay K. Bhatia**, City Polytechnic of Hong Kong, Hong Kong
Dr **Bryna Bogoch**, Bar Ilan University, Ramat Gan, Israel
Dr **Mark Brennan**, Charles Sturt University, New South Wales, Australia
John Carroll, Solicitor, Australian Capital Territory, Australia
Dr **Malcolm Coulthard**, University of Birmingham, England
Professor **Brenda Danet**, The Hebrew University of Jerusalem, Israel
Dr **Diana Eades**, The University of New England, Australia
Dr **Robert Eagleson**, New South Wales, Australia
Dr **John Gibbons**, The University of Sydney, Australia
Dr **Laurence Goldman**, The University of Queensland, Australia
Professor **Sandra Harris**, Nottingham Trent University, England
Wendell A. Harris, Philadelphia, USA
J. Dyson Heydon QC, Selbourne Chambers, New South Wales, Australia
Alex Jones, The University of Sydney, Australia
Professor **William Labov**, The University of Pennsylvania, USA
Yon Maley, Macquarie University, Australia
Dr **Francis Nolan**, University of Cambridge, England
Her Honour **Judge Margaret O'Toole**, Compensation Court of New South Wales, Australia
Professor **Bethyl A. Pearson**, Grand Canyon University, USA
Dr **Jane Simpson**, The University of Sydney, Australia
Dr **Wilfrid Smith**, University of Ulster at Jordanstown, Northern Ireland
Dr **Michael Walsh**, The University of Sydney, Australia

General Editor's Preface

For a Series Editor a good point to begin might be to argue why John Gibbons' comprehensive editing of **Language and the Law** should find a natural home in the *Language in Social Life Series*. Why in addition to its considerable explanatory value to professionals concerned with the law this book contributes distinctively to a particular understanding of how language functions in society.

By language *in* social life we have in mind how the critical study of language in its everyday, as well as here in its professional and institutional usages, enables us to illuminate and explain issues of social concern within such professions and such institutions. More specifically, enabling us to explore using a range of linguistic tools the ways in which our communication is both constrained by the structures and forces of those social institutions within which we function as members and how, in a parallel manner, such institutions and our roles within them are defined and maintained by particular language use.

Such an agenda evokes three points of reference, a triangle of forces if you like, which interconnect at particular crucial moments in critical communicative sites, all three of which points are necessary for the elucidation of that mutually defining relationship between language and social life we have so far asserted: the description and interpretation of language as discourse, the explanation of social structure, and the ethnographic understanding of the context of particular professional and institutional practices. It is crucial that each of these reference points is defined in relation to each of the others. Language, for this Series, is no autonomous construct, simply a set of forms, but language defined as discourse, as action; similarly society is no mere mosaic of individual existences locked into stratified structures but defined as a dynamic structuration of relationships, roles and practices characterised by struggles for power; professions defined in terms of memberships linked to institutions whose conventional behaviours are ideologically shaped by such social relations, realised and regularly confirmed by particular discourses.

On this view, then, language is characteristically a social practice, not some phenomenon external to society to be adventiously correlated with it. Language as discourse is not merely the delicate description of the products of language, texts, but also a sensitive exploration of the conditions surrounding and imbuing the production and the interpretation of language of which the text as product is only the most obvious part. Language in social life, therefore, and in this Series, marks a movement away in language study from a focus only on the descriptive towards an exploration of the interpretive, including the participants in the linguistic process and seeking to reconcile the cognitive, the social and the textual. Above all, the Series exists to explore the contention that our understanding of the social order is most easily and conveniently achieved through a critical awareness of the power of language; to recognise that access to and participation in the power forums of society depend largely on a mastery of their discourses and through that knowledge and that communicative competence to enable the achievement of personal, social and professional goals.

Given the above, and given the popular, professional and academic attention paid to the language of the law, there is perhaps a certain inevitability in the selection of the Law as a field of social life for exploration. As several of the authors indicate, and John Gibbons reinforces in his editorial Introductions, many of the essential concepts of the law are shared by linguists; the two professions draw in part on a common epistemology. Not that language *is* the law or the law language, but undeniably it is through language and as much through specifically focused everyday language as through specialist terminologies that the law is constructed, evidenced and transmitted. Not that the connection is only synchronic; as some of the papers exemplify in considerable detail, this association of language with law offers the reader also a diachronic perspective on how, historically speaking, literacy and law can be seen to have enjoyed parallel development.

Implicit in the thinking underpinning the *Language in Social Life Series* is a concern with disadvantage, inequity and social disorder, not because one would want naively to attribute to language either ultimate causes of such disadvantage and disorder, or more romantically perhaps because we believe that a greater critical awareness of how language functions in social contexts will magically permit the restoration of the social and personal equilibrium that many, especially the disadvantaged rightly seek. Nonetheless, it is just that explanatory and critical dimension that charaterises books within the Series, and no more so than this present one. Indeed, Part Two of **Language and the Law** explicitly focuses on language and disadvantage before the law and does so not only by adducing representative cases that target the linguistic sources of inequity, but also by throwing into relief and debating the fundamental legal question of the relationship between law and justice. Language, it turns out, is a valuable tool in such a professional discourse. John Gibbons rightly calls for vigilance in our monitoring of the practices of the law. As he would no doubt agree, vigilance, like awareness, is not enough. We need *informed* vigilance, in short, we need linguistic evidence.

It is precisely the nature of such evidence that is especially targetted in Part Three of the book, focusing as it does on *forensic linguistics*. There is however a temptation in dealing with the analysis of evidence that we focus closely, perhaps too closely on the text, the observable data and product of the law. Much recent work has, naturally enough perhaps, taken this line, imaginatively utilising a broad range of linguistic techniques, prosodic, lexical, syntactic and semantic, and a full range of increasingly sophisticated techical resources in the service of grounding legal arguments in accurate description. For a language in social life, however, as I have argued earlier, the text is not enough. Equally important are the conditions of production and interpretation of the text. Under what conditions was this text produced and interpeted, by whom, when, where and why? Evidence also needs this interpretive dimension if it is to be used to explain behaviour. However, obtaining that linguistic evidence is fraught with difficulty, not just in terms of its recording and its presentation but, crucially, in terms of the difficult role relationship between researcher and researched that the contexts of this book imply. John Gibbons alludes to this dilemma facing forensic linguists in his Introduction. As with all language in social life, the moral and the social cannot be excluded from the textual.

Characteristic of the books in the *Language in Social Life Series* is their attitude to the relationship between theory and practice and to the connections to be made between the language specialist and the professional practitioner. In **Language and the Law** we see both of these precepts carefully honoured. Not only are the papers themselves evidence of the close contact between linguists and lawyers but the introduction of specifically invited legal commentaries greatly enhances the editorial apparatus of the book. More than that, if offers as far as is possible in a two dimensional book some reflection of the debate that any such interdisciplinary endeavour ought to engender. For linguist readers what we see here is the critical application of their tools of trade put to the test in the workshop of another profession. As in all proving exercises, the tools themselves change and are revalued under stress. As linguists we discover what our tools can do and what they cannot. As lawyers, we may venture that to the measure that language is the stuff of law then language in social life is not arcane but germane to the legal enterprise. Certainly for both audiences and for the wide population whose access to justice is made or barred by the language of the law, the resources in these papers and in the uniquely comprehensive bibliography provide the wherewithal for social as well as narrowly legal explanation.

Professor Christopher N Candlin
General Editor
Centre for Language in Social Life
Macquarie University, Sydney.

Acknowledgements

We are indebted to the following for permission to reproduce copyright material:

Cambridge University Press for extracts from *Anglo Saxon Wills* by Dorothy Whitelock (1930); William Power for his statement and evidence used in the article 'Powerful Evidence for the Defence: An Exercise in Forensic Discourse Analysis' by Malcolm Coulthard.

PART I

LANGUAGE CONSTRUCTING LAW

INTRODUCTION

Language constructing law

John Gibbons

Goldman in his chapter for this book makes the very important point that many legal concepts, such as accident and liability, are based upon concepts which appear universal across human languages, for instance happenings which have an agent and those which do not (agentive and non-agentive happenings are grammaticalised as transitivity or ergativity). The basic concepts of the rights and obligations of a member of a community are deeply embedded in the fabric of language itself, and existed before there were codified laws. Furthermore, the concepts which now construct legal systems such as 'guilt' and 'murder' are available to us only through the medium of language. There is then a very important sense in which language constructs the law (hence the title of the first part of this collection).

Laws are in essence attempts to control human behaviour, mainly through a system of penalties for law breaking. The law exists to discourage murder and theft, and bad faith in business dealings among other offences. There are two main aspects of the law – the legal code, and legal processes. The legal code is not designed to cover a single instance of human behaviour, but rather a range of related behaviours in a delimited range of situations. The main problem is saying neither too much, and thus having an oppressive legal code, nor too little, and so licensing instances of behaviour that are unacceptable. This is of course very much a language problem. Legal proceedings are usually concerned with testing the applicability of the generalisations found in the legal code to individual instances of behaviour or to particular cases. This is managed with very small exceptions through language, so for example trials are linguistic events. Language is then central to the law, and law as we know it is inconceivable without language. Many lawyers pride themselves

3

upon their mastery of language, and regard such mastery as a critical skill for legal professionals.

The first part of this book examines this relation between language and the law, in particular the nature of the language of the law and the sources and reasons for this nature. Maley's chapter is given first because it presents a masterly survey of the current uses of language in the law, thereby framing all the chapters which follow. I shall return to it repeatedly in my discussions. Of particular note is Figure 1.1 which summarises and clarifies the various text and discourse types encountered when analysing the language of the law.

The chapters in Part I illustrate various phases in the development of the language of the law, as these mirror literacy development in the culture of which the law is part. Cultures can be seen as moving through pre-literate, literate and post-literate stages (sometimes more than once, as seems to have happened in Western Europe where the literate Roman Empire was replaced in many places by largely illiterate cultures until the Renaissance). The chapters which constitute Part I range across these stages as follows:

Pre-literate	Transition	Literate	Transition	Post-literate
Goldman	Danet and Bogoch	Maley Bhatia Harris	Pearson and Berch	(Danet and Bogoch)

THE PRE-LITERATE STAGE

Goldman's chapter describes aspects of a pre-literate legal system. It shows that there are well-established formalised social processes for legal disputation through which judgments are obtained. These do not appear to be different in type from other decision-making processes of a political or administrative type. Furthermore, while there is a discourse or genre for disputation, Goldman makes it clear that there is not a specific legal register or jargon. In discussing the absence of a defined term for 'liability' he writes 'None of the terms . . . can be said to represent some specially adapted or developed register'. Instead he demonstrates most convincingly that the resources of everyday language are used to express this complex concept. One characteristic of the law in pre-literate cultures is the relative lack (although not a total absence) of *codification* of the law. This means that few concepts have undergone the process of re-ification (usually nominalisation) into specific legal terminology which is typical of literate societies. Goldman also shows how even trained anthropologists can be sufficiently ethno-centric as to mistake the absence of codification for the absence of the concept.

THE TRANSITION TO LITERACY

It is Danet and Bogoch's chapter which most directly addresses the relationship between literacy and the language of the law. They examine the development of the language of wills in a society where literacy was becoming more established, namely Anglo-Saxon England. They plot the changes which occurred as oral wills became written. As much work in this area has already shown (see, for example, Tannen 1982), the transition involved a movement away from dependence on immediate physical context to much lower context dependency. Danet and Bogoch also uncover a change in the functionality of written texts, from being an adjunct to and record of the spoken text, to the modern condition where it is the written text which actually performs the function of willing property. The linguistic consequences of these developments are several, for example in a spoken will assumptions can be made about shared knowledge – those present will know when the will was made, and what property the testator has. In a written will such assumptions are less valid, so such details as dates, and specific details of property must be included. Those present at an oral will would also naturally be addressed directly, using for example the second person pronoun, while this is less appropriate in the more objective written will. The acceptance of the increased speech act functionality of written will, which is noted also in Maley's chapter, makes unnecessary the curses used to strengthen oral Anglo-Saxon wills. Increased functionality is also manifested through the development of a stable text type or genre. This is predictable, since Martin (1992) and others have established that genres develop in order to perform specific socio-cultural functions. Danet and Bogoch show that neither the presence nor the ordering of the stages of wills had fully stabilised in Anglo-Saxon England, each seems to be generated afresh with little of the uniform routinised language of the modern written will – in other words the codification process was not complete. This lack of a codified genre to perform the function of bequeathing is also reflected in meta-comments upon the text itself. In their discussion section Danet and Bogoch arrive at the important conclusion that without acceptance of the performativity and conventional codification of written legal documents the systems of written law which have become the current international standard would be impossible.

THE LITERATE STAGE

The advantages of codifying law, precedent and other legal documents in a stable written form are obvious. It means that the legal system is less dependent upon the (possibly flawed) memories or judgments of individuals. Halliday (1985a&b) suggests that some of the linguistic consequences of written codification are increased nominalisation, grammatical metaphor and lexical density. Increased nominalisation entails nouns replacing verbs, which is related in turn to grammatical metaphor, since processes (e.g. 'to pay') which are most naturally expressed as verbs often become nouns (e.g. 'the payment'). An advantage of this re-ification of processes and actions is that it makes them much easier to organise into an argument. It also means that they can be qualified and modified more easily – adjectives are more productive and plentiful than adverbs, verb participles such as 'intended' and 'referred to' can be used, and nouns can modify other nouns (e.g. 'service payments') much more freely in English than one lexical verb can modify another lexical verb (?paid to serve ?paid for serving). In legal documents these tendencies are often exploited to produce extraordinarily complex noun phrases – Crystal and Davy (1969: 205) give the following example: 'The payment to the owner of the total amount of any instalment then remaining unpaid of the rent hereinbefore reserved and agreed to be paid during the term . . .'.

Halliday (1985a) also suggests that increased complexity at the phrase level is usually accompanied by reduced syntactic complexity in the sentence or clause complex. Unfortunately, unlike scientific English, the language of the law appears to have the worst of both worlds, combining complex phrases with complex sentence syntax. Both Maley's and Bhatia's chapter provide examples from legal documents and explanations of this, and elsewhere (Gibbons 1990) I have detailed the syntactic complexity of police cautions. As Bhatia's chapter suggests, the reason for this complexity appears to be that legal language is often trying to cover all possible combinations of conditions and contingencies. Language complexity increases greatly when an attempt is made to unify all these within the confines of a single sentence. The pursuit of precision has also led to both retention of archaic relics of Norman French and Latin such as 'corpus delicti' and 'demise' to create specialised terms, and the agglomeration of synonyms in search of semantic exactitude, for example 'give, devise and bequeath' (compare the elegant simplicity of Danet and Bogoch's Anglo-Saxon wills) 'cease and desist' and 'fit and proper'. Bhatia's chapter, and Danet (1980a) provide many other illustrations of the complexity of the language of the law.

Unfortunately, the pursuit of precision has produced obfuscation. This linguistic complexity has met widespread criticism from lawyers (see the Law Reform Commission of Victoria 1987), the public at large and linguists (see, for example, Labov and Harris's chapter in this volume). It has been ridiculed by satirists as varied as Jonathan Swift (*Gulliver's Travels*), Charles Dickens (*Bleak House*) and Groucho Marx (*Animal Crackers*). Its lack of intelligibility is well established (see Charrow and Charrow 1979, and Labov, this volume). The response has been to attempt to simplify the language, either in an *ad hoc* fashion (see Philips 1985) or in a more organised way through the Plain English movement (see Danet 1990; Eagleson 1991; and Maley's comments, this volume).

The most developed area in the study of the contemporary language of the law is not written texts however, but the language of the courtroom. Maley's chapter summarises much of the important work done by O'Barr and his associates at Duke

University, where there is a continuing programme of research into this topic, and by researchers such as Atkinson and Drew (1979). Maley also provides fresh insights into courtroom language from genre analysis. A main theme that emerges from such work (see Maley) is the great disparity of power within the courtroom, in particular between the legal professionals on the one hand, and the general public, particularly plaintiffs, defendants and witnesses, on the other. This is mainly a product of the social situation in the courtroom, but it is also in part a result of the use of the complex legal language discussed above. These disparities in power are both revealed and imposed through language.

Disparities in power are not limited to the courtroom, however. In private consultation with lawyers non-lawyers may feel disempowered – an experience I have had as an expert witness. Contacts with the police are another area where power disparities are in evidence. Before going any further, however, it is necessary to show how power differentials are manifested through language in legal settings. Fairclough (1989: 18) in his book in this series, gives the following telling example from an interview in a police station.

This text is part of an interview in a police station, involving the witness to an armed robbery (w) and a policeman (p), in which basic information elicitation is going on. w, who is rather shaken by the experience, is being asked what happened, p is recording the information elicited in writing.

  (1) p: Did you get a look at the one in the car?
  (2) w: I saw his face, yeah.
  (3) p: What sort of age was he?
  (4) w: About 45. He was wearing a . . .
  (5) p: And how tall?
  (6) w: Six foot one.
  (7) p: Six foot one. Hair?
  (8) w: Dark and curly. Is this going to take long? I've got to collect
      the kids from school.
  (9) p: Not much longer, no. What about his clothes?
  (10) w: He was a bit scruffy-looking, blue trousers, black . . .
  (11) p: Jeans?
  (12) w: Yeah.

How would you characterize the relationship between the police interviewer and w in this case, and how is it expressed in what is said?

The relationship is an unequal one, with the police interviewer firmly in control of the way the interview develops and of w's contribution to it, and taking no trouble to mitigate the demands he makes of her. Thus questions which might be quite painful for someone who has just witnessed a violent crime are never mitigated; p's question in turn 1, for example, might have been in a mitigated form such as *did you by any chance manage to get a good look at the one in the* instead of the bald form in which it actually occurs. In some cases, questions are reduced to words or minimal phrases – *how tall* in turn 5, and *hair* in turn 7. Such reduced questions are typical when one person is filling in a form 'for' another, as p is here; what is interesting is that the sensitive nature of the situation does not override the norms of form-filling. It is also noticeable that there is no acknowledgement of, still less thanks for, the information w supplies. Another feature is the way in which the interviewer checks what w has said in 7. Notice finally how control is exercised over w's contributions: p interrupts w's turn in 5 and 11, and in 9 p gives a minimal answer to w's question about how much longer the interview will take, not acknowledging her problem, and immediately asks another question thus closing off w's interpellation.

(Fairclough 1989: 18)

Harris's chapter takes this discussion an interesting step further. She reveals how the power inequalities in court are both manifested covertly in patterns of language behaviour, and are also overtly expressed, and in some cases disputed. She shows how magistrates attempt to assert equality between the parties in court, while defendants express the power imbalance between themselves and the magistrate. O'Toole in her response asserts that problems of defendants in the courtroom derive from the complexity of legal language (discussed above) as well as power inequity.

THE TRANSITION TO A POST-LITERATE STAGE

With the development of modern media of communication, notably television and video recording, entertainment and information are increasingly received and stored in an audio-visual form. As a consequence, in richer countries there are emergent trends in some areas towards a post-literate stage. Danet and Bogoch's chapter contains a short but fascinating section which discusses this move and its consequences, with brief reference to some example of video recorded wills. Pearson and Berch document in some detail how the written deposition (a form of sworn written evidence) is being steadily replaced by the video deposition. It is interesting to note how the changes produced by literacy in Anglo-Saxon wills are being reversed. For example, video depositions can be much more context-dependent, and make use of material in the physical context such as models and charts, thus strengthening the communicative effectiveness of the deposition. Information from facial expressions, bodily gesture, and paralanguage such as pausing and intonation, which was largely lost in the written form can now once more be captured. This can have the advantage of increasing the flow of information, and may often reduce ambiguity, but there are disadvantages in the fact that this type of information is easily misinterpreted. A video deposition also gives more clues as to the social and ethnic identity of the witness, an advantage in that it gives additional insights to judge, jury and lawyers, but a disadvantage if it triggers ethnic and social prejudice. Pearson and Berch recognise the inevitability of the move into a post-literate world, but advise us to tread slowly and with caution.

ONE

The language of the law

Yon Maley

INTRODUCTION

Jane Prince, MSc CPsychol

In all societies, law is formulated, interpreted and enforced: there are codes, courts and constables (Goody 1986: 132). And the greater part of these different legal processes is realised primarily through language. Language is medium, process and product in the various arenas of the law where legal texts, spoken or written, are generated in the service of regulating social behaviour. Particularly in literate cultures, once norms and proceedings are recorded, standardised and institutionalised, a special legal language develops, representing a predictable process and pattern of functional specialisation. In the Anglo-Saxon common law system, a discrete legal language has been apparent since post-Conquest England, which in many essentials has persisted to the present day. A description and explanation of the present-day forms and organisation of the language of English and English-derived law needs then to begin with a brief account of its origins.

The common law

It seems that there has never been a time since the Norman Conquest when the English of the law has been in tune with common usage. It has always been considered a language apart and there are good historical reasons why this should be so. The institution of English law, as we know it, dates from the

11

Norman Conquest. There was English law before the Norman Conquest but there was no distinct profession, no centralisation of justice (Mellinkoff 1963: 46). These things, plus a wealth of legal concepts and procedures, the Normans brought with them and gradually established in Britain. The written language of the law after the Conquest was at first Latin and English. Latin was predominant and gained ground steadily. By the time William the Conqueror died, Latin was the language of formal written documents. It was not classical or medieval Latin, however, but a variety of Latin, law Latin, that included many latinised English and Old French words. For example, the Old English, 'morðer', a secret killing, became 'murdrum', and hence the modern 'murder' (Kiralfy 1958: 96). By the fourteenth century, French had taken over from Latin as the language of the Year Books (the earliest law reports) and statutes, strangely enough when French as a language for communication was dying out and the English language was rapidly replacing it. Mellinkoff (1963: 101) suggests that one reason for the use of French in legal documents was the urge to have a secret language and to preserve a professional monopoly. There is of course strong precedent throughout history and in various cultures for the powerful and elite reserving for themselves a special language which serves both to set them apart socially and to reinforce and perpetuate power by depriving the less powerful classes of access to its mysteries, whether or not this motivation was present in the minds of the lawyers in the thirteenth and fourteenth centuries.

It was not until 1650, by *An Act for Turning the Books of the Law, and all Processes and Proceedings in Courts of Justice into English* (455 (1650) 11 Acts and Ordinances of the Interregnum) that English became the official language of the law. By that time a host of Old English, Latin, Norman-French and Middle English terms had become fixed in the vocabulary of lawyers. Over the centuries since then there has been a continual process of Anglicisation, but particularly in vocabulary, in the specialised, technical lexicon of the law, the effect of its varied origins is still apparent.

It would be a mistake to suggest, however, that the language of the law reached its definitive form in the Middle Ages and has remained unaltered ever since. It has been affected, as have all other forms of English, by the great moves of culture and taste that differentiate one period of history from another. Probably it reached its heights, or depths, of verbosity or prolixity in the early eighteenth century, supported by such long-standing practices as the notorious piecemeal system: the longer the document, the greater the drafting fee (Mellinkoff 1963: 188). Since then there has been a slow but perceptible process of simplification (Bhatia 1987b). Despite these efforts at simplification and clarification, the gap between legal discourse and everyday discourse is still very wide. Present day legal discourse retains its identity as a highly specialised and distinctive discourse type or genre of English. It has a certain ubiquity too. The legal discourse of the legal systems of England, Canada, the United States of America, Australia and New Zealand, which are derived from the English common law system, are manifestly similar.

The expressions of this discourse type are to be found in a variety of legal situations. There is not one legal discourse but a set of related legal discourses. Each has a characteristic flavour but each differs according to the situation in which it is used. There is judicial discourse, the language of judicial decision, either spoken or written, which is reasonably flexible and varied but none the less contains recognisably legal meanings, in predictable patterns of lexicogrammar. These judicial decisions, collected in reports, make up what is known in the English-derived common law system as case law. There is courtroom discourse, used by judges, counsel, court officials, witnesses and other participants. This is interactive language, peppered with ritual courtesies and modes of address, but otherwise perhaps the closest approximation to everyday speech of all public legal discourses. There is the language of legal documents: contracts, regulations, deeds, wills, Acts of Parliament, or statutes, quintessentially legal and formal. And there is the discourse of legal consultation, between lawyer and lawyer, lawyer and client.

Legal discourse

In the past twenty years, there has been a great efflorescence of interest in the language of the law from linguists, sociolinguists, ethnographers, discourse analysts, ethnomethodologists, and semioticians (for overviews see Danet 1980a and 1990; Shuy 1986; Bhatia 1987a). Much of the comment has been critical and has been directed at its bizarre and inaccessible forms; a related criticism is directed to the social consequences of the inequalities of power it realises. Lawyers themselves, particularly those of a reforming bent, have also begun to look more closely and critically at its characteristic forms and patterns[1]. As a result of the analyses and critiques a great deal of legal language has been described and to a certain extent explained. However, because the language of the law is not one homogeneous discourse type but a set of related and overlapping discourse types, and because such a range of different theoretical models has been applied to each, but never to the whole, each analysis speaks only for itself. Whatever coherence or consistency may underlie or inform the language of the law as a whole is not available to view.

It seems then that there would be some advantage in attempting to provide an overview of the language of the law and its internal or constituent discourses, approaching each discourse type from a similar point of view and a consistent framework and set of concepts.

The approach

I propose to explore the nature and scope of the language of the law from a particular theoretical perspective. The approach taken is semiotic and functional, and derives from the functional-systemic model developed by M.A.K. Halliday (1978; 1985a). A semiotic system is a system for meaning; its signs, by which meaning is communicated, may be linguistic or non-linguistic, or a mixture of both. In a given society, these signs are not free-floating but found in characteristic configurations in social situations. Linguistically, the configuration of meanings con-stitute a discourse type (a register or genre) which is realised in texts by lexicogrammar, textual organisation and a structural shape (a 'generic structure potential', Hasan, in press) that is identified with the genre. There is then a relationship between the discourse type and the social situation which needs explication. In the Hallidayan model this relationship is derived

from the values or components of the social situa
tenor and *mode*. These are very broad, general
context. What is claimed is that the nature and purpo
going activity (field), the nature and speech r
participants (tenor) and the type of channel for communication
(mode) are related to the meanings typical of the discourse type.
That is to say, in all social situation-types, certain categories of
meaning are functional, serving to express matters of content, the
field; the dynamics of social interaction and point of view, the
tenor; and the processes of text production and organisation, the
mode. These related meanings or functions of language are the
ideational, the *interpersonal* and the *textual* respectively. The
ideational has two further sub-functions: the *experiential* and the
logical. The former serves to represent experience and therefore
the content of language by means of syntax and lexicon; the latter
serves to represent relationships such as coordination and
subordination.

Figure 1.1, below, attempts to model in a simplified and non-
exhaustive way the chief structures and processes of the common
law legal system and their associated discourses. As the figure
shows, a number of different situation types arise sequentially
and form groups which can be characterised as 1) sources of law
and originating points of legal process; 2) pre-trial processes; 3)
trial processes; 4) recording of judgment in law reports. There is a
potential feedback loop between (4) and (1).

A typical, and simplified, sequence might be that a social
conflict between parties comes under the rubric of a rule of law,
either a statutory or a common law one. If the parties decide to
litigate, each party will consult a lawyer and the case will be
prepared, with all the attendant documentation. If the next step is
taken, then the parties appear in court and a trial before a judge,
and sometimes a jury, follows. At the end of the trial, the judge
will give judgment which is an integral part of the trial process
itself. However, if the judgment has any significance in terms of
extending or restricting a rule of law, or establishing a rule of
statutory interpretation, then it is reported and becomes part of
the huge volume of precedents that constitute case law. There is
some circularity in the process: once a case is reported and
becomes a precedent for later cases, it is then a source of law and
potentially an originating point for a new trial process with a
new set of parties.

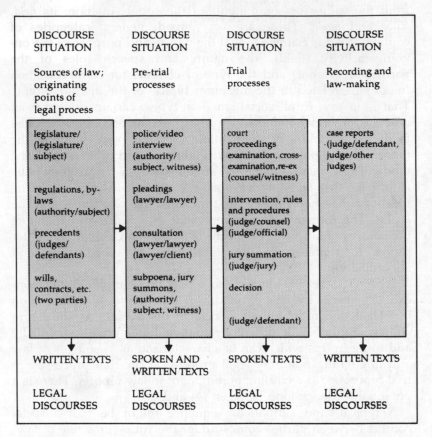

DISCOURSE SITUATION	DISCOURSE SITUATION	DISCOURSE SITUATION	DISCOURSE SITUATION
Sources of law; originating points of legal process	Pre-trial processes	Trial processes	Recording and law-making
legislature/ (legislature/ subject)	police/video interview (authority/ subject, witness)	court proceedings examination, cross-examination,re-ex (counsel/witness)	case reports (judge/defendant, judge/other judges)
regulations, by-laws (authority/subject)	pleadings (lawyer/lawyer)	intervention, rules and procedures (judge/counsel)	
precedents (judges/ defendants)	consultation (lawyer/lawyer) (lawyer/client)	(judge/official)	
wills, contracts, etc. (two parties)	subpoena, jury summons, (authority/ subject, witness)	jury summation (judge/jury) decision	
		(judge/defendant)	
↓ WRITTEN TEXTS	↓ SPOKEN AND WRITTEN TEXTS	↓ SPOKEN TEXTS	↓ WRITTEN TEXTS
LEGAL DISCOURSES	LEGAL DISCOURSES	LEGAL DISCOURSES	LEGAL DISCOURSES

Figure 1.1

The sequence is not inevitable. Wills and contracts, for example, once drafted and made effective, may never give rise to legal process; or, after consultation with lawyers, the parties may settle the dispute privately; some, perhaps a majority of cases, are recorded but not reported and collected in law reports. But these different structural and discourse situations exist, as a potential, where needed, for the regulation and facilitation of social life.

In what follows, I shall consider three of the possible discourse situations and their discourses: *legislation, trial proceedings,* and *judicial judgments.* I shall begin by providing a general description of the discourse situation, showing the important relationships between institutional functions, purposes and goals and institutional roles; that is, a general description of the field and tenor. There will be no attempt to cover all possible aspects of the discourse, only those that are seen to be criterial, or to have clear functional connections with their context.

LEGISLATION: CERTAINTY AND FLEXIBILITY

The discourse situation

An apparent paradox often addressed by jurisprudence and legal textbooks within the English and English derived common law traditions is posed this way: how can the law be certain and stable and yet achieve flexibility? Certainty is demanded by justice and the rule of law which require predictability of outcome: like cases must be decided alike. When the facts are the same, the outcome should be the same. But no set of facts is ever quite the same and the question often arises: does the new set of facts arising from different times and different circumstances really fall within the ambit of the same legal rule as the earlier set? What are the mechanisms by which the legal rule can be adjusted, made flexible, in order to accommodate the new set of circumstances? How is the rule extended or restricted in order to do justice to this particular case?

Two kinds of rule are involved in the application of rules of law to particular circumstances: the rules of legislation and codes of law; and common law rules derived from the decisions of judges, often called 'judge made' or case law. Both constitute important and interconnected areas of legal discourse. I shall begin with a discussion of legislation since it is the largest and most powerful source of law in a society; also, legislative discourse is the most complex and esoteric of all forms of legal discourse. Its forms have been shaped by its history, its institutional functions and ideologies – not the least of which are the requirements of certainty and flexibility.

Statutes, then, (or Acts of Parliament) are 'systematically interrelated sets of rules' (MacCormick 1990: 544), usually rules of both substance and procedure. The systematicity relates primarily to experiential content, to a focus on a particular area of social life or behaviour. The general function of legal rules, the function that provides them with their *raison d'être*, is to regulate – in the broadest sense – social behaviour. And the need to endow the rules with both certain and, where necessary, flexible meanings is ancillary to this larger function.

Legal rules emanate from the Queen in Parliament or the sovereign legislative body but are actually drafted by public servants (usually draftsmen) to conform to the intentions of the legislature; they are addressed formally to the subjects (or a group of subjects) of the sovereign power, but they are interpreted by other lawyers and more importantly, when there is a dispute, by the courts. Their special status derives from the fact, as we shall see in the next section, that their interpretation of the meanings of the statute or its enactments is the only 'correct' one; more importantly, it is the enforceable one. The discoursal correlates of these situational features are formality, associated with the sovereign subject relationship; and technicality associated, at least in part, with the specialised, professional readership.

Legislative discourse

Generic structure

Discourse types or genres characteristically organise their content, their message, within broadly recognisable structural shapes; that is to say, we can categorise the texts that are the products of the discourse process according to the configuration of structural elements that they exhibit. Current linguistic work on narratives, jokes, story telling and conversation in general proceeds on the assumption that an essential part of our recognition of these as distinct genres is based on the fact that each has a distinct internal organisation or structure. In her analyses of the nursery tale and service encounters as discourse genres, Hasan uses the principle of a 'generic structure potential'. This postulates that each genre is characteristically associated with a set of obligatory and optional structural elements which stand in a certain relation to each other, for example relationships of sequence or recursivity (Hasan 1984). The notion of a 'potential' is important, for it draws attention to the capacity of language to serve as a resource for meaning, which is differently drawn from or instantiated in different kinds of context, or contexts of situation.

In the texts that instantiate legislative discourse, these structural regularities are apparent. All modern statutes follow a regular form (Maher et al. 1971: 207; Enright 1983: 54) which constitutes their generic structure. The actual configuration of elements, both obligatory and optional, may vary from jurisdiction and certain types of statute have a specific generic structure. However, some generalisations across the different types and jurisdictions can be made. There is first pre-material, giving long title, year and number, short title, preamble and an enacting formula. The body of the statute follows, divided into numbered sections, subsections and paragraphs. Larger units may be used; for example, a definitions part or division, followed by a substantive part and a procedural part. Schedules are appended as end material. Definitions may occur here as a schedule, if they do not constitute a separate part in the body of the Act. Some elements are optional, e.g. short title and preamble, division into parts, but the sequence of elements is invariable.

Interpersonal meanings: performativity

The speech functions adopted in legislation clearly typify its nature as 'text-in-action' (Halliday 1985a). Consider the enacting formula which precedes all English statutes:

> Be it enacted by the Queen's Most Excellent Majesty, by and with the advice and consent of the Lords Spiritual and Temporal, and the Commons, in this present Parliament assembled, and by the authority of the same, as follows:

A similar enacting formula is used in Australia and the United States of America substituting, of course, the relevant legislative bodies.[2] It is a fine example of an explicit performative speech act, a saying which is at the same time a doing. In *How to Do things with Words*, Austin (1962) showed how this category of speech act explicitly performs linguistic acts that are also social acts. In this case, the saying of the words, the enactment formula, performs the institutional act of enacting. Philosophers and linguists have subsequently explored this aspect of the speech act in law (Kurzon 1986; Maley 1987; Danet and Bogoch, this volume). We note how the substance of the formula specifies one part of the appropriate contextual conditions for its successful performance, that is, the appropriate participants. The archaic jussive subjunctive form expresses clearly the relationship between the text and the source of the discourse – it is expressed as if it were a perpetual, speaking command from the sovereign power to its subjects. In modern jurisprudence it is well accepted that law-as-command is not an accurate representation of the nature of law in general or of legislation in particular, but the jussive subjunctive form sustains the older view. In linguistic terms (Searle 1969) it has the indirect illocutionary force of certifying that the correct participants and conditions accompany the saying of the speech act, at the same time as its explicit force is a command that the contents of the statute become law. Now the enacting formula may be no more than a quaint relic, but it provides the frame of power, distance and status which endows legislative texts with their formal, imperious quality.

The enacting formula makes law the entire text which follows it. As Kurzon points out (1986: 11), the subject 'it' is no more than a place holder: 'the real subject, extraposed to the end of the sentence, is the entire text of the statute'. Because of its enveloping and framing role, the enactment formula functions as a macro speech act (Van Dijk 1977; Maley 1987: 28ff). The individual sections within the statute are also performatives each with its own implicit performative, or as lawyers say 'operative' verb (Coode 1848).

The body of the statute which follows has as its central task the identifying and empowering of rights and duties relevant to the domain of experience it is regulating. There are two chief ways of doing this – by saying what must be done and what may be done, what are called in law mandatory or directory and discretionary or permissive rules. Linguistically this is achieved by the use of the modals 'may' 'shall', and 'must', which carry the

meanings of permission, ordering and prohibi
20). Consider:

e 26. This Act shall come into force on 1st January 197
27. This Act may be cited as the Interpretation Act 1
(Interpretation Act 1978,

These two short provisions are respectively mandatory and permissive. For centuries the distinction between what must be done and what may be done has been carried by 'must' and 'shall' as opposed to 'may', although always subject to interpretation by the courts whether the legislature really intended to be either mandatory or permissive or discretionary. Modern statutes sometimes omit to mark the distinction. For example:

15. Where an Act repeals a repealing enactment, the repeal does not revive the enactment previously repealed unless words are added reviving it.

(Interpretation Act 1978, United Kingdom)

The section appears to be mandatory, but less explicitly so.

Other types of sections where 'must', 'may' or 'shall' do not necessarily occur are those which define an offence:

1.(1) A person, whatever his nationality, who, in the United Kingdom or elsewhere,
(a) detains any other person (the hostage), and
(b) in order to compel a State, international governmental organisation or person to do or abstain from doing any act, threatens to kill, injure or continue to detain the hostage, commits an offence.

(Taking of Hostages Act 1982. United Kingdom)

Typically, in defining sections the legal verb, e.g. 'commits', is present, non-deictic tense, uttering or performing a continuing rule defining the offence or crime e.g. hostage-taking.

Performativity and modality are the linguistic means which express the institutional ideology of the role relationships involved in legislative rule-making. In themselves, they have no role in achieving certainty. However, since it is assumed that the rule once uttered is forever speaking, the rule acquires continuity and permanence as an authoritative text, a major contribution rds certainty. The text is fixed and 'frozen'. It exists erformatively, until it is altered or repealed. The meaning of the rule is to be found in the very words of the rule and there is very limited recourse possible to other authority to determine the meaning of the rule.

Experiential and textual meanings

The most common source of certainty, however, is in experiential and textual meanings and organisation; that is, in the expression of its content and in its textual presentation. The development of referential linguistic resources and their textual deployment represent institutional discoursal strategies to achieve certainty by making the rule both precise and explicit. The draftsman aims to refer exactly and comprehensively to identifiable categories of participant, process and circumstance in that part of the world subject to the law's jurisdiction (see Bhatia, this volume). The competing goal of flexibility is, as we shall see, also achieved experientially, by an appropriate generality and vagueness of reference.

The first and most obvious way to regulate a domain of social experience or activity is to develop a specialised and technical vocabulary which will conceptualise the semantic field as a set of related terms which articulate it by means of superordinate and hyponymous terms, and fixed or semi-fixed collocations. The semantic field of homicide, for example, is articulated in this way. In most jurisdictions, murder and manslaughter are kinds of homicide; the terms 'murder' and 'manslaughter' are thus co-hyponyms of the superordinate 'homicide'. And in most jurisdictions, further distinctions are possible, particularly in kinds of manslaughter. The participants, processes and circumstances by which these crimes are distinguished and defined may differ from jurisdiction to jurisdiction and have certainly altered from one historical period to another (Maley 1985a: 152).

Terms like 'murder' or 'manslaughter' are not terms of art, since their meaning is not invariable. Technical language in the sense of words with fixed and definite meaning is generally considered to be one of the most distinctive features of legal discourse in general. However, the amount of technicality in legal discourse generally, and legislative discourse in particular, depends greatly on the subject matter. In some areas of the law, such as property, contract and tort, the key concepts originate early in the history of the common law, dating back to medieval times. Statutes or other documents dealing with these subject matters fairly bristle with technical and arcane terms. On the other hand, some statutes contain relatively few technical terms. A statute on the taking of hostages, for example, or on importing prohibited substances is not – apart from some procedural terms – necessarily technical lexically. Usually, most modern statutes include definition sections, which set out the key terms used throughout the statute and provide definitions *for the purpose of that statute*. Experiential meanings are, as Goodrich suggests (1987: 149) established intentionally, by stipulating the meaning that the legislature intends the term to have for the purpose of the particular statute, or by reference to a judicial pronouncement on what was the legislature's 'true' intention.

There are syntactic and grammatical correlates of technicality. One feature of the technical legal vocabulary of English is the high number of nominalisations representing processes. Procedural sections in particular are likely to use such terms, and to incorporate them into passive clauses, frequently with agents deleted. Thus:

> **558(2)** A recognizance mentioned in subsection (1) shall be conditioned upon and subject to such terms and conditions as the Court shall order.
>
> (Crimes Act 1900, New South Wales)

Thematisation of the procedural terms in a passive clause is common, as in s558(2). Also:

> **419** On the prosecution of a person for bigamy, the first marriage shall not be proved by the evidence of the husband, or wife, of such marriage alone.
>
> (Crimes Act 1900, New South Wales)

The circumstantial phrase 'on the prosecution of a person for bigamy' foregrounds a previous process economically, deleting unwanted or irrelevant information, i.e. the prosecuting agent.

The section below incorporates a number of typical drafting practices in all common law countries.

> (1) A person who attempts or incites another to commit, or becomes an accessory after the fact to an offence (in this subsection called 'the principal offence') commits –
>   (a) if the principal offence is an indictable offence, the indictable offence; or
>   (b) if the principal offence is a simple offence, the simple offence,
> but is liable on conviction –
>   (c) to a fine not exceeding half of the fine; and additionally or alternatively,
>   (d) to imprisonment for a term not exceeding half of the term,
> to which a person who commits the principal offence is liable.
> (2) A person who conspires with another to commit an offence (in this subsection called 'the principal offence') commits –
>   (a) if the principal offence is an indictable offence under section 6(1) or 7(1), the indictable offence, but is liable on conviction to the penalty referred to in section 34(1)(b); . . .
>   (Section 33, Drugs Act, Western Australia 1981)

Experientially, the section has some technical terms ('accessory after the fact', 'indictable offence'), and is a general rule ('a person who . . .'). The present tense of the rule ('attempts', 'commits', 'is liable') provides continuity over time. There is also a typical pattern of participants processes and circumstances – in legal terms, the legal subject, the legal operative verb and the conditions.

In addition, textual features, in the sense of the management and packaging of information, are intended to make the section explicit and precise and therefore certain.

There is first the layout of the section. Older statutes present each section as a continuous and usually unpunctuated single sentence. This modern section retains the convention of a single sentence section but breaks up the component clauses of the clause complex into separate numbered and lettered paragraphs and uses punctuation freely. The layout serves as a visual device to identify and separate the component parts of the rule. Yet, as in earlier statutes, the entire section is presented as one sentence. The retention of the one sentence section is directly traceable to institutional methods of interpretation, since lawyers believe that it is easier to construe a single sentence than a series of sentences

(Renton 1975), and that there is therefore less potential for uncertainty. That is, the textual, micro-organisation of the statute is also attributable to institutional goals and beliefs. One may wonder how well based these beliefs are, since in order to fit all the component parts of the rule into a single sentence, draftsmen frequently have recourse to complex patterns of subordination and embedded non-finite clauses (Crystal and Davy 1969: 201; Gustafsson 1975: 8; Bhatia, this volume). This syntactic complexity, as well as nominalisations and technical terms which also contribute to the tightly packed character of the legal sentence, makes for texts of very high lexical density (Halliday 1985b). Even with devices of layout and graphology, the syntactic complexity – probably more than technical terms – renders legislative texts incomprehensible to all except the specialist reader and increases the possibilities for uncertainty.

Patterns of cohesion devices are another textual, i.e. discoursal feature, intended to make the section more precise and explicit, and therefore certain. Repetition rather than pronouns has always been the preferred cohesive device in legislative drafting, and is used freely here ('the principal offence', 'the indictable offence').

A second textual and cohesive device in section 33 occurs in subsection (2)(a) where reference is made to information found in other sections of the statute. Bhatia (1987b: 9, and this volume) suggests that this kind of 'textual mapping' is increasingly a feature of modern legislation which attempts to reduce the amount of information to be packed into a section by means of referring either backwards and forwards in the text to related, essential information.

Despite the lexicogrammatical and textual contributions to precision, section 33 is not, as it turns out, entirely clear or certain. Its uncertainty derives from an intertextual clash between it and the section referred to in the final subsection, which provides a different penalty for the same offence. Uncertainty or ambiguity of this kind is probably attributable to faulty drafting, and illustrates that other factors can intervene to render a section uncertain in some way. However, whether it works or not, intertextuality in the sense of overlapping references, both implicit and explicit, between texts is a most pervasive feature of drafting practice. Most statutes have to be read and understood against a background of related legislation, as well as principles and standards which may be considered applicable and which come from the common law; for example, the principle 'the public good'.

Deeming and legal fictions

Section 33 contains another noteworthy feature which contributes not to certainty but to flexibility, in the sense of extending the scope of the existing system of rules. To the ordinary reader, there is something a little strange about a rule that provides that a person commits an offence if he/she merely attempts or incites another person to commit the offence. The oddity lies in the fact that section 33 is what is known as a 'deeming' section. In a decision which interpreted and applied this section, the presiding judges commented: 'In other words, a person who attempts to commit an indictable offence is deemed to commit the indictable offence, but is liable to only half the penalty.'[3]

This provision, which 'deems' something to be the case, which it patently is not, is an example of one of many legal fictions in English and English-derived law. Legal fictions occur in many legal systems, and according to the historian, Maine, have a very long history reaching back at least as far as Roman law (Maine 1972: 15): they may be procedural, jurisdictional or substantive.

In general, a legal fiction is a kind of enabling or facilitating device which enables a lawyer to say, 'X is Y', or, more precisely, 'For the purposes of this enactment or statute, X is deemed to be Y'. Because deeming clauses of this kind bring together two disparate elements into a temporary text-specific equative relationship, they have affinities with metaphor. Just as a literary metaphor enables readers to think of an entity as being in some sense the same as another and thus enlarges the system of meaning relations for the literary work, so the legal fiction allows lawyers to treat disparate entities as similar and thus enlarge the legal meaning relationships for the purpose of the particular statute or section. A new rule for a new circumstance does not have to be made. The existing rule applies, simply by 'deeming' one circumstance, participant or process to be the same as another.

Flexibility, in the sense of a temporary text-bound extension of a rule, is apparently the motivation behind the wording of section 33. It provides that for *the purposes of conviction*, a person who incites etc. is the same as a person who actually commits the offence, (i.e. X is Y) but goes on to provide that *for the purposes of sentencing*, a lesser penalty applies in his case (i.e. X is not Y).

Fictions such as the deeming clause, above, or metaphors in literary and other genres are temporary and text-bound. But their effect can be more permanent. Just as some metaphors create new meanings permanently when they are adopted into the language (e.g. the *eye* of the needle, the energy *wave*), legal fictions can create new legal entities. The corporation is an accepted legal category; it is no longer a legal fiction (Pollock 1969: 167).

Judicial discretion

Legal fictions are one way by which flexibility can be imported into rules, but, in fact, their use is fairly restricted in modern legislation. Deliberate flexibility, as opposed to unintentional ambiguity, is most commonly achieved in the drafting of legislation by the use of subjective terms like 'wilful', 'reasonable', 'negligent', 'unconscionable'. Such terms provide judges with discretion to decide whether the relevant behaviour was, in their judgment, 'reasonable', and so on, in the circumstances. For example, a provision regarding the abrogation of a contract can allow a judge to consider whether the contract or a provision of it 'to have been unjust in the circumstances relating to the contract at the time it was made' (Section 7, Contracts Review Act 1980, New South Wales) – see Fagan (1990). What is 'unjust in the circumstances' is as much a matter of opinion as of fact, and clearly such provisions provide scope for judicial subjectivity.

The tension between certainty and flexibility

Fictions and subjective, vague terminology are devices of drafting practices, of the way in which texts are produced, which give either flexibility to the rule or discretion to later courts to define their scope and meaning. They contrast with the other, and more typical, kinds of drafting devices earlier described, those employing technical terms, repetition, single sentence sections with involved syntactic structures, which are intended to achieve certainty in the legal rule. Despite the care, or the best intentions, of their drafters, sections written for certainty can become just as uncertain as those written for flexibility. Every case of statutory interpretation which comes before a court is an instance of uncertainty: it may be ambiguous, vague, absurd, or in conflict with other rules. Pearce (1974: 1) claims that both in Australia and England, approximately 40 per cent of the work of the court requires a ruling upon the meaning of a particular piece of some legislative instrument. Figures of this proportion give real substance to the view of many critics of the law, that the pursuit of certainty in legal rules is both unrealistic and dishonest (Frank 1963; Goodrich 1987). Some lawyers and draftsmen lay blame for these unintended uncertainties on the 'imperfections', the 'diseases' or 'inherent frailty' of language.[4] Mere words, apparently, are not up to the job of providing precise rules.

An alternative approach to the linguistic sources of uncertainty in statutory rules stems from H.L.A. Hart's conception of the 'open texture' of language. Words, in particular general words like 'vehicle', 'residence', 'plant', have both a core of meaning and a penumbra of uncertainty (Hart 1961: 119). In the penumbra where language takes on an open texture or vagueness (1961: 120), there is room for judicial discretion, for solving 'hard cases'. Hart's views are, however, controversial – see Dworkin (1977) and (1986); Cohen (1984).

Insofar as it is a linguistic explanation for uncertainty in texts, Hart's view of the core and penumbra takes up the problem of how the sense of lexical items correlates with their referential scope. In legislative discourse, a legislator/draftsman has a problem in deciding the appropriate level of generality with which to draft the legislative rule (actually, the same is true for the judge who formulates a common-law rule). Typically, legislative rules are intended to be general rules, applying to a class of individuals, rather than to a single individual. The more generalised such rules become, the greater the difficulty of determining what items are included with their scope. They are not embedded in any meaningful context of utterance and the surrounding linguistic context (the section or paragraph expressing the rule) may or may not be helpful. In addition, ordinary usage or dictionaries may be silent on the point. Such situations give rise to Hart's 'hard cases' and what Stone (1968) has called 'judicial leeways', an area of interpretation and judicial decision making.

Interpretation

In a recent article discussing methods of interpretation of European Community legislation, Millett commented: 'Methods of interpretation do not exist in a void but develop in relation to the legislation which falls to be interpreted' (Millett 1989). EC legislation tends to be general in its scope, and more in line with continental drafting practice, which aims for clarity and broad outlines. Domestic legislation in common law countries (the drafting of constitutions aside) is quite different. Typically, the generality of the rule is offset by detailed lists of either participant, process or circumstance, which strive for an ideal of certainty and not necessarily (indeed, more often not!) clarity (see Bhatia, this volume).

It is only when one asks *why* certainty should be such a virtue in one system and not another that the real institutional motivation is apparent for the difference in drafting practices, and the entailed differences in interpretive practices. The institutional role of the judge and the function that the judge performs within the institutional structure is different in each case. The continental system is prepared to allow more scope for the interpretation of law by the courts (Renton 1975: 52). They are able to look to intent rather than to form in a way that has traditionally been denied to the common law judges in England and Australia, although interpretive practices in the United States of America have always been freer and less constrained by the words of the text. None the less, the text remains the paramount source of interpretation in all common law systems (Hurst 1982: 46). The traditional ideology has been that judges only interpret; they do not usurp the role of the legislation, but seek the communicative intention of the legislature, i.e. the meaning, from the words of the statute itself. So the common law draftsman/legislature tends to put as much information as possible into the act or section, covering every possible situation that may arise so that the judge will not be tempted to interpret freely and in effect legislate. In fact, as we have seen, judges do make law, informally and perforce, when they rule on the meaning of disputed sections (or when they formulate principles of common law. See 'Judicial discourse', below). But detailed methods of drafting keep them in check and limit the scope of such informal law-making.

To assist them in making the 'correct' choice, judges frequently invoke the aid of a barrage of interpretive techniques, which are supposed to assist them to identify the legislature's meaning and which represent a set of institutional strategies for resolving uncertainty. There is not space here to describe their full scope and operation. They are fully set out in a number of legal textbooks (e.g. *Craies* 1971; Dickerson 1975) and linguists too have shown their semantic properties (Bowers 1985, 1990; Maley, 1987).

To a linguist, the semantic problems dealt with by the courts involve some very familiar concepts. Consider the case, for example, of *Corkery* v. *Carpenter* [1951] 1 K.B. 10, where the Court considered the scope of the following provision:

12. Every person who in any highway or other public place, whether a building or not, is guilty while drunk of riotous and disorderly behaviour, or who is drunk while in charge on any highway or other public place of any carriage, horse, cattle or steam engine, or who is drunk when in possession of any loaded firearms, may be apprehended, and shall be liable to a penalty not exceeding forty shillings, or in discretion of the court to imprisonment with or without hard labour for any term not exceeding one month.

(*Licensing Act* 1872 (UK))

The defendant, Shane Corkery, was undeniably, by any standards, drunk as well as disorderly. But was the bicycle he was riding, and in charge of at the time, a 'carriage' within the meaning of the Act? Clearly, if Hart's notions are invoked, this would be a penumbral rather than a core meaning of the term. The court held that the object of the Act was the protection of the public and the preservation of public order and within those purposes a bicycle was a carriage: the words of the Act were wide enough to embrace a bicycle under the expression 'carriage'. Note how the rule is both general and detailed. There are general terms (*person, public place, carriage, firearms*) and subjective terms (*riotous and disorderly*); as well there are detailed lists (*carriage, horse, cattle or steam engine*), specificity (*any highway or public place*) and phrasal repetition.

The judges are here wrestling with issues raised by semantic structures in particular texts: the limits of synonymy, the proper scope of hyponymy or inclusiveness of meaning; of change of meaning; of contextuality; of intertextuality. There are a number of grounds on which the decision can be made, and a corresponding number of leeways (Stone 1968) for flexibility.

Once a decision has been made, the meaning of the words of the statute is what the judge says it is. There is a certain Humpty Dumpty like quality about the meaning of statutes and other documents whose meaning is judicially determined – which has not escaped the attention of critics of the law and legal discourse. It is in the interpretation of statutes that judges achieve stability and flexibility, and methods of interpretation interact with methods of drafting. So the question or paradox with which this section began is resolved in this way: the law will remain stable and certain if the words of the statute are certain; it will be flexible to the extent to which it incorporates general and discretionary terms. If ambiguity, i.e. uncertainty, does arise textually, then stability is more likely to be achieved if the words are interpreted literally. Literal interpretation will choose the plain meaning of the words in the section, or strictly follow previous decisions, no matter how socially uncomfortable the effects of the decision may be. If the statute is interpreted creatively then flexibility is achieved. Creative interpretation will look to the wider effects and contexts of the section and determine the meaning accordingly. This is not the place to debate which approach is preferable; it is probably true to say that the last decade has seen in America and Australia and to a lesser degree in England a considerable swing towards both an acceptance of the creative role of the judge, and a willingness to consider looking at the wider context in which the statute operates to determine not so much its true, as its sensible (and some might hope, its socially sensitive) meaning.

COURTROOM DISCOURSE: POWER AND CONSTRAINT

The discourse situation

Before a case can be decided, however, it must be argued in court before a magistrate, a judge or a bench of judges. The courtroom is the forum whose basic and unavoidable role is to *decide*, to make a decision, on any issue brought before it concerning the legality of social behaviour, either criminal or civil. The behaviour may invoke either a common law or a statutory rule.

Despite the relevance of what courts do to the lives of those who are subject to their jurisdictional power, the courtroom is, for most people, a strange and alien setting. Anyone who visits a court for the first time and witnesses a typical day or even an hour's proceedings is usually overcome by a sense of having ventured into an arcane and immensely busy world – particularly if the court in question is a lower, i.e. magistrate's or local court. Some participants are noticeable by their verbal activity (counsel and witness), or by their physical position (judge or magistrate(s)), and in some cases by their clothing, i.e. robing (judge, counsel). Others are almost entirely silent (jury). Around them scurry a host of apparently lesser characters, whispering, conferring, taking notes or just listening (court officials). There may be an armed police officer, a reminder of the fact that verbal justice sometimes needs reinforcement. Everyone, except the newcomer – and frequently the witnesses – seems to know what he or she should do.

Semiotically, the strongest meanings communicated by the physical setting of the room and behaviour of those in it are those of hierarchical power. The physical layout of the room expresses, as it is intended to, a 'symbolic recognition of the authority of the court' (Goodrich 1988: 143). The judge or magistrate(s) occupies a dominant, focal position, usually (in England and Australia) sitting under an insignia-topped canopy which marks their position as a representative of sovereign justice. The opposing parties, each represented by counsel, face the judge or magistrate ('the bench'), each occupying a delimited area and space of table. Of the chief participants, only counsel move freely in the inner space, or well, of the court. If there is a jury, its members sit together on one side. Many observers have seen a metaphor here of trial-as-battle where two opponents seek to secure supremacy over each other (Danet and Bogoch 1980), each represented by his/her champion, the counsel, whose task it is to joust before an impartial audience (the judge and/or jury) and secure a decision. There must be a winner.|

The underlying institutional structure which allows such a metaphor to be made is the adversarial system of common-law trial proceedings. The European, i.e. continental system, is differently structured, employing what is called an 'inquisitorial' system. An English judge, in comparing the common-law adversarial system with the European 'inquisitorial' system, has observed: | _Trial of_ _strength_ | _Trial of_ _inquiry_ .

> The essential difference between the two systems – there are many incidental ones – is apparent from their names: the one is a trial of strength and the other is an inquiry. The question of the first is: are the shoulders of the party on whom is laid the burden of proof, the plaintiff or the prosecution as the case may be, strong enough to carry it and discharge it? In the second the question is: what is the truth of the matter. In the first the judge and jury are arbiters: they do not pose questions and seek answers; they weigh such material as is put before them, but they have no responsibility for seeing that it is complete. In the second the judge is in charge of the enquiry from the start; he will of course permit the parties to make out their cases and may rely on them to do so, but it is for him to say what he wants to know.
>
> (Devlin 1979: 54)

However, |if the common law trial is a trial of strength like a joust or a battle, it is a battle fought not with swords but with words. The oral trial is the centrepiece of the adversary system (Devlin 1979: 54) and the rules which regulate the oral proceedings are essentially verbal: they are the rules of evidence and other exclusionary rules which constrain the semiotics of the situation.| These are the rules which are implied by the adversary system and which are intended to make it not only workable but equitable. |They stipulate what must be said, what may be said – and of course by whom and in what order (Maley and Fahey 1991: 3)| That is to say, the ideational, interpersonal and textual meanings of this discourse type are strictly constrained.

| Perhaps the most common perception, and criticism, of courtroom discourse concerns the inequalities of power which

underlie these rules of speaking, and which are symbolised in the physical layout and trappings of the courtroom itself. All participants in the process are to some extent constrained but differentially. The situation is essentially hierarchical, extending from the judge or magistrate, at the top and most powerful, through the counsel to the witness who is commonly seen by critics of the trial process as being powerless, even degraded (Danet and Bogoch 1980; Penman 1987, in press; Harris, this volume). Power is exercised primarily by those who have the most right to speak, and to choose, control and change topics. The judge has greatest power: his rulings on evidence and procedure are decisive. Conventionally, however, in a trial or even in a lower court, the judge or magistrate intervenes minimally through the examination process (whereas in the inquisitorial model, it is the judge who asks questions).[5] The elicitation of the relevant facts in the case is achieved by counsel questioning the defendant or plaintiff and the witnesses, who are constrained to answer questions only and not volunteer information. Counsel control topic management: they choose and pursue and change topics, subject always to the laws of evidence and considerations of relevance. Silence is an option which the common law system allows, but its legal and psychological/ strategic force is equivocal, as Kurzon (1990) has shown. In the counsel-witness dyad, counsel and witness speak directly to each other, but neither party is speaking exclusively or even primarily to each other. The jury (or the judge in a non-jury trial) is the non-interactive participant, the indirect but crucially important target of the exchange of meanings (Drew 1985; Bülow-Møller 1991).

The essentially discoursal nature of court proceedings has led to the rise of another, perhaps more powerful metaphor than that of the trial as battle. That is the metaphor of trial as story-telling. The initial impetus in this area came from Bennett and Feldman's pioneering study (1981) in which they claimed that in a criminal trial a jury interprets the evidence presented to it from the opposing sides and constructs a story. That is to say the jury accepts from the opposing versions or 'stories' of the event placed before them a single story which fits with their everyday knowledge of what people are likely to do and should do. It is true that in many cases, counsel, particularly defending counsel, may be more concerned to throw doubt on the prosecution story than to construct an alternative version, but in raising a 'reasonable doubt' in the minds of jury members, an alternative version is implied. The trial-as-story metaphor, despite a certain vagueness about the linguistic and discoursal criteria for storiness, has proved to be a very fertile and valuable one and has been the framework around which a great deal of analysis and comment has been made of courtroom language from writers in law (White 1985; Jackson 1988a, b) and linguistics (Kurzon 1985; Den Boer 1990; Maley and Fahey 1991: 4). It has the value of focusing attention on the discoursal strategies of all participants, but particularly those of counsel and witness; the ways in which both counsel and witness exploit the discoursal resources available, given the discoursal constraints laid upon them, and the inequalities of power that these represent.

Courtroom discourse

Generic structure

Courtroom discourse is spoken and interactive. The adversarial nature of the trial process is the immediate determinant of its structural elements: the different stages which structure the proceedings. These ensure that for each witness there will be an examination-in-chief, by his own supportive counsel (this is called direct examination in USA) a cross-examination, by the adversarial counsel, and then a re-examination from the supportive counsel, if he/she thinks it necessary. As well, each counsel typically, in a trial of any weight, will open his case, by a summary, an opening address, and will close the case, after all his witnesses have been examined, by a closing address. In a trial before a jury (all criminal trials and some civil proceedings) there will be as well a summation or direction from the judge, directed to the jury.

These different stages are obligatory elements of the generic structure. There may be as well other optional kinds of interactive episodes; for example judge to counsel, judge to witness, counsel to counsel, judge to jury.

Although each stage is crucial to the overall process, the

examination stage is usually perceived to be the core of the trial process, an arena of opposition and drama. It is the stage which has attracted the greatest attention from those legal and linguistic observers concerned with the distribution of power, and with forensic strategies.[6]

The examination process and interpersonal meanings: interactive strategies

Given that virtually all the exchanges in examination in chief, cross-examination and re-examination are conducted by question and answer turntaking, it is not surprising that much research has focused on question form employed by counsel and its effect on response form. Some studies have attempted to measure the 'combativeness' and 'coerciveness' of question types (Danet and Bogoch 1980; Woodbury 1984) used by counsel. Confirmation seeking questions, for example, may be either polar in form or declarative, and with or without tag; their predicted or entailed answer is either a confirmation or denial, i.e. yes or no. Clearly these are more likely to constrain a witness's reply than an information seeking question, i.e. a 'WH' question. Of the confirmation seeking questions, declaratives with tags are the most constraining: 'You saw him there, didn't you?'. Or 'You saw him there. Is that correct?' When witnesses attempt to go beyond a minimal response they can be checked.

It is, however, important to realise that two kinds of examination process are in fact involved in courtroom proceedings. It is true that the adversary system encourages combative and aggressive questioning by counsel, and limits answers to narrowly perceived parameters of relevance, but it is also true that for each opposing counsel there is a supporting one.

In the text below, from an Australian trial, counsel is cross-examining a key witness for the prosecution, a criminal who has turned police informer. The witness is familiar with the witness box and its perils, but the counsel, well known for his successful advocacy, has an important point to pursue:

Counsel: And I suppose it would be fair to say that as they came
              to recognise the extent of your knowledge about

	overseas drugs, so they became more and more interested?
Witness:	No, that would be incorrect. They already knew where I stood, much prior to July of 1982.
Counsel:	You say that their own intelligence was sufficient to let them know how important you were even before you spoke to them?
Witness:	They had been following me . . .
Counsel:	Is that right or not?
His Honour:	Just a moment, Mr B. I am allowing the witness to answer that question.
Counsel:	With respect, Your Honour . . .
His Honour:	I am allowing him to answer it.
Counsel:	I am asking that my objection be noted.
His Honour:	Every objection that you have ever made in this case has been noted, Mr B.
Counsel:	I must be allowed to make it, with respect, or it does not go down.
His Honour:	Would you say what you were saying, Mr C?
Witness:	They had been following me, monitoring telephones that I was associated with and raiding premises that I was associated with since 1979.

In this exchange, the counsel, Mr B wants to explore the nature of the relationship between the witness and the Australian Federal Police ('they'). He asks a question about the extent of the Australian Federal Police's intelligence about his activities, phrasing it in the form most favoured by cross-examining counsel: a declarative with a rising tone which seeks confirmation, not information, as a response. When the witness fails to provide a straight confirmation or denial (Yes or No) he seeks to curb the answer. But the judge intervenes and allows the witness's account. That is 'They knew of my involvement *because* they had been following me.' It is an implicit explanation which the judge allows presumably because of its potential relevance to the issues.

This exchange shows that to give an account of the facts, as here, is to provide a version of events. Here each party to the exchange is stressing different aspects of the witness's involvement with the Federal Police: the witness stresses what the police did ('they had been following me . . .'; the counsel stresses interaction between police and witness, what was shared knowledge and what the police did on behalf of the witness, ('to let them know how important you were even before you spoke to them'). These meaning choices (police as actors versus witness as actor and sayer) are tactical, consonant with the version of events that each is expressing.

Consider now the same witness with his supportive counsel in examination in chief (direct examination):

Counsel: After having given those documents to Mr H, did you see Mr H again?
Witness: Yes, I did.
Counsel: When was that?
Witness: About the second or third week of June.
Counsel: Did you have a conversation with him regarding M?
Witness: Yes, I did.
Counsel: What did you say?
Witness: I said to him, 'There seems to be some holdup with the M money. The chap didn't turn up. I'll have to wait for the weekend and go out and see M.'
Counsel: Then Mr H said something to you?
Witness: That is correct.
Counsel: After that meeting with Mr H, when was the next time that you saw him?
Witness: In July of 1983.

Here the pattern of question and response is quite different. The exchanges are congruent and cooperative, and the counsel and witness together build up the story they are presenting. This sequence is intended to establish for the benefit of the judge and jury a sequence of events in an illegal conspiracy. Counsel is not permitted to 'lead', to ask questions which presuppose their answer, so his questions typically alternate between indefinite polars ('Did you then say something?') and open information seeking questions ('What did you say?'). The witness, right on cue, responds with the required information, in the desired sequence. His experience as a witness is revealed in the easy and appropriate way in which he quotes conversations, that is in direct, as against indirect, reported speech, thus conforming to evidential requirements. Note how the question 'Then Mr H said something to you?' is answered only by a confirmation. He does not elaborate unless his counsel gives him the prompt, e.g. 'What did he say?' The sequence has all the signs of a carefully rehearsed performance.

These examples show the relevance of the story-telling model to the description of courtroom discourse, and how the different structures of examination create different interactional contexts in which the stories can be told. Figure 1.2 shows their relationships.

Witness strategies

Figure 1.2 shows how the discourse structure of the trial comprises two distinct dialogic modes. There is a cooperative and supportive mode in examination in chief, and a combative and adversarial mode in cross-examination (and re-examination). The opposing versions of the story emerge from the different interactional contexts. Because the supportive cooperative mode offsets the adversarial, combative one, it follows that witnesses do have opportunities in direct examination to give their own version of events – but with two important provisos. First, they and their counsel need to be in tune and to some extent at least, rehearsed. It is said that good counsel never ask a question to which they do not know the answer or which cannot be turned to some advantage. Second, witnesses need confidence or experience or both, to render them credible in the eyes of the judge and jury. O'Barr's (1982) studies have shown the value of certain 'powerful' modes of speech, i.e. confident standard speech, in

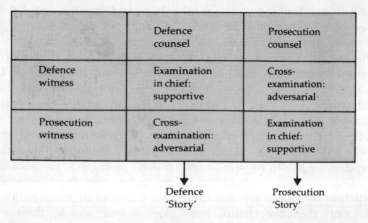

	Defence counsel	Prosecution counsel
Defence witness	Examination in chief: supportive	Cross-examination: adversarial
Prosecution witness	Cross-examination: adversarial	Examination in chief: supportive

Defence 'Story'   Prosecution 'Story'

Figure 1.2

comparison to 'powerless' modes, i.e. fragmented, non-standard speech. Some ethnic or special groups (for example children) are often confused, surprised and affronted by the unfamiliar procedures, and are unable to exploit the opportunities offered them to tell their story (Maley and Fahey 1991: 16; Brennan, this volume; Eades, this volume).

Experiential meanings: the construction of reality

From the discussion above it is clear that strategies of courtroom story-telling involve not only matters of speech function and role but of content. The question and answer sequences are only the vehicle, the textual organisation, on which the story, or stories, is built. It is experiential meanings which carry the content of the story or stories: who did what to whom, where, when, how and for what purpose (Hasan, in press b). Through the transitivity patterns of the clause which realise the different choices of participant, process and circumstance, the opposing stories are constructed by the courtroom discourse. Traditionally, in textbooks and reference works on the law of evidence and courtroom process generally, this process of construction is explained as a matter of establishing the 'facts'. Of course, all discourse is selective of the 'facts' it relates, whether true or not, and necessarily so in the interests of brevity and relevance. To that extent, all discourse presents or constructs only a version of reality. In courtroom discourse, brevity and relevance are institutional requirements, established and maintained by the rules of evidence and they greatly constrain the meanings and therefore the versions of reality, i.e. the stories, that can be constructed. The texts in the previous section have shown some of these constraints in operation. It is beyond the scope of this study to detail them here: Penman (1987) has shown how these evidentiary rules seek to enforce the maxims of the Cooperative Principle (Grice 1975). However, some generalisations about the scope of their content can be made. Cross-examining counsel rarely ask questions about the witness's thoughts, intention, purposes. Questions are very much restricted to verifiable matters: physical, verbal, visual processes and their associated participants. Hearsay is inadmissible. Counsel in examination in chief, on the other hand, may pose a question to their own witness about thoughts and intentions. So, one story may focus solely on the actions of a particular witness; the opposing story may seek to establish the motivation of the witness, in the sense of exploring the circumstances and reasoning behind his/her actions. One story emphasises material, verbal and behavioural processes, the other intertwines these with mental processes.

Transitivity patterns provide the framework of each story's version of events. Lexical choices make these patterns specific and connect them to particular contexts. The actual lexical choices made by opposing counsel also reveal the extent to which their stories are at variance with each other, and show the extent to which experiential and interpersonal meanings are mapped upon each other in texts. In her analysis of the choices made by counsel in an abortion trial, Danet (1980b) showed how the interpersonal colouring of referential words e.g. 'baby' versus 'fetus', constructed the different realities. A baby implies a mother, and a positive, culturally valued context; a fetus implies a womb and a neutral, sanitised medical context.

The constraints on experiential meanings (what can or cannot be said) and interpersonal and textual meanings (by whom, how and in what order) have consequences for discourse strategies. The single question and answer exchange is slow and limiting. It may take a long 'line of questioning' for counsel to establish a relevant fact, incident or motive. Hasan (in press a) has argued that relevance (in the Gricean sense) is rarely a matter of a single exchange and the illocutionary force of its parts. It is a discoursal notion which is built up in contextualised texts. Studies in courtroom discourse have also stressed that the relevance of any exchange in a sequence of exchanges can only be assessed in terms of that sequence, and *its* relevance to a topic or component of the story, i.e. location, motive, key incidents, character (Harris 1984b; Drew 1985; Bülow-Møller 1991) or even in relation to the lawyer's macro-organisation of the case (Valdes 1986).

JUDICIAL DISCOURSE: OPINION AND OBLIGATION

The discourse situation

When a case is decided, the dispute between the parties is settled, or an offence or crime has been found or not found. This may mean either that a story has been accepted or rejected or that the court has decided on the disputed meaning of a section within a statute and made a decision accordingly. As we saw earlier (Introduction) the decisions of courts have significance for later cases, since the principle of law applied, particularly if it is a common law principle, may serve as a precedent for later cases.

Judges give their decision and order verbally in court to the litigants involved; important, i.e. legally significant judgments are later published, tidied up a little by the judges, in Law Reports. There may be criticism of the principles for selection for such cases (Goodrich 1988: 147) and often there certainly is criticism of the justice, validity or wisdom of individual judgments, but none the less these are legally significant documents. The judgments of the higher appellate courts, in particular, represent the substance of the common law. Because of the huge body of case law that this represents, stretching back several centuries in many cases, and because of its social significance, I shall here concentrate on this area of discourse.

The structural and ideological differences between common law systems and European continental systems which underlie the management of court proceedings also have consequences for judicial judgment, particularly at the appellate level. Wetter (1960) in a comparison of appellate judgments in USA, England, France, Sweden and Germany shows how the different role of the judge in these systems has produced entirely different discourse styles. The judicial role and its realisation in discourse reflects in particular 'the shaping force of the procedural setting and institutional composition of courts, their actual working conditions, legal education, the current styles of advocacy, and the structure of substantive law' (1960: 52). In short, they emerge from and are part of different legal cultures (Friedman 1975: 223). Continental judges are likely to be officials and bureaucrats: their decision-making is correspondingly restrained and frequently rigid in style and format. In the common law tradition, judges have been trained as advocates and their training has focused on the construction and balancing of argument. As a separate wing of government, common law judges have assumed an independence and an individuality unmatched elsewhere, at the same time as they have developed guildlike skills of argumentation and reasoning and mastery of the specialised vocabulary. Such qualities can be perceived as valuable, an expression even a flowering of a time-honoured tradition. In the perception of other more critically minded observers, they represent an exercise of elitist and exclusionary discourse practices (Goodrich 1987).

There are of course differences even within the common law tradition in the way in which judgment is given and reported. None the less, one shared tradition of common law judgments, whatever their jurisdiction, is the *individual* tenor of judgments. That is to say, common law judges do not regard the application of the principles of law to the facts of the case as a purely mechanical process. Reasoning is involved, a kind of reasoning by analogy (Levi 1949), and choices abound (and will have been pressed by counsel) for the premises or bases on which the reasoning will proceed. A number of judges may come to the same conclusion, but by different reasoning processes; or they may come to entirely different conclusions.

In giving judgment, a judge could, of course, simply declare the principle of law which is applicable to the instant case. The principle of law is called the 'ratio decidendi' or reason for deciding. But common law judges do not discharge their obligations so simply. Not only do they declare the law, they make explicit the reasoning processes which have led them to that decision, the cases they have considered, the analogies they have considered and rejected – in short, their individual 'fullest examination'. There is, then, both a declaratory and a justificatory purpose or function (Maley 1985b: 169).

What the individual tenor means in practice, is that there may be as many as five full, i.e. lengthy judgments delivered for a case on which a bench of five judges has sat, usually as a higher appellate court. Each judge gives his opinion as to what the correct principle of law is for the case, as well as an account of his reasoning; a majority verdict prevails. Often, a judge will concur with his brother judge or judges and refrain from offering a separate judgment which at least has the advantage for later lawyers (and law students) of making fewer judgments available from which principles of law or precedents must be sifted. Obviously, this is not an economical system, but it is time-honoured and highly prized by common law judges. I have argued elsewhere that the giving of reasons, the revelation of analogies and argumentation which support a principle of law serve a legitimating function in the law (Maley 1989: 83). In delivering judgments, appellate judges have in mind a wider audience than the individual litigant in the case before them (Kitto 1975: 9). Rather judges are thinking of the scrutiny of their peers both present and future. If the judgment contains an important principle of law, then the judges may well be speaking to posterity. Even if they lack a taste for immortality, judges are well aware that their judgments can be confirmed or overturned in later cases, so there is a strong incentive to be careful and explicit.

In summary, judicial decisions are an important source of law in common law countries, since the reasons for the decision provide a precedent which can be applied to the facts of later cases. The historical role of common law judges, in deciding cases, is to say what in their opinion is the correct principle of law to be applied and to reveal the reasoning processes by which they have come to that decision. Judgments serve both a declaratory and a justificatory function.

Judicial discourse

Generic structure

The freedom which the common law judge enjoys, in particular the appellate judge, reflects first of all in the flexibility of the generic structures of judicial discourse. None the less, all judgments share a set of structural elements, and therefore can be said to have a generic structure potential. These elements are quite easily identified (Enright 1983; Bhatia 1987a) and can be itemised:

Facts, an account of events and/or the relevant history of the case;
Issues, either of fact or of law or both;
Reasoning;
Conclusion, the principle or rule declared applicable for the instant case;
Order or Finding

(Maley 1985b: 160)

All the elements are obligatory in a single judgment or the first judgment of a majority judgment. In a set of judgments on a particular case, a concurring or dissenting judge may choose, but rarely does, to omit Facts. If the Facts element is present, it precedes Issues and Reasoning which logically form a fixed sequence. Issues and Reasoning are iterative or recursive. Conclusion and Order typically occur initially or finally.

Interpersonal meanings: point of view and modality ✗

The freedom which common law judges have assumed historically and jealously retained |ensures that each judge speaks to some extent in his own voice, as it were. Individual styles vary considerably in judgments, but, no doubt because of the social gravity of the occasion or speech event, a consistently lofty and formal tenor is typical, particularly in the written appellate judgments that form the core of case law./ In the English higher courts, formal modes of address are retained, even in the published reports, and the judges refer to 'their learned brethren', 'my noble and learned friend'.

|Within the judgment, the individual tenor and institutional functions are reflected in an intricate pattern of different forms of modality. Consider the text below, taken from a famous House of Lords' judgment in 1932 which formulated an important principle on the duty of care in tort (see also Goldman, this volume). It is well known to every law student and lawyer, and frequently quoted in later judgments.

> At present, I content myself with pointing out that in English law there *must* be, and is, some general conception of relations giving rise to a duty of care, of which the particular cases found in the books are but instances. The liability for negligence, whether you style it such or treat it as in other systems as a species of 'culpa', is **no doubt** based upon a general public sentiment of moral wrongdoing for which the offender *must* pay. But acts or omissions which any moral code **would** censure *cannot* in a practical world be treated so as to give a right to every person injured by them to demand relief. In this way rules of law arise which limit the range of complainants and the extent of their remedy. The rule that you *are to* love your neighbour becomes, in law,

you *must* not injure your neighbour: and the lawyer's question, who is my neighbour? receives a restricted reply. You *must* take reasonable care to avoid acts or omissions which you **can** reasonably foresee would be likely to injure your neighbour. Who, then, in law, is my neighbour? The answer **seems** to be: persons who are so closely and directly affected by my act that I *ought* reasonably to have them in contemplation as being so affected when I am directing my mind to the acts or omission which are called in question . . . **I think** that this sufficiently states the truth if proximity be not confined to mere physical proximity, but be used, as **I think** it was intended, to extend to such close and direct relations that the act complained of directly affects a person whom the person alleged to be bound to take care **would** know **would** be directly affected by his careless act . . .

(*Donohue v. Stevenson* [1932] A.C. 562 per Lord Atkin)

We note here the first person speech role which orientates the judgment from Lord Atkin's point of view. He discusses the relevant principles of legal obligation as he sees them. Because he is talking of obligation the semantics of modality are invoked. Halliday (1985: 86) distinguishes between two kinds of modality which he calls modalisation (often just modality) and modulation. Modalisation expresses the varying degrees of probability and usuality, while modulation expresses the various degrees of obligation and inclination. Both modalisation and modulation may be either objective or subjective; that is to say while both are expressed from the viewpoint of the speaker, they can nevertheless be expressed as though they are objective or subjective. In Lord Atkin's speech above, where modulation has been underlined and modalisation is in bold typeface, the two can intertwine as when he projects '[persons] that I *ought* reasonably to have in contemplation' from 'the answer **seems** to be . . .', the latter being an example of an objective modalisation, and the former a subjective modulation. That is, Lord Atkin is saying what in his opinion the law *should* be.

Modalisation and modulation are the chief linguistic means of expressing the justificatory and declaratory functions of judgment (Maley 1985b: 169) but of course carry interpersonal meanings as well. While the different forms of modality are pervasive in most judgments, the density of their distribution is likely to be uneven. Modulations are most likely to occur in the *conclusion* and *order*, usually prefaced or modified by modalisations. The interplay of modalisation and modulation is extremely common.

Modalisations in general are more widespread throughout the entire judgment. The *facts* element will contain least. Since it is now the accepted version of the extra-court reality, there is no need for an assessment of probability and as yet no need for an assessment of legal obligation that the facts give rise to.

Trial as story

The facts element is always presented as a narrative. Usually it is a version not only of the events that have given rise to the legal proceedings in the first place, but as well a narrative of the previous proceedings (charging, sentencing, arguments in lower courts, sentencing and so on). Each judge who includes a facts element in the judgments delivered seriatim on a particular case does so in his or her own way. The main events or facts may not be in doubt but each judicial story will express small but subtle differences. The selection of experiential, interpersonal and textual meanings realise differences in perceived relevance, emphasis and point of view. In this way, also, the judge exercises his right to see the case in his own way. Jackson (1988a, b) has argued that there is involved in the notion of trial as story not only the story-in-the-trial but the story-of-the-trial, and that all the participants comprehension of the case depends upon an interweaving of these substantial and pragmatic aspects. It seems then that the narrative versions presented in the facts element represent the judicial perception of these interwoven strands.

Intertextuality

A number of different aspects of intertextuality pervade judicial discourse. As in legislation and courtroom discourse, all discourse is carried on against a framework not only of shared knowledge of the institutional culture, but of knowledge of a more specific kind, that is, of the relevance of other institutional discourses to the particular issue. The entire operation of precedent, which is the basic facilitating concept of the common law legal system, is a matter of intertextuality. Previous discourses, or selected parts of previous discourses, become crucial to the interpretation of present discourses. Any principle of law, formulated by a judge in a particular case, will have a relationship to another earlier one, or more likely a set or line of earlier principles. Thus the principle formulated by Lord Atkin, above, was to some extent built upon earlier principles, that is, formulated with earlier principles and cases firmly in mind. Because Atkin's decision or principle represented something of a leap from these earlier ones, even though it was closely related to them, it became an important principle in the law of tort. All future discourses on the law of tort, all future principles are related to, or dialogic with, this principle (Bakhtin 1981).

CONCLUSION: THE POSSIBILITIES FOR REFORM

The preceding outline of three central areas of legal discourse has attempted to show how the discourses of law are integral to a particular kind of legal system and legal culture. I have argued elsewhere that any reformation of legal discourse must take into account the contingency between language change and legal, i.e. institutional change. That is not to say that such change is neither possible nor desirable; only that reform can only be achieved by the cooperation of relevant government and legal authorities and with a recognition of the adaptation and compromises involved. In a recent review article, Danet (1990) has outlined developments in the plain language language movement in the USA, England, Australia and some European countries. Her review of the literature indicates that the plain language movement has made substantial progress in the simplification and reorganisation of many business and government documents. The task of simplifying legislation remains more intractable and virtually untouched, despite government initiatives (Eagleson 1991). It is not simply a matter of conservatism; amending existing legislation in any volume of the Statute book is a daunting and expensive task. But the more difficult problems arise from the institutional situation outlined above. Given the detailed, explicit nature of much legislation, a change in words can result in a change of meaning and consequent uncertainty. More general rules would be simpler and more comprehensible but there are attendant problems of vagueness and applicability, the 'open texture' that Hart has evoked (see above, 'The tension between certainty and flexibility'). Yet there are signs that governments and their draftsmen are prepared to do what they can (Bhatia, 1987b; Eagleson 1991) and may in the future do even more.

Reform of the discoursal procedures of the courtroom also raises questions of structural reform, since discoursal patterns and traditions of advocacy are derived from the adversarial system and the rules of evidence. Realistically, governments are unlikely to contemplate dismantling the adversary system, which in any case is for many people a valuable and cherished institution, encapsulating traditional values like 'the golden thread' of British justice (see Carroll, this volume). But here again concessions are being made, when a glaring need for them arises, as it has in the question of the evidence of children (see Brennan, this volume). There is a real possibility that some relaxation of evidentiary requirements may create a more flexible and productive atmosphere for these particularly vulnerable witnesses (see Carroll, this volume; Eades, this volume).

No one would deny that the language of the law should, wherever possible, attempt to shorten the gap between it and everyday language that is the source of much incomprehension, frustration and frequent disadvantage. That task will be made easier if observers and critics of the legal process are able to distinguish between the criterial forms of legal language, that is to say, those that are integrated deeply into institutional structures practices and ideologies and which may or may not be open to reform; and those that are unhelpful, peripheral, and therefore dispensable. *It is important to bridge the gap for democratic purposes.*

NOTES

1. See Mellinkoff (1963), Friedman (1964, 1975) for a traditional approach; Goodrich (1987); Kelman (1987) from the viewpoint of critical legal studies.
2. Kurzon (1986: 10) provides other versions of the enacting formula.
3. *R.* v. *Marinovich, Romeo and Ricciardello* [(1990) 46 A Crim R].Western Australia. For legal fictions, generally, see Fuller (1967).

50 LANGUAGE CONSTRUCTING LAW

4. Commonwealth of Australia, Attorney General's Department (1982). *Extrinsic Aids to Statutory Interpretation*, Australian Govt Publishing Service, Canberra.
5. *Jones* v. *National Coal Board* [1957] 2 Q.B. considered the scope of the judge's role. See also 'The judge who talked too much', in Denning (1980: 58).
6. On strategies and power in courtroom discourse see: Atkinson and Drew (1979), Drew (1985), Harris (1984a), Harris (this volume), Harris (1987), Bülow-Møller (1991), Philips (1984), Woodbury (1984), O'Barr (1982), Dunstan (1980).

TWO

Accident and absolute liability in anthropology

Laurence Goldman

Therefore every death is an accidental one, even death from illness. Or to put it more precisely, no death is, since to the primitive mind nothing ever happens by accident, properly speaking [p.43] . . . the very idea of accident is inconceivable to the primitive mind [p.45].

In fact, *there is no such thing as chance*. The idea of accident does not even occur to a native's mind, while on the contrary the idea of witchcraft is always present [p.50].

(Lévy-Bruhl 1923)

A PLEA FOR ACCIDENT

This paper presents an ethnographic account of the grammar and pragmatics of 'accident' in the forensic discourse of the Huli of Papua New Guinea. It explores how actors model and maintain the reality of accident interpretations through their conversational behaviour. Such linguistic building materials offer indispensable resources for constructing and accessing cultural philosophies of action, mind and responsibility. In English, our notions of accident frequently discriminate between **actions** that are under the control of agents, and **happenings** that are essentially non-agentive in nature. But they can also signal views about the moral and legal dimensions to the doing of actions. This is because accidentality terms like *inadvertently, coincidentally*, or *accidentally* provide us with an account of the mental element – intention, will, desire, deliberation, purpose, etc. – in some event. When describing some incident or process as an 'accident', or having 'occurred/been done accidentally' rather than 'deliberately' or 'intentionally', we conflate information not just about causation, and perhaps (if pertinent) degrees of culpability and fault to be imputed, but also about the element of consciousness that intruded into the event. To talk of 'accidents' is then to engage in a mode of theorising about 'mind' in the world. For this reason, investigating indigenous categories of coincidence must assume a paramount place in any treatment of the vastly ramified topics of causation and culpability. What cannot be recognised, however, cannot be known. If, as I argue within, we indeed know very little about accident from a cross-cultural viewpoint it is because anthropologists have too often allowed themselves to talk about this concept at the expense of, and removed from, how speakers themselves talk *with* and *through* accident.

The images of chance found in the Huli case considered below reflect two interrelated facets of the data. First, such angles of vision are here focused on the topic of death. Second, their viability is being established and tested in a context of ideological conflict. 'Accident' is perceived through, and emerges from, opposition with volitional 'murder'. Accident is as accident does, so that from the processes of rebuttal and refutation we can more easily identify its sociocultural and pragmatic character.

In our English vocabulary of conduct, the sense that adverbial qualifications like *intentionally*, *wilfully*, *deliberately*, or *purposefully* have is in part determined by their recognised antitheses. There is an imprecision about the statement that 'x did y *voluntarily*' until we have comprehended precisely what was excluded – e.g. *duress*, *persuasion* or *compulsion*. In Austin's (1956) linguistic work, focused as it was on the grammar of certain philosophically important expressions of excuse, action-modifiers like *accidentally*, *mistakenly*, *inadvertently* or *unintentionally*, were analysed as 'moral adverbs'. Their role as excuses could be gauged both from how they functioned to rule out or exonerate one from responsibility, and their contrast with complementary terms that served to aggravate or assign responsibility. Thus exculpations were analysed alongside inculpations as an exemplification of how the 'abnormal will throw light on the normal'.

The philosophies of conduct and mind are inextricably linked, for mentalistic notions like *intention*, *motive* and *reason* play a role in both the identification and description of human actions. They have a bracketing effect on how we dissect a stream of doings and how this gets communicated to others. Our descriptions reflect the intentions we impute, those avowed or denied by the actor, and those which guide our verbal interactions. The choice of 'arson' as against 'setting alight', 'murder' as against 'killing' is suffused with intentionality. Actions implicate intentions because intentions explicate actions. In this respect the battery of modifiers like *inadvertently* or *absent-mindedly* articulate cultural ideas of 'heed' (Ryle 1949); they are about minding and the application of mind. Accidents are tested by enquiring about motive.

In linguistics, examining the scope, ambiguity, and co-occurrence restrictions of accidentality adverbs has long been appreciated as central to the analysis of action verbs and processes of causativisation (i.e. where, for example, an intransitive verb like 'burn' gets changed to a transitive form). What can modify what, what combinations or dissociations occur, can help uncover the type of cause-consequence relation – whether direct/indirect, intended/incidental, directive (verbal persuasion)/manipulative (actual physical force) – signalled by particular causal affixes. We look both to the presence, absence and behaviour of contrasting purposive adverbials, as well as to how agency, responsibility and control are buried in the interstices of linguistic form. Our linguistic expectations here are to a degree conditioned by cultural understandings of what is 'normal'; in Huli it is more usual to set houses alight than people, as in Western societies it is more usual to tread on snails than babies. This accounts for the rejection, or reaction of puzzlement, to statements such as 'x set person y alight inadvertently' or 'x trod on the baby accidentally' in the respective speech communities. But there is more to their queerness than this. The fact that there is a whole range of English verbs that cannot be qualified by accidentality adverbs points to an inherent component of censure and condemnation. The incongruity of such configurations as 'x cheated *accidentally*', or 'x lied *unintentionally/accidentally*' rests on the observation that we cannot blame and excuse, ascribe and withdraw fault, in the same breath. Equally there seems another whole class of verbs which sit uncomfortably with accidentality adverbs and where the semantic confusion would be precisely that of doing something 'accidentally on purpose'. Thus verbs such as *cook*, *compose*, *write* or *build* rarely figure in constructions such as 'I accidentally cooked a meal/I accidentally wrote a letter'.

There are less obvious linguistic encodings of inadvertent/ incidental causation, agency and blame. Beyond adverbial qualifications lie case marking patterns (ergative/instrumental, comitative, etc.), word order preferences, causal affixes, contrafactual constructions, and transitivity paradigms to name some of the parameters considered here. As indices of a legal philosophy, any distillation of accident in Huli law talk is compelled to consider them.

For jurisprudence, marking boundaries between various types of accident is pivotal in determining the applicability and scope of legal liability. Accident law (tort law) in the Anglo-American legal system deals with the entitlement of a victim of accident to damages from an injurer. To fall within the purview of some liability rule, however, the accident must be deemed to be of a given type. In this process the law appears centrally concerned to distinguish between the following general categories of accident.

Accidents not caused by human conduct

Those consequences, either harmful or beneficial, where some human conduct (act or omission) or contrivance is not held to be causally involved. That is, the happening is of a type whose probability or severity is unaffected by the behaviour of any injurer's or victim's behaviour. It is this sense of independently interacting causal chains, or confluences of forces, which we convey by such expressions as 'it just happened' or 'accidents will happen, it's no one's fault'. Moreover, the immunity of such events from any human control is frequently emphasised by the adjectival qualifications 'pure, freak, absolute, or complete' with the close synonyms 'luck, chance, coincidence and accident'. Accidents are pure in the sense of being free from human control or contamination. In this type of accident, results have been set in motion often by inanimate entities incapable of volition but capable of their own propulsion; the semi-agentive forces of wind, smoke, fire or water are typical examples. In the legal arena these 'inevitable accidents' may constitute a defence of 'no actus reus (criminal deed)', 'superseding cause' or 'novus actus interveniens' to negative or break the chain of imputed causation between some act and resultant harm.

Accidents caused by human conduct

Accidents are also those unintended or inadvertent consequences of conduct that may itself have been volitional – accidental harm resulting from negligence, mistake, recklessness, or death *per infortunium* – or non-volitional as in the circumstances of automatism, physical compulsion, self-preservation, insanity, shock or intoxification.

Misfortunes, mishaps and accidents 'overtake' or 'befall' people; they may be good or bad, evoke envy or pity. But only actions (which presume agents) can be talked about or evaluated as right or wrong, praiseworthy or blameworthy. Accident, along with its sibling defences of mistake or duress, represents the 'cash value' (Hart 1949) of such legal notions as the *actus reus* (criminal deed) and *mens rea* (state of mind accompanying such acts). To determine the types of harm which are considered to have resulted from the unreasonable risks created by a defendant, and which are thus subject to some liability rule, the law has recourse to four principal notions which can be summarily stated as follows:

1. *Duty of care*: to take reasonable care to avoid acts or omissions likely to injure another. This includes the duty of affirmative care (aid and rescue) where the defendant is the source of some danger, where a plaintiff is deemed to be under the latter's protective pale, or where the defendant's position/status gives rise to such duty. This duty of care, however, is grounded in specific relationships only and the law does not, for example, impose a positive duty to act on a bystander who sees a small unrelated child drowning. This omission to save a life would be non-culpable since the harm is unconnected with the bystander's conduct.
2. *Remoteness of damage*: a reasonably proximate connection has to exist between some injurer's act and the harm; the consequences must not be too 'remote'. Although tests based on 'necessary' causation or the 'but for' principle (i.e. but for the act of x the harm to y would not have occurred) are utilised, inquiries are just as frequently hypothetical.
3. *Contributory negligence*: refers to the plaintiff's failure to meet his/her proscribed level of care and which is deemed legally contributory to some resultant harm. This is a defence

which can be pleaded to diminish or abrogate the 'duty to care'.

4. *Voluntary assumption of risk*: proceeds on the basis that no wrong is done to one who consents: *volenti non fit injuria*. The risk assumed may be implied or explicit, and tended to operate as a defence in consensual relations as for example between a host driver – passenger, or occupier – visitor.

These legal precepts are notoriously uncertain, discretionary and hydra-headed when used to determine the scope of liability. Nevertheless, they all function to mark a boundary between the general categories of accident delineated above. That is, between *coincidental accidents* – where the probability and severity of the event is unaffected by any level of care or conduct of some injurer (Shavell 1987) – and *non-coincidental accidents* where the converse circumstances obtain. In law then, accidents must be of a certain kind that do not usually occur without human negligence to attract damages, a sentiment encapsulated in the legal maxim *res ipsa loquitur*. In effect, legal reasoning reflects here the more broadly understood distinction between actions and superventions. The defence of accident is a rebuttal raised to contend either that (a) the conduct of an accused had no causal connection with the fact of which complaint is made; or (b) that fact is an 'unintended consequence' of some act.

The history and development of legal systems, both Western and non-Western, to recognise and assimilate 'accident' in their calculations and canons of liability impacted on, for example, psychology. Thus Piaget (1932) espoused the theory that what held good for the evolutionary genesis of legal responsibility was paralleled in the social and moral learning of the child. The objectivity of 'primitive' law which ascribed responsibility to involuntary acts, accidents, as well as acts committed without negligence or imprudence manifested the 'infantile' perception of a world from which all chance had been proscribed. The fortuitous and coincidental belong here to the agnosticism of adult life where subjective intentions are usually taken into account in ascribing responsibility.

This brief survey of 'accident' provides the necessary background for an anthropological excursion into this topic. Accident is endowed with a quite profound place in the structure and development of world-views, so we must remain sensitive to the diverse ways in which it manifests itself in discourse, and the diverse discourses in which accident appears. However, if the conventional wisdoms of anthropology are to be believed, this whole project should be a non-starter. For to depict a small-scale non-Western society in which accident impacts on the limitations and scope of liability, and which is not couched in the mystically premised dialogue of evil, witchcraft or sorcery, is in itself to offer a critique of a doctrinal legacy the main articles of which are that:

1. Concepts of coincidence and accident are absent from non-Western theories of action or misfortune. That in respect to human fatalities, the possibility of resorting to 'chance' appears inconceivable – 'because nothing that so harms a human being can be truly accidental' (cf. Evans-Pritchard 1937: 63ff.) (Chowning 1987: 156; cf. also Rasmussen 1989). Processes of ideological conflict between agentive (murder) and non-agentive (accident) causal models appear unknown, unheeded or unimportant. The anthropology of misfortune is historically couched then in the language of mysticism, magic and predestiny.
2. The ethnographic data from African, Melanesian and North American cultures show them to be uniformly of the classic no-fault liability mould with respect to how they treat accidental deaths. The canon of *absolute liability* (henceforth AL) – often grounded in the maxim that 'a man acts at his peril' – obviates any inquiry into fault or motivational bases. Accident and absolute liability are here antithetical brethren. Under this principle of AL, one is liable for the harmful results of one's actions (or omissions) whatever the circumstances regarding knowledge about such harm, knowledge that one is committing a prohibited action, or whatever the state of mind in which the act is done. Whether from an insensibility, unwillingness or inability to conceive the unintentional infliction of harm, traditional legal systems look only to the *consequences* of events, and their human or supra-human causal nexus. 'This ethic leaves little place for the accidental' (Glasse 1968: 111). The preclusion of 'accident' defences in the above regions reposes on structural, historical and logical arguments indicating both social anomie (Koch 1974, 1984; Moore 1972) and mental anomie (Horton 1967; Schieffelin

1976; Bowden 1987) were 'accident' permitted to enter into calculations of responsibility.

3. That even where concepts of the accidental appear (*contra* [1]), and even where events are 'unforeseeable and unpreventable' (Ryan 1961: 134), this does not serve to expunge liability but merely reduce the compensatory ramifications. This is still then a far cry from the naturalistic vocabulary of *coincidental accident* and seemingly discontinuous with the Western jurisprudential concepts of *volenti* or 'remoteness of damage' referred to above.

4. In line with the above, the orientation of discourse in the legal proceedings of these societies is towards *consequences* not *intentions*. In assessing liability there is a restricted focus on actors' psychological states of mind (*mens rea*). 'In determining responsibility, Huli rarely consider a person's motive or intent' (Glasse 1968: 111; cf. also Ochs 1988; Just 1990; Koch 1974; Epstein 1967). Accordingly, intentions, like exculpatory arguments, have a low (if not imperceptible) discourse profile.

There will be incredulity among non-anthropologists that so many societies seemingly operate without naturalistic models of explanation that allow for chance and coincidence. For comparative jurisprudence, that absolute liability exists anywhere in such pure form will appear implausible; while for linguists and philosophers, that speakers in any language can converse about actions and happenings in a manner empty of the import of intentionality will seem if not incomprehensible then unacceptable. Setting side questions about the accuracy of data purporting to show the absence of concepts of coincidence, the radical flaw in the above pattern of theorising concerns misconceptions about actions and their descriptions. Hardly any action is just the making of a physical movement, for what differentiates the stretching of a limb as against a 'victory salute' is convention, culture, and intent. Moreover, most of the verbs of action we use to describe events communicate some aspect of intentionality as simply part of their meaning. It would indeed be very difficult to account for human conduct by relying purely upon 'behaviouristic' terms. To suggest that in talking about 'consequences' one somehow avoids discussing intent is to both ignore and fundamentally misconstrue how speakers describe human behaviour, for it is intentions that tell us why some conduct counts as one action as against another. Furthermore, it quite falsely portrays forensic discourse in non-Western societies as devoid of all why-questions aimed at eliciting rationales – i.e. reasons for acting (cf. Goldman 1988, 1993). The lacuna in our ethnographic knowledge of accident is thus a direct reflection of the theoretical cul-de-sac into which it was driven. No finer example of *fallacia accidentis* – of the confusion between essential and accidental (συμβεβηκός) properties in cognitive systems – exists in the discipline.

And yet it is precisely here, in the interface between accident concepts and ascriptions of liability, that law and language studies can directly confront the concerns of traditional legal anthropology. In this view, the plea for Huli excuses – for the existence of a legal category of accident in Huli – is an anti-thesis on two counts. First, it offers a critique of the myth of absolute liability in anthropology. Second, it opposes the idea that we should view accident here as some proto- or pre-legal phenomenon – as somehow contributing to a more general historical understanding of the development of legal forms. The power of the linguistic evidence adduced suggests that accident is always likely to be implicative for liability ascription as a linguo-cultural reflex of the universally appreciated distinction between agentive and non-agentive happenings. We are then ineluctably transported beyond the forensic to the realm of language ontogenesis, to universal semantic notions and the way they are grammaticalised and deployed. This is why language and law go hand in hand in an investigation of accident concepts.

LEGAL ANTHROPOLOGY: ACCIDENT AND ABSOLUTE LIABILITY

Given the bold claims made above it is necessary to briefly sketch what anthropologists have had to say about accident before directly engaging the Huli materials. The resurgence of interest in, and noticings of, cultural instances like Samoa where 'legal assessments of wrongdoing do not rely on properties of mental states, and verbal conjectures on this topic are not part of legal proceedings' (Ochs 1988: 220; cf. also Just 1990) signifies the continuing vitality of the classic themes of intent, causality and culpability. The contrast is invariably drawn here with Western systems where assignment of liability attends to speakers' intentions, not just consequences of actions. The familiar distinction between what a person does and the mental state with which it is done gives way to an uncompromising focus on the harm done – 'the Law of wrongs starts from the fact that damage has occurred' (Gluckman 1965: 232). The primary concern or 'impulse' (Morris 1973: 35) is to repair and redress rather than any assessment of fault. Such noticings reflect the ubiquity of AL which, along with self-help and collective responsibility have been judged to be 'especially characteristic of *primitive* legal systems' (Moore 1972: 51).

The history of AL in anthropology has been admirably discussed in the writings of Moore (1972), Gluckman (1965), Elias (1956) and Epstein (1967). There are two points which merit attention in connection with this literature:

1. The apt reconsiderations of AL which tempered early findings on African law were in the main concerned to show the importance of fault and *mens rea* to the issue of damages. Typically, the data indicated either (a) that no distinction appeared to be drawn between intentional and unintentional killing as among the Kikuyu, Kamba (Dundas 1915; Elias 1956) and certain Nigerian tribes (Diamond 1951: 282); or (b) the distinction is recognised but no sanction followed an accidental homicide as among the Ngwato and Kgatla (Schapera 1970: 261); or (c) though *mens rea* is taken into account as in Barotse 'they do not lessen the damages for accident' (Gluckman 1966: 233); or (d) as in the majority of cases and the Nuer, the significance of intention is restricted to ameliorating the quantum form, timing or acceptance of compensation (cf. Schapera 1970: 51; Diamond 1951: 113; Ibik 1969: 315; Howell 1954). The principle of AL for accidental harm was thus never challenged, merely refined and there was certainly never any suggestion in the African literature that a concept of accident might negative liability.

2. In the much later Melanesian literature we find a wholesale importation of the above African models. For example, Barnett (1973; cf. also Gordon and Meggitt 1985: 197) notes that the 'Melanesian view about compensation for injury caused to person or property is far more like one of absolute liability

than liability based on fault [p.64] . . . they believe in absolute liability even for injury or death caused by accident [p.74]'. Indeed, there seems little to choose between on the one hand the African data from Schapera (1970: 51) on the Tswana, Epstein (1967: 383) on the Zambia and Gluckman (1955: 205; 1965: 232) on the Barotse – concerning the irrelevance of motive – and on the other hand the Melanesian/Polynesian data from Ochs (1988: 111) on Samoa or Koch on the Jalé who appear not to 'distinguish between intent, negligence, inadvertence, and accident as aggravating or extenuating circumstances' (1974: 86). It appears then from these accounts that there is a basic isomorphism in forensic reasoning in Africa and Melanesia/Polynesia which is impervious to quite fundamental discontinuities in sociocultural and sociopolitical structures. I simply do not accept this.

While in the above mentioned ethnographies accidents were treated as a residual factor, in the extreme hypotheses it was banished altogether. Thus we find both Moore and Koch propounding the same thesis that AL in 'primitive' systems acts to constrain abuses of freedom since everyone knows they must eventually pay for the consequences of their actions. Moreover, 'the plea of accident or good intention will not excuse one' (Moore 1972: 67) for if 'alleged or actual accidents were to confer immunity, the maintenance of regulated social life would become a precarious enterprise' (Koch 1974: 90), or in Koch's later version 'public peace would be impossible' (1984: 121). Since accident defences or concepts would result in social anarchy they were held to be non-existent. Because the anthropologists felt accidents were functionally deleterious to society they presumed their subjects held the same views and consciousness of these self-evident legal truths.

Apart from plunging societies into the abyss of social disorder, another strand of thinking lay behind the banishment of accident. AL was grounded in small-scale kinship dominated systems which emphasised duty to others. Intentions were held to be read off given sets of relationships; thus any killing by an enemy was always a 'murder'. The assessment of *mens rea* independent of such social ties 'takes a long period of development' (Gluckman 1965: 217). Importantly, we glimpse here the familiar precept that defences of accident had to evolve or emerge, and on the basis of this chasm the rigid dichotomy between Western and non-Western systems of thought was established. Moreover, legal anthropologists could feel confident in these evolutionary premisses because they accorded with theories of misfortune generated elsewhere in the discipline; most notably in the fields of religion and comparative cognitive systems briefly sketched below.

Witchcraft, disease and misfortune

> Witchcraft participates in all misfortunes and is the idiom in which Azande speak about them and in which they explain them. Witchcraft is a classification of misfortunes.
>
> (Evans-Pritchard 1937: 64)

The above quote, reflecting earlier ideas about 'evil geniuses' (Lévy-Bruhl 1923) behind deaths from accidents, depicts the destiny that accident was to have in anthropology. Misfortunes were handled within the framework of religio-cosmological beliefs. Witchcraft was both a vision of natural causes as well as the language into which fortuity was translated. Accident was swallowed whole by the conventional wisdom that witchcraft beliefs provided explanations of the *why* of misfortune, disease and death. To ask about accidents was to contribute to discourse on the problem of evil, and on the multiplicity of human and mystical causal agents behind 'adversities of all kinds' (Turner 1964: 2). In the face of such mystical reductionism the position that legal anthropologists took on accident was merely acknowledging the time-honoured association of causality first with animism, and then with witchcraft. Traditionalistic thinking, it was held, sustained a single over-arching explanatory framework incapable of ideological conflict. Drawing on some recent Melanesian studies Chowning (1987: 156) notes for the Kove that 'any sudden death . . . any *fatal* [emphasis added] or serious accident to an adult will be attributed by at least some observers to sorcery . . . because nothing that so harms a human being can be truly accidental'. Elsewhere in the literature this thoroughgoing agentive model is rationalised in terms of mental stability. Sorcery/witchcraft beliefs are 'psychologically satisfying explana-

tions of misfortunes' (Bowden 1987: 109) as if somehow accident
is anathema to the Melanesian mind. Such psychological profiles
are also drawn by Schieffelin (1976: 101) when describing the
Kaluli where 'all deaths, whether due to illness, old age, or
violent accident' are caused by witchcraft. In effect, all deaths are
murders. Death cannot here be 'fortuitous, it must have a cause
or it is unintelligible' (p. 147). We are being asked to accept that
indigenous notions of accident are absent even though a
fortuitous fatality (*contra* Schieffelin) is not *per se* non-causal,
though it may be non-agentive. The idea of accident would
wreak both social anarchy and psychological turmoil. In its most
famous guise, accident is 'inconceivable because it is psychologically intolerable' (Horton 1967: 174).

'Primitive mind' theories

> It is evident that to minds so constituted the theory of an accident
> would be the last that would present itself, or rather that it would
> never present itself
>
> (Lévy-Bruhl 1923: 47)

A second major historical strand influencing theories of
accident derived from research into comparative thought structures. Lévy-Bruhl's ideas on the recalcitrant nature of the
'primitive mind' to tutelage in the notion of accident found
willing champions in Piaget and indeed many a famous
philosopher. For example, in Austin's consideration of 'ancient
models' (1956: 29) of causality he describes the agentive
perspective of 'primitive man . . . [for whom] every event has a
cause, that is every event is an action done by somebody – if not
by a man, then by a quasi-man or spirit'. The separation of an
event (i.e. a non-agentive happening) from an action was for
Austin a 'later' development in mankind. The existence of, and
recourse to, explanations of coincidence is once again depicted in
terms of evolutionary development. For tribal peoples, the notion
of chance is inconceivable for 'to entertain it would be to admit
that the whole episode was inexplicable and unpredictable: a
glaring confession of ignorance' (Horton 1967: 173; cf. also
Gluckman 1970: 324).

The above overviews reveal the extent to which accident became bogged down in an impasse of evolutionary suppositions about pre-scientific mentality, and how the theory of AL – with its hopelessly inadequate and muddled appreciation of indigenous ideas of intention, inadvertence and inevitable accident – was simply part of this whole picture. There is no room in these schemas for doctrinal pluralism, opportunism or cohabitation of naturalistic (the inexorable laws of nature, fate and inevitable accident) and voluntaristic (agentive) causal models.

Set against this myth that concepts of accident are absent from non-Western epistemologies the texts presented in Table 2.1 raise a host of issues. While the cultural settings vary so far as was possible similar examples have been selected to illustrate the supposed chasm in legal reasoning about causality, coincidence and culpability. As we move from A through B and the New Guinea extracts C–F we seemingly traverse that line where pure accident is both recognised, and where such recognition acts to break the chain of causation between an act and some imputed damage. Certainly, the need to integrate an understanding of causality and responsibility with notions of accident is implicit but here 'as with most New Guinea peoples, the recognition of pure accident as a cause of death is limited' (Ryan 1961: 121). The no-fault liability systems of the Jalé, Mendi and Wola are but instances of a regional type to which the Huli can also claim membership: 'everyone in Huli society is held responsible for the consequences of his or her actions . . . In determining responsibility, Huli rarely consider a person's motive or intent. They show little concern for extenuating circumstances; it is the consequences of an act they consider' (Glasse 1968: 111). In the apparent submission to the principle that 'a man acts at his peril' Winfield's Mediaeval man meets New Guinea man.

There are a number of grounds, however, for being less than satisfied with the apparent parallels between Anglo-Saxon and African/Melanesian legal systems. The question is legitimately raised as to whether these kinds of account – the best the discipline has to offer – are really the stuff of which comparative ethnological theories are, or should be, made? We might ponder, say, the role of voluntary assumption of risk in C[III] in Table 2.1 which is an accident type that occurs in all the selected texts. How formal is the act of 'invitation', and what evidence must be adduced to show that it was extended, or that

Table 2.1: Accident and liability: selected ethnographic reports

A. [Anglo-American Law: Shavell 1987 pp. 110–11]

Likewise, suppose that X invites Y to his home for dinner and that on the way Y slips on ice and breaks his leg. Here too we would be inclined to say that the accident was in some sense coincidental to, or was not closely related to, the injurer X's act, the dinner invitation, even though the invitation caused the accident . . . it is just as probable that Y will break his leg going to X's as it is that he will break his leg going to the movies; a dinner invitation will thus not increase the probability of the type of accident 'Y breaks his leg going somewhere'.

B. [Anglo-Saxon Law: Winfield 1926 on Leges Henrici]

'A man acts as his peril', it is said . . . it means that whatever a man does will, if it injures someone else, make the doer guilty of a breach of law. To put it quite plainly, he is liable for every conceivable harm which he inflicts on another. Such a proposition is merely ridiculous . . . They [Leges Henrici] are a queer collection, and show to a modern eye a good deal of muddling of intent with negligence, or perhaps even with inevitable accident. If A by sending another, is the cause of death on the message, A is liable; so too if B meets his death when A has summoned him, or is slain by arms placed by A.

C. [Mendi Law, Papua New Guinea: Ryan 1961: 124–5]

The question here is that of the allocation of responsibility: if deaths must be paid for, who is going to pay? The deciding principle relies on a concept similar to that of 'invitee' in English law. If a man has invited a victim of the accident into the situation which led to his death (or injury), then the inviter (and hence his sub-clan, or wider social group) is liable for any compensation that may be incurred. To give some examples . . .

II A invites B to accompany him on a journey on which B is killed. A is liable.

III A's house collapses, killing B while the latter is visiting him. A is liable.

D. [Wola Law, Papua New Guinea: Sillitoe 1979: 222–3; 1981: 76]

The Wola carry the concept of responsibility for violent death beyond war casualties to accidental deaths where someone else is involved in some way. A person may assume responsibility for an accidental death under various circumstances . . . A man asked a friend to accompany him on a journey and crossing a vine bridge his friend fell into the Was river and drowned; the man was held responsible for the death (and gave wealth to the deceased's

Table 2.1: *continued*

relatives). Two men went hunting together and one of them fell to his death out of a tree while ferreting out a marsupial; the other man was held responsible for the death . . . The Wola explain that the other party is responsible in such cases because they should have been more concerned for the welfare of the dead person [and anyway, who is to know (that) there was not (foul play and) deliberate murder?].

E. [Jalé Law, Papua New Guinea: Koch 1974: 86–88, 189]

Jalé reasoning deduces jural liability from a doctrine of effective action . . . in evaluating only the consequences of the injurious act the Jalé do not question a person's guilt or innocence – his psychological state – when they establish formal liability, that is, his obligation to provide restitution or indemnity to the injured party. . . . What the Jalé consider an effective action need not be the cause of a person's injury or death. . . . But the Jalé extend the causative link even further. For example, if someone invites another man to join him on a hunting trip or a ratan-collecting expedition across the Central Ranges and this man suffers a fatal <u>accident</u>, the initiator of the venture must pay a 'guilt' pig to the deceased's agnates.

F. [Kiwai Law, Papua New Guinea: Landtman 1927: 182–3]

According to custom a person is often held responsible for <u>accidental</u> deaths, for instance, a man who has invited somebody else to accompany him on a journey or a hunting or harpooning expedition, if his companion perishes . . . on account of the responsibility involved, a man does not like to ask a friend directly to join him on a venturesome undertaking, the other man must go of his own accord.

G. [Lozi Law, Africa: Gluckman 1955: 205–6; 1963: 197–8]

Their standard of negligence is indeed so high that it appears as if their law does not recognise moral guilt in assessing damage, as has been frequently stated for all primitive law. Responsibility appears to be absolute (1955). . . . These and other moral rules they share with us; and the rules are axiomatic, they cannot be demonstrated. An example of such a rule is equivalent to the Roman Law maxim, *volenti non fit injuria*: a man who willingly exposes himself to injury, cannot sue for damages if he is then injured. The Barotse maxim is, 'If you are invited to a meal and a fish-bone sticks in your throat, you cannot sue your host.' Under this rule (which they say is patently fair), they will not allow damages to a man who is injured in a fishing-party when men enter a pool at the dry season, and blindly hurl bundles of spears to get catfish buried in the mud. Nor will they allow damages to a man injured on a hunt (1963).

it has primary status as 'cause'? With particular respect to C, D, E and F, what is the rule concerning liability in the circumstances where there is some consensual agreement to go hunting between two or more persons? In the event that one dies, are the other parties jointly liable? There need not of course be any uniformity of principle across these disparate societies, but F suggests the importance of *volenti* in a way that is seemingly at odds with the other comparable examples. However, even where a defence of *volenti* appears as in G, the account can at best leave questions unanswered, and at worst manifest internal confusion. Thus Epstein inquired of *volenti* in Lozi (G) that 'If I am a guest in my neighbour's hut, is he under a duty to exercise reasonable care to see that I come to no harm or do I have to accept all the consequences of my visit' (1973: 651). Although it may appear from the cited extract that Lozi invoke this presumption of voluntary assumption of risk to abrogate liability, the statement that immediately precedes another version of these facts suggests an altogether quite different basis for the same outcome: 'They [Lozi] also recognise some actions as *purely accidental* [emphasis added]' (Gluckman 1955: 206). Accident and *volenti*, however, are by no means equivalent principles of defence but the descriptions of Lozi law offer no further clues to their relative weight or contribution.

In view of the above it would be hard not to agree with Bohannan (1969) that at fault is the method of exposition whereby fundamentally Western ideas are translated into Lozi/Mendi instead of translating fundamentally Lozi/Mendi ideas into English. But those who eschew the importation of Western legal ideology on the grounds that it distorts the content of native concepts fare little better. Lip-service is paid to the anthropological cliché concerning the contextual significance of specific social relationships and yet in not one of the extracts is the relationship between injurer and victim specified in terms of kinship, affinal or non-kinship based ties. We might further inquire of D, for example:

1. What significance lies behind those instances where Wola apparently 'assume' responsibility, and those instances where it is 'ascribed'?
2. While it appears from the beginning of the text that Wola espouse the principle of strict liability for accidental deaths,

we are told somewhat later that the basis of liability concerns a failure 'to have been more concerned for the welfare of the dead person'. But this suggests at the very least a duty to care and perhaps even a duty to rescue. In either event, the concept of negligence appears relevant in which case the analysis may well have benefited from an approach that is more comparatively constructed.

3. If a co-hunter has then a duty to care, can this be waived in given circumstances such that a defence of *volenti* abrogates such duty? Does the harm which results have to have been foreseeable?

Sillitoe wants to argue that the system is of the classic no-fault liability mould, with perhaps 'invitation' (given the reference to Mendi cases in Sillitoe 1979: 222) identified as the 'but for' causal condition. The Wola, in contrast, appear to want to argue that responsibility is grounded on a finding of fault – breach of a duty to use reasonable care. If the latter holds true, what exculpatory import is given to any subsistent notion of accident? The brevity of the texts, the omission to provide any exegesis of native terms, categories or conversation militates against any clear understanding of the important issues they broach.

All this is symptomatic of the deeper problems which besets C–G. In the attempt to elicit principles from observed, recounted or hypothetical cases – and here your guess is as good as mine – and to illustrate these by reduction to easy-to-read formulae, a distortion has inevitably crept in which, in this era of reflexivity about the ethnographic enterprise, would be deemed negligent or reckless. In different versions of the same facts details appear and disappear at the whim of the analyst; but such literary changes have an impact on the legal analysis. Just as there is an important difference between accident and *volenti* in G, so in Sillitoe's two versions of the journey example the precise role of invitation, facts of the accident, and social ties are obscured:

A man asked a friend to accompany him on a journey and crossing a vine bridge his friend fell into the Was river and was drowned
(Sillitoe 1979: 222)

In another case two men were crossing a vine bridge together and one fell through it and drowned . . .
(Sillitoe 1981: 76)

These and other (see bracketed sections in Table 2.1:D) small but significant changes are of precisely the kind that, according to AL theorist concerned with social structural variables (i.e. kin relationships) would appear to make the difference. But Sillitoe's accounts are not alone in this fault. What is 'invitation' in E, appears as 'inducement/initiation' in the longer case record (No. 26, 1974: 189) of which E is seemingly (?) a precis. Furthermore, in subsequent citations of E, Koch specifies the accident type as a 'fatal fall from a cliff' (1984: 108). Ethnographers are adding and deleting information at will in a way that obscures our perception of jural ideology, and dashes hopes for a comparative ethnological theory of liability. We are not told, and even shielded from, how the ethnographer derived his/her knowledge, and what this consists of. Consider the coda in the following two descriptions of the same event in Jalé. Here a woman has recklessly walked in the path of a tree felled by a man called Kevel:

> My informants insisted that Kevel had to indemnify the woman's relatives because 'the branch fell by his own hand', even though the accident occurred through the woman's own fault
>
> (Koch 1974: 88)

> The woman's kinsmen were entitled to indemnification because 'the branch fell down by his hands', even though the accident occurred 'through the woman's own fault'
>
> (Koch 1984: 107; Case 2)

One does not need to be a Queen's Counsel in order to appreciate the fact that there is distortion of the grossest kind. In the first coda we are told that it was Koch's informants who held this view of liability, but not that they witnessed the event, participated in it, or were promoting personal or political ends. One presumes the reported speech marks are not verbatim quotes but emphasised summary descriptions. Did Koch witness this dispute? In the second version, given a decade later, the source of 'informants' is omitted and the last five words are now also included in speech marks. Moreover, such changes give the reader the impression that we are being presented with a standardised viewpoint when it is clear that this is certainly not the case. It is precisely on this type of speech impoverished ethnography that those researchers working with transcripts of naturally occurring talk, and indeed law and language paradigms, press their claims of greater objectivity.

Succinctly stated, the evidence for AL is quite unsatisfactory. Beyond omissions of data, internal inconsistencies and plainly incorrect parallels, we must recoil at the lack of conceptual discrimination found in the use of the term *accident* (underlined occurrences in Table 2.1). Presenting the indigenous viewpoint through native terminology is the first task of the legal anthropologist and here, as Bohannan noted, 'the power of the word is greater than the power of the gloss' (1969: 402). It is far from clear in C–G whether 'accident' is at the level of description of the judicial system, as a possible rendering of indigenous notions, or at the level of interpretation as a counter in ethnographers' prose. Are we to infer that concepts of, and/or terms for, accident are absent in all these cultures? That this is not the case seems evident from the following fact. Even in a society like the Kaluli of New Guinea, where apparently all deaths are murders, the following direct speech exchange has been recorded:

[As the mother leaves the room, in a soft voice to Mε li]: He will accidentally cut himself. Stay here and watch over adε

(Schieffelin 1990: 115)

Clearly, and contrary to the reports cited previously, Kaluli do have a concept capable of being translated with an adverb of accidentality.

The questions we might ask of the data are legion (cf. Goldman 1993) but there are reasonable grounds for supposing that anthropological theories of AL are tenuous and display a lack of understanding of notions such as omission, mistake or coincidence. It must strike us as somewhat puzzling that the very architects of AL openly conceded that in regard to accident there was a gap both within their own, and the encompassing discipline's, data base (cf. Koch 1974: 89; Diamond 1951: 285–6; Gluckman 1966: 134; 1965: 204). This can be seen clearly in the following passages. For Africa generally it was noted that researchers

had not dealt well with liability for omissions to act so that another suffers damage, nor have they discussed adequately liability for damages caused by what we call negligence, inadvertence (failure to take due care), and accident

(Allot et al. 1969: 68)

while for the Lozi specifically, Gluckman informs us

unfortunately I did not record a rich enough variety of cases tried in court for me to illustrate how Barotse judges handle in practice problems of damages arising from negligence or accident, or from damages committed unintentionally through ignorance

(Gluckman 1965: 232)

We should be clear that it is data on the concept of accident, *and not necessarily the concept itself*, which is scarce. Epstein's succinct formulation of the problem provides further evidence:

What needs to be explored further are those cases where the damage sustained was an unforeseen consequence, or the result of negligence, the failure to take due care . . . Such cases, too, are apt to fall into the category of what we call accidents. In many African societies, as is well known, personal misfortunes or accidents are commonly attributed to witchcraft . . . The relationship between the definition of duty, the operation of witchcraft beliefs, and the emergence of a legal concept of accident which precludes liability poses a problem . . .

(Epstein 1967: 383)

Little by way of a solution to this problem has emerged in the intervening decades. Our knowledge of the nature, place and role of accident in non-Western legal systems has suffered at the hands of AL theories. The evidence thus far presented indicates that anthropology, rather like Piaget's pre-causal child, 'is still very far from allowing its share to chance in the nexus of events . . . and because accident is more of a problem for him [read 'anthropologist'] than us [read 'Huli'] . . . he tries to do away with the accidental element as such' (1926: 178). We are bereft of any insight into the spectrum of qualifications on the simple descriptive statement 'x did y'; we know little about variations in excuse-offering terms, their semantic overlaps or graduated differences in intentionality or inadvertence. It is as if all the languages mentioned were somehow empty of the types of qualification which both articulate and adjust relationships between action and responsibility. It is as if the human predicament is everywhere the same in the face of given contingencies.

The thrust of my argument is that anthropological approaches to accident, whatever their sub-disciplinary affiliations, have necessarily to display understandings and sensitivities drawn both from formal linguistics as well as from other speech-focused approaches. If 'accident' is to have the ethnographic stage it may well deserve it will be necessary to analyse its linguistic manifestations. So the interpretative venture must properly stand at the crossroads between the disciplines of linguistics and legal anthropology.

THE CASE OF THE HULI

Ethnographic background and case particulars

The Huli people live in the Southern Highlands of Papua New Guinea. Now numbering over 90,000 they have sustained rapid socio-economic change since the early 1950s. Disputes rank as amongst the most prolifically produced cultural artefacts in Huli and are a conspicuous everyday event. Informal gatherings of people for the express purpose of 'talk' – referred to herein as 'moots' – may convene spontaneously following an incident, or be subject to a degree of scheduling. Most frequently they take place on cleared grounds (*hama*) making them both public and highly visible events. They are characterised by a predominance of males who may come and go at will. There is no overall choreography to the affair, no distinctly conceived or named episodic phases of examination or cross-examination, and no pre-patterned system of turn-taking. The talk has far less ping-pong than that of Western courts which is predominantly structured in terms of neat dialogic units like questions and answers. Apart from the groups of opposed litigants, most other participants will membership themselves as 'middle-men' to preserve their neutrality and help mediate the conflict. Mediation, then, is unequivocally a male-dominated activity. But there is no pre-specification of turn type – that is how one phrases one's talk – and no restricted access to turns at talk. In this system of conflict resolution, outcomes emerge through consensus after protracted debate. Huli is an egalitarian society and there are no authorities capable of making or implementing judgmental decisions. Extended descriptions and analyses of dispute talk can be found in previous publications (Goldman 1983, 1986a, b, 1988, 1993).

The language data presented below is taken from an audio-recorded dispute that occurred in Ialuba valley in 1978. In essence, the case concerns two elderly and unrelated women, Ngualima (sometimes referenced as 'Kenobi's wife') and Gegai, who were in the habit of residing together in the former's house. One night the house caught fire, and while Ngualima and all her livestock (pigs normally occupy the rear of women's residences) managed to escape unharmed, Gegai died in the fire. For Gegai's son, Hanai, and indeed all the male dominated audience, this was simply an accident. There seemed nothing untoward about the incident to suggest Ngualima was in any way liable for the death of her friend. For Gegai's step-daughters, Kibime and Dagome, Ngualima had deliberately locked Gegai in the house, following some quarrel, and set them on fire. This version is supported by such indicators as the fact that (a) neither Ngualima nor the pigs endured any burns at all; and (b) the pigs appeared to have made a quite orderly exit from the burning house and were not, as one might expect, scattered around the adjacent gardens. The perspectival conflict is that between murder and accident, each encompassing quite different snapshots of responsibility and liability. Accident stands out in bold relief here because of the antithetical nature of these two angles of vision in this case.

'Accident' in Huli: a preliminary statement

Mindful of the point that the subject matter of this dispute is that supposedly rare, if not impossible, African/Melanesian species 'a significant and fatal pure accident' we might commence our investigations by considering the following transcript extracts (see Appendix to this chapter for a list of abbreviations):

[1] [Lines 166–187]
HANAI
1 *Anduane   kago   ibu   **mememe***
2 owner be-3ps-PST+EMPH she+ABS **accidentally**
   dedagoni
   burn-3ps-PtST+EMPH
3 God is there, she (Gegai) got accidentally burnt
4 *Anda   dalu   daga*
5 house+ABS burn+SUB2 burn-3ps-HAB
6 When houses burnt then people used to get burnt
7 *Wiya   dagua   dedagoni*
8 put-3ps-PST like burn-3ps-PtST+EMPH
9 What was there got burnt like this
Unidentified Male
10 *Iba   piaga*=
11 water go-3ps-HAB
12 People used to drown=
HANAI
13 =*Iba   piaga*=
14 water go-3ps-HAB
15 =People used to drown=
Male (as above)
16 =*Ira **longai***   *piaga*=
17 trees **misadventures** go-3ps-HAB
18 =Misadventures occur involving trees=
HANAI
19 =*Ira **longai***   *piaga*=
20 trees misadventures go-3ps-HAB
21 =Misadventures occur involving trees=
Male (as above)
22 =*Uli*   *piaga*=
23 caves/holes go-3ps-HAB
24 =People used to fall into holes=
HANAI
25 =*Uli*   *piaga*
26 caves/holes go-3ps-HAB
27 =People used to fall into holes
28 *Nde kira kirali   kirahowa   mendego   pilaga*
29 then two-together two+ABL second+EMPH fall-3ps-HAB
   wiyagoni
   put-3ps-PST+EMPH
30 Whilst two people were together one used to fall down
31 *O biagoale bidagoni*
32 o that+Def do-3ps-PtST+EMPH
33 Like the event(s) referred to it (this one) has happened

[2] [Lines 326–336]
DALU
1 *Ai andame   dagaale*
2 ai house+INST burn-3ps-HAB+Def
3 Like this people used to get burnt by house
4 *Dindi anda ngua biaga ndo*
5 We never customarily built houses under the ground
6 *Kaba anda biaga ndo*
7 We never customarily built houses of tin/metal
8 *Anda paliaga biagoale paleria dayadago*
9 Whilst sleeping in houses they used to burn down

The message of the passages is clear – accidents *are*. What is explicated is a recognised set of happenstances, contingencies or 'accident-types': 'people getting burnt by houses' [1:6;2:3,9], 'tree-accidents' [1:16,19], 'cave-accidents' [1:22,25] and 'drownings' [1:10,13]. The texts define known risks, familiar harms occurring in the state of the world known to Huli and thus are comparable to our concepts of 'car/skiing/aeroplane/bus-accidents'. The human condition is depicted as one of 'proneness' to mishaps of these types; one might even say they are accidents waiting to happen. They have the property that some human conduct or contrivance is not held to be causally involved, these accidents are of a type whose probability or severity may be unaffected by the behaviour of any injurer's or victim's behaviour. What is enumerated above is a category of *coincidental accidents* the complete involuntariness of which relieves liability *even where another person is present or involved in some way* [1:30].

This vision of reality is quite naturalistic, indicating the normality in Huli of various non-agentive happenings. The argument of the non-aligned mediator Dalu supports this vision. He emphasises in [2] that houses/people frequently burn because Huli houses, unlike those introduced by colonial administrators, are built of flammable materials. It is an argument highly reminiscent of the Lozi principle of non-liability for damage by fire: one cannot 'control fire in houses made of grass' (Gluckman 1955: 205). The import of the text, however, lies elsewhere. Of major significance is the thesis that a misfortune/accident is not unusual, rare or remarkable simply because it eventuates in death or involves someone else in some way. The principle of AL – of formal liability for accidental harm – is directly challenged by such data. The prevalence of the habitual (HAB) verb form in 1 and 2 is noteworthy in terms of speakers' linguistic choices. The habitual expresses that which customarily takes place and is linked to statements of accepted truths embodied in norms, proverbs, aphorisms, etc. Its marked occurrence in [1] and [2] thus reinforces the idea of the regularity/normality of certain types of misfortune. Component statements utilise non-transactive (i.e. one-participant structures involving no causal transaction, cf. Kress and Hodge 1979) clauses and verbs that remove consideration of agency as a topic of debate. Causality is opaque, and this vision of supervening misfortune is promoted by strategic choice of the intransitive 'burn' (*da*) as against the transitive/causal verb form *dela* ('burn'). The antithetical visions of death which the case displays – as between coincidental accident and murder – are realised through the key descriptive options of lexical anti-causative

[3]   (1947; cf. also 1:1)
      Inaga   ainya   dayadago
      1+GEN mother+ABS burn-3ps-PST+EMPH
      My mother got burnt

and derived causative constructions

[4]   (2137) *Kenobi one   biagome inaga   ainya   delara*
             Kenobi wife that+ERG 1+GEN mother burn+CAUS-3ps-
             au   laruda
             PRES like say-1sg-PST
             I said, 'Kenobi's wife is burning my mother'
      (2282) *Kenobi one   biagome i   ainya   andaheba*
             Kenobi wife this+ERG your mother+ABS house+COM
             delarabe?
             burn+CAUS-3ps-PRES+lgv
             Kenobi's wife is setting your mother alight along with the house?

These two forms of the verb 'burn' compose a dispute paradigm: 'a set of words which are the options available for use in defining this situation, each of which marks an alternative ideological position' (Trew 1979). The options are here dramatising opposed conceptions about the relationship between responsibility, intention and actions. As such they define distinct kinds of victims' powerlessness in the face of life-threatening events.

When modification occurs with an adverb that expresses accidentality, such as *mememe* [1:1], then choice is constrained. Importantly, as is explained below, in Huli accidental causation of the type 'I accidentally burnt y' cannot be expressed with a causative construction, but like Telegu (Rao and Bashir 1985: 236) must be realised with an intransitive verb construction as in [1:1]. Accidents in Huli are happenings not actions. To fully appreciate what is involved in the above we must needs attend to the semantics of causative constructions in this language an endeavour which linguists have long understood is facilitated by consideration of the scope, ambiguity and co-occurrence restrictions of adverbial qualification. I shall further show that this dispute paradigm is correlated with other lexico-syntactic choices. For example, in the language of accident we find 'house' marked by the instrumental case suffix (i.e. *andame* 2:1). Attention is thereby focused on an inanimate object not capable of intentions, and thus ordinarily incapable of being held liable. Under this perspective death results from an autonomous self-caused event like 'house-fires'. Contrastingly, in the language of murder, 'house' is invariably suffixed with the comitative case (i.e. *andaheba* 4(b)). This allows speakers to shift focus back onto an agent such as Ngualima; here, the house along with its female occupant (Gegai) are both victims of a controlled and deliberate act of arson. Such shifts then have strategic value in the dispute game.

Moral adverbs: the family group 'accident, inadvertence, mistake and misadventure'

Austin's (1956) much celebrated and programmatic treatment of the grammar of certain philosophical expressions of excuse alerted us to the point that modifiers like *accidentally*, *inadvertently* or *unintentionally* mark distinctions in the doing of actions. These acts of qualification have most usually a moral quality insofar as the relationship between actions and excuses or blamings is grounded in culturally shaped ideas about the nexus responsibility, mind (intention) and behavioural phenomena. But Austin also reminded us that language sets traps for the linguist and philosopher. Austin utilised self-conscious intuitions and retrospections; imaginary situations were supplemented by recourse both to the dictionary and the technical jurisprudential vocabulary of tort law where ordinary expressions were often employed in extraordinary ways. In this reliance on intuitive resources conclusions were drawn about the meaning of expressions that were often due to an implied, if overlooked and unforeseen, context of utterance. Such a dichotomous classification between 'ordinary' and 'forensic' expression seems wholly inappropriate to Huli dispute talk. None of the terms examined below can be said to represent some specially adapted or developed register. Moreover, the idea that a field of discourse can determine in advance of investigation a set of relevant words and idioms ignores the potential significance of free-associations, combinations, and synonyms that typify naturally occurring speech. The basis of the ethnographic method is to reveal speaking persons in social processes; intuition is eschewed for a focus on language as social fact and social action.

Evidence of a Huli concept of accident first emerged in the case of *Wanili* vs. *Ogoli* (Goldman 1986a: D.2). The dispute concerned an incident in which Wanili's teenage son Baro had drowned while out with another male friend. Wanili recounted her reactions in the following terms

[D.2. lines 140,203]
Ibu   **tiga tiga**   *iba*   *piyagoni*   *lalu*   *piru*
he straight straight (redup) water go-3ps-PST say-SUB2 go-1sg-PST
I said, 'He (Baro) **straight** drowned' and I went off
:

lya ilame   *iya*   *kirali*   *honowinidago*   **mememe**   *iba*
we both+ERG we two people gave birth-RP **accidentally** water
 piyadago
go-3ps-PST
We bore him together and he **accidentally** drowned

Of particular note is the counterbalance between the two adverbs *tiga tiga* (straight) and *mememe* (accidentally). The lexeme *tiga* connotes that which is true, straight, right or just. It here signals that there was no abnormality, nothing untoward about the fatal contingency. The drowning was kosher in the precise sense that there was no impropriety of the type which involved human error or control; its 'purity' thus circumscribes liability from attaching to some human candidate. We find an exact duplication of viewpoint and expression in the burning accident under discussion:

[Lines 190,1940]
Ayu andame   **tiga tiga**   dene   ebere   ngago
now house+INST straight straight burn-RP that one place-3ps-PRES
Now she has been burnt **straight** by the house
:

Mememe   dayago   layene
accidentally burn-3ps-PST say-3ps-PST
He (Hanai) has said, 'She (Gegai) got *accidentally* burnt'

Importantly, *mememe* is not marking the aberrant non-standard case with regard to death in these contexts but rather amplifying the resonance of 'normality' given out by the modifying adverb 'straight'. This is precisely the type of free-association of action-modifiers referred to above. *Mememe*, the most common of the accidentality adverbs we encounter in Huli, covers then those situations where outcomes are independent of human control, and which may be either harmful or beneficial in nature. The sense of 'blamelessness' is implicit. *Mememe* contrasts here with *longai* (1:16–21) which always has some negative import and thus is more appropriately glossed by the terms 'mishap' or 'misadventure'. *Longai* tends to occur in constructions with instruments like axes, bows, sticks or trees, or in directives like *longai poleni*: 'don't venture there an accident might occur'. The various nuances of *mememe* can be gauged from the following passages. In reference to natural processes like plant growth it carries the meaning of 'by itself' or 'of its own accord':

[5]   (Goldman 1983: 164 line 298)
    . . . *anda mememe*   *holebira*
    grow   accidentally be-3ps-FUT
(When you plant coffee in your garden) it will sometimes accidentally grow

while in [6] the element of chance or lack of design is emphasised (but here bereft of any hint of lack of care)

[6]   (Lines 1799–1808)
    While we are here nothing is being said
        Ibu mememe   *mobai*   *holebiragoni*

it   **accidentally** CAUS+reveal be-3ps-FUT
It might get accidentally revealed
/While we are saying nothing the source of this dispute might
accidentally come out/

The connotation of 'coincidence' is particularly clear in the
sarcastic reference of the speaker in [7] to the fact that Ngualima's
pigs neither scattered everywhere after fleeing the burning
house, nor appeared to have sustained any burns at all.

[7]   (Lines 1812–1819)
Everything of yours (Ngualima) went outside but not one of the
hairs of your pigs was even nearly burnt
When that happened the pigs didn't jump to the other side of the
gardens and they weren't scattered eating the gardens
everywhere
Ibu **mememeore**   *ogoni*   *biyadago*
it   *accidentally*+INT that do-3ps-PST
It really accidentally happened
/That must really be some **coincidence**/accident/

The sarcasm posits the unacceptability of a scenario such as
this being the product of fortuitous and coincidental forces. The
evidence of the pigs' well-being, it is implied, is more consistent
with a controlled and directed exit involving Ngualima.

There are no less than eleven instances of *mememe* in the
transcript and all reveal slightly different facets and depths to this
world-view. While it might appear in [8–10] the coincidental
accident meaning of *mememe* is merely being reaffirmed, there is
far more to the grammar of accident in these locutions than is
perhaps immediately noticeable.

[8]   (Line 207)
Mandagi   *dedaligo*   *ibu*   *nde* **mememe**
together burn-PrST+CONTRF+EMPH she then accidentally
pongo balu
date hit-SUB2
They would have got burnt together but it was her day and she
accidentally (died/got burnt)
[9]   (Lines 3062–3076)
O biago denedale ogonibi lalu hale ho hendedamilegoni
If that one (Ngualima) had got burnt then you would have heard
it and seen it

Ayu o bedago   *denedale*
now o sit-3ps-PrST burn-RP+CONTRF
If she (Ngualima) had got burnt
If Hanai's mother (Gegai) had gone outside then we would be making talk
That one (Ngualima) is burning
/We would be pointing to Ngualima and saying she is the one who is burning/
Ogonibidege o dayagola lalu bedale
If she (Ngualima) had got burnt then we would have talked here (just the same)
NGIBE
Au   *bidalego*   **mememe**   *biyago*
like do-3ps-PrST-CONTRF accidentally do-3ps-PST
If it was like that then it would **accidentally** have happened
[10]   (Lines 1024–7)
Ibu   *andame*   *dene*   *biago*
she+ABS house+INST burn-RP that one+ABS
hora harimidagoni
bury-1pl-PST+EMPH
She (Gegai) got burnt by means of the house and we buried her
Amugubi da pagu   *bidalegoni*
that one burn additional do-3ps-PrST+CONTRF+EMPH
That one (Ngualima) might have got burnt too

They demonstrate that in the construction of a theory of accident no dispreference is observed for guessing, proposing, testing or disputing hypothetical situations – i.e. what might have transpired. Speakers are here philosophically ruminating upon, analysing and discussing causation through the medium of *contrafactual constructions*. Given a state-of-the-world in which Gegai died, an opposing scenario is contemplated where the roles of victim/ injurer are reversed. Another world is hypothesised which is only minimally distinct from that now obtaining; it is a reasoning process grounded in the presumption of 'all things being equal then if p were the case q would happen'. This process is realised through the counterfactual (CONTRF) conditional construction which in Huli is marked by the postpositional suffix *-le/-li* on either/both conditional clause (medial) verb or principal (final) verb. Conjuring up these possible worlds helps support the lack of 'necessary causation' in this incident: that a victim would have suffered the harm even if an injurer had acted differently or the roles had been reversed. This posits a state of nature whose metaphysical rationale need not invariably entail, even for fatalities, any notion of omnipresent evil or human/ supra-human malice aforethought.

The sociolegal import of this linguistic strategy is that it signifies an argumentative style that aims to display both neutrality and fairness. It offers a perspective that proclaims 'let us consider the other side; if things had been different then . . .', such that the occurrence of Gegai's death is mooted as independent of the will, control, or foreseeability of any human actor. A parallel can be drawn here in the use of contrafactual constructions between Huli and Western legal reasoning in respect to accident and liability. In Anglo-American law, the consequences that will follow from some injurer's act will be adjudged to depend on the particular state-of-the-world that obtained or might have obtained. Considerations of this kind determine, for example, that a person is not liable for harm whatever level of care shown *if the consequences would have happened regardless*. Hypothetical reasoning is utilised to construct a definition of *coincidental accident*. The contrafactual and its inherent class of reversible worlds is part of a set of linguistic options. These include use of the instrumental suffix (*-me*: see [10]) and intransitive 'burn'. They represent a material culture expressing the *verismo* of accident in this case. The tone of [8] goes beyond the hypothetical to intimate a passive fatalism signalled by the phrase 'her day for dying'. An economy in which we have fatalistic philosophies and accidentality adverbs bespeaks volumes about the standing of 'coincidence' in Huli world-views. They provide the most persuasive thesis for natural accident negating legal liability that could be mustered.

Close synonyms of *mememe* are *minalu/minana* and *kogobo*, though this latter term is only used in the Koroba region of Huli. In many instances *minalu* and *mememe* are interchangeable as in example [11] provided by interviewees

[11]   (Informant contrived)
   (a) *Ira minalu/mememe podaya*
      tree accidentally   break-3ps-PST
      The tree accidentally broke
   (b) *Anda minalu/mememe deneya*
      house accidentally   burn-RP
      The house accidentally burnt

while in other constructions it conflates both the sense of 'accident' or 'of its/his own accord' with a statement about the mentalistic (i.e. 'mind') properties. It can impart a nuance of unintentional result either because the subject lacks sense of a conventional type –

> Nogo **minalu**   mabu   piya
> pigs accidentally garden go-3ps-PST
> The pigs went into the garden of their own accord

taken in the context of the belief that pigs lack human 'sense or mind'

> Ibu   nogoha   mini nawi
> her   pigs+Loc   mind Neg+place
> Her (Ngualima's) pigs of no mind (all disappeared)

– or because one normally does not intend, though it may be foreseen, for such a result to occur

> [12] (47)
> Ibini   **minalu**   deneyago
> she+REF   **accidentally**   burn-RP+EV+EMPH
> Iole . . .
> say+PURP . . .
> To say, 'Herself got accidentally burnt' . . .

But the sense of 'accidental' registered in [12] by the adverb *minalu* is different from that of *mememe* thus far encountered. What is suggested is that there was an 'absence of mind' in an event that involved some human agent; in this regard it establishes the existence of a *non-coincidental accident* class. Thus the various modifying adverbs are not freely and inconsequentially interchangeable in all contexts. [12] employs the contemplative idiom of 'heed'; there was a failure to exercise due care, caution or attention and an inadvertent unwished for result occurred. Words do not easily shake off their etymology in Huli so that we may entertain the thesis that these meanings are morphologically encoded:

MI [MIND]

*MI*NI	*MI*NA
[with mind, sense]	[without mind, sense]
*MI*NIWI	*MI*NAWI
[wise, sagacious	[elderly, senile
mini (mind)+*wi* (placed)]	*mina* (no mind)+*wi* (placed)]
*MI*TANGI (BIA)	*MI*NANA/*MI*NALU
[thoughts, thinkings, to think	[without thought, absence of mind,
mi (mind)+*tangi* (cap)+(do)]	unintentionally/accidentally
	mi (mind)+*na* (nom. suff.)+*lu*
	(long)]

I am not of course suggesting that contemporary uses of a word can necessarily be established by appeals to their etymologies. Rather, I am indicating that the mooted etymologies of any of the above Huli terms *happens in these cases* to correspond with understandings gained from conversationally contexted analysis. Given this note of caution, and the systematic way in which sound-symbolism is a pervasive facet of the expression of synonymy and antonymy in the language (cf. Goldman 1983), the semantic relation of 'mind' (*mi*) to various accidentality adverbs seems indicated in the above. Contrasting states-of-mind are being marked by morphologically related lexemes manifesting final position variations – most notably the *ni* vs. *na* nominal suffixes. They are different terms and yet the same in some senses; their participation in 'mind' is here iconically reflected by the sharing of the element *mi* (mind). The variant *minalu* has the morph *lu* (long, entangled) found in such terms as *lulu* (long-long: mad, crazy), *lu lungu ya* ('holding mad': senile) and *de lubia ha* (to trick/deceive). In the adverb *minalu* then there may also be an inherent nuance of deceit, duplicity or falseness quite in keeping with the notion of untoward happenings.

It is important to again reiterate that both accidentality adverbs (i.e. *mememe*/*minalu*) qualify happenings not actions, 'getting burnt' not 'burning someone', so there is here a discontinuity with similar English modifiers that can qualify action verbs like 'jump' or 'burn'. *Minalu*, in contrast with its siblings, makes a more definitive statement about intentionality or premeditation in actors who might otherwise have displayed some rational deliberation. In this regard it is particularly suited to strategies where notwithstanding the unforeseen nature of the happening, some censure (if such is to be ascribed) can be imputed to the injurer/victim. In contrast *mememe* signifies *blamelessness* because the event was outside the control of any human actor – i.e. a *pure* accident. Both accidentality adverbs say something about causation and responsibility, the one quite explicitly, the other by reference to what is known or guessed about inner mental activities. This is highlighted in [12] where the reflexive 'herself' (*ibini*) has a pragmatic function analogous to reflexive complements in English which are often employed to stress the property of ' self-volition' in some act: e.g. She went back into the house *herself*.

The speaker in [12] makes reference to the belief that Gegai had first left the burning house and then returned to collect some of her belongings and had burnt to death. There is an element of volition, desire or self-will about Gegai's decision to return to the burning house and thus she had some part in her own tragedy. Mediators are thus offering up the alternatives of (a) a 'blameless' accident in the sense of pure chance; or (b) an accident in which the victim suffers through contributory negligence. No firm commitment need be given as to which of these related viewpoints should prevail for both serve to abrogate the liability of Ngualima. The presence of the reflexive pronoun in [12] indicates 'personal responsibility for an act, autonomy in one's actions, and isolation in the sense that the person is doing something that does not involve others' (Strathern 1979: 250).

Minalu as a description of this incident can never be drained of mentalistic import. It shows Gegai's state-of-mind to be one of 'mind loss' and as such she bears responsibility for her own death. Legal talk about accident in Huli inescapably addresses at some stage motivations/intentions of injurer/victim.

At a higher level of generality superordinate terms like *ko*: 'bad' can be used to convey a sense of untoward result. Thus one may 'make a mistake' (*bia ko*), 'say a mistake' (*la ko*), see or hear incorrectly (*hale/handa ko*). Mistakes that are, however, tantamount to *inadvertence*, where in the execution of one act another unwished for act is committed, can be more precisely imparted by the Huli adverb *taba laba* (*taba*: 'carried') as in [13] (where the subject NP may optionally take ergative case-marking):

[13]   (Informant contrived)
*Agali naigo **taba laba***   *baya/delaya*
man there inadvertently hit/set alight
That man inadvertently hit/set alight.

One may thus inadvertently hit a person when firing at a tree, or set alight a garden one mistakenly believed should have been set alight. Significantly, the acceptability of [13] but not [14] can be further explained by the fact that the latter seeks to qualify a volitional act of setting alight with an adverb that expresses fundamentally the exact opposite.

[14]   **Agali naigo **mememe***   *baya/delaya*
man   there accidentally hit/set alight
That man there accidentally hit/set alight.

The semantic anomaly is that of 'accidentally on purpose'. What is being kept apart is the pure (coincidental) accident of *mememe* from the non-coincidental accident of *taba laba*. In [13] the action is deliberate, the performance of some act intended, but the specific target or desired result is somehow incorrect.

A further set of expressions occur which bleach the ideas of inadvertent and accidental result. They have an adjunct+pro-verb (APV) form, tend to co-occur with a quite specific and limited class of objects, and are morphologically (adjunct) verbs of failure or mishap. These are

(a)   *habolo puwa*   e.g. *walime habolo puwa anda delaya*
                        – the woman missed and burnt the house (by accident)
(b)   *koba puwa*   e.g. *nogo koba puwa baya*
                        – it missed and hit the pig (by accident) [used mainly of arrows, sticks or stones]
(c)   *gola puwa*   e.g. *ayu gola puwa dibaya*
                        – the axe came off and cut (by accident)

In the discourse of conduct there is considerable subtlety in the way Huli can convey the accidental dimension of some behaviour and the repercussions this has for the imputation of fault. We begin to construe from the above the manner in which language constrains choice, but also the manner in which speakers manipulate and synchronise resources to convey their snapshot of an event's accidentality. Moreover, we can perceive the workings of a central classificatory axis – coincidental:nonco-incidental – common to both Huli and Western legal reasoning.

Much was made in my introduction of the need to consider excuses in the light of expressions which aggravate or impute responsibility – that x was done *deliberately, designedly, wilfully, intentionally*, etc. And yet I have said nothing about, nor proffered any example of, Huli inculpations. In fact there is a complete absence of purpose adverbials in the language. When we examine then what can and cannot be modified (e.g. as in [14]), we begin to uncover certain conventional presuppositions involved in 'doing an action' in Huli. For verbs like *dela* (causative/transitive 'burn'), to set alight is just to set alight *intentionally* and it always presumes a volitional human agent in control such that [14] is infelicitous. To be clear, I am not attempting to explain the non-occurrence of purposive adverbials through some redundancy principle; neither am I claiming that all verbs that cannot be qualified by some accidentality term share the property of an inherent free-will component. An act that fails to be done 'accidentally' does not *ipso facto* qualify as having been done 'deliberately', and *vice versa*. Notwithstanding these caveats, the presupposition of intentionality is valid for the focal term *dela* because the sense of a human agent acting with deliberateness is morphologically signalled by the causative affix *-la* found in the verb. One implication here is that theses about whether some legal discourse does/does not attend or orientate towards the topics of intention/motivation have to show sensitivity to how actors might thus read intent from verb form and choice.

Causative constructions in Huli: syntax and semantics

Huli is a non-Austronesian verb final language with the characteristic Papuan distinction between medial and final verb forms. Switch-reference devices operate such that verb morphology signals features such as non-coreferentiality between the subjects of subordinate and main clause verbs. Verb morphology is thus complex and inflects for person, number, tense, mood and aspect. As is the case with many other so-called ergative languages (cf. Dixon 1979, Comrie 1978, Plank 1979) Huli is syntactically accusative. Ergativity is expressed through nominal case marking, with the two core cases being ergative (ERG) – where the NP is marked (optionally) by the postposition – **me** (homonymous with the instrumental case) – and absolutive (ABS) – where a NP has zero marking. Most commonly, ergativity is explicated in terms of the core syntactic arguments of transitive subject **(A)**, intransitive subject **(S)** and object/patient **(O)**

[15]   **NP(S)**   **V(intr)**
ABS
inaga   ainya   *dayadago*
1+GEN mother+ABS   burn-3ps-PST+EMPH
[16]   **NP(A)**   **NP(O)**
ERG   ABS
Kenobi one biagome   *inaga ainya*
Kenobi wife that+ERG   1+GEN mother+ABS
V(tr)
delara
burn+CAUS-3ps-PRES

In [16] the ergatively marked NP serves to emphasise the intentional actor behind some action, the 'who' of a planned transaction. The causative dimension of a reported event is thereby in focus and in reference to Gegai's death is thus highly blame implicative. For this reason, as has been commonly noted (Dixon 1979: 80), the ergative suffix tends to be prevalent in the environment of accusatory speech. But agency, causation and culpability are independent ingredients which may just happen to be conflated in the cocktail of a case marker like -*me*. Not all causation is agentive in the sense of controlled by some animate actor – non-agentive or stative causation involves causing events or states like thunder or anger – and 'fault' may be ascribed to some inanimate object by analogical extension. This critical point is exemplified in [17] which figured prominently in the step-daughters' claims for compensation. Here blame and causal involvement (rather than pure agency) appear to be stressed

[17]   (508)
I   anda ibugua   dedagoni   i honolebere
your house it+**ERG** burn-3ps-PtST+EMPH you carry-2sg-FUT
larogodagoni
say-1sg-PRES+EMPH

YOUR HOUSE IT, she is burnt and you will pay compensation
I am saying
(It happened in your house and she is burnt. You'll pay
compensation I'm saying)

At the same time, its discoursal saliency as an accusatory
marker surely derives from the manner in which it *indirectly*
implicates a blameworthy human by virtue of their known
association to the focused object 'house'. [17] then embraces both
the sense of a cause-consequence relation and 'fault' as encoded
in the foregrounded ergative NP. Comparison can be made with
[18] where a seemingly similar statement is made but where the

[18]   (478)
    O wali   naigo i   andaga   dayadago . . .
    o woman there your house burn-3ps-PST+EMPH
    That woman (Gegai) got burnt in your house

blame implicativeness of the adverbial phrase 'in your house'
comes from the context of use. The reference is to location of
death and does not necessarily imply the causal responsibility of
house + *house owner*. In another context the same statement
might be devoid of any fault imputation in a way that [17] *can
never be*. The three instances of 'house' found above distribute as
follows:

I anda ibugua	('your house it')	
your house it+**ERG**		_____ *emblems of accusation*
Andaheba	('with the house')	
house+COM		_____ *emblems of accident*
Andame	('by the house')	
house+INST		

Understanding responsibility and liability in this case entails
appreciating how context and morphology interactively construct
blame. There is semantic continuity between -*me* in its role as
agent marker in a transitive clause, and its occurrence as a clitic
element on a verb as a clause marker signalling cause-effect
relationships. In the following [19] this linkage type expresses a
'because of that' relationship, where the ergative morpheme

functions as a clause marker as opposed to its other (but related) role as NP(A) case marker

[19]   (1568)
Inaharu   paliarigomehowa   inaga   ainya
you+ERG+Def sleep-2sg+ERG+ABL 1+GEN mother
homenedago
die-RP+EMPH
You slept together and because of that my mother is dead

Beyond illustrating the importance of attending to phenomena such as case-marking patterns, [15–19] also reveal the very close links between the notions of instrumentality, agentivity, causality and culpability in the Huli language. We need to expand this picture by briefly considering causativisation processes.

Lexical and nonlexical causatives in Huli

In accordance with morpho-syntactic structure, and as is common for strongly agglutinative languages, Huli has the following causative types:

1. *Lexical*: morphologically irregular verbs whose causative meaning is not signalled by any causative morpheme, and which are nonproductive; e.g. *ba*: 'hit/strike/kill'.
2. *Synthetic*: derived causative verbs (affixial) of which there are two distinct types: (i) prefixal causation marked by the morpheme *mo-*; and (ii) suffixal causation marked by the semi-productive *-la* that serves to transitivise a small and unpredictable class of intransitive verbs that lack distinct lexical causatives.
3. *Analytic*: full periphrastic constructions restricted to the expression of permissive causation (i.e. 'to give opportunity or to fail to prevent' as in the English verb '*let*') and marked by *lela*: 'let (talk)/permit/allow'.

The dispute paradigm as defined above is constituted by the opposition of causative/non-causative verbs '*dela/da*' so that my specific task in the following is to uncover the degree of volitionality imputed to an actor in event descriptions which employ these verbs. In part this entails an understanding of the

behaviour – scope and co-occurrence restrictions – of accidentality adverbs, the corresponding absence of purposive adverbials, and in part the semantic discontinuities between the
causative affixes *mo-* and *-la*.

Prefixal causation

The causative morpheme *mo-* allows for both agentive and non-
agentive causation, and for incidental/inadvertent results. Inanimate agents incapable of volition may figure as subjects in such
constructions.

[20]   (433; 316)
    bi   motimbu   timbu timbu harimigoni . . .
    talk CAUS+big big big be-2pl-PST+EMPH
    You have caused the talk to be/become really big . . .

[21]   (Informant contrived)
    Ki ku   biagome   i   moembeda   hara
    happiness that one+ERG me CAUS+forget be-3ps-PRES
    That happiness made me forget

[22]   (Informant contrived)
    Hari kulu   biagome   i   mopila   haya
    thunder that one+ERG me CAUS+fall be-3ps-PST
    The thunder caused me to fall/to be fallen

The possibilities of adverbial qualification have already been
noted for [6] where causation is incidental and references an
autonomous event independent of any planned involvement of
agents. In fact *mo-* functions across a spectrum of roles in the
causative domain as a transitiviser, causativiser or intensifier of
the verbal idea. The above is sufficient to clarify some of the
relationships between pairs of affixal causatives as in [23]

[23]   (Contrived)
    (a)   *mobira   ha*   vs.   (c)   *berela*
        CAUS+sit be-STM   sit-StSTM+CAUS
        cause to be seated/sit

    (b) *mohoma*   *ha*   vs. (d) *homela*
          CAUS+die be-STM   die-StSTM+CAUS
          cause to be dead/die   cause to die

The causatives of (c) and (d) always require a wilful human agent whether acting on animate or inanimate causees. By contrast, the productive causatives of (a) and (b) allow for both incidental causation, inanimate causers, and directive (i.e. persuasion that is non-contactive) rather than manipulative (i.e. physical force) coercion. [23c] would accordingly be used in relation to babies, whereas [23a] is used in relation to adults; [23b] may take an inanimate causer like a tree or, in its metaphorical mode, human agents acting on inanimate objects as in 'making an issue die/be dead', while [23d] always selects a human subject acting on another human subject.

The main point is that because *mo-* allows for stative causation and incidental/inadvertent results, the manner in which responsibility$_1$ [causal authorship/agency] and responsibility$_2$ [moral/ legal liability] map onto each other is here highly contingent on the type of causer and causee involved. Nothing can be read concerning intentions or fault from form alone.

Suffixal causation

In the causativisation process the suffix *-la* is a semi-productive morpheme which serves to transitivise a small set of intransitive verbs which lack distinct lexical causatives. In this function the morpheme is bound, and a verb is produced that semantically behaves like a lexical causative. The following semanto-syntactic features indicate the contrast with *mo-*:

1. *-la* always requires an animate causer.
2. No coreferentiality of causer/causee occurs.
3. Causation is always direct and frequently manipulative, but never directive in nature.
4. Causee may be inanimate.

-la always implies an antecedent act of volition by some human agent. The performance of the act is conscious, wilful and deliberate, such as to have involved a *decision*. In such prototypical transitive events, the responsibility$_1$:responsibility$_2$

relation is never (unlike with *mo-*) contingent. Purpose adverbials are thus implied and inherent. The control implications of this morpheme are that results 'may not be considered an accident. The object of deliberate control is free neither to act deliberately nor act accidentally' (Givón 1975: 79). Thus when speakers use the causative *dela*: 'burn' the idea of any inadvertence or accidental action cannot be entertained. Specifically, intention is read into, and from, verb form and choice which thus bears directly on our interpretations about causation and culpability in the language of accident in this case. Constructions like [14] and [24] are ill-formed in Huli and totally absent from the dispute transcript

[24] *Ibugua   anda/wali   mememe   delaya
she/he+ERG house/woman accidentally burn-CAUS-3ps-PST
She/he accidentally burnt the house/woman

These features constitute constraints on the co-occurrence of such verbs with accidentality adverbs. Somewhat analogously with the case of *mo-* (causative affix)/*mo* (SV), *la* is a common constituent of a whole range of Huli verbs which have the structure of adjunct [-concrete noun] + pro-verb (PV). It carries the sense of 'cause' and nearly always signals active verbs as in the cutting/ breaking forms given below

lere la	– rip	*gandu la*	– cut
pambu la	– smash	*galo la*	– chew
taga la	– break	*yanga la*	– spread

The possibility is raised then that the morpheme *-la* is also derived from a periphrastic verb meaning 'cause'. There is more, however, to this morpheme in terms of its relevance to socio-legal issues than is at first apparent.

Permissive causation

The cross-linguistic literature on the syntax and semantics of causative constructions indicates a high degree of correspondence between the direct coercive marker and its capacity to further signal permissive or delegative causation as for Lahu *ci* (Matisoff 1976), Japanese *sase* (Shibatani), German *lassen* and Hungarian *kem cc-*: 'force someone to go/allow, permit to go' (Hetzron 1976: 380). Huli is quite regular in this regard and all the derived causative verbs listed below can further take the meanings covered by the English 'let' of giving the opportunity, permission, or simply failing to prevent

Nga(place)	→ *Ngela*	*Bira*(sit)	→ *Berela*
Pu(go)	→ *Pela*	*Da*(burn)	→ *Dela*
Ibu(come)	→ *Ibila*	*Ha*(stand)	→ *Hela*
Palia(sleep)	→ *Palela*		

[25]   (Informant contrived)
    I ambolo   *berelaro*
    I baby   sit-CAUS-1sg-PRES
    a. I sat the child up
    b. I left/let the child sitting/sit

The conflation of permission/coercion in a single lexical item or morpheme suggests a wide appreciation of the correlative nature of *acts* or *forbearances*. A theme such as 'rescuing a burning woman' can be positively or negatively stated, but 'failings to prevent' (i.e. omissions or forbearances) are not the same as 'not doing *simpliciter*' (Von Wright 1963: 45; cf. also Ross 1968: 115). Omissions imply both the possibility of positive action, and the *decision*, choice or preference, not to interfere on some given occasion. For non-action to count as a voluntary omission, these conditions have to be fulfilled. In the normative modality of permission – where it has the sense of forbearing to act – forbearing to preserve a life has the same result as a conscious decision to actively destroy life. Both the forbearance and the action result in death, one positively the other negatively defined. Coercive/permissive causation have, then, similar ground conditions in respect to human agency and volitionality which appears indexed here by the morpheme '*la*'.

These linguistic noticings provide one window, one means of access, onto what is acknowledged to be the least understood component of liability systems – the culpability of acts of omission. Generally, omissions tend to lack the visibility of normative enunciation. They would appear not to be enshrined in rule-formulations and as such do not leap out at the anthropologist. And yet intuitively we know that, given a dispute context, a statement such as 'you just let her burn to death' presumes an intentional forbearance and is blame implicative. If such notions as duty of affirmative care (of rescue) exist in Huli then permissive constructions provide one type of evidence for this. In this regard [26–27] reinforce the step-daughters' overall depiction of Ngualima's 'attitude' towards Gegai. Not rescuing the burning woman, when she (Ngualima) could have, directly highlights her *state-of-mind*

[26] (1690; cf. also 3374)

KIBIME:

... *ibu   do   **ngelowa**   ibu   unu   tagira   pialuhowa*
she burn placed+SUB3 she there outside go-SUB2-ABL
She (Gegai) was burning and having left her she (Ngualima) went outside

[27] (3305)
... *inaga ainya   agi   biyene   do   paya anda*
1+GEN mother what do-3ps-PST burn close inside
helaribe ...
be+CAUS-2ps-PST+lgv
What happened with my mother that you closed her inside and left her burning?

The omissions indicated in [26–27] do not unequivocally allow us to infer a legal duty to rescue such that liability is attached to Ngualima, but they are part of a total package of guilt which Kibime/Dagome construct. The permissive causative is thus a member of a set of linguistic means – which set includes ergative NPs, comitative 'house', transitive 'burn', etc. – utilised by the proponents of the 'murder' point of view. It is complemented in this dispute by judicious use of the abilitative construction which marks actions that are able/unable to be carried out. It is formed by attaching +*behe* to the verb stem. In [28] the negated benefactive suggests an accusation, while [29] clarifies the sense in which 'opening the door' for Gegai was a possible course of action for Ngualima that, it is implied, *she decided to forbear*

[28]   (1384)
KIBIME:
I   nadugua   hari
you Neg+open-STM BEN(be-2sg-PSt)
You didn't open the door (for Gegai)

[29]   (2930)
. . . *duguabehegodago*
open+ABIL+DEC+EMPH
she (Ngualima) could have opened (the door on the evidence)

If the permissive imbues an action with fault, it does so by virtue of what the abilitative suggests was possible to control, and perhaps even, by innuendo, *should have* been controlled. The point of this excursion into causativisation is to explain what it means for a Huli to hear or use transitive 'burn' in respect to what is understood or communicated about some causer's volitionality or state-of-mind. The analysts' interpretations and glosses are thus openly revealed as having proceeded to place such constructions within the natural economy of causatives in the language remaining sensitive both to proto-history and wider cross-linguistic patterns.

CONCLUSION

The technique of primitive law is characterised by the fact that the relation between the conduct and its effect has no psychological qualification . . . No relationship between the state of mind of the delinquent and the effect of his conduct is necessary.

(Kelsen 1945: 65)

The contention that absolute liability prevails in tribal polities is now some two centuries old. The validity of this wisdom is critically dependent on the presumed absence of concepts, legal or otherwise, of 'accident' in these same societies. And yet anthropology has been able to tell us very little about this topic precisely because it has thus far failed to attend to the subtle ways in which language incorporates and encodes accident. Notions of causation, agency, volitionality and culpability are notoriously slippery and theoretically enmeshed. But if we are not to be halted by the paralysis that perfection seeking can impose, any attempt to disentangle these issues has to confront the types of linguistic data examined here. Our understanding of legal concepts and ratiocination in non-literate societies must be shown to have derived through some consideration of the talk *with, through* and *of* accident, coincidence or whatever. The reality of accident is being constructed through the very activity of talk about accidents.

In terms of the conventional wisdoms enumerated in my introduction, the data suggest that, most certainly in Huli, any debate about accident is also a debate about relevant mentalistic parameters such as premeditation, deliberateness, etc. Accidents are never conceived in a vacuum of understandings about human/suprahuman volitions. The relevant questions for anthropologists to address then are not whether society x or y has/has not a concept of accident, but rather what is done with it, by whom, and in what contexts and with what effects. In other words, accident is taken out of the playing field of variables that can or cannot be predicted to occur in given socio-cultural circumstances, and placed back in the camp of semantic or linguistic universals. Accident would thus invariably be implicative – whether acknowledged or ignored – for all jural ideologies. At this level of forensic reasoning, and with specific respect to accident, the data suggest an isomorphism in Huli and Western legal systems. Cultural definitions, scales and the interactional rhetoric of accident appear similar and are underpinned by the recognition and workings of the dichotomy between *coincidental* and *non-coincidental* accident categories. In this there lies hopes for a truly comparative ethnological theory of liability. And it is one that does not attempt to theorise in splendid isolation from any detailed investigation of accidentality concepts, terms or TALK.

APPENDIX: LIST OF ABBREVIATIONS

ABIL	ABILITATIVE
ABL	ABLATIVE
ABS	ABSOLUTIVE
BEN	BENEFACTIVE
CAUS	CAUSATIVE

COM	COMITATIVE
COND	CONDITIONAL
CONTRF	CONTRAFACTUAL
Def	DEFINITIVE
DESID	DESIDERATIVE
EMPH	EMPHATIC
ERG	ERGATIVE
EV	EVIDENTIAL/EXISTENTIAL VERB
FUT	FUTURE
GEN	GENITIVE
HAB	HABITUAL
HORT	HORTATIVE
Igv	INTERROGATIVE
IMP	IMPERATIVE
INST	INSTRUMENTAL
INT	INTENSIFIER
Loc	LOCATIVE
Neg	NEGATIVE
NOM	NOMINATIVE
POSS	POSSIBILITATIVE
PRES	SIMPLE PRESENT
PrST	PRESENT STATIVE
PST	SIMPLE PAST
PtST	PAST STATIVE
PURP	PURPOSIVE
redup.	REDUPLICATIVE
REF	REFLEXIVE
RP	REMOTE PAST
SA	SENSED ASPECT
STM	STEM
StSTM	STATIVE STEM
SUB1	SUBORDINATE CLAUSE [simultaneous action]
SUB2	SUBORDINATE CLAUSE [consecutive/ simultaneous action]
SUB3	SUBORDINATE CLAUSE [consecutive action]
SUB4	SUBORDINATE CLAUSE [reason]
V	VERB
1/2/3	FIRST/SECOND/THIRD PERSON
sg.	SINGULAR
pl.	PLURAL
du./dl.	DUAL

D.	= dispute number D.1:35 is to read as dispute no.1, line 35
:	indicates omitted speech
(line 4;5,6,9)	the first number references the attached citation, while the following numbers are other related occurrences of the same feature in focus
*	indicates grammatical unacceptability of the sentence
//	encloses free translation
=	indicates a lack of interval between the end of one person's utterance and the commencement of the next turn

THREE

Orality, literacy, and performativity in Anglo-Saxon wills[1]

Brenda Danet and Bryna Bogoch

INTRODUCTION

This chapter presents a case study in the history of legal language. Its goal is to elucidate aspects of the transition to the use of writing for legal purposes in the Middle Ages. Drawing on ideas from sociolinguistics, discourse analysis and speech act theory, we analyse the language of sixty-two Anglo-Saxon wills in Old English. The linguistic features of these wills are contrasted with modern wills. Two main themes are highlighted: incipient performativity of the written document, and context-dependence of the text. We discuss self-consciousness about writing; the linguistic realisation of the act of bequeathing; secondary means to strengthen the performative potential of the written will, notably witnesses and curses; the degree of planning evident in the text; patterns of reference to property and persons; the lack of attention to dating; and emotional involvement of the testator.

Speech, writing and the history of legal language

As creatures of the late twentieth century, we take it for granted that legal affairs should be conducted, recorded, and even constituted in writing. We find it hard to imagine how the business of society could ever have been conducted *without* the written word. Thus, it seems natural and right that legally binding acts such as business contracts, wills, or apartment leases should be committed to writing. Similarly, we take it for granted that the laws of modern states are written down, rather than passed on through purely oral tradition, as is the case in customary law.

How did writing come to enjoy this kind of authority? How did human societies make the transition from the constitution of legally binding acts in oral ceremonies, as is characteristic of pre-literate societies, to their constitution via writing in literate and post-literate ones? We are a long way from understanding this important aspect of the history of human communication, and of the history of legal language.

This chapter reports on a case study of the transition to literacy in medieval Europe. We examine a corpus of transitional legal texts from Anglo-Saxon England, in order to illuminate how written legal acts emerged from oral ones in the Middle Ages. The period investigated dates from the fifth century AD to the conquest of England by William the Conqueror in 1066 AD. During this period, it was customary for kings to issue grants or leases of land in oral ceremonies. Similarly, members of the feudal aristocracy, as well as high-ranking personages in the Catholic Church such as bishops and archbishops made wills in oral ceremonies. In both cases, witnesses were present. Frequently there was manipulation of physical objects. For example, the transfer of land might involve the symbolic transfer of a clod of dirt from the property in question, or the transfer of a knife from one person to another (Clanchy 1979).

This case study takes as its corpus the complete set of Anglo-Saxon wills in Old English, sixty-two in number, which have survived to the present day. Our concern is with the emergence of linguistic features of documents which indicate that society is moving toward a view of writing as a form of *constitutive social action*, and of the products of writing, written documents, as autonomous material objects having a life of their own. We will show that the linguistic features of Anglo-Saxon wills differ sharply from those which characterise modern ones. In some ways these wills retain links to pre-literate times; in others, they anticipate the eventual institutionalisation of writing. Our theoretical approach draws on recent work in sociolinguistics, discourse analysis, and speech act theory.[2]

Ancient and medieval literacy

The struggle to institutionalise writing did not begin in the Middle Ages, nor was the process of transition from oral to literate culture a smooth, linear one. There is a good deal of evidence that literacy had been more widespread in ancient Greece and Rome than it was in the so-called 'Dark Ages' in Europe (Harris 1989; Thomas 1989; Graff 1987a). It is therefore more appropriate to think of literacy as 'reborn' in the medieval period (Stock 1983). Apparently, medieval societies had to relearn some of the lessons about writing and its potential uses which had already been learned in earlier civilisations.

The processes by which the conventions of medieval oral culture were broken down, and by which literate practices came to supersede them, had important parallels with the development of literacy in the ancient world (Stock 1983: 32–4). Many ancient societies used writing for economic, political, administrative, and legal purposes. For instance, thousands of clay tablets from Sumer (c. 3500 BC) with legal documents inscribed in cuneiform writing have survived to the present day (Kramer 1956; cited in Goody 1986: 168). In addition, such seemingly modern aspects of documentation as standardisation of form and language, the making of duplicate or triplicate copies, and use of documents as legal evidence already existed at different times in the ancient world (see Goody 1986).

The use of documents as legal evidence dates back at least to the Old Kingdom of Egypt, of approximately 2150 BC (Baines 1983), and to the Code of Hammurabi, King of Babylonia in the eighteenth century BC (Goody 1986: 77). The Old Kingdom of Egypt also made written records of court proceedings, and created monumental copies of documents to display publicly (Baines 1983). If these steps toward literacy had been taken in the past, readers may want to ask, why is it important to study the medieval period? As Stock (1983) has argued, it was only in this period that literacy was to become so widely and *irreversibly* institutionalised in the West: 'Up to the eleventh century, western Europe could have returned to an essentially oral civilization. But by 1100 the die was cast' (Stock 1983: 18). We view the present research, then, as a case study of a process taking place in different areas all over Europe, at different rates, with somewhat different emphases in each area.

Law, language and literacy in Anglo-Saxon England

Despite the 2000 or so documents and literary works that have come down to us from the Anglo-Saxon period (Clanchy 1979; Wrenn 1967; Blake 1977), English society between the fifth and eleventh centuries was largely an oral society. It was not simply that the majority of people were unable to read or write in any language. Outside the Church, writing was largely regarded as mere graphic marks on parchment, and thus, no authority was vested in written texts (Galbraith 1935). The ability to read Latin or any other language was not related to social position or prestige. In fact, Galbraith (1935) notes that none of the kings of Anglo-Saxon England, with the exception of Alfred and possibly Ceolwulf, were able to read or write. The ability to write was not even considered essential for the *literatus*, that is, the elite clergy who were educated in Latin. Only scribes were allowed to put quill to parchment, although their exact role in the composition of documents is not known.

While the ability to read remained unnecessary for most social functions until the end of the Anglo-Saxon period, *access* to the written word became increasingly important (Baüml 1980). Initiated by the clergy as aids to remembering transfers of property in which the Church was the beneficiary, the use of documents eventually extended to records of other governmental and commercial transactions as well (Clanchy 1979; Graff 1987b). Although writing was gaining in importance, the spoken word remained the primary mode of legal transactions, and disputes in court were resolved using procedures like oathtaking and ordeals. As we began to suggest above, the conveyance of land and bequest of property continued to be primarily oral acts, performed according to specific ritual and formulas and witnessed by trustworthy individuals (Whitelock 1979; Hazeltine 1986 [1930]). Records of such acts were regarded with suspicion, and in many instances, this distrust was justified, because the lack of standards for authentification made forgeries simple and common (Clanchy 1979).

THE PRESENT STUDY: AN ANALYSIS OF THE LANGUAGE OF ANGLO-SAXON WILLS

Rationale for choosing wills

The sixty-two wills analysed in this chapter cover a briefer span than the full Anglo-Saxon period. The earliest surviving Anglo-Saxon will in the corpus is dated 805 AD; the last one was created approximately at the time of the Conquest in 1066.[3] These wills have been the focus of considerable interest on the part of social and legal historians, linguists and literature scholars interested in the development of the English language and the emergence of English prose, and students of the history of literacy, though none have approached them with the micro-sociolinguistic perspective developed here. Stock (1983: 48) notes that 'the acculturation of writing within oral tradition is well recapitulated *in nuce* in the history of the Anglo-Saxon will.' It was feasible to analyse the complete available corpus intensively. The total number available – sixty-two – was manageable, and on the average, the wills were rather short documents of about 300–350 words. We were also attracted by the idea of examining an entire corpus of a given genre of document, rather than having to sample it, since nothing is known of what the total original number of such documents may have been.

Another consideration was the fact that these documents represented early beginnings of the eventual diffusion of writing for private purposes to individuals other than the highest ranking royalty. The other two main categories of Anglo-Saxon documents which have survived besides the wills are land transfers – grants and leases – and royal writs. Both of the latter types of documents were mainly produced by and for kings. While during the period studied here it was mainly aristocrats and high-ranking Church officials who made wills, as noted above, by the thirteenth century even serfs had seals, and thus were using documents for legal or quasi-legal purposes (Clanchy 1979).

The most important reason for choosing wills, however, was that initial impressions of these texts had suggested that we would find in them strong evidence of their transitional nature, and of a struggle to realise the performative potential of writing.

Since the legal act of bequeathing was conducted orally, documents were after-the-fact records of the binding event that already had taken place. The dominance of oral practices is further reflected in the fact that, like other kinds of documents, written wills were often read aloud after they had been drafted. This custom is evident in a passage from the will of Æthelstan, dated 1015:

> *Nu bidde ic ealle þa witan. þe minne cwyde gehyron rædan. ægðer ge gehadode. ge læwede. þ hi beon on fultume. þ min Cwyde standan mote.*[4]

> Now I pray all the councillors, both ecclesiastical and lay, who may hear my will read, that they will help to secure that my will may stand.
>
> (Will of Æthelstan, 1015 AD; Whitelock 1986 [1930]: 62–3)[5]

Thus, we hypothesised that analysis of the language of the wills would, first of all, reveal evidence of links to the oral ceremony, and would contain 'oral residue', defined by Ong (1971, 1982) as

> habits of thought and expression tracing back to pre-literate situations or practice, or deriving from the dominance of the oral as a medium in a given culture, or indicating a reluctance or inability to dissociate the written medium from the spoken.
>
> (Ong 1971: 146)

At the same time, we expected to find evidence of the growing realisation of the potential of documents not merely to record but actually to perform socially binding acts.

Legal differences between Anglo-Saxon and modern wills

Although the documents analysed in this study are routinely called 'wills' by scholars of the Anglo-Saxon period, there are important legal differences between them and modern wills. First of all, as Hazeltine (1986 [1930]) pointed out, a modern will is a unilateral act of disposition of property to take effect after death.

Anglo-Saxon wills, in contrast, often resembled contracts; individuals contracted with the Church to look after their souls after death, in exchange for transfer of property. Thus, these wills are often bilateral acts, in which Church officials were explicitly involved, often even named in the will. Legal historians claim that there is a second important legal difference between Anglo-Saxon and modern wills, namely, that modern ones are revocable – they can be changed, whereas Anglo-Saxon wills were generally treated as irrevocable (Hazeltine 1986 [1930]; Sheehan 1963; Kurzon 1986).[6]

As we have begun to suggest, an important legal difference between Anglo-Saxon and modern written wills is that Anglo-Saxon ones were, as the legal historians put it, merely evidentiary, rather than dispositive. They were supposed to serve only as supplementary evidence of what had occurred in the oral ceremony, rather than to constitute the binding act of making a will themselves. In the case of modern wills, on the other hand, the written document typically constitutes the binding act. In England written wills became legally binding only in the seventeenth century. A Statute of Wills passed in 1540 allowed written wills to override certain customary arrangements regarding the transfer of specific types of land. However, written wills were not actually required until the Statute of Frauds in 1677 (Kiralfy 1958).

The linguistic features of Anglo-Saxon wills

What, then, are the linguistic characteristics of Anglo-Saxon wills that reveal their status as transitional documents? Figure 3.1 lists seven linguistic features and summarises the relevant contrasts between modern and Old English wills. While no one will has all of the features described below, most have at least several of them.

After a brief look at the phenomenon of self-conscious meta-comments about writing in these documents, we will devote the rest of the chapter to two main themes: the implicit struggle to realise performativity in the documents, and the context-dependence of the text. With respect to the issue of incipient performativity, two topics will be discussed: the linguistic

FEATURE	ANGLO-SAXON WILLS	MODERN WILLS
Meta-comments about writing	yes	no
Realisation of act of bequeathing	linked to oral ceremony	autonomous
Opening strategy	non-standard	standard
Consistency	inconsistent	consistent
Secondary means to strengthen act of bequeathing	carried over from oral practice or transitional	writing-specific
Witnesses	reference only, or touching the document	signature
Curses	present	absent
Evidence of planning	present with lapses	present
Patterns of reference	situated	explicit
Dating	no date	date specified
Involvement of testator	high	low
Direct address	present	absent
Evaluative expressions	present	absent
Hedging	present	absent

Figure 3.1

realisation of the act of bequeathing, and the mobilisation of secondary devices to strengthen this act. As for autonomy of the text, or lack of it, we will examine, in turn, evidence of planning in the wills, patterns of reference to property and persons, dating, or rather the lack of a date in most documents, and the use of expressions which indicate high involvement of the testator. Issues of performativity are central, by definition, in any document of potentially constitutive intent. Autonomy, in contrast, is a more general concept, which may characterise both a scientific research article, written in a strongly decontextualised manner, as well as a performative legal document.

Meta-comments about writing

One striking difference between modern wills and at least some of the Anglo-Saxon ones is the overt reference to the act of writing itself. Whereas modern documents take the act of writing completely for granted, Anglo-Saxon wills include phrases which reveal self-consciousness about writing and written documents. For example, the will of the reeve Abba opens with a record of instructions to the scribe

Ic abba geroefa cuðe 7 writan hate hu min willa is þæt mon ymb min ærfe gedoe æfter minu dæge.

I, Reeve Abba, declare and command to be written what are my wishes as to the disposal of my property after my time.
(Will of Abba, 835 AD; Earle 1888: 109–110; trans. Whitelock 1979: 40)

Imagine the bizarreness of a modern will in which the text began with a record of the instructions of the testator to the lawyer to prepare the will! It is as if a modern will would begin, 'I hereby instruct my lawyer to draft this will.' Other types of meta-comments about writing are found in Anglo-Saxon land grants, though not in the wills. For example, the scribe may bemoan the fallibility of human memory and comment that creating a written record prevents important matters from falling into oblivion.

Not only do wills contain self-conscious comments about the act of writing, but they often make explicit references to the oral ceremony which constituted the actual act of bequeathing. Thus, the will of Æthelwold concludes:

þonne wylle ic þæt þæt sie gedeled for mine sawle swa swa ic nu þam freondum sæde þæ ic to spræc.

Then I wish it to be given out for my soul *just as I now said to my friends with whom I spoke.*
(Will of Earl Æthelwold, 946–955 AD; Harmer 1914: 33)

Similarly, the will of Ealdorman Alfred refers explicitly both to written and to verbal or oral statements.

And swa hwylc mon swa ðas god. 7 ðas geofe. 7 ðas gewrioto. 7 ðas word. mid rehte haldan wille. ond gelestan.

And whatsoever man will rightly observe and perform these
benefactions and gifts and these *written and verbal statements* . . .
(Will of Ealdorman Alfred, 871–888 AD; Earle 1888: 151; trans.
Whitelock 1979: 539)

Linguistic realisation of the act of bequeathing

Viewed through the eyes of speech act theorists (Austin 1962,
1970; Searle 1969, 1979), bequeathing is a type of *performative
utterance* – a speech act in which 'saying is doing', a form of
action in which *saying makes it so* (Austin 1962, 1970). In Searle's
(1969, 1979) modification of Austin's approach, he suggested that
utterances can be used for five basic purposes. As we have begun
to suggest, some types of speech acts use words to describe the
world or actions; in others, saying the words is a means either to
bring about a change in the world (i.e. to get someone to do
something), or to constitute a new relationship. Thus, to say 'I
made a will' or 'He made a will' is to match words to the world,
to report on a past event – what Searle (1979) calls an 'assertive'.
In contrast, in the proper circumstances, to declare 'I hereby will
and bequeath' is literally to engage in the act of making a will.
Searle's preferred term for the latter type of speech act is
'declaration':

Declarations bring about some alteration in the status or condition of
the referred to object or objects solely in virtue of the fact that the
declaration has been successfully performed.
(Searle 1979: 17)[7]

Speech act theorists typically write in an ahistorical fashion.
Their general theories of language use assume that the institutional arrangements which make acts of declaration like bequests
binding and authoritative are *in place*. Thus, declarations involve,
in Searle's words, 'an extra-linguistic institution, a system of
constitutive rules in addition to the constitutive rules of
language' (Searle 1979: 18). We have already pointed out that
written wills did not become fully binding in England until the
seventeenth century. Thus, in Searle's terms, we may say that in
the Anglo-Saxon period, the extra-linguistic arrangements for a

fully successful written performative act of bequeathing were not yet in place.

Modern written wills, which are full declarations in both the linguistic and the extra-linguistic senses, tend to have a standard form, and in particular to have a formulaic opening. Thus, modern British wills employ one of two prototypical openings, 'I John Smith hereby will and bequeath,' or 'This is the will of me, John Smith' (Kurzon 1984). As might be expected of a period of early experimentation with writing, the openings of Anglo-Saxon wills are anything but standard: indeed, they are remarkably varied in form and substance. Only a tenth of the wills open with a strategy which resembles that of a modern will, as in the will of King Alfred the Great:

Ic Ælfred Westseaxena cinge mid godes gife 7 mid ðisse gewitnesse gecweðe hu ic ymbe min yrfe wille æfter minum dæge . . .

I Alfred king of the Westsaxons by the grace of God and with this witness declare how I wish to dispose of my inheritance after my death . . .
(Will of Alfred the Great, 873–889 AD; Earle (1888): 144–45; trans.
Whitelock 1979: 534)

This type of opening is cast in the first person present, like those of modern wills. Contrast this with the seemingly similar opening of the will of Æthelstan, one of the six sons of King Æthelred:

On godes ælmihtiges naman Ic Æþestan Æþeling gesutelige on þysan gewrite hu ic mine are and mine æhta geunnen hæbbe.

In the name of Almighty God I Æthelstan the Atheling declare in this document how I *have granted* my estates and my possessions . . .
(Will of Æthelstan, 1015 AD; Whitelock 1986 [1930]: 56–7)

Although this opening also starts off like a modern will, the second half reveals that Æthelstan has already bequeathed his property, in a previous oral ceremony. In fact, then, this opening is a mixture of a narrative report with a second act of declaring.

The opening to Æthelstan's will illustrates another characteristic of many Anglo-Saxon wills, the lack of consistency of person and tense in the realisation of the act of bequeathing. While this will is consistently in the first person, it mixes the present and past tense.[8] Other openings are inconsistent in person but not in tense, as in the following example:

> *Leof Æþelwold ealdarman cyþ his leofan cynehlaforde Eadred cynge hu ic wille ymbe þa landare þe ic æt mine hlaforde geearnode.*

> Sire Earl Ethelwold declares to his dear Lord Eadred the King how I wish to dispose of the land that I acquired from my lord.
>
> (Will of Æthelwold, 946–955 AD; Harmer 1914: 33)

In a modern will, the voice and tense, not only of the opening strategy, but of the text as a whole, must be consistent. In the will of Æthelstan, the inconsistency of tense results from the link with the oral ceremony. In other cases, inconsistency seems to be a product of lack of care in the organisation of the document, or of the scribe's confusion as to what stance he is supposed to take *vis-à-vis* the substance of the document. Is he supposed to be primarily a transcriber of the testator's own words or stance, or is his mandate to provide a third-person summary of what the testator said? Or is he, as we would argue, experimenting with the transfer of performativity to writing, but perhaps uncertain as to how to do so? In some cases, the scribe is not confused at all, and the opening strategy, as well as the entire text, are consistent in person and tense but cast in the third person, resulting in a full-fledged *narrative*. Consider, for instance,

> *Æðelnoð se gerefa to Eastorege 7Gænburg his wif arræddan hiora erfe beforan Wulfre de arcebiscope 7 Æðelhune his mæsseprioste 7 Esne cyninges ðegne.*

> Æthelnoth the reeve at Eastry and Gænburg his wife have disposed of their inheritance before Archbishop Wulfred and Æthelhun his priest and Esne the King's thegn.
>
> (Will of Æthelnoth and Gænburg, 805 AD; Robertson 1956 [1939]: 4–5)

Here, the scribe is telling the story of the oral ceremony, taking the stance of a reporter rather than attempting to render the performative act of the testator directly. In other instances the scribe constantly switches person or tense, or both. In still others a nearly consistent scribe 'slips up' just once or twice, as in the will of Wynflæd (950 AD; Whitelock 1986 [1930]: 10–15). Except for one act of granting in the first person, this unusually long will is entirely in the third person.

If Anglo-Saxon wills were unequivocally intended only as a record of the oral ceremony that preceded them, a third-person narrative version, or even a sketchy list of donations, together with some identification of the testator, would have been entirely adequate. Yet, as Table 3.1 demonstrates, first-person texts outnumber third-person ones. Although just under a fifth of all sixty-two wills are fully in the first person, a high 40 per cent are almost entirely in the first person, with just an occasional 'lapse' into third person. In contrast, only a fifth are entirely in the third person, with a similar proportion almost consistently in the third person. Thus, *three out of five wills are cast in the voice of the testator* – either in entirely consistent fashion, or nearly so. While the absolute numbers are obviously quite small, making any such comparison somewhat risky, we wish to argue that the trend towards first-person renderings indicates that testators and scribes were attempting to invest the written document with performative power.

Second-order performatives: witnesses and curses

It was quite common practice in medieval times to place freshly completed documents upon a church altar, or to copy them into a

Table 3.1. The representation of voice in Anglo-Saxon wills (percentages)

Voice	Percentage
Entirely first person	19
Almost entirely first person	40
Entirely third person	21
Almost entirely third person	19
	99
	(62)

holy book (Clanchy 1979; Tabuteau 1988). In our terms, these quasi-magical acts were intended not simply to protect the document as object but to enhance its performative power. Although none of the wills in the present study explicitly mentions that the document was actually placed on an altar or written into a holy book, it is possible that at least some document-makers employed these strategies.[9]

However, the wills do contain explicit evidence of two other types of efforts to strengthen the primary performative act of bequeathing. First, the text sometimes reveals that witnesses were involved in the confirmation of the document, as opposed to merely witnessing the oral ceremony. Second, curses directed to anyone tampering with the will are mobilised in order to strengthen the bequest.

Witnesses are sometimes explicitly mentioned in the wills as having been present and heard the oral declaration. Such references to witnesses do not have implications for performativity of the document, because they only report on the act of witnessing the oral ceremony. However, in other cases, a list of witnesses appears with a cross next to each name, much like a list of signatures in present-day wills. A phrase such as *ic . . . ðis write 7 ðeafie 7 mid cristes rode tacne hit festniæ* ('I . . . consent and write and confirm it with Christ's cross') is often added. Although these are not signatures in the modern sense because all writing on the document, including the ostensible signatures and the cross, was done by the scribe (Clanchy 1979), there *is* performative significance to the fact that witnesses often touched their sword or hand to the cross, as is indicated by the following passage:

> *sind gewritan gewitenesse 7 hiera handa seitene . . .*
> (Will of the thegn Alfred, 932–939 AD; Robertson 1956 [1939]: 54–5)

Robertson (1956 [1939]: 55) translates this sentence as 'the witnesses and their signatures are recorded'. However, the literal translation, 'the witnesses are written and their hands touched', comes closer to communicating to the reader the performative role of the witnesses specifically in relation to the document. Touching the cross is thus a medieval equivalent of the modern signature. It is a transitional act, from the viewpoint of the history of literacy, since it both reveals close links with the physical manipulation of symbolic objects common to oral ceremonies, and points toward literacy in that individuals are relating to graphic marks on the parchment.

There is another phenomenon in the wills which has important implications for performativity of the document, and which has not received the full attention it deserves, namely, the inclusion of curses in the *sanctio*, or concluding section. Twenty-five of the sixty-two wills contained such curses, addressed to anyone who tampers with the will. Here is a vivid example:

> *and se þe mine quyde beryaui þe ic nu biquepen habbe a godes ywithnesse beriaued he worþe þises erthliche meryþes godes and ashireyi hine se almiyti driyten þe alle sheppe shop and ywroyte uram alre haleyene ymennesse on domesday. and sy he bytayt Satane þane deule and alle his awaryede yueren into helle Grunde and þer aquelmi and godes withsaken bute ysweke and mine irfinume neuer ne aswenche.*

> And he who shall detract from my will which I have now declared in the witness of God, may he be deprived of joy on this earth, and may the Almighty Lord who created and made all creatures exclude him the fellowship of all saints on the Day of Judgment, and may he be delivered into the abyss of hell to Satan the devil and all his accursed companions and there suffer with God's adversaries, without end, and never trouble my heirs.
>
> (Will of Wulfgyth, 1046 AD; Whitelock 1986 [1930]: 86–7)

These curses are both an expression of widespread magical beliefs and practices, often pagan in origin, and of the strong influence of Catholicism on public life. This was a period in which religion and magic were inextricably fused, as is evident in the practices of putting documents on altars or copying them into holy books. Curses were commonly used in many aspects of everyday life. A form of 'word magic', they served as an attempt to exert control over the supernatural and social world.

Curses were apparently a common part of oral wills and grants of land. They were mobilised in these ceremonies because Anglo-Saxons believed that they could strengthen the acts of declaring or bequeathing performed in them. At the very least, then, the curses in the documents are closely related to the ones that were part of the oral ceremony. Are they, then, simply a form of oral residue? Are they merely a *report* of the oral curse, rather than a new, independent curse in writing? In most cases, we feel the answer to these questions is negative. Curses are mobilised to strengthen the performative potential of the *document*: they are second-order performatives mobilised in support of first-order ones.

In another paper (Danet and Bogoch, 1992), we explored in depth the hypothesis that curses are especially likely to be mobilised in documents which are struggling toward performativity, and when the acts at issue are of a public rather than a private nature. In order to test this hypothesis, we compared wills with two other types of Anglo-Saxon documents, land grants and royal writs.[10] Like wills, land grants involve public ceremonial acts which create new, legally binding situations. In speech act terms, both therefore involve declarations (Searle 1969, 1979). Writs, in contrast, are private letters, a kind of assertive, in speech act terms, whose purpose is to notify or inform some particular individual of an event. Thus, we expected that curses would be more common in the wills and land grants than in writs. Another line of reasoning also led us to the same expectation. Since writs were private letters to specific individuals, kings might care less about their long-term preservation than in the case of documents of public import, such as wills and grants, and therefore would be less likely to mobilise curses to protect them.

Our findings supported these predictions. We found that about six out of ten Anglo-Saxon land grants and leases have a curse, and about four out of ten wills include one. In royal writs, on the other hand, curses are much rarer – less than a fifth of all writs include one. Thus, these results strongly support the thesis that curses appear in written wills as part of the effort to transfer performativity to the document. Another pertinent finding is that curses appeared more frequently in eleventh-century wills than in those of the ninth and tenth. Whereas only a third of the thirty-three ninth- and tenth-century wills contained a curse, over half of the group of twenty-nine eleventh-century ones did so. Had curses merely occurred as residue from oral rituals, we would have expected to find their incidence to decline as time went on. Indeed, as Tabuteau (1988: 219) notes, curses continued to be used into the twelfth and thirteenth centuries in Norman wills.

It is evident that in modern practice curses are no longer mobilised to strengthen wills or other legal documents. We moderns rely on other devices to heighten performativity, such as the signature, especially the notarised signature, the seal or stamp, and the signatures of witnesses to the signing of the document by the parties.

Degree of planning

There are many other linguistic aspects of Anglo-Saxon documents which differ sharply from the model of the modern legal document. These other aspects are not related to performativity, but to the more general notion of autonomy of the document, its decontextualisation from the interpersonal setting in which it was created. The first of these features examined here is that of textual structure. Like official or legal documents generally (Biber 1988), modern wills are texts which generally reflect a high degree of planning. They have a regular structure and the information presented in them is laid out in ordered fashion. To what extent is this true for transitional texts like Anglo-Saxon wills?

Anglo-Saxon scholars report that wills are characterised by a basic three-part structure; the three parts are known, respectively, as the *notificatio*, the *donatio*, and the *sanctio* (Sheehan 1963; Whitelock 1986 [1930]). According to Sheehan (1963), the *notificatio* introduces the testator, states his/her purpose or the function of the document itself, and very often cites the authority backing the will. The *donatio* details the provisions of the will, sometimes also including boundaries of lands donated. The *sanctio* is a closing section. As pointed out above, it often contains curses directed to anyone attempting to tamper with it, and sometimes includes a blessing as well. Additional concluding components may also list the location of copies of the documents, as was typical of chirographs,[11] provide lists of witnesses who were present at the oral ceremony, or who heard the written version read aloud and confirm its provisions,[12] or cite other, outside endorsements of the provisions of the will.

Modern editing conventions, taken for granted by modern literates, help readers to discern the presence of structure in these texts, through the employment of devices such as paragraphing. Thus, in Whitelock's (1986 [1930]) collection, the Old English is printed in run-on fashion, just as the texts were written on the original parchment, while in the modern English translation each of the three basic parts often begins with a new paragraph; or at least paragraph indentations divide up the text into smaller chunks, whose relation to the text as a whole can be more easily grasped than if the entire will were one run-on text. The lack of chunking through paragraphing is itself obviously evidence of a very early stage in the development of a concept of textuality.

Structure is very much in evidence, despite the lack of graphic aids to help the reader to discern it. Fifty-four of the sixty-two wills contain a *notificatio*, and three-fourths have some sort of concluding section, either a traditional *sanctio* or some other material which indicates that the scribe or testator have stepped back from the details of the *donatio* and are attempting to provide a sense of closure or completion (Herrnstein-Smith 1968). Consider, for instance, the will of Wulfgeat. Although it does not contain a traditional *sanctio*, it ends with a general, concluding request which goes beyond the *donatio*:

> 7þeo wellinc æt þære wic into Dunnintune. 7 Æþelsige. leof cyð þis mine hlaforde 7 ealle mine freondum.

And the spring at Droitwich is to belong to Donington. And, dear Æthelsige, make this known to my lord and to all my friends.
(Will of Wulfgeat, c. 1006 AD; Whitelock 1986 [1930]: 56–7)

The will of Wulfsige (1022–1043 AD) is a good example of a well-organised text with a simple, clear-cut structure. The three basic parts are present, and in standard order. Moreover, the information within the *donatio* is also carefully organised. The complete text of this will is presented in Figure 3.2.

The *notificatio* states the general purpose of the text in straightforward fashion:

> Her switeleþ on þise write wam Wlsi an his aihte.

Here in this document it is made known to whom Wulfsige grants his possessions.
(Will of Wulfsige, 1022–1043 AD; Whitelock 1986 [1930]: 74–5)

The text then lists all the provisions of the will, moving smoothly from disposition of land – the estate at Wick – to serfs, and finally to goods of various kinds. The expression *þat is erst* (literally

[H]er switelep on þise write wam Wlsi an his aihte. þat is erst for his soule þat lond at Wiken into seynt Eadmundes biri þa tweye deles 7 Alfric Biscop þe þridde del. buten ane gride and .XII. swine mesten þat schal habben Wlwine hire day. and after hire day into seynt Eadmundes biri 7 alle þo men fre for vnker bother soule. And ic an mine kynelouerd .II. hors. and Helm and brinie. 7 an Swerd and a goldwreken spere. and ic an mine lauedy half marc goldes. an mine Nifte ann ore wichte goldes. And habbe Stanhand alle þinge þe ic him bicueðen habbe. and mine brother bern here owen lond. 7.II. hors mid sadelgarun. and .I. brinie and on hakele. And se þe mine cuiðe awende god almithin awende his asyne from him on domesday buten he it her þe rathere bete.

Here is this document it is made known to whom Wulfsige grants his possessions. First, for his soul, two-thirds of the estate at Wick to Bury St. Edmunds and the third part to Bishop Ælfic, except one yardland and mast for twelve swine which Wulfwyn shall have for her life, and after her death [it shall go] to Bury St. Edmunds; and all the men are to be free for the sake of the souls of us both.

And I grant to my royal lord two horses and a helmet and a coat of mail, and a sword and a spear inlaid with gold. And I grant to my lady half a mark of gold, and to my niece an ore's weight in gold. And Stanhand is to have everything which I have bequeathed to him, and my brother's children their own land, and two horses with harness, and one coat of mail and one cloak.

And he who alters my will, may Almighty God turn away his face from him on the Day of Judgment unless in this life he will quickly make amends for it.

Source: Whitelock, 1986 [1930]: 74-75

Figure 3.2 The will of Wulfsige, 1022–1043

'that is first', translated by Whitelock simply as 'first') at the beginning of the *donatio*, a common one in the wills, is evidence of conscious attention to the sequence in which items of information are presented. It is a linguistic device which enhances *cohesion* of the text (Halliday and Hasan, 1976). Another cohesive device is the use of the conjunction 'and' to link the various parts of the *donatio*. As Ong (1982) has pointed out, this simplest of cohesive devices is very typical of oral discourse in non-literate societies and in unplanned, spontaneous speech. His term for this phenomenon is 'additiveness'. Modern testators would be unlikely to string together their various bequests in this way. The curse in the *sanctio* also begins with 'and', a common occurrence in the wills.

Surprisingly, the will of King Alfred the Great, which was

produced for a king who was highly literate – a rarity at this time – ends quite abruptly, without a closing of any kind.[13]

In four wills the text is clearly disorganised, even though all three parts are present. Here is a colourful example from the will of a woman called Ælfgifu:

> And ic biddæ minnæ cinelaford for godæs lufum, þæt næ forlæte minæ mænn þe hinæ gesæcen, and him wyrðæ syn. and ic ann Ælfwerdæ anræ sopcuppan. and Æþelwerdæ anæs gerænodæs drincæhornæs.

> And I beseech my royal lord for the love of God, that he will not desert my men who seek his protection and are worthy of him. And I grant to Ælfweard a drinking-cup and to Æthelweard an ornamented drinking horn.
> (Will of Ælfgifu, 966–975 AD; Whitelock 1986 [1930]: 22–3)

Considering that the creation of documents was such a novelty, that writing on parchment was a laborious physical act, and that it was very difficult to make changes, these texts are remarkably well organised. Perhaps the degree of planning evident in them is not so surprising, after all, when we take into account the use of wax tablets by scribes during this period. From antiquity and, in fact, even well into the High Middle Ages, scribes used such tablets to draft texts or make notes (Clanchy 1979; Rouse and Rouse 1989). It is extremely likely that Anglo-Saxon scribes drafted wills on such tablets. The fact that texts are clearly structured supports this claim. However, if the texts were meant solely as evidentiary documents, why would the scribe or the testator care what form the final document took? It may be that the relatively good organisation of these texts is another shred of evidence that the performative potential of documents was beginning to be recognised.

Explicit versus situated reference

One of the most striking features of the language of Anglo-Saxon wills is the phenomenon of context-dependence: testators refer to property and persons in ways which assume that others will know who or what is meant. In many instances, shared knowledge of members of the community would be necessary in order to 'decode' the text, and to carry out the wishes of the testator. Such patterns of reference are situated in the flow of interpersonal communication among persons who have an ongoing face-to-face relationship.[14]

We look first at patterns of reference to property bequeathed. The will of Bishop Theodred of London is especially rich in context-bound references. Among the goods which he bequeaths are those which are to go to his lord after his death:

> . . . *tua hund marcas arede goldes and tua cuppes siluerene. and four hors so ic best habbe, and to suerde so ic best habbe* . . .

> . . . two hundred marks of red gold, and two silver cups and four horses, *the best that I have*, and two swords, *the best that I have* . . .
> (Will of Bishop Theodred, 942–951 AD; Whitelock 1986 [1930]: 2–3)

To modern eyes, Theodred's bequest is quaint: how is one to know which horses and swords he considered his 'best'? Only those who knew Theodred well could carry out his wishes.

The will of Æthelstan (1015 AD; Whitelock 1986 [1930]: 56–63) distinguishes between 'the sword with the silver hilt which Wulfric made', and 'the silver-hilted sword which belonged to Ulfketel'. Although these descriptions appear more objective because they include objective information – swords with silver hilts – here too, shared knowledge would also be necessary in order to transmit the right sword to the right person.

Another aspect of context-dependence is the practice of referring to people without identifying them in any way. This contrasts sharply with modern practice, which employs a variety of devices to identify individuals, such as the giving of first and last name, title, address, identification numbers, and so on. We have examined both how testators themselves are presented, and how other persons mentioned, generally beneficiaries, are identified.

Most commonly, testators are presented by name only, as in

This is Ælfgifu's request to her royal lord
(966–975 AD; Whitelock 1986 [1930]: 21)

This is Ælfgar's will
(946–951 AD; Whitelock 1986 [1930]: 7)

Here it is made known how Siflæd grants her possessions after her
death
(c. 1066 AD; Whitelock 1986 [1930]: 93)

Almost as common is the combination of name and title or
role. Kings, archbishops and bishops regularly refer to themselves this way, as well as some lesser persons. Examples are:

I Alfred, King of the West Saxons
(873–889 AD; Whitelock 1979: 535)

I, Bishop Æthelmær, declare to all men . . .
(1047–1070 AD; Whitelock 1986 [1930]: 93)

In just two cases testators were designated as 'the son of . . .':

This is the will of Leofwine, Wulfstan's son
(998 AD; Napier and Stevenson 1894: 122)

In the Lord's name. I, Thurstan, Wine's son, make known to all
men . . .
(1943–1044 AD; Whitelock 1986 [1930]: 81)

Only in one case is the testator identified by place of residence:

This is the will of Wulfgeat of Donington
(c. 1006 AD; Whitelock 1986 [1930]: 55)

As for beneficiaries, they are sometimes identified by their
name and blood relationship to the testator. Thus, Wynflæd
'bequeaths to her daughter Æthelflæd her engraved bracelet and
brooch' (950 AD; Whitelock 1986 [1930]: 11), and Bishop Theodred
grants an estate 'to my sister's son Osgot' (942–951 AD; Whitelock
1986 [1930]: 3). In other instances, beneficiaries are identified by
their social role, like some of the testators, as in 'my servant
Viking' (will of Thurstan, 1043–1044 AD; Whitelock 1986 [1930]:
83), 'a woman-weaver and a seamstress the one called Eadgifu,
the other called Æthelgifu' (will of Wylflæd, 950 AD; Whitelock
1986 [1930]: 11), or 'Æthelric the priest and Ælfric the priest and

Æthelsige the deacon' (will of Leofgifu, 1035–1044 AD; Whitelock 1986 [1930]: 77). However, it is extremely common to refer to beneficiaries by name only, or only by social role, with no additional identifying information. Here is the opening donation in the will of Wulfgar:

> I, Wulfgar, grant the estate at Collingbourne after my death to Æffe for her lifetime.
> (Will of Wulfgar, 931–939 AD; Whitelock 1986 [1930]: 52–3)

While it would be reasonable to guess that Æffe was his wife, this is made explicit only in a separate endorsement which was appended to the text.

Witnesses to the bequest are also often presented in context-dependent fashion. Compare the wills of Alfwold, Bishop of Crediton and of Wulfgyth:

> 7 þises is to gewitnesse wulfgar ælfgares sunu. 7 godric becrydian. 7 eadwine mæssepreost. 7 alfwold munuc. 7 byrhtmær preost.

> And of this are to witness: Wulfgar, Ælfgar's son, and Godric of Crediton, and Eadwine, mass-priest, and Alfwold, monk, and Bryhtmær, priest.
> (Will of Ælfwold, Bishop of Crediton, 1008–1012 AD; Napier and
> Stevenson 1894: 23)

> þisses is to ywithnesse Eadward king and manie oþre.

> Of this King Edward and many others are witnesses.
> (Will of Wulfgyth, 1046 AD; Whitelock 1986 [1930]: 86–7)

Whereas in the former case, each witness is carefully listed, along with additional information to identify him, in the latter, the text explicitly mentions only the most important person present, the king, and simply notes that 'many others' were also present. Similarly, the will of Thurstan states, e.g., 'These are the witnesses . . . in Suffolk: Leofstan the dean and all the community of Bury St. Edmunds . . .' meaning, presumably, that all the monks at that monastery were present (Will of Thurstan, 1043–1044 AD; Whitelock 1986 [1930]: 83).

Although testators, beneficiaries and witnesses tended to be referred to only by name, and although the same names tended to be used over and over – a fact that makes for confusion for modern scholars – the persons mentioned in these wills would not have had difficulty identifying them. Theirs was a local world, in which 'everyone knew everyone else', and in which documents were never meant to be autonomous.

Still another expression of context-dependence is the occasional reference in the wills to previous, generally oral agreements, without explicitly specifying the conditions of those agreements. As noted earlier, the will of Ealdorman Alfred mentions 'written and verbal statements', but supplies no explanatory information about the latter (will of Ealdorman Alfred, 871 AD; Earle 1888: 151; Whitelock 1979: 539). Similarly, that of Ealdorman Æthelmer concludes:

And ic gean syððan minum wife ealles ðæs ðe ic gean ge on lande ge on æhtum to þam forewordun þe wit mid wedde unc betweonan gefæstnodon . . .

And finally, all that I grant to my wife, whether estates or goods, I grant *according to the terms which we settled by a compact between us.*
(Will of Ealdorman Æthelmer, 971–983 AD; Whitelock 1986 [1930]: 26–7)

Even the literate King Alfred (or his scribe) had not yet fully internalised the notion of an autonomous document. He too refers to such an agreement without further explanation.

Dating

The literate practice of dating documents by a universal standard serves to objectify them and to disassociate them from the immediate context in which they were created. This practice is relatively recent. Even well into the twelfth century, documents were rarely dated in England. Moreover, during the Anglo-Saxon period there was, as yet, no standard way of reckoning time. Our current, taken-for-granted system of reckoning the year from the birth of Christ was only one of several competing systems (Earle 1888; Zerubavel 1981; Harrison 1973; Parise 1982). There were also modes of reckoning by the year of the rule of emperors or kings; fifteen-cycles called Indictions, reckoned from 312 AD, the reign of Constantine; nineteen-year cycles called epacts, etc. Dating from the birth of Christ appeared in England as early as the seventh century and became increasingly popular after the publication of the Venerable Bede's *De ratione temporum* in 725 (Zerubavel 1981; Earle 1888).

Latin documents such as land grants tended to be dated, using one or more of these methods, well before documents in the vernacular. However, only one of the sixty-two Old English wills, that of Leofwine, is dated – by modern criteria, 15 April 998. Actually, no less than eight different time-reckonings are supplied in this will:

> þys wæs gedon þæs geares fram ures drihtnes gebrydtide.

> anni dni indic epac ccur ciclos dies XIIII. lun
> DCCCCXCVIII XI XX V VIII XVII kl mai
> dies pasce tun ipsius
> XV kl mai XVI
> This was done in the year 998 of our Lord's birth, etc.
> (Will of Leofwine, 998 AD; Napier and Stevenson 1894: 122)

In some cases, testators and scribes locate the making of the will in time by mentioning local events or events in their personal lives, a common practice not only in the Anglo-Saxon period but well into the Norman one. Three wills were made as testators embarked on pilgrimages to the Holy Land.

> þis is seo feorewearde þe Vlf 7 Madselin his gebedda worhtan wið [ ] 7 wið sce PETER, þa hig to Ierusalem ferdon.

> This is the agreement which Ulf and his wife Madselin made with [God] and with St. Peter *when they went to Jerusalem.*
> (Will of Ulf and Madselin, 1066–1068 AD; Whitelock 1986 [1930]: 94–5)

Other wills relate the documents to local events or customs which are common knowledge to contemporaries:

> 7 heregyð bibeadeð . . . ðæt sie simle to higna blodlese ymb twelf monað agefen

And Heregyth enjoins . . . that payment always be made annually
when the community are bled.
(Will of Abba, 835 AD; Earle 1888: 108; Whitelock 1979: 42)

A curious example is the reference to the 'shad season' in the
will of Wulfric. He grants certain lands to Ælfhelm and Wilfheah
'on condition that when it is the shad season, each of them shall
pay three thousand shad to the monastery at Burton' (Will of
Wulfric, 1002–1004 AD; Whitelock 1986 [1930]: 46–7).

Involvement of the speaker

Still another way in which these texts reflect the dominance of
oral practice is the high degree of involvement of speakers which
is given expression in the text. Involvement is apparent in the
practice of addressing persons directly, as if they were present in
a face-to-face conversation; in the use of evaluative expressions
which reveal feelings and attitudes, rather than merely supplying
information in dry fashion; and in the tendency to hedge or
qualify one's utterances.[15]
In about a fifth of the wills, testators address individuals –
usually beneficiaries or their feudal lord – in the second person,
as if they were talking to them, a practice we are unlikely to find
in a modern will.[16] A typical example appears in the will of
Wulfwaru:

Ic kyðe þe leof her on ðisum gewrite hwæs ic geann into Baðum to Sce
Petres mynstre . . .

I make known to you, Sire, here in this document, what I grant to St
Peter's monastery at Bath . . .
(Will of Wulfwaru, 984–1016 AD; Whitelock 1986 [1930]: 62–3)

Any instance of addressing a person directly can perhaps be
considered a form of appeal or persuasion, but in this instance
the exhortative quality of this text is further illustrated in the
curse addressed to would-be violators of Ælfhelm's wishes:

se man se þe minne cwyde wende. but þu hyt sy leof. 7 ic hæbbe

geleauan þ þu neelle. god afyrre hine of his rice. buton he þe hraþor
ongen wende.

That man who shall alter my will, *unless it be you, Sire, and I am*
confident that you will not, may God drive him back from His kingdom,
unless he will quickly alter it back again.
(Will of Ælfhelm, 975–1016 AD; Whitelock 1986 [1930]: 32–3)

Like virtually all the curses occurring in Anglo-Saxon legal
documents, this one is cast in 'whoever' form; it states, 'Whoever
tampers with the conditions of this will, let something bad
happen to him'. The interjection of a direct appeal to the lord,
perhaps flattering him into complying with Ælfhelm's request
not to tamper with the will, disrupts the formal invocation of
heavenly wrath on potential violators, and injects a conversational note into the otherwise awesome curse.

A second way in which these texts reveal the high involvement
of testators is in the use of evaluative adjectives, adverbs and
adverbial expressions which offer information on the subjective
or emotional state of the speaker, or on subjective judgments by
him or her. Some of the examples already presented to illustrate
other points are also pertinent here. Thus, references to one's
'best' sword or veil, discussed in the section on explicit versus
situated reference, convey subjective judgments. But there are
other kinds of evaluative adjectives too. For instance, Wulfric
refers to his '*poor* daughter' and to his '*little* estate'; he concludes
by saying that he believes his lord to be 'so *good* and so *gracious*'
that he will not violate the will (will of Wulfric, 1002–1004 AD;
Whitelock 1986 [1930]: 46–51). Mantat the Anchorite greets his
king and queen 'very *joyfully with God's joy*' (Will of Mantat the
Anchorite, c. 1035 AD; Whitelock 1986 [1930]: 66–7). The Ætheling
Æthelstan thanks his father 'in all *humility*' for permission to
make his will (will of Æthelstan, 1015 AD; Earle 1888: 226; trans.
Whitelock 1979: 596). Ketel threatens potential violators of his
wishes with the curse,

7 *And gif ani man si so disi þat wille mine quide bereuen. god him fordo on*
domesday and alle his halegan.

And if anyone be so *foolish* as to wish to detract from my will, may
God and all his saints destroy him on the Day of Judgment.
(Will of Ketel, 1052–1066 AD; Whitelock 1986 [1930]: 90–1)

A related phenomenon is the tendency to hedge or qualify one's statements. The most dramatic example occurs in the will of King Alfred. After a long, detailed specification of how he wishes his property and his money to be allocated, he confesses:

> 7 ic nat naht gewislice hwæðer ðæs feos swa micel is, ne ic nat ðeah his mare sy; butan swa ic wene.

I know not for certain whether there is so much money, nor do I know if there is more, but I think so.
(Will of Alfred the Great, 880–885 AD; Earle 1888: 148; trans. Whitelock 1979: 536)

This is no minor hedge: modern testators know that they should only bequeath benefits which they are sure they possess!

DISCUSSION

We have demonstrated in this chapter that Anglo-Saxon wills differ sharply in their linguistic features from the model of the modern autonomous will. They are saturated with oral residue, illustrating in a host of ways the symbiotic relationship between the document and the oral ceremony which preceded it. While various researchers, primarily historians, have occasionally remarked on this or that linguistic feature, this is, to our knowledge, the first intensive, systematic study of the language of transitional documents. We believe the main contribution of this research to be the analysis of the evidence for incipient performativity of the document. Our results reveal that it is simplistic to characterise documents as merely evidentiary. It is necessary, then, to distinguish between the official legal status of the document and the communicative work that the document is beginning to accomplish.

We do not mean to imply that Anglo-Saxon testators and scribes actually knew that they were revolutionalising the conventions for making a will, or intended to do so. These processes of legal and linguistic transition took place *without* the full awareness of participants. By experimenting with new means – written documents – to strengthen the old ways, they inadvertently helped to encourage the demise of the oral ceremony itself. In the last analysis, the full institutionalisation of writing can only take place if and when understandings about the performative potential of writing, and linguistic conventions for the constitution through writing of binding social acts converge with legal changes superimposed from above. Perhaps these legal changes can only occur if the linguistic ones have first taken place. Clearly, this is an issue which requires further investigation.

The need for comparative studies

The portrait of the transitional legal document which emerges from the above analysis is probably not unique to wills, or even to Anglo-Saxon materials. As noted at the beginning of this chapter, the shift to written documentation, and to the constitution of binding legal acts through writing, was taking place at different rates all over Europe. McKitterick (1989) analysed the diffusion of writing in the Frankish kingdoms of the Carolingian period (eighth and ninth centuries). She claims that the Carolingians had already passed from reliance on memory to reliance on the written word for a wide variety of societal functions. Although the status of documents varied somewhat between kingdoms, she concludes:

> even if these charters are not wholly dispositive in function, what we
> are observing in these documents is first of all the practical
> manifestation of prescriptions contained in the law codes concerning
> records, and secondly a transition from charters as documents
> establishing record and proof of ownership to charters which *in
> themselves constitute the legal transaction.*
> (McKitterick 1989: 75, emphasis added)

It would be interesting to compare the language of Anglo-Saxon documents with those of other medieval societies such as the Carolingian kingdoms. We could ask, for example, do the same types of oral residue occur in Carolingian ones as in Anglo-Saxon ones? How do the linguistic features of Carolingian documents change, as they move toward autonomy and full performativity? The need for comparative studies is further brought out by the comments of Tabuteau on the status of documents in eleventh-century Normandy. In her opinion, 'the principal role of charters in eleventh-century Normandy was as memoranda of the transactions recorded' (Tabuteau 1988: 221). Even though the Norman period is later in time than either the Carolingian or the Anglo-Saxon ones, Tabuteau appears to suggest that writing for legal purposes was less fully institutionalised in Norman times than in the Frankish kingdoms of the Carolingian period. Is this discrepancy due to the different criteria used by different researchers, or is it, rather, an illustration of the non-linear nature of the transition to literacy in Europe, or of the different rate of change in different geographical areas? What was the impact of the Norman invasion of England on the language of English legal documents? Was there a 'great leap forward' toward the linguistic realisation of performativity, with the advent of larger-scale social organisation?

It would also be intriguing to compare medieval transitional documents with a corpus from an ancient culture. As we noted in the introduction to this chapter, a number of ancient societies made extensive use of writing for legal, administrative and commercial purposes. Thus, we might ask, for instance, do Sumerian or ancient Greek legal documents have some of the same linguistic characteristics as those identified in this study? What aspects of these early documents offer evidence of experimentation with the performative potential of writing? In what ways are they too context-bound?

Such analyses might help us to isolate the universal versus culture-specific aspects of the institutionalisation of writing. Other research questions which could be asked include the following: to what extent are the linguistic means mobilised to perform the act of bequeathing, or any other type of constitutive act, universal, and to what extent are they culture-bound? Which elements associated with performativity are common to both speech and writing, and which are writing-specific? Which elements, if any, are absolutely required for the realisation of performativity, and which are simply the result of convention in a particular cultural setting? It is apparent, for example, that the first person present is not always essential – modern contracts between two parties are typically drafted in the third person present.

It is also evident that the use of curses as second-order performatives is culture-specific; we moderns are not very likely to include them in our wills. They disappeared over time, as processes of secularisation, rationalisation, and the differentiation of the religious and legal spheres undermined the belief in the magic power of the word. It would be fascinating to explore whether drafters of ancient legal documents also employed curses to strengthen their performative power.[17]

Autonomy of the document

The language of Anglo-Saxon wills was contrasted with a model of the autonomous text which has crystallised in Western literate practice. Like any model, this model is an idealised one. It remains an empirical question to what extent modern wills in England, or elsewhere, for that matter, in fact conform to this model. No doubt, some people, particularly those of low levels of education, who have not internalised this model, and who have not had much practice in writing in the manner of essayist literacy (Scollon and Scollon 1981) compose wills which in various ways hark back to the transitional model. Some might, for example, refer to possessions in a context-bound manner; or they might occasionally make evaluative comments or address personal comments to selected persons, in the conversational style we saw to characterise many Anglo-Saxon wills. How much deviation from the model, and what kinds of deviation can be tolerated without invalidating the document? To answer such questions, one might investigate the fate of wills whose linguistic anomalies or ambiguities led to their being contested in court. Such studies might help to clarify the nature of the interrelations between performativity and autonomy of the document, two concepts we have treated as independent, on the whole.

It is interesting to note in this connection some of the changes which the Plain Language movement has been making in the language of contemporary legal and bureaucratic documents. This movement, which gained momentum in the West in the last fifteen to twenty years, seeks to reform the language of documents to make it more readable, more accessible to the public. Language reformers have been reintroducing, for example, the use of the second person, sometimes quite consciously attempting to make the language closer to everyday speech. Redish (1985: 125) even goes so far as to define Plain English as language *'that reads as if it were spoken'*.

Video wills: from oral to literate residue

An especially fascinating research question which will increasingly be asked in the future is: what will be the linguistic features of *video wills*? A thousand years after the experiments with writing analysed in this chapter, we creatures of the late twentieth century are once again experimenting with new modes of communication which challenge deeply internalised assumptions about orality and literacy. Just as primary orality was transformed in the Middle Ages by new literate practices, so literacy is now being transformed in ways we hardly begin to grasp by a new tertiary[18] orality made possible by mechanical reproduction of electronic media.

One of the most striking instances of these developments is the phenomenon of living video wills. This innovation began to proliferate in modern societies, starting about the end of the 1970s (Negev 1990), though it is still the exception rather than the rule, and the legal status of such wills is not established. Testators arrange to have a videotape made of themselves, either reading aloud a previously composed written document while looking into the camera, or speaking directly and spontaneously to their beneficiaries and bequeathing their property to them. We can already see that reading aloud a decontextualised, written text is a form of *literate* residue! Instead of exploiting the possibilities of the new medium, testators who do this are unthinkingly following obsolescent literate practice. At the same time, by using video technology they may be contributing to the eventual demise of the document as the binding legal act.

In one instance, cited in a recent newspaper article in Israel, a wealthy widower began his video will with the following opening in Hebrew:

Ka'sšer tir'u et hatmunot haele, kvar lo eheye baxaim. B'heyoti bidea çlula umeyuševet, ani miçave bizot al rixuši l'axar moti.

When you see these pictures, I will no longer be alive. Being of sound and stable mind, I hereby bequeath my property after my death.[19]

Then the testator began to point to the objects bequeathed and even requested that the camera zoom in on some of them, to make clear his intentions. Asking for a 'zoom' shot is a good example of exploiting the potential of the new medium. Note also that in this example we have a brand-new opening, consisting of an improvised, informal 'video-specific' strategy, combined with the standard written performative formula, the one regularly used by lawyers in Israel, but now spoken aloud.

Will decontextualisation of the text become obsolete, when it is again possible to speak directly to one's heirs, to express one's emotions, and to point physically to objects bequeathed? Will video wills eventually replace documents as the binding will? And if so, will the process be much faster, in this era of rapid social change, than in the case of the transition to documents in medieval and Renaissance Europe?

Video wills raise a host of other questions (see Pearson and Berch, this volume): In what ways will they serve as supplementary evidence, if not as the binding will itself? Under what conditions will courts grant them status as acceptable evidence? How will the need for authentification and conventionalisation be met, under these new conditions? What will replace the literate strategy of having witnesses sign their names to legal documents? Another change might be renewed tolerance for relatively loose textual organisation – 'asides' to the audience, for example. Certainly, we can anticipate self-conscious meta-comments about the use of videotape, such as 'I'm glad that videotape makes it possible for me to communicate with you directly, after my death.'

Already, we have identified four innovative strategies improvised by testators to protect video wills. One testator put a clock before the camera, to show the time at the start and finish of the film, and thereby prevent cutting a portion of it. Another filed a copy of the film with his lawyer and kept a second, signed copy at home. In a third case, the lawyer made sure to film the testator while he signed the written will. And when a testator had to start again, he preserved both versions of the video will, to show that no tampering had occurred.[20]

These speculations on video wills put the findings of this

chapter in fresh perspective and heighten our awareness of the complex relations between orality and literacy. It is our hope that this research will stimulate others to extend the interdisciplinary study of the history of legal language.

NOTES

1. We acknowledge with gratitude the support of this research by the Israel National Academy of Sciences, Fund for Basic Research, and by the Israel Ford Foundation–Educational Trustees. Among those whose comments and encouragement have benefited this work, we would like to thank Barbara Kirshenblatt-Gimblett, Jeffrey Kittay, and Tamar Katriel. Special thanks to our research assistant, Eugene Sotirescu, for his help with Old English.
2. For speech act theory the basic references are, of course, Austin (1962, 1970) and Searle (1969, 1979). We also draw on the large literature on the similarities and differences between speech and writing. See, e.g., Biber (1985, 1988); Chafe and Tannen (1987); Tannen (1982); Akinnaso (1982a, 1985).
3. Contemporary printed editions of these wills are available, usually with a modern English translation on the page facing the original Old English. Texts were gathered from five sources. Thirty-nine wills come from Whitelock (1986 [1930]). An additional seven come from Harmer (1914); twelve were taken from Robertson (1956 [1939]), and another two from Napier and Stevenson (1894). The sixty-first will was taken from the text known as the will of the Reeve Abba (Harmer 1914). This document actually contains two separate wills, that of the Reeve Abba himself, and that of his wife Heregyth. Finally, the sixty-second will was published separately (Roxburghe Club 1968). We thank Michael M. Sheehan for providing access to this text.
4. In all citations of passages in Old English, we have followed the orthography practices of the editors of the collections in which these documents appear, reproducing the inconsistencies in the original.
5. Modern wills might also be read aloud, but only to a gathering of the beneficiaries after the testator's death.
6. We believe that this point is debatable. Although legal historians like Sheehan (1963) and Hazeltine (1986 [1930]) do claim that these wills were irrevocable, evidence in the wills themselves suggest otherwise. For instance, King Alfred mentions in his will that he had destroyed earlier wills, and some testators explicitly make provisions for the possibility of change. Thus, the will of Wulfgar states,

And I grant two hides of the estate at Buttermere, after my death,
to Brihtsige and one to Ceolstan's sons, if they show me due
obedience till then.
(Will of Wulfgar, 931–939 AD; Robertson, 1956 [1939]: 52–3)

Specifying such a condition obviously presupposes that the testator
leaves himself or herself room to change the will.

7. Actually, acts of bequeathing are somewhat different from other
   types of declarations. In Kurzon's (1986) view, a will is a declaration
   of intention, which is only carried out after the testator's death.
   Thus, he would argue that 'saying' does not instantly 'make it so',
   even if all the conditions for the act of making a will are fulfilled.
8. There are two tenses in Old English, a present and a preterit, which
   in most cases is used as a simple past (Carlton 1970). What we refer
   to for convenience as the past is actually the preterit used to describe
   past action.
9. Several documents in Robertson's (1956 [1939]) collection contain
   explicit references to such practices. Thus, a charter of King
   Æthelbert concludes:

   'it came to pass that King Æthelbert on Friday, two days before
   Easter, with joyful heart laid this charter of freedom with his own
   hand upon the high altar at the monastery in Sherborne, in the
   presence of all the assembled brethern . . . and also of his kinsmen
   . . . and of his other councillors . . .
   (Charter of King Aethelbert to Sherbourne; Robertson, 1956 [1939]:
   21)

10. For the purposes of this comparison, a total of 247 documents were
    examined – the sixty-two wills which constitute the focus of the
    present study, as well as 112 writs appearing in Harmer (1914), and
    seventy-three land grants. With the exception of a few early texts
    taken from Earle (1888), all land grants come from Whitelock (1979).
11. Chirographs were documents cut into three parts in puzzle-like
    fashion, so that authentification could be determined by fitting them
    together. Sometimes the word 'chirograph' was itself written
    between the copies on the parchment, and then cut, to further
    reduce the chances of tampering with the document.
12. These witnesses were not signatories, as no one wrote on the
    document except the scribe. Persons listed as witnesses were not
    necessarily all present at the same time.
13. For the text of the will of King Alfred, see Earle (1888): 144–149;
    trans. Whitelock (1979: 534–7).
14. For reviews of literature on context-dependence versus decontex-

tualisation, see, e.g. Biber (1985, 1988); Tannen (1982); Chafe and Tannen (1987); Chafe (1985).

15. On the dimension of involvement versus detachment, see, e.g. Chafe and Tannen (1987); Chafe (1985); Biber (1985, 1988).

16. Two wills were entirely written in what is known as 'writ' form. This is a type of royal letter, which opens with a greeting and which is entirely cast in the second person, like a modern letter. See Harmer (1914) and the wills of Mantat the Anchorite (c. 1035 AD; Whitelock 1986 [1930]: 67) and of Leofgifu (1035–1044 AD; Whitelock 1986 [1930]: 76–7).

17. There is preliminary evidence of the prominence of curses in many aspects of ancient culture, for instance, as a form of protection in ancient building inscriptions, in political treaties, to foster compliance with laws (the code of Hammurabi ends with a massive list of curses), and on boundary stones marking the conveyance of property. For suggestive examples of curses in ancient culture, see Danet and Bogoch (1992).

18. Secondary orality, according to Ong (1982), is the orality which persists, in modified form, when literacy becomes institutionalised. Thus tertiary orality (our term, but consistent with Ong) means orality in a third era – that dominated by the electronic media.

19. Cited in an article, 'Now Video Wills', by Eilat Negev, *Yediot Axronot*, 12 January 1990. See Negev (1990). We are grateful to Tamar Katriel for calling this article, as well as the phenomenon of video wills, to our attention.

20. Obviously, if video wills eventually acquire full legal status, provisions will be necessary to establish which of two versions would be the binding one.

FOUR

Cognitive structuring in legislative provisions

Vijay Bhatia

Legislative writing has acquired a certain degree of notoriety rarely equalled by any other variety of English. It has long been criticised for its obscure expressions and circumlocutions, long-winded involved constructions and tortuous syntax, meaningless repetitions and archaisms. To the specialist community these are indispensable linguistic devices which bring in precision, clarity, unambiguity and all-inclusiveness and so on; however, to the non-specialist this is a mere ploy to promote solidarity between the members of the specialist community and to keep non-specialists at a respectable distance and is hence regarded by them as nothing more than pure linguistic nonsense bringing into professional discourse pomposity, verbosity, flabbiness and circumlocution. The truth, however, lies somewhere in between. In this chapter we shall examine a few instances of legislative provisions in an attempt to unravel the mysteries underlying this complex artefact and to answer the question why legislative provisions are written the way they are. In order to appreciate the complexity of legislative statements, we need to have a better idea of the communicative purpose(s) these statements are meant to serve and the constraints that are imposed on the drafting of these provisions.

COMMUNICATIVE PURPOSE

Legislative writing is highly impersonal and decontextualised, in the sense that its illocutionary force holds independently of whoever is the 'speaker' (originator) or the 'hearer' (reader) of the document. The general function of this writing is directive, to

136

impose obligations and to confer rights. As legal draftsmen are well aware of the age-old human capacity to wriggle out of obligations and to stretch rights to unexpected limits, in order to guard against such eventualities, they attempt to define their model world of obligations and rights, permissions and prohibitions as precisely, clearly and unambiguously as linguistic resources permit. Another factor which further complicates their task is that they deal with a universe of human behaviour, which is unrestricted in the sense that it is impossible to predict exactly what may happen within it. Nevertheless, they attempt to refer to every conceivable contingency within their model world and this gives their writing its second key characteristic of being all-inclusive.

Legislative writing differs significantly from most other varieties of English, not only in terms of the communicative purpose it is designed to fulfil, but also in the way it is created. In most other written varieties, the author is both the originator and the writer of what he creates, whereas in legislative provisions, the parliamentary draftsman is only the writer of the legislative Act, which originates from the deliberations of a Parliament in which he is never present. Similarly, in most varieties the reader and the recipient for whom the document is meant are the same person, whereas in the case of legislative provisions, the document is meant for ordinary citizens but the real readers are lawyers and judges, who are responsible for interpreting these provisions for ordinary citizens. The result of this unique contextual factor is that the parliamentary draftsman finds his loyalties divided. On the one hand, he has to acknowledge his loyalty to the will of the Parliament and, on the other hand, he must use linguistic and discoursal strategies to help the intended readership towards what Candlin (1981) refers to as 'the equalising of interpretative opportunity'. In other words, he is required to use linguistic resources and discoursal strategies to do justice to the intent of the Parliament and also to facilitate comprehension of the unfolding text for ordinary readership at the same time. Reconciling the two is not always an easy task. His predicament is well summed up in the words of Caldwell, an experienced practitioner in the field:

> there's always the problem that at the end of the day there's a system of courts and judges who interpret what the draftsman has done. It is

very difficult to box the judge firmly into a corner from which he
cannot escape . . . given enough time and given enough length and
complexity you can end up with precision but in practice there comes
a point when you can't go on cramming detail after detail into a bin
. . . you've got to rely on the courts getting the message and deducing
from what you have said or it may be often from what you haven't
said, what implications they are to draw in such and such a case
(quoted in Bhatia 1982: 25)

So, in spite of the seeming impossibility of the task, no effort is
spared in legislative provisions 'to box' the reader 'firmly into a
corner'. This is generally achieved by making the provision clear,
precise and unambiguous. However, that does not seem to be the
end of the story, because these provisions are meant to apply to
real life situations and are invariably interpreted in the context of
a particular dispute. Any specific interpretation will be dependent on and constrained by the facts of the case, which provide
the context for its interpretation and it is possible that such an
interpretation may not necessarily be the same as the one
intended by the Parliament. In order to guard against such
eventualities, the draftsman tries to make his provision not only
clear, precise, and unambiguous but all-inclusive too. And it is
this seemingly impossible task of achieving the dual characteristic of clarity, precision and unambiguity on the one hand, and
all-inclusiveness on the other hand, that makes legislative
provisions what they are.

TYPES OF LEGISLATIVE PROVISION

Gunnarsson (1984: 84) distinguishes three types of legislative
rules.

1. *Action rules*, which are applicable to only a set of specified
   descriptions of cases and are mainly meant to impose duties
   and obligations, to give rights, to prohibit actions, to assign
   power to certain members or bodies of the executive or other
   parties, or to state the law or just the penalties imposed on
   specific actions. A typical example will be the following:

   [1] When any person in the presence of a police officer commits or

is accused of committing a non-seizable offence and refuses on the demand of a police officer to give his name or residence or gives a name or residence which the officer has reason to believe to be false, he may be arrested by that police officer in order that his name of residence may be ascertained.
(Section 32(1) of Criminal Procedure Code, Republic of Singapore, 1980)

2. *Stipulation rules*, which define the domain of application of a particular act or any section of it, as in the following example:

[2] Sections 35 to 46 of this Act do not apply to a tenancy at any time when the interest of the landlord belongs to a housing association which is a registered society.
(Section 49(3) of the Housing Act 1980, UK)

3. *Definition rules*, which are applicable to the entire Act and are primarily meant to provide terminological explanation, as in [3] below:

[3] In this Chapter 'landlord authority' means –
(a) a local authority;
(b) . . . a housing association which falls within section 15(3) of the 1977 Act;
(c) a housing trust which is a charity within the meaning of the Charities Act 1960;
(d) A development corporation;
(Section 42(1) of the Housing Act 1980, UK)

However, a number of such definition rules, as Swales (1981b: 109) points out, go well beyond such an objective and are treated as 'the Law itself *tout court*' and he cites the following example from the Law of the Sudan defining 'kidnapping':

[4] Whoever takes or entices any minor, under fourteen years of age if a male or under sixteen years of age if a female, or any person of unsound mind out of the keeping of the legal guardian of such minor or person of unsound mind without the consent of such guardian or conveys any such minor or person of unsound mind beyond the borders of the Sudan without the consent of some person legally authorized to consent such removal, is said to kidnap such a minor or person of unsound mind.

He points out that the above definition is the law and provides eight different routes to kidnapping. Gunnarsson (1984: 84) also claims a somewhat similar position when she says that definition rules have implications for action. Whatever the relative merits of the claims, on one thing both of them agree that the bulk of legislation consists of action rules rather than the other two. So our discussion will primarily focus on them, which I have elsewhere (Bhatia 1982, 1983) called legislative provisions.

SYNTACTIC PROPERTIES OF LEGISLATIVE PROVISIONS

It has been claimed (Swales and Bhatia 1983) that syntactic and discoursal features of legislative writing are, in various ways, interconnected, in the sense that the apparent legal requirement of expressing something by means of nominal expressions and a variety of qualifications would bring in syntactic discontinuities, thus making the discoursal structure of the sentence not only complex but compound as well. Therefore, it is necessary to look at some of the predominant syntactic features of the legislative provisions before we go to the discoursal features of this genre. Let us begin with a typical instance of this genre:

[5] For the purpose of ascertaining the income for any period of any person who has incurred expenditure on lawfully searching for, or for discovery and testing, or winning access to any mineral deposits in Singapore, there shall, if the person has within that period permanently abandoned such activities without having carried on any trade which consists of or includes the working of deposits in respect of which the expenditure was incurred, be deducted the amount of the expenditure wholly or exclusively incurred by that person in connection with such activities as if the expenditure were incurred at the time when such activities were so abandoned:
Provided that no deduction shall be made –
(a) in respect of the value at the date of the permanent abandonment of such activities of any machinery or plant used in such activities or, if the machinery or plant is subsequently sold or transferred, any sum of money or other consideration received by that person in respect of it;
(b) to the extent that any sum of money or other consideration is received by such person from the sale of any rights or other

benefits derived from such activities, or from the use of any such machinery or plant by any other person;
(c) in respect of any sum which is, apart from this section, allowed to be deducted in computing for the purposes of income tax, the gains or profits of any such person;
(d) in respect of any expenditure met directly or indirectly by the Government or by any government, public or local authority, whether within Singapore or elsewhere, or by any person other than the person claiming relief.

> (Section 14A(1) of The Income Tax Act, 1984,
> The Republic of Singapore)

This legislative provision is from the Singapore Income Tax Act and is about the deductions allowed in relation to certain expenditure on abortive mining operations. As any other instance of legislation, this also displays a number of syntactic and discoursal characteristics typical of the genre. Let us consider some of the most important syntactic properties, particularly those which will help us understand regularities of organisation in this genre.

Sentence length

To begin with, the whole section consists of a single sentence of an above-average length: 271 words-long as compared with the average 27.6 word-long sentence in written scientific English (Barber 1962).

Nominal character

Legislative sentences are more nominal in character than the ones generally encountered in ordinary everyday usage. Swales and Bhatia (1983) claim that example [6] below is likely to be preferred in this writing than its more typically verbal version given in [7] below.

[6] The power to make regulations under this section shall be exercisable by statutory instrument which shall be subject to

annulment in pursuance of a resolution of either House of Parliament.

(Ch.25/78: Nuclear Safeguards and Electricity (Finance Act) 1978)

[7] A statutory instrument can be used to make regulations under this section and such a statutory instrument can be annulled if either House of Parliament passes a resolution to that effect.

Although Example [5] gives some indication of nominalisation, as in the use of 'permanent abandonment of such activities', it is not highly nominal in character. A more typical example of the nominal character of this genre will be the following section from the Wills Act, 1970 of the Republic of Singapore.

[8] No obliteration, interlineation or other alteration made in any will after the execution thereof shall be valid or have effect except so far as the words or effect of the will before such alteration shall not be apparent, unless such alteration shall be executed in like manner as hereinbefore is required for the execution of the will; but the will, with such alteration as part thereof, shall be deemed to be duly executed if the signature of the testator and the subscription of the witnesses be made in the margin or on some other part of the will opposite or near to such alteration or at the foot or end of or opposite to a memorandum referring to such alteration and written at the end or some other part of the will.

(Section 16 of The Wills Act, 1970, Republic of Singapore)

In this case we have eleven instances of nominalisation where five different verbs have been nominalised, of which one, i.e., *alteration* has been used six times. The use of such nominalised expressions helps the writer to bring in a greater degree of precision and all-inclusiveness in his legislative statements. Nominalisation certainly helps a legal draftsman to make his provisions more compact and yet precise and all-inclusive; however, it also has the adverse effect of making it more dense and hence difficult to interpret. It takes a lot more time and effort and expertise to unpack, as it were, each nominalised phrase. This is obvious from the following rather innocent-looking provision from the Republic of Singapore Wills Act.

[9] No will shall be revoked by any presumption of an intention on the ground of an alteration in circumstances.

(Section 14 of the Wills Act, Republic of Singapore)

(For a more detailed account of the use of nominal expressions in academic and professional genres, see Bhatia 1991.)

Complex prepositional phrases

The next striking syntactic feature of the legislative genre is the use of what Quirk et al. (1972: 302) refer to as complex prepositional phrases. They give its structure as P–N–P (Preposition + Noun + Preposition). Some of the typical examples from legislative writing include *for the purpose of*, *in respect of*, *in accordance with*, *in pursuance of*, *by virtue of*, etc. The first two of the list have been used a few times in example [5]. The use of complex prepositions rather than the simple ones, for example, 'by virtue of' instead of 'by', 'for the purpose of' in place of 'for', and 'in accordance with' or 'in pursuance of' instead of a simple preposition 'under' are preferred in legislative writing simply because the specialist community claims, with some justification, of course (see Swales and Bhatia 1983) that the simple ones tend to promote ambiguity and lack of clarity.

Binomial and multinomial expressions

Binomial and multinomial expressions have also been typically associated with legislative texts (see Gustafsson 1975, 1984). What I mean by binomial or multinomial expression is a sequence of two or more words or phrases belonging to the same grammatical category having some semantic relationship and joined by some syntactic device such as 'and' or 'or' (see Bhatia 1984: 90). Typical examples include 'signed and delivered', 'in whole or in part', 'to affirm or set aside', 'act or omission', 'advice and consent', 'by or on behalf of', 'under or in accordance with', 'unless and until', and 'consists of or includes', 'wholly and exclusively', 'the freehold conveyed or long lease granted' and many many others. The provision in [5] offers a few more. These include some very much more complex and interesting ones, such as 'machinery or plant', 'sold or transferred', 'any sum of money or other consideration', 'from such activities or from the use of any such machinery or plant', 'directly or indirectly', 'by the Government or by any government, public or local authority . . . or by any person other than the person claiming relief', 'within Singapore or elsewhere', and many more. It is not very difficult to see why legal draftsmen have a special fascination for expressions like these. This is an extremely effective linguistic device to make the legal document precise as well as all-inclusive. Here is an excellent example from the Prevention of Corruption Act 1947 from India.

[10] Where in any trial of offence punishable under section 161 or section 165 of the Indian Penal Code or of an offence referred to in clause (b) of subsection (1) of section 5 of this Act punishable under subsection (2) thereof it is proved that an accused person has accepted or obtained, or has agreed to accept or attempted to obtain, for himself or for any other person, any gratification (other than legal remuneration) or any valuable thing for any person, it shall be presumed unless the contrary is proved that he accepted or obtained, or agreed to accept or attempted to obtain that gratification or that valuable thing, as the case may be, as a motive or reward such as is mentioned in the said section 161, as the case may, without consideration or for a consideration which he knows to be inadequate.

(Section 4(1) of the Prevention of Corruption Act 1947, Government of India)

In order to better appreciate the use of binomials and multinomials to achieve all-inclusiveness in legislative provisions, let us take a look at a different version [10A] (see p. 145) of example [10]. The left-hand column of the provision gives one way each of accepting any gratification and of determining whether such a gratification has been accepted without consideration. However, if we read through the entire provision from left to right and downwards, we find that it lists at least $(3 \times 4 \times 2 \times 2)$, i.e. 48 different ways of accepting gratification and nothing less than $(4 \times 2 \times 2 \times 2)$, i.e. 32 ways of accepting that gratification without consideration. Binomial and multinomial expressions, therefore serve as a useful tool for making legislative statements all-inclusive.

Initial case descriptions

Legislative statements typically begin with fairly long initial case descriptions. The legal subject is conventionally delayed by the introduction of a long case description in the form of an adverbial clause beginning with 'where', 'if' or sometimes

[10A]

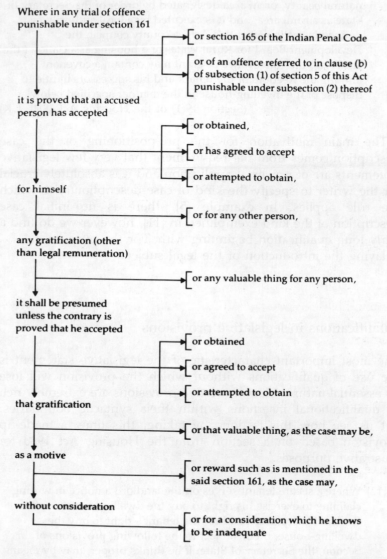

Where in any trial of offence punishable under section 161

or section 165 of the Indian Penal Code

or of an offence referred to in clause (b) of subsection (1) of section 5 of this Act punishable under subsection (2) thereof

it is proved that an accused person has accepted

or obtained,

or has agreed to accept

or attempted to obtain,

for himself

or for any other person,

any gratification (other than legal remuneration)

or any valuable thing for any person,

it shall be presumed unless the contrary is proved that he accepted

or obtained

or agreed to accept

or attempted to obtain

that gratification

or that valuable thing, as the case may be,

as a motive

or reward such as is mentioned in the said section 161, as the case may,

without consideration

or for a consideration which he knows to be inadequate

'when'. Here is a rather extreme example from the Housing Act 1980, UK.

[11]   Where a conveyance or grant executed in pursuance of this chapter is of a dwelling-house situated in a National Park; or an

area designated under section 87 of the National Parks and
Access to the Countryside Act 1949 as an area of outstanding
natural beauty, or an area designated by order of the Secretary of
State as a rural area, and it is executed by a local authority (as
defined in section 50 of this Act), a county council, the
Development Board for Rural Wales or a housing association ('the
landlord') the conveyance or grant may contain a covenant
limiting the freedom of the tenant and his successors in title to
dispose of the dwelling-house in the manner specified below.

(Section 19(1) of the Housing Act 1980, UK)

The main motivation for the pre-positioning of the case
description comes from the requirement that very few legislative
statements are of universal application and it is absolutely crucial
for the writer to specify the kind of case description(s) to which
the rule applies. In example [5], there is no initial case
description of the kind exemplified in [11], however we do find a
fairly long qualification beginning with 'For the purpose of . . .'
delaying the introduction of the legal subject.

Qualifications in legislative provisions

The most important characteristic of the legislative statement is
the use of qualifications without which the provision will lose
its essential nature. Most legislative provisions are extremely rich
in qualificational insertions within their syntactic boundaries.
Let us see how this is done by taking, this time, a made-up
provision based on a section from the Housing Act 1980 for
illustrative purposes.

[12] Where a secure tenant serves on the landlord a notice in writing
claiming to exercise his right to buy the dwelling-house, and if
the landlord refuses to admit the tenant's right to buy the
dwelling-house, then, subject to the following provisions of this
Section, the Secretary of State, if he thinks proper, may by means
of a written notification make special regulations in pursuance of
his powers under Section 15 of this Act for the purpose of
enabling the tenant to exercise his right to buy the dwelling-
house (notwithstanding anything contained in Section 51 of the
Land Registration Act 1925) within a period of six months from

the date of such a refusal, provided that the dwelling-house, or any part of it, is not being used for charitable purposes within the meaning of the 'Charitable Purposes Act 1954'.

In very simple words, this provision is meant to give powers to the legal subject, in this case, the Secretary of State, to make special regulations. But he is not given the authority to make special regulations as and when he likes. The attached qualifications make the provision extremely restricted. In fact, without these qualifications the legislative provision will be taken to be of universal application and it is very rare that a rule of law is of universal application. The qualifications seem to provide the essential flesh to the main proposition without which the provision will be nothing more than a mere skeleton, of very little legal significance. In the words of Caldwell, a very senior practising parliamentary counsel:

if you extract the bare bones . . . what you end up with is a proposition which is so untrue because the qualifications actually negative it all . . . it's so far from the truth . . . it's like saying that all red-headed people are to be executed on Monday, but when you actually read all the qualifications, you find that only one per cent of them are.

(quoted in Bhatia 1982: 51)

Syntactic discontinuities

It is not simply the presence of qualifications that makes legislative provisions an interesting genre but the way these qualifications are inserted within the syntax of the legislative sentence. It is understandable that if one needs to incorporate a variety of qualifications within a single sentence one would like to have as many syntactic points to insert them as are possible. But one consideration that makes this task even more difficult is the fact that if qualifications on the one hand make the main provisional clause more precise and clear, they can also promote ambiguity if they are not placed judiciously. That is the main reason why legal draftsmen try to insert qualifications right next to the word they are meant to qualify, even at the cost of making their legislative sentence inelegant, awkward or even tortuous. If they can help it it will never be ambiguous. The result of all this effort is that these qualifications are inserted at various points where they create syntactic discontinuities rarely encountered in any other genre. In example [5] we have a rather longish qualification

> if the person has within that period permanently abandoned such activities without having carried on any trade which consists of or includes the working of deposits in respect of which the expenditure was incurred

inserted immediately after the modal 'shall' thus creating discontinuity within the main verb phrase 'shall be deducted'. So far as qualificational insertions are concerned, legal draftsmen do not consider any phrase boundaries sacrosanct, be it a verb phrase (as in [5]), a noun phrase, binomial phrase or even a complex prepositional phrase. Let us look at some of the examples from the British Housing Act, 1980.

Discontinuous noun phrase

[13] A secure tenant has *the right* –
    (a) if the dwelling-house is a house, *to acquire the freehold of the dwelling-house;*
    (b) if the dwelling-house is a flat, *to be granted a long lease of the dwelling-house*

               (Section 1(1) of the Housing Act, 1980, UK)

Discontinuous binomial phrase

[14] Where a secure tenant serves on the landlord a written notice claiming to exercise the right to buy, the landlord shall (unless the notice is withdrawn) serve on the tenant, within *within four weeks, or,* in a case falling within subsection (2) below, *eight weeks,* either
    (a) a written notice admitting the tenant's right; or
    (b) a written notice denying the tenant's right and stating the

reasons why, in the opinion of the landlord, the tenant does
not have the right to buy.
(Section 1(5) of the Housing Act, 1980, UK)

Discontinuous complex prepositional phrase

[15] Any power of the Secretary of State to make an order or
regulation under this Act shall be exercisable by statutory
instrument *subject*, except in the case of regulations under section
22(1), 33(2), 52(3), 56(7) or paragraph 11 of Schedule 3 or an order
under section 52(4), 60 or 153, *to annulment* in pursuance of a
resolution of either House of Parliament.
(Section 151(1) of the Housing Act, 1980, UK)

Discontinuous constituents with fairly long qualificational
insertions like these and many others embedded within them
add considerably to an already complex syntactic character of the
legislative sentence and cause serious psycholinguistic problems
in the processing of such provisions, especially in the case of
non-specialist readership (see Bhatia 1984, for a detailed discussion of this aspect of legal writing).

COGNITIVE STRUCTURING IN LEGISLATIVE PROVISIONS

Having looked at some of the important lexicogrammatical
features of this genre, we shall now consider how these features,
particularly the complexity of intervening qualifications, are
reflected in the cognitive structuring that is typically associated
with the legislative provision. Looking more closely at the law-
making process, we find two important aspects of it. The first, of
course, is the main provisionary clause, by which we mean
essentially two things. One, the legal subject, i.e. the person or
the party which is the subject of the provision. In other words,
the person who is either given a right or some power to do
something or is being prohibited from doing something. And,
the second is the legal action, i.e. the nature of power or right he
is given to do or prohibited from doing, that flows from the

provision. But, the main provisionary clause, by itself, can only provide the bare bones. The essential flesh is provided by what we earlier on referred to as case description, by which we mean the nature and specification of circumstances to which the main provisionary clause applies. Crystal and Davy (1969) give a good indication of this when they claim that most legal sentences have one of the following forms.

If X, then Y shall do Z,

or

If X, then Y shall be Z,

where 'If X' stands for the description of case(s) to which the rule of law applies, although they do not say so explicitly, 'Y' is meant to be the legal subject and 'Z' indicates the legal action.

George Coode, as early as in 1848, made a significant contribution to this aspect of law-making when he identified four essential elements in legal statements and placed them in the following order:

(Case) Where any Quaker refuses to pay any church rates,
(Condition) if any church warden complains thereof,
(Subject) one of the next Justices of the Peace
(Action) may summon such Quaker.

Although Coode's analysis of the legislative sentence is insufficiently developed for application to all legislative sentences, particularly those with multiple and complex modifications, it certainly is of considerable value, because of the attention it pays to the sentence structure and the arrangement of qualifying clauses in the 'best' position.

Both, Coode (1848) and Crystal and Davy (1969) point out the essential nature of the legislative sentence, however they oversimplify the picture. Although it is true that the three essential elements in the syntax of the legislative provision are 'the case description', 'the legal subject' and 'the legal action'. 'Condition' as pointed out by Coode (1848) is also very important, if not obligatory. However, as Bhatia (1982, 1983) points out, legislative statements can and most of them do have a number of qualifications, other than the case description, which provide essential flesh to the bare bones. Basically, there are three types of qualifications and they tend to provide three different types of information about the rule of law. The first type are *preparatory qualifications* which outline the description of case(s) to which the rule of law applies. The second type are *operational* qualifications which give additional information about the execution or operation of the rule of law. And, finally there are *referential* qualifications which specify the essential intertextual nature of the legislative provision. In the words of Caldwell, a practising parliamentary counsel:

> very rarely is a new legislative provision entirely freestanding . . . it is part of a jigsaw puzzle . . . in passing a new provision you are merely bringing one more piece and so you have to acknowledge that what you are about to do may affect some other bit of the massive statute book
>
> (Reported in Bhatia 1982: 172)

Qualifications, therefore, form an important part of the structuring of the legislative statements. In fact, most legislative provisions can be written and understood in terms of a two-part interactive move-structure, consisting of the main *provisionary clause* and the attendant *qualifications* of various kinds, which are inserted at available syntactic positions within the structure of the main clause. To illustrate the two-part move structure, let us take a very simple example from the British Housing Act 1980.

[16] Where the dwelling-house with respect to which the right to buy is exercised is a registered land, the Chief Land Registrar shall, if so requested by the Secretary of State, supply him (on payment of the appropriate fee) with an office copy of any document required by the Secretary of State for the purpose of executing a vesting order with respect to the dwelling-house and shall (notwithstanding section 112 of the Land Registration Act 1925) allow any person authorised by the Secretary of State to inspect and make copies of and extracts from any register or document which is in the custody of the Chief Land Registrar and relates to the dwelling-house.

(Section 24(5) of the Housing Act, 1980, UK)

Cognitive structuring as used here is an excellent tool to interpret the regularities of organisation in order to understand the rationale for the genre. In legislative provisions cognitive structuring displays a characteristic interplay of the main provisionary clause and the qualifications inserted at various syntactic openings within the structure of a sentence (Bhatia 1982).

The example above gives not only a clear indication of the complexity of individual qualificational insertions in the legislative genre but also some indication of the variety of such qualifications. In order to have a more explicit display of the structural organisation of the genre and to understand the rationale for such an organisation, let us look at another version of the same text.

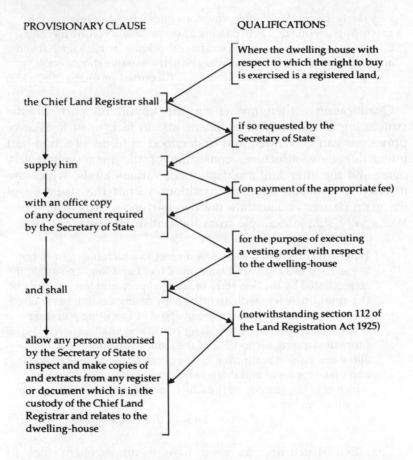

PROVISIONARY CLAUSE   QUALIFICATIONS

Where the dwelling house with respect to which the right to buy is exercised is a registered land,

the Chief Land Registrar shall

if so requested by the Secretary of State

supply him

(on payment of the appropriate fee)

with an office copy of any document required by the Secretary of State

for the purpose of executing a vesting order with respect to the dwelling-house

and shall

(notwithstanding section 112 of the Land Registration Act 1925)

allow any person authorised by the Secretary of State to inspect and make copies of and extracts from any register or document which is in the custody of the Chief Land Registrar and relates to the dwelling-house

Both the density and the complexity of qualificational insertions serve a typically legal function in this genre in that each one of them is meant to answer legal questions and doubts, and offer clarifications about various aspects of the main provision. Any adequate structural description of the genre should explain this phenomenon. Therefore, it is more appropriate to think in terms of a two-part *interactive* cognitive structure consisting of the main provisionary clause and the qualifications rather than the linear organisation of the moves as found in the case of a number of other genres (see Swales 1981; Bhatia 1982, 1991). The analysis of cognitive structuring is interactive here in the sense that the move *qualifications* typically interacts with several aspects of the move *provisionary clause* at various positions, answering a number of questions that can be legitimately asked in the context. The main function of these inserted qualifications or conditions is to make the legislative provision precise, clear, unambiguous and all-inclusive (see Bhatia 1982, 1987). We shall take our final example, which we have already quoted as [12] to illustrate the complexity of qualificational insertions. The following version of this example [12A] gives a more vivid account of the range of qualifications and the role they play in the structuring of the legislative provision (see p. 154). (See Bhatia 1982, 1983 for a detailed account of the role of qualifications in the legislative statement).

CONCLUSIONS

In the preceding sections, I have made an attempt to demonstrate that legislative statements have a conventionalised communicative purpose mutually shared by the practising members of the specialist community. This shared communicative purpose is largely reflected in the way legislative statements are conventionally written and read by the members of the community, particularly in the way some of the syntactic and discoursal resources are used in this genre. The typical use of complex-prepositions, binomial and multinomial expressions, nominalisations, the initial case descriptions, a large number and variety of qualificational insertions make syntactic discontinuities somewhat unavoidable in the legislative statements and, to a large extent, account for the discourse patterning that is typically displayed in such provisions.

I have also tried to suggest that legislative statements have good reasons to be what they are, and one should try to understand this genre on its own terms rather than by imposing standards of ordinary expression from the outside, as it were, on

[12A]

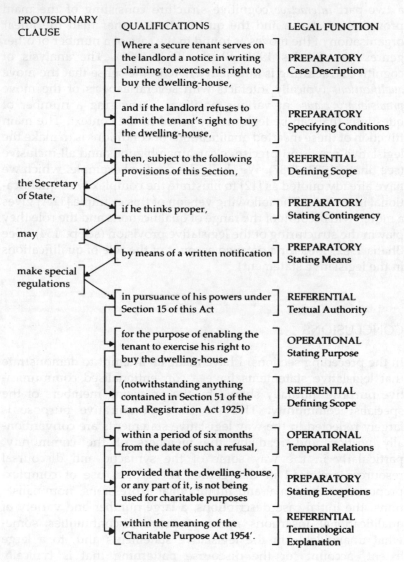

PROVISIONARY CLAUSE	QUALIFICATIONS	LEGAL FUNCTION
	Where a secure tenant serves on the landlord a notice in writing claiming to exercise his right to buy the dwelling-house,	PREPARATORY Case Description
	and if the landlord refuses to admit the tenant's right to buy the dwelling-house,	PREPARATORY Specifying Conditions
	then, subject to the following provisions of this Section,	REFERENTIAL Defining Scope
the Secretary of State,	if he thinks proper,	PREPARATORY Stating Contingency
may	by means of a written notification	PREPARATORY Stating Means
make special regulations	in pursuance of his powers under Section 15 of this Act	REFERENTIAL Textual Authority
	for the purpose of enabling the tenant to exercise his right to buy the dwelling-house	OPERATIONAL Stating Purpose
	(notwithstanding anything contained in Section 51 of the Land Registration Act 1925)	REFERENTIAL Defining Scope
	within a period of six months from the date of such a refusal,	OPERATIONAL Temporal Relations
	provided that the dwelling-house, or any part of it, is not being used for charitable purposes	PREPARATORY Stating Exceptions
	within the meaning of the 'Charitable Purpose Act 1954'.	REFERENTIAL Terminological Explanation

a genre which has its own specialised concerns and specific constraints under which they are written and read. Many of the attempts to reform legislative writing in the Western world have largely been ineffective because of their failure to recognise the value of an ethnomethodological position that the legislative provision reflects a sphere of practical reasoning which needs to be understood in its own terms. However, one often gets a feeling, quite justifiably in many cases, that this concern on the part of the specialist community for clarity, precision, unambiguity, on the one hand, and all-inclusiveness, on the other, has been taken rather too seriously and, perhaps, too far. It is true that legislative writing has a long and well-established tradition and the style of legal documents has become firmly standardised with the inevitable result that the legal draftsmen tend to become comfortable with tried, tested and time-honoured linguistic expressions and style of writing over a period of time. This becomes particularly significant where each subsequent generation of parliamentary draftsmen is trained by the preceding one while on the job.

It is also true that there have been some improvements in style that have taken place in the past few decades, especially in the way textual-mapping devices are used to reduce information load at a particular point in the provision (see Bhatia 1987) but such reforms have been few and far between and, hence have gone unnoticed by ordinary readers. On the part of the specialist community, therefore, there is a need to show two kinds of concern. First, a need to show greater awareness of their loyalty to the real readers of legislative documents. Second, a need to use linguistic resources more consistently, particularly in the case of those where certain linguistic forms are traditionally associated with some very specific meanings (see Swales and Bhatia 1983). This is particularly desirable in the use of what specialists call 'proviso-clauses'. This practice will create fewer problems of interpretation for many of the readers, the specialists as well as the non-specialists. There is also a greater need to make more effort to use long syntactic discontinuities more sparingly, perhaps as an exception rather than a rule.

FIVE

Ideological exchanges in British magistrates courts

Sandra Harris

> Magistrate: This court is a *reasonable* court – trying to do *justice* to
> both sides in some dispute
> Defendant: Well it's like – me – trying to argue with you – I just
> can't can I – so if he's an official I just can't argue with
> him
> Magistrate: But you can put your point of view – as I hope you can
> to me
> Defendant: I dunno where I am you know
> (Excerpts from audio recordings of the Nottinghamshire County
> Magistrates Courts)

COURTROOM LANGUAGE AND IDEOLOGY

Anyone with any experience of the court system, whether as defendant, lawyer, judge, member of a jury or merely observer, must inevitably acknowledge the importance of language to the legal process. Indeed, it is difficult to imagine a context where verbal behaviour plays a more crucial role. At all levels, language penetrates the legal system, and the law perhaps more than any other is a profession of words, ultimately and utterly dependent on some form of linguistic negotiation (e.g. Atkinson and Drew 1979; O'Barr 1982; Drew 1985; Maynard 1984).

Moreover, few would deny that the courts also are a significant ideological site, where decisions are taken on a day-to-day basis which affect the lives of thousands of ordinary people, especially in the lower court divisions. This legal process of decision-making operates on several levels. In the most practical sense, it affects the actual behaviour of those involved in courtroom cases.

Disputes are settled, and directives are given that defendants must act in accordance with court dictates. But, equally important, courtroom decisions – even in the lowest divisions – provide for those involved in court procedure a tangible connection with more abstract concepts inherent in the legal process and embodied in an underlying but usually implicit ideological framework which grounds such decisions in legitimacy (Harris 1988, 1989).

> The mantel of democratic legitimacy may be only a mantel, but that does not make it unimportant, any more than the appearance of fairness in a class-based legal system is irrelevant to substantive justice; the need to keep up appearances has historically afforded very important and consequential protections to people who might otherwise have been entirely powerless.
>
> (Simonds 1989: 185)

Concepts such as 'justice', 'equality before the law', 'impartiality of judgment', 'legal rights and obligations' are fundamental not only to the effective working of the legal system but to the perception and maintenance of Western political democracy as we know and experience it. These are also highly ideological concepts, and courtroom interaction becomes an interesting and potential source of ideological conflict and confrontation which is made visible through the process of linguistic negotiation and thus can be the subject of analysis. This is particularly true of certain sections of British magistrates courts, where defendants speak for themselves directly to magistrates without the intervention or mediation of lawyers or other professionals. Also made 'visible' is the manifest nature of power and control, in a context where mainly middle-class magistrates and clerks interact with defendants who are predominantly working class or unemployed.

In his work on the theory of ideology, Thompson (1984) has pointed to the crucial connection between ideology and language and proposed that the study of language must necessarily occupy 'a privileged position' within the theory of ideology. Indeed,

> to study ideology is, in some part and in some way, to study language in the social world. . . . The theory of ideology, thus enriched and elaborated through a reflection on language, enriches in turn our view of language.
>
> (Thompson 1984: 3)

One of the reasons why the concept of ideology has had such a vexed history and has proved so difficult to pin down theoretically is the failure to locate it clearly in language rather than in a more abstract realm of beliefs and values detached from any particular context of expression. This is not to suggest, of course, that ideology only exists in language (see Eagleton 1991). Clearly, a broad range of social practices can be identified as ideological. However, seeing ideology as pertaining to that which can be *said*, to the specific expression of linguistic forms and meanings in historically specific situations, has considerable methodological advantages. It is somewhat surprising then that, until recently, there has been relatively little work on what constitutes ideological discourse or even work on language produced in primary ideological sites such as the courtroom, where participants have a great deal at stake and ideological conflicts are both significant and predictable. (But see Hodge and Kress 1988; Wodak 1989; Fowler 1991; Fairclough 1992.)

Work on discourse and ideology also highlights the intersection of language and power and a definition of ideology which focuses on 'the ways in which meaning (signification) serves to sustain relations of domination' (Thompson 1984: 4). A large number of the studies produced within the last ten years or so on courtroom discourse have revealed significant patterns of power and control in court (e.g. O'Barr 1982; Harris 1984; Philips 1984; Woodbury 1984; Adelsward et al. 1987; Adelsward 1989), control exercised primarily as a communication strategy extensively used by lawyers in the questioning of witnesses and defendants. Fewer studies have specifically addressed the question of ideological discourse in a courtroom context (Sumner 1979; Goodrich 1984, 1987; Jackson 1985) and fewer still have made extensive use of empirical evidence in the form of recorded data as a means of investigating ideological processes.

The *purpose* of this chapter, then, is:

1. To offer a tentative definition of ideological discourse through the examination of specific instances of courtroom interaction which are manifestly ideological.
2. To suggest how ideological processes in court operate in a complex way on several different levels simultaneously (see Fairclough 1985). A number of writers have commented on the

need for studies which bring closer together and attempt to relate in a meaningful way macro analyses of the social order and micro studies involving individual actors (e.g. Thompson 1984; Agar 1985, 1990; Fisher and Todd 1986).

3. To analyse, in some detail, recurrent patterns of opposing propositions voiced respectively by magistrates and defendants, making use of Halliday's (1978) analysis of context into field, tenor and mode and, more specifically, the semantic realisation of the first two categories as the ideational and interpersonal components.

The data base is a series of audio-recordings, involving twenty-six cases and five different magistrates, of the Arrears and Maintenance Division of a British magistrates court. In addition to the clear contrast in most instances between the social class of defendants and magistrates, all twenty-six cases have a common goal, i.e. eliciting an 'offer' from the defendant of what he or she will pay in future towards his/her fine or maintenance. There is, in consequence, a high degree of consistency in the purpose and structure of court sessions which lessens the likelihood of making gross errors of interpretation. This data is supplemented by recordings of the Criminal Division of the magistrates court.

PROPOSITIONAL AND PRAGMATIC LEVELS OF DISCOURSE

Even when ideological processes are clearly located in language, there is little or no general agreement about precisely how these are realised linguistically or what kind of analysis is most helpful. Thompson (1984) suggests three very broad levels through which linguistic constructions may be studied with a view to explicating their ideological features: narratives, argumentative structure, and syntactic structure. These are examined only very tentatively by Thompson. Kress (1985), distinguishing between 'text' and 'discourse', proposes that ideological content is expressed in linguistic form in two ways,

First, as the sign of ideologically determined selections made by the speaker or writer – in other words, as an index of ideological activity.

Second, as the expression of ideological content expressed by a linguistic form in the context of other forms in a text. This content becomes specific because of the copresence of the other forms in a text that narrows and determines the meaning of any given linguistic form.

(Kress 1985: 31)

He goes on to argue that discourses, which are more abstract 'social units', are realised in texts, which are 'linguistic units', and that texts thus may be the location for contradictory or disparate discourses. In this sense, the language of law becomes a generic discourse which is realised in a wide variety of particular texts, i.e. legal documents, courtroom interaction, the law reports, and so on. Abstract legal concepts, such as 'justice' and the 'rule of law', belong to the discourse, which according to Kress is . relatively fixed and stable but may be questioned, contradicted, or debated in particular texts.

What these writers point to in differing ways is a separation between the propositional (including lexical) and pragmatic levels of linguistic analysis, and the fact that ideological processes would appear to operate in important ways on both levels (see also Hartley and Montgomery 1985; Martin 1986; Fairclough 1989). A useful starting point is Halliday's (1978) analysis of context into the component parts of field, tenor and mode. Halliday defines 'field' as the nature of the activity that participants are engaged in, including the 'subject matter'. What is being talked about is realised semantically primarily in the ideational component, which in Halliday's terms becomes the explicit means by which language encodes the cultural experience.

If we turn specifically to courtroom interaction, it seems clear that magistrates and clerks put forward propositions (convey meanings) which are demonstrably ideological in terms of 'what they are about'. Such propositions can be defined tentatively as ones which:

1. are not explicitly and empirically verifiable in terms of their truth value;
2. function in context to maintain the status quo, to reinforce and reify existing relationships of power and domination;
3. are to a greater or lesser degree 'naturalised', made to seem like 'common sense'. This naturalising process, first described

by Marx, has been widely commented on (see Fairclough 1985).

Given this definition, the following utterances (each spoken by a different magistrate to a different defendant) can be said to contain distinct ideological propositions:

1. This court is a *reasonable* court – trying to do *justice* to both sides in some dispute.
2. This (fine) must be paid off and it's paid off before any pleasures which you think are your right – the law says you pay your fines first.
3. Now – uh – the Bench are very pleased – and I record this – that you've got a job – because now you're becoming a useful citizen – able to contribute to the nation and look after yourself.

or, conversely

Don't you think that it's up to you to use some of that fourteen pounds (defendant's unemployment benefit) rather than everybody else sitting in this court – and everybody else in the country (to make the defendant's maintenance payments)

Whilst I don't wish to belabour the substance of these particular propositions, the concepts of a court based on 'reason' and dispensing 'justice' are, as previously suggested, fundamental ideological assumptions, referred to frequently by politicians and others as well as by magistrates and judges as essential not only to the maintenance and credibility of the legal system but to the very existence of our social and political democracy. A challenge to the 'justness' of a court thus constitutes the grounds of an ideological dispute by proposing a construction of reality which is inevitably an oppositional one. The other propositions – that defendants are obligated to pay their fines before pleasure and that to be employed is to be a useful citizen (and its negative correlative) – likewise belong to an ideological discourse which is often, at least in British magistrates' courts, invoked by magistrates in one form or another. While ideological pro-positions may not be so clearly manifest in all magistrates' utterances, it is both useful and possible to identify consistent ideologies operating at the *propositional* level.

Turning to the pragmatic level, Halliday defines 'tenor' as

inclusive of participant relationships and of both social and discourse roles. Tenor is realised semantically as the interpersonal component, the participatory function of language which serves to establish and maintain social relationships. The interpersonal component is, thus, realised specifically by those linguistic features which express speaker attitudes towards propositions and towards hearers.

Returning to the previously cited ideological propositions, we can say that in (a) the magistrate is putting forward an assertion without qualification and that 'court' is emphasised in the structuring of the message as both theme and rheme. In (b) the 'message' is structured as a directive in declarative form, containing a high value modal ('must'), and that the directive is repeated as an embedded imperative ('you pay your fines first'). In (a) a negative polar question functions as a request, with the ideological element embedded as a proposition within a highly conducive syntactic form. Such choices on the part of the magistrate define participant relationships from a position of authority and control, with the emphasis on the directive.

Moreover, in each of these utterances the speaker is not expressing the proposition as an individual actor but in his/her institutional role as the representative of, respectively,: in (a) the 'court'; in (b) the 'law'; and in (c) the 'Bench'. That the force and legitimacy of these propositions is that of the particular institution and beyond that the legal system (the rule of law) is made clear in the shift in person from 'Bench' to 'I' in (c).

This notion of institutional force and authority applies also to the performance of speech acts. One of the most noticeable features of the data base is the presence of recurrent patterns of particular speech acts, i.e. questions, directives, threats. These speech acts are ideological in a court context in ways in which they may not be in other settings in that:

1. They are predictable in a sense which rarely if ever happens in ordinary conversation. Large numbers of questions and directives occurred in all twenty-six cases, and the majority of cases contained identifiable threats.
2. Their force and validity derive from the institution rather than the individual. Any challenge is that force and/or validity is thus a challenge to the operation of the institution and not the individual representative (magistrate or clerk).

IDEOLOGICAL CONGRUENCE AND DISPUTE: TWO CASES

The extracts which follow involve an almost identical context, inasmuch as this is possible in a natural language situation. They took place in the same court, though with different magistrates presiding. Both defendants are male, working class and middle aged; both have been judged as guilty by a previous court and fined for the same type of offence – road traffic; both defendants have been ordered to pay fines of a fixed amount and have failed to pay. In each case, having explicitly established that the non-payment is indisputable shared knowledge, the magistrate requests an account of the defendant's failure to pay.

Case one

(C: clerk; D: defendant; M: magistrate)
C: Thank you – is it correct that on the 16th of June last year you were fined a total of ninety pounds in respect of three road traffic offences and also ordered to pay costs of four pounds ninety-two pence – making a total of ninety-four pounds ninety-two pence – is that correct?
D: yes sir – it is
C: and you were ordered to pay by weekly instalments?
D: yes
   [utterances omitted]
M: why haven't you been paying more than this – what – will you give us a reason?
D: *well actually* you worships *like* I've uh you know about a year and a half I fell out of – well my wife left me *like* – and I've been all – *you know* I just started drinkin' and *that like* and uh – go to the pub one night and seen her and we've got back together again now so
M: but you see – you've committed this offence – and this is a *commitment* – a *court* commitment [2] and – you *should of – have* been paying this – it's no *excuse* that you've just had domestic troubles and gone off drinking and things – this *should have been* – as I understand it there's been nothing paid – in the last six months of last year – is that right Mr –
   [to the clerk]
C: the last two payments – one pound

M: yes but that's this year
C: this year yes
M: and the offence was June of last year [2] so June to December
   you've paid *nothing* – and your reason is – that you've got
   domestic problems and you're all anyhow with your money and
   you went off drinking – now this is not good enough
D: no I realise that your worships like – now I'm setting myself
   straight again now my wife is with me like – now I'm willing to
   pay it off you know every week like
M: well do you take this seriously
D: of course I do your worship – ⌈ really do
M: ⌊ because you know you *can* go to
   prison for non-payment of fines
D: I realise that your Honour

Propositions

The defendant's initial response to the magistrate's request for an
account takes the form of a narrative which only indirectly
addresses the matter of payment. When the magistrate counters
with his own reformulation of his narrative ('and your reason is,
etc.') + evaluation ('this is not good enough'), the defendant
accepts her evaluation ('no I realise that'), including her
inferences that he has been unwilling rather than unable to pay
his fine ('now I'm willing to pay it off you know every week
like'). He puts forward no opposing proposition of his own.

Lexical choices and semantic orientation

In his initial 'account', the defendant uses a series of highly
mitigated forms and hedges (well, actually, like, you know) +
terms of address ('your worship', 'your honour') which explicitly
and repeatedly acknowledge the status and role of the magistrate.
This is set against the magistrate's classification of the defendant's narrative as an 'excuse', her stress on 'commitment' and
'court' and her repeated use of mid-value modals ('should have
been paid'). The defendant does not dispute this classification.

Interaction

On this level also the defendant is cooperative. He gives an account when requested and answers the magistrate's polar question ('well do you take this seriously?') with the positive proposition intensified. He also acknowledges her 'accusation' with an admission of guilt and accepts her subsequent threat. On all three levels, ideological congruence is achieved. The defendant ultimately offers the 'goods' which are central to the immediate purpose of the court session and accepts his obligation to pay. Ideological processes are thus significantly represented in the linguistic negotiation, in what is actually *said*. Whether this ideological congruence extends to the defendant's non-linguistic behaviour, i.e. he pays his fine, cannot be determined from the data base but only from the court records.

Case two

(C: clerk; D: defendant; M: magistrate)

C: thank you – and I think in May of this year you were before the court for motoring offences when you were fined thirty-five pounds and for costs fifteen pounds making a total of – fifty and uh you were ordered to pay within twenty-eight days – you haven't as yet paid anything or been in touch with the court – can you explain why you haven't paid and what your situation is at the present time

D: yes – the reason I haven't paid – is – [A] that I haven't got the fifty pounds and also secondly that I feel that I was totally *unfairly judged to be guilty at the time* – I saw my solicitor about it and he said that he didn't think it was [2] worth going any further – said it would only cost me more money which I couldn't afford – I brought the solicitor from Derby in the first instance which cost me fifteen pounds – and I asked him to get – if it was possible to get my delayed because I felt so strongly about it that I wanted to take the matter further [2] and at that point it is resting with him and at the present time I've been trying to get in touch with him but he was away for three weeks [2] and *I still feel most strongly about it*.

[utterances omitted]

M: you're not prepared to make the court an offer – of payment [2]

because I think I should tell you that ⌈the alternative is going
to prison Mr

D: ⌊if I do [   ]

D: fair enough – if I do I'm condoning *injustice* – which I think it was
in the first place

M: hmm – well – we can't re-try the case

D: even – even the prosecutor at the time – at the recess when the two
magistrates went out – of whom I think your companion was one –
stated at the time that the case should never have even been
brought up – that he agreed entirely with my action

M: hmm – we can't re-try the case I'm afraid

D: so I've got to pay it – and accept *injustice*

M: yes – well it's up to you – I say ⌈the alternative could very
well be prison

D: ⌊which says a lot for

D: which says a lot for British *justice*

M: hmm

[5]

D: there is a lot *could* be said – but obviously I would be had for
contempt of court – if I said it – which I don't propose to say

M: hmm

D: which I feel very very – *bitter* about the whole situation

M: hmm

D: you *were* actually on the Bench

M: no that's nothing to do with it – the composition of the Bench
when the case was heard has nothing to do with it and we can't
re-hear the case – it's just not possible – the decision has been
made and you've missed your opportunity – to appeal – that's
open to everybody – and if you're dissatisfied with the appeal in
the Crown Court you can go further – those are the lines along
which you *should have gone* [2] if you felt – uh this injustice – that
injustice was being done – but regrettably now the time has

D: but I could not afford to take it further at the time

M: hmm well

D: so I just have to accept *injustice*?

M: um – um well it's up to you Mr ⌈H – uh – uh – I'm putting it to you

D: ⌊((   )

M: again – are you um – are you going to *make* an offer – uh – uh to
discharge this debt?

[6]

D: would you in my position?

M: I – I'm not here to answer questions – you answer *my* question

D: one rule for one – and one for another I presume

[3]

M: can I have an answer to my question – please
[6]
M: the question is – are you prepared to make an offer to the court to discharge – this debt
[2]
D: what sort of minimal offer would ⌈ be required
M: ⌊ it's not a bargaining situation
it's a *straight* question [2] Mr H – can I have the answer
D: well I'll just pay the court a pound annually
M: that's not acceptable to us
D: what would be acceptable to the court
M: no we don't find – uh we want a sensible offer Mr H

Propositions

This defendant responds to the request for an account of his non-payment directly, restating the presupposition in the magistrate's question ('yes – the reason I haven't paid is'). Though he does appeal to his inability to pay, more importantly, he explicitly puts forward a proposition which challenges one of the basic ideological 'givens' of the legal system, i.e. that the court was unfair and he was wrongly judged to be guilty'. His narrative is focused on the latter proposition rather than his inability to pay, and his only use of a mitigating form is 'I feel', which is repeated as an intensifier in order to make explicit his attitude to his own proposition ('I still feel most strongly about it'). The defendant maintains his opposing proposition, that to pay his fine would be to condone, accept injustice. He responds to the magistrate's reference to the appeals procedure with a further counter-proposition ('but I could not afford to take it further').

Lexical choice and semantic representation

What happens on this level is a semantic dispute over the parameters of the case and the construction of particular meanings. The defendant defines what is being talked about as 'injustice', and attempts to establish 'justice' as the topic and frame of reference for proceeding with the case. The magistrate refuses to accept this definition by explicitly distancing himself from the defendant's classification ('if you felt – uh this injustice – that injustice was being done'). The initial version commits the speaker to the acceptance of 'injustice' in a way that the re-phrased version does not. The defendant twice re-asserts his classification of the court's behaviour as 'injustice', finally put forward as a positive proposition for the magistrate to confirm or deny ('so I just have to accept injustice'). By either confirming or denying the defendant's proposition, the magistrate would be accepting 'injustice' as a presupposition and a legitimate frame of reference. Consequently, he does neither ('well – it's up to you Mr H'), and re-classifies what is being talked about as a 'debt' which must be 'discharged'.

Interaction

It is on the interactive level that the underlying ideological framework of participant relationships becomes most visible, with an explicit dispute over the implicit 'rules' of discourse in court. This occurs at the point when the magistrate regains the initiative, with his request for an 'offer' ('are you going to make an offer – uh – uh – to discharge the debt?'). The dispute involves the defendant in contravening the unstated discourse rules in three ways: (1) Defendants must answer questions, which is a more court specific version of the more general rule that the space after the question belongs to the hearer; (2) the defendant's response ('would you in my position') involves a personal appeal to the magistrate as an individual rather than in his symbolic role as the representative of the legal system; (3) differential access to particular speech acts, i.e. questions, is made explicit. Defendants can only ask questions in court subject to certain constraints. The magistrate in his response makes explicit this differential access to questions ('I'm not here to answer questions – you answer *my* question'), which the defendant acknowledges with reference to its ideological implications of power and dominance ('one rule for one – and one for another I presume'). This is followed by a further dispute over the rights of speakers in relationship to questions ('it's not a bargaining situation – it's a *straight* question').

Thus the ideological dispute in this case is manifested in: (1) on the propositional level, sets of opposing propositions put forward respectively by the magistrate and the defendant, and; (2) divergent lexical classifications with regard to what is being talked about and the definition of particular acts; (3) on the pragmatic level, a dispute over speakers' rights to particular speech acts and their sequencing. The defendant's 'choices' at each level construct a form of resistance to the dominant ideology and pose an explicit challenge to the power of the court; the magistrate's 'choices' re-inforce his authority and control.

CONCLUSION

In summary, then, ideological processes in court are expressed in complex ways and operate on both the propositional and pragmatic levels, including propositional content, choices of mood and modality, and recurrent choices of particular lexical items. Interactively, differing rules with regard to speaker rights are enforced, along with sequencing constraints. Ideology is also expressed by consistent choices involving particular speech acts, i.e. in this court, the magistrate's use of questions, directives, accusations, threats.

It is not the case, however, that such choices and constraints are necessarily ideological whenever and wherever they occur. Indeed, settings which are not significant ideological sites, such as service encounters, may also involve constraints and patterns of interactive and lexical choice which may well be of purely local significance and related only to immediate goals of the setting. For example, questions in an information booth or in a greengrocers, are likely to be asked by the customer rather than the person serving; directives may be given by a travel agent. Nor is it the case that such choices and constraints have no local significance in court; obviously they do have this as well. But such speech acts and, particularly, sequences of speech acts are also ideological in court, in part because the existing constraints are much more powerful in their operation and are nearly always enforced when breaches occur. They serve not only to maintain the control of the clerk or magistrate in the immediate discourse context but also to sustain an ideological construction of reality which is crucial to the perceived legitimacy of magistrates' decisions.

SIX

Video depositions: linguistic endorsement and caveats

Bethyl A. Pearson and Rebecca White Berch

BACKGROUND

What is a deposition?

A deposition is a procedure for recording witnesses' oral statements for later use in legal proceedings. Accompanied by counsel, the deponent appears, is placed under oath, and responds to questions from attorneys from both sides of the case. Parties may inquire into any matter that is relevant to the case and is not privileged. Although no judge is present, attorneys may make objections, which a judge will rule upon before the material objected to is used in a trial.

Attorneys representing either side of the case may initiate a deposition to: (1) provide the basis for further factual exploration, (2) obtain admissions for impeachment (a tactic for discrediting a witness's testimony if he or she can be shown to have made prior inconsistent statements), (3) commit a witness to a particular version of the facts, (4) perpetuate testimony in case the deponent will not be available for the trial, (5) 'preview' the witness to see whether he or she will appeal to jurors, (6) demonstrate to the opposition either the strength of one's case or the prowess of one's attorney or (7) substitute for testimony at trial regardless of the witness's availability.

Historical attitudes toward videotaped deposition

Under current federal and many state laws in the United States of America (Fed. R. 30(c) Civ. P.; Ariz. R. Civ. P. 30(c)), depositions must be recorded stenographically by court reporters unless the court grants one party's request or all parties stipulate audio or video recording. Furthermore, the party seeking to take a video deposition must get consent from the party to be deposed or go to court to get an order requiring the deponent to submit to a videotaped deposition.

Surprisingly, even this tightly constrained option of audio/ video recording, which was endorsed in 1980 (Fed. R. Civ. P. 30(b) (4) (1970) (amended 1980, 85 F.R.D. 521, 52 (1980)), represents a distinct mellowing in point of view. Until 1970, the Federal Rules of Civil Procedure and the parallel rules of most states restricted the use of video: unless all parties agreed otherwise, depositions could only be taken stenographically. Since few parties would agree, few non-stenographic depositions were taken. However, a suggestion in 1967 that non-stenographic depositions be allowed upon notice by the scheduling party lent support to a ruling in 1970. That allowed a party to obtain a court order to take a deposition by 'other than stenographic means' (Fed. R. Civ. P. 30(b) (4), 48 F.R.D. 509, 510 (1970). By 1977, some courts had begun to encourage the use of video depositions, at least implicitly (Advisory Committee Notes, 80 F.R.D. 323, 337, 1979), and, since the 1980 amendment, they have granted increasing permission to use video, despite the fact that non-stenographic deposition 'as of right', that is, as a legal right, much less as a requirement, is still disallowed.

The historical reluctance of the courts to embrace video technology and the caution implied even in the recent warming of their attitudes toward video are a direct reflection of the fear that 'these methods give rise to problems of accuracy and trustworthiness' (Advisory Committee Notes, 48 F.R.D. 509, 514 (1970)). However, these 'problems' generally refer either to equipment failure or to fear of abuse of the technology in altering deposition testimony, outcomes that are proving unfounded because courts have also imposed technical safeguards: restrictions on staging techniques, background, time clocks, camera angle, etc.

Oddly, in their debate on the acceptability of video, the courts have gradually endorsed video depositions for reasons of greater efficiency and reduced expense, but they have overlooked two far more important reasons for favouring the use of video: (a) video provides more of the linguistic and communicative content of the deponent's testimony than stenography, and (b) stenographic recording probably has a margin of error which equals or exceeds the potential errors in non-stenographic means (*Marlboro Products Corp.* v. *North Amer. Phillips Corp.*, 1972).

This chapter argues that because video provides the paralinguistic and visual signals of the metacommunicative frame in which utterances are made (Bateson 1972), video depositions should be required in place of stenographic depositions. However, this chapter also argues that a specific condition that video should *not* be required *if the deponent can satisfy the court that the deposition should not be videotaped* should accompany such an amendment.

With this caveat, we pose the perhaps equally serious question members of the law profession should be asking: *not* whether video deposition is 'accurate and trustworthy', which the inclusion of visual and paralinguistic cues under the eye of careful technology would seem to guarantee, but when it may be *too* accurate and trustworthy. That is, under certain circumstances the visual and paralinguistic cues to interpretation of the testimony present in video and absent from stenographic recording, such as a witness's non-standard pronunciation, may diminish the credibility of the deponent. In certain cases stenographic depositions better skirt the prejudices and inaccurate interpretations of jurors who hear and see the closer-to-live testimony of video, and should be preferred over video. In endorsing video, we therefore also caution the lawyers and judges who will determine standards that 'satisfy' the exemption of its use against underestimating the powerful subjective forces of (non)verbal evaluation video entails.

We outline the linguistic and non-linguistic motivations for supporting video depositions more fully below. We also justify the attachment of an 'escape clause' to the likely amendment. First, however, we summarise the results of a survey which empirically validate the hunch we had that the use of video depositions is increasing.

ARIZONA ATTORNEYS' ATTITUDES TOWARD VIDEOTAPED
DEPOSITIONS

We conducted a survey to test the regional validity of the
apparent nationally increasing tendency for the courts to favour
videotaped depositions. We wanted to determine Arizona attorneys' attitudes toward video depositions and to ascertain specifically why and how often attorneys choose video over stenographic
recordings. Findings would provide a basis for a realistic assessment of the future of video depositions in the courts.

We used a written attitudinal survey with Likert-type scaled
attitude questions to survey over 200 litigation attorneys
attending continuing legal education (CLE) seminars in Phoenix
and Tucson during the fall and summer of 1989.[1] We found that
although the lawyers have minimal training and experience with
video and they use it infrequently, their training and experience
with video is increasing, and the more they become familiar with
it, the more they favour its use.

The attorneys we sampled represent a relatively young
'emerging bar' in that they have been in practice on an average of
five years. During this time, nearly half of the respondents (112 or
46 per cent) indicated that they had participated in a video
deposition. However, the depth of their experience was rather
limited; most had participated in only one or two. Only six
respondents (7 per cent) had participated in more than ten.

Attorneys also indicated that they most often participated in
video depositions in personal injury cases. Witness unavailability
was the leading reason that video depositions were requested for
a majority of respondents (92 or 89 per cent).

Only 48 of 236 respondents (20 per cent) had training in how to
take video depositions, and most of those (82 per cent or 37)
received their training through CLE seminars. Only 7 per cent
received training in law school. Yet 80 per cent indicated that they
plan to take training, and fully 88 per cent agreed that the use of
video was likely to increase in all types of litigation in the future.

At the same time, only 55 per cent agreed that the federal and state
rules should be changed to permit the routine use of video
depositions. Not surprisingly, the percentage favouring amending
the rules increases to 62 per cent among those who have participated in a video deposition, and to 72 per cent among those who
have training in how to take a video deposition. The implication for

the court system is that as attorneys, through participation and training, become more comfortable with video technology, the pressure on the system to modify the rules will increase.

MERITS AND LIABILITIES OF VIDEO DEPOSITIONS

If the survey outlined above accurately indicates the national trend, which we believe it does, the national support for the use of video depositions ultimately will demand an amendment of the Federal Rules of Procedure 30 to **require** its use. For this reason, video depositions merit more detailed evaluation on the basis of insights of experts in several related and potentially cross-fertilising disciplines – anthropology, communication, law, linguistics, psychology, and sociology – in order to understand what conditions should rightfully require or rightfully exempt their use. We will conclude that in a majority of cases, the paralinguistic and visual channels of communication provided by video enable the hearers of the message to better form an opinion about the message and the deponent who sends it.

General advantages

Video has several general advantages over stenographic deposition that are only loosely related to issues of authenticity of communication. As suggested above, these are the types of advantages to which the court has been particularly receptive. We briefly review them in order to explain more fully why the use of video depositions is on the rise.

It is more efficient to tape a video deposition than to have the proceedings recorded stenographically. Video can be reviewed immediately after the deposition has been taken, or even during breaks in the proceedings if need be. It usually takes court reporters anywhere from several hours to several weeks to transcribe stenographic notes, depending upon the length of the deposition.

Videotape effectively broadens the scope of witness availability and enhances authority of the testimony. Expert witnesses, such as medical doctors or public officials, often are unavailable to testify at trials because of scheduling conflicts.[2] Videotapes may be made in the doctor's office to maximise the convenience for the witness, to help ensure the witness's cooperation, and to enhance the expert's air of authority. In addition, taking a deposition at the doctor's office may allow the doctor to use as evidence demonstrative on-location aids such as models, charts, skeletons, or X-rays, or immovable machinery or equipment that would be difficult or impossible to transport to court. Use of demonstrative evidence is lost, for all practical purposes, in a stenographically recorded deposition.

A video deposition may also substitute for an available witness on occasions for which timing is an important tactical consideration. Some trial lawyers keep a videotaped deposition as a backup in case a witness is late getting to court. A video deposition also helps late in the day, if the attorney wants to wait to present live testimony until the morning, when the jury is most alert, but his or her witness cannot return then (McElhaney 1988).

In addition, jurors absorb and retain testimony better from video depositions when they receive the information both visually and aurally. Studies have shown that when jurors see and hear evidence simultaneously, they are able to recall 65 per cent of the testimonial evidence after a three-day interval (Belli 1982). If jurors hear testimony with no accompanying visual cues, their recall falls dramatically to about 10 per cent after the same three-day period (Belli 1982). Videotaped depositions meet the test of both engaging the jurors' minds and keeping them involved with the testimony so that they remember it during deliberations, which may occur days, weeks, or even months after they hear the testimony. This increased retention level may have persuasive implication for the outcome of a case.

Another prime advantage of video is the cost, although there is some debate on this issue (Rypinski 1982). A video deposition usually costs from $300 to $1200, varying with the length of the deposition, but this may actually be less than stenographic depositions when the total cost in the litigation is evaluated. Costs of presenting expert testimony by videotape are less than the costs of presenting the expert in person; a video deposition costs less overall than paying for an expert to sit in court for several hours or days. For example, travelling to court and waiting once he got there consumed 73 per cent of the 'testimony' time for which a psychiatrist billed. Furthermore, in a case involving multiple defendants, a tape used for one defendant's trial may be cost-effectively re-employed in a subsequent trial. Finally, a video deposition often results in a higher, faster settlement.

Evidence also shows that witnesses and lawyers behave more professionally when on camera; furthermore, because they do not wish to appear to jurors as attempting to obstruct the flow of testimony, attorneys make far fewer objections in video depositions (Kaufman 1983).

Moreover, fully 80 per cent of male jurors and over 75 per cent of female jurors favour videotaped depositions, according to a recent National Bureau of Standards study (Whitney 1988). Farmer et al. (1976: 59) claim that the majority of jurors found video deposition to be 'significantly more interesting, easier to pay attention to, more refreshing, clearer, and more stimulating than the transcript method'.

Video has certain advantages over live testimony. Unlike live testimony, video can be edited to eliminate inadmissible evidence before the jury has the opportunity to view the deposition. Jurors remember evidence once it is presented; despite instructions to disregard inadmissible evidence they are unable to do so (Miller and Fontes 1978).

In addition, witness schedules and other tactical considerations often require that testimony at trial be presented out of chronological sequence. But presenting evidence out of order sometimes confuses jurors. Videotaped depositions provide a partial solution. They enhance a lawyer's case by facilitating presentation of evidence in a logical proof sequence (Suplee and Donaldson 1988). Further, in long cases, portions of individual videotaped depositions may be integrated by subject matter to minimise juror confusion (*Beard* v. *Mitchell* 1979).

Finally, the court and attorney expense consumed by attorney arguments in the courtroom over objections is eliminated. Judge, jury, and counsel time is used more efficiently and flexibly because the jury need not wait around while counsel debate evidentiary objections. For very long depositions, the judge and counsel need not be present while the jury views the videotape.

Despite some criticism that (a) video may dehumanise a trial (Miller and Boster 1977), (b) jurors are potentially conditioned to the fictional emphasis of TV (Miller and Fontes 1978), or (c) jurors may display over-attention or deference to witnesses who appear on TV (Miller and Fontes 1978), the merits of videotaped depositions strongly outweigh their liabilities in the general categories summarised here. We now turn to the more communicative issues.

Communicative elements captured by video depositions

Video recording of depositions captures many potential cues to meaning that stenographic copy cannot record. These comprise visual and paralinguistic cues, many of which are non-verbal. Although researchers do not agree on the comparative influence of verbal versus non-verbal cues in communication, none would deny the communicative value of the 'body idiom' (Goffman 1959) and other extra-lexical cues.

Birdwhistell (1970: 197) claims that 'no more than 30 to 35 per cent of the social meaning of a conversation or an interaction is carried out by the words', while Mehrabian (1972) counts verbal communication as carrying only 7 per cent of the impact of the message, with paralinguistic carrying 38 per cent, and visual, 55 per cent. Aron et al. (1986: 429) equalize these claims, reporting that 'the generally accepted figure among scientists who have researched the field carefully runs to 60% for non-verbal and 40% for verbal.'

Given this tipping of the scales toward greater influence of non-verbal over verbal communicative cues, we are not surprised that Key (1975) claims it is not the rational, verbal language which moves people to action, but rather the attitudes communicated through paralinguistic and visual cues. It may be more surprising, however, that, according to Zunin and Zunin (1972), most people decide the credibility of others within the first four minutes of viewing. Furthermore, there is evidence that in cases in which verbal and visual cues conflict, jurors tend to disregard the verbal communication, and instead rely upon the paralinguistic and visual cues (Bandler and Grinder 1979).

We believe that a witness's impact on the jury is a direct function of the communication cues he or she emanates. As jurors view the way in which a witness responds to questions, they receive cues about that witness's confidence, competence, and trustworthiness – cues that relate directly to several judgments the jurors form about that witness's credibility, persuasiveness, and honesty. Video rightly makes these communication cues available.

Unfortunately, the inclusion of these powerful cues in video does not always guarantee their accurate interpretation by a jury. Within American culture alone, only a few discrete visual movements, such as the hitch-hiker's thumbing sign, the 'A-OK' sign, a few postures, and some facial expressions such as anger, disgust, and surprise, have generalised meaning that is easily understood in isolation from other communication cues. Most paralinguistic and visual cues have no specific or universal meaning in themselves. Rather they derive meaning by endorsing each other in congruent cue clusters (Matlon 1988).

Furthermore, many of these cues are culture or subculture dependent and are, therefore, subject to ambiguous or incorrect interpretation by members of other groups, especially by people who harbour biased attitudes toward accented speech and other non-mainstream communicative behaviour. In addition, many innocent indicators of nervousness or anxiety can be easily misinterpreted as indicators of deceit. Because jurors lack familiarity with the witness they are called upon to evaluate, they may not be able to distinguish whether the postural or paralinguistic signs of anxiety revealed in a video deposition relate to witnesses' resistance to a particular question or whether those cues reflect their situational anxiety in the deposition setting. Anxious witnesses, therefore, become particularly vulnerable to sending messages that are not the intended ones.

Beyond these difficulties in interpretation, jurors have differing abilities to observe and decode communication cues. Researchers have found that untrained jurors' abilities to accurately detect deceptive communication vary widely. Some jurors have a sophisticated 'third eye' (Houts 1981) that enables them to accurately detect and interpret cues, while others are less perceptive.

For example, some evidence suggests that gender-based differences exist in ability to detect communication cues. Hall (1978), in a review of seventy-five studies, claims moderate, but consistent female advantage in non-verbal decoding accuracy. Burgoon (1985) also claims that, as a group, female jurors are better than male jurors in decoding paralinguistic and visual cues, regardless of the age or gender of the witness. He says, too, that the ability to detect deception logically improves with age and, in addition, a juror with an extroverted personality enjoys greater interpretative ability than an introverted juror. Halberstadt (1985) suggests that jurors from groups that historically have been oppressed, including Blacks and women (Henley 1977), may develop better decoding skills as survival tools. Finally, jurors from particular occupations may be more perceptive. Those who have backgrounds in nursing, acting or the visual arts professions seem to exhibit greater decoding ability (Hayano 1980).

Given the wide-ranging potential for variability in jurors' interpretations of the visual and paralinguistic cues reviewed below, the proposed general 'accuracy and trustworthiness' of video requires some qualification. Evidence reveals a clear need for an 'escape clause' from the requirement of video deposition and implies that more training of lawyers and judges in the application of the amendment is necessary.

In the following section we discuss individual cues to communicative meaning and their often problematic interpretation. Because our study deals with the advent of video in the United States, the studies that we cite use American subjects, unless otherwise noted.

Visual cues

The bulk of evidence from rank ordering visual versus vocal channels indicates a strong bias toward the primacy of visual modalities (Burgoon 1985). Facial expressions in particular are primary vehicles for emotive messages surrounding persons and events. Expressive messages may be intentional or unintentional, but are argued to universally include happiness, sadness, fear, anger, disgust, surprise, and combinations of these six basic emotions (Ekman 1982). Visual cues, especially gestures, may also encode emphasis; 'it appears that the body is responsible for signaling the intensity of affect while the face signals the specific evaluative state' (Burgoon 1985: 371). Visual communication cues are not recorded by stenographic transcription. One body of research indicates some consensus in the interpretation of certain visual cues; other research findings, however, suggest a great deal of disparity, not only in correlations between these cues and witness truthfulness,[3] but in cross-cultural uses and interpretations as well.

A witness's head and eyes emit many visual communication cues, but, unfortunately, according to Ekman and Friesen (1969), they may provide the least accurate clues to deception. Some evidence demonstrates that in Western culture, at least, smiling behaviour differs between those who are telling the truth and those who lie. Although Miller and Burgoon (1982) find no difference, Mehrabian (1971) and McClintock and Hunt (1975) claim that witnesses who lie tend to smile more.

None the less, facial expressions are not a particularly accurate source of communication cues for several reasons. Witnesses may be able to disguise them by intentional control (Fugita et al. 1980). Facial communication, particularly smiles, can be 'put on' to mislead jurors. Also problematic is the fact that smiling has different meanings for members of other cultural groups and those meanings might mislead Western jurors. For example, according to Japanese tradition, smiling often connotes sorrow, anger, or embarrassment.

Eye contact in Western culture is favourably associated with honesty and credibility (Andersen 1985), although for a Native American, for example, direct eye contact is negatively evaluated (Scollon and Scollon 1981). Many American jurors believe that a witness who looks away while speaking is lying (Lewis and Pucelik 1982). Research indicates, however, that when lying, sophisticated witnesses tend to look more steadily at the receiver than when telling the truth (Friedlund et al. 1987). However, witnesses can be trained to control eye gaze in order to give the appearance of truthfulness. Furthermore, avoidance of eye contact may occur for reasons such as nervousness, fear or embarrassment – reasons unrelated to lack of truthfulness (Bandler and Grinder 1979).

Other eye behaviours such as blinking and pupillary change, are only minimally susceptible to witness control because they are involuntary. According to Zuckerman and Driver (1985) persons who are lying exhibit fewer blinks than truth-tellers, and their pupils contract suddenly. However, jurors probably would not be able to observe much of this behaviour from the videotape.

Knapp (1980) claims that deceiving witnesses tend to use more rapid hand movements and other adapter gestures, such as touching the face and other body parts, than witnesses who tell the truth. Nose touching, according to Morris (1977), correlates strongly with deceit. Those witnesses who do not tell the truth also manipulate objects, such as jewellery or clothing, more frequently, although problems of interpretation arise in the fact that people who are anxious perform the same behaviours (Matlon 1988). Knapp et al. (1975) claim that a deceitful witness tends to use fewer illustrative or other gestures to reinforce verbal communication, but individuals vary in their ability to control their hand movements (Roberts 1987).

Posture and body orientation are visible in video. Most studies show that lying witnesses shift position more often than truthful communicators (Ekman and Friesen 1969). Furthermore, seated body orientation, although susceptible to control, is one of the communication cues witnesses least control (Mehrabian 1972). Witnesses who are not telling the truth seem to lean forward less (Mehrabian 1971). In addition, a deceitful witness's body tends to angle away from his or her audience (Knapp 1980). This suggests that a truthful witness could be expected to face the questioning attorney directly. This deception indicator, however, could be misinterpreted if the attorney sits to the side of the camera, and the witness is perceived as avoiding and deceiving the attorney. Standardisation of technique is in order.

Paralinguistic cues

Although paralanguage has been defined in different ways by various researchers (e.g. Ekman and Friesen 1969; Mehrabian 1972; Harrison 1974; Key 1975), for the purposes of this chapter we include the following within paralanguage: volume, pitch change, tempo or rate of speech, extent, that is, how drawn out or clipped the speech is, non-verbal vocalisations, speech fillers (e.g. um, hmm), and voice quality, that is, whether the voice is shrill, smooth, shaky, or gravelly. Here we also include intonation and stress, traditionally structural, prosodic cues to meaning (Lyons 1977) and 'accent'.

Studies have shown that paralinguistic cues are better predictors of deception than visual cues (Wiegman 1985). Deceptive communications tend to be higher pitched and shorter than truthful communications (Apple et al. 1979), although this tendency may cause problems for some speakers from other cultures. For example, a high-pitched voice is considered admirable for women in Japanese culture. Deceptive communications also contain more disfluencies, such as hesitations and fillers (Druckman et al. 1982), and hesitation cues may be one of the best indicators of deception. Matlon (1988) found that hesitation cues were more strongly associated with lying than any other non-verbal cue except pupil dilation. At the same time, however, vocal non-fluencies also increase under stress and may wrongly negatively affect witness credibility.

A deceptive witness tends to speak more slowly than a truth teller and delays responses to questions (Ekman et al. 1976). However, when a witness becomes anxious, that anxiety may also manifest itself in longer response times, slower speech and longer pauses (Smith and Malandro 1985).

As for prosodic cues, questioning intonation at the end of declarative sentences may negatively affect the jurors' perceptions of the witness's credibility; rising intonation may be viewed as overly tentative (O'Barr 1982). On the other hand, more intonation in general seems to affect witness credibility positively (Matlon 1988).

Other intonation patterns may cue very different meanings for the same lexical items. For example, if during the taking of a deposition the attorney asked the following question of a criminal defendant and received the following response, the presence or absence of prosodic and visual cues in the answer could affect the jury's assessment of the deponent's communication.

Q: When the police arrived at your door and announced that they wanted to search the premises, you granted them permission to enter, did you not?
A: Yeah, sure.

The answer may be intoned in two ways, one indicating easy affirmation, the other suggesting sarcastic *dis*affirmation, both presumably supplemented by disambiguating visual cues. Of course, the witness may still be deceiving, and there is no guarantee that jurors will perceive the intended meaning.

'Accent' is another feature that may have a great impact on witness evaluation. In particular, a witness with a non-mainstream accent or regional dialect may be perceived as less credible (Smith and Malandro 1985). Research in attitudinal behaviour strongly suggests that members of dominant societal groups respond favourably to speech and language patterns similar to their own and less favourably to non-standard varieties of subordinate groups (Street and Hopper 1982). Sebastian and Ryan (1985) argue that degree of accent is a cue for stereotyping and categorising: the greater the accent the more negative the evaluation.

In particular, evidence points to severe negative evaluations of Black and Hispanic accent and speech patterns in the United States (e.g. Light et al. 1978; Carranza 1982), despite the proliferation of recent research on these varieties (e.g. Baugh 1983; Kochman 1981). Negative evaluations of the accented English of non-native speakers other than Hispanics are also prevalent (e.g. Anderson-Hsieh and Koehler 1988), and many prejudices remain toward lesbian and gay patterns of verbal and non-verbal use (e.g. Hayes 1981). Language attitudes thus are closely tied to ethnic, racial and cultural stereotypes, stereotypes which may be reinforced by a video deposition, but guarded in a stenographic recording.

A final communicative feature of video that is separate from visual and paralinguistic cues but also important, is conversational turn-taking. Video more fully captures the interactive nature of spoken discourse and the sometimes shifting balance of power between interactants as they negotiate the exchange. With video, jurors can see and hear overlaps, talk-overs and interruptions that are impossible to capture on the written page. They can then better interpret messages by judges and lawyers, and ascertain, for example, if the witness is being badgered.

Conclusion

According to the constitutional laws upon which the American judicial system is founded, live testimony before a jury of one's peers is the standard, preferred over any kind of deposition testimony. In line with this stated preference for live testimony, the federal judicial system and most state systems have passed rules giving deference to the decisions of factfinders who have had the opportunity to receive visual and paralinguistic evidence (Fed. R. Civ. P. 52).

Clearly, since (a) video recording would seem to more closely approximate this 'live' standard than stenographic recording possibly could, (b) American judicial systems have opted in favour of encouraging factfinders to avail themselves of visual and paralinguistic evidence, (c) video has numerous technical and evidentiary advantages, and (d) the survey of Arizona litigation attorneys indicates increasingly favourable attitudes toward video depositions, the courts likely will continue to approve the increasing use of video depositions to the point of requiring their use as a general rule.

We favour video depositions as a requirement because video provides a fuller and more explicit communicative framework for the witness's message than stenography does. The judicial system should allow jurors to receive more than a portion of a communicative message when technological advances make it possible for them to perceive a much larger part of the communication. This outcome implicates the very function of the justice system – to search for the truth.

Furthermore, we take seriously the evidence that jurors have more confidence in decisions they make based upon seeing the deponent than they do in decisions that are based upon stenographically transcribed testimony. Despite the room for misinterpretations, the jury's confidence in their judgments is a prime societal consideration for the legal system.

Yet our endorsement bears a cautious attachment. Videotaped depositions should not be required in all circumstances. Some kind of 'escape clause' is crucial because while it may be argued that video favourably supplies more of the communicative message that should be available to jurors for their own interpretation, just as it is from witnesses who testify live, video has been shown to contain the potential for serious risks of misinterpretation. That is, jurors may misinterpret the visual and paralinguistic cues they receive. Features that may indicate anxiety or nervousness are similar to those that reflect deceit. In addition, features that are favourably evaluated in a particular culture may be unfavourably evaluated or differently interpreted in another culture. Furthermore, attitudes and biases of jurors toward members of subdominant groups may have an unjustly negative influence. Therefore, the opportunity for the deponent to satisfy the court that a deposition should not be video recorded is integral to our support of the standard use of video depositions in litigation practice.

We recognise the difficulties in the two-pronged option we present here. While we target video testimony as a goal, we sense that stenography has certain built-in protective biases. Having offered some complexities surrounding the issue, we encourage the legal profession to devote greater attention to the behaviours discussed here than it has in the past. Despite the increasing evidence demonstrating the impact of non-verbal and non-lexical features on communication, legal education provides attorneys with little information about communication behaviours. Still less does it discuss the application of those behaviours to the legal context (Bailey, cited in Taylor et al. 1984). And certainly, the profession could apply this knowledge far beyond the domain of depositions.

We hope that the issues we have reviewed here will contribute to increased awareness of the implications of any changes in the civil rules of procedure either to increase or decrease the use of video depositions. Only by taking advantage of available cross-disciplinary insights can we make informed choices for the future.

NOTES

1. For a full report on the instruments and findings of the survey, including statistical cross-tabulations, the authors should be contacted directly.
2. In Arizona, approximately 75 per cent of videotaped depositions done by one deposition service are of medical experts, according to an interview with S. McFate, President, McFate Deposition Service in Phoenix, Arizona (15 August 1989).
3. The cues to deception discussed in this section are applied to juror interpretation with caution because many of the procedures employed in the deception research manipulate lying by giving research

participants instructions to lie, or permit the participants to make up fictitious responses (see Hocking 1976). This situation is fairly far removed from the naturalistic lying taking place in either stenographic or videotaped depositions. Future study using witnesses in deposition setting should lend insight.

SEVEN

Lawyer's response to language constructing law

Margaret O'Toole

The chapters by Maley, Bhatia and others provide valuable insights into features of legal language; such analysis is not widely known among practising lawyers. However, I have responded here mainly to Harris' chapter 'Ideological exchanges in British magistrates courts' because she addresses a subject within my daily experience. I sit as a trial judge, determining questions of fact and law in applications made by workers who claim to have suffered personal injury, arising out of or in the course of employment. On occasions, a litigant appears in person. Workers and witnesses who give oral evidence are predominantly from lower socio-economic backgrounds. Many speak a first language other than English. Frequently their answers to counsel's questions (particularly in cross-examination) are brief and ostensibly compliant.

My response to Harris is made with the understanding that I am furnishing a reader's impression of edited, transcribed extracts from utterances by Magistrates, Defendants and Court Clerks in 'the Arrears and Maintenance Division of a British Magistrates court'. An opportunity to hear and observe the speakers' paralinguistic cues and demeanour might provide other impressions of register and meaning.

My reservations about Harris's chapter arise from two sources. First, I believe she mistakes the primary role of these proceedings, and second, she posits or assumes significant levels of mutual understanding between the exemplified Magistrates or Court Clerks and the Defendants who appeared in person.

In Britain and Australia the judicial system, particularly courtroom proceedings, forms part of a social mechanism comprised of the Legislature, the Executive (including prisons, police, and inspectors), and an independent Judiciary, which seeks orderly dispute resolution. A court does not legislate and it does not enforce the law, it can only interpret and apply the law. Harris and others correctly observe that the structure of court proceedings and language used by judicial officers in the courtroom seek 'to maintain control' over the behaviour of witnesses or parties. However, the only direct control that a court exerts is upon courtroom behaviour. If a court does 'cause a change in the defendant's actual behaviour' outside the courtroom, that is because a party follows a certain course or because law enforcement officers or some other branch of executive government enforce a court's sentence or judgement. Statements by a Magistrate that 'the law says that you pay your fines first' or 'you're becoming a useful citizen [because] . . . you've got a job' articulate judicial encouragement to agree to take a certain course and hence to conclude the court proceedings. Frequently, but by no means invariably, the defendant or a civil litigant will follow the course to which s/he has agreed.

Turning to the issue of mutual understanding, Harris emphasises 'the clear contrast in most instances between the social class of defendants and magistrates' and posits that this contrast is the cause of their 'widely differing perspectives of social reality and the ideological meaning of the situation (in the courtroom)'. She relates 'the manifest nature of power and control . . . exercised primarily as a communication strategy extensively used by lawyers in the questioning of witnesses and defendants' to the social gulf between 'mainly middle-class magistrates and clerks [who] interact with defendants who are predominantly working-class or unemployed'. I assume that Harris' reference to 'social class' includes formal academic education or its absence, but she does not distinguish or give weight to education or other experiences which might provide access to the language of the courtroom.

Utterances of British Magistrates and Court Clerks transcribed by Harris contain many examples of the specialised legal register which is typical of people with some legal or judicial training. Their language in 'Case 1' and 'Case 2' includes the following expressions – *before the court, offences, fined, costs, order to pay* – all of which have a precise legal meaning as well as a meaning in common parlance. There are also phrases such as 'in respect of' which are infrequently used by laymen.

There is ample evidence that such legal language is not fully understood by laymen. Both Maley, and Danet and Bogoch refer to Mellinkoff's (1963) *The Language of the Law*, which identifies nine major characteristics of the language of the law including 'frequent use of formal words . . . deliberate use of words and expressions with flexible meanings . . . frequent use of common words with uncommon meaning'. Mellinkoff (1963) posits that 'the language of the law . . . is a convenient label for a speech pattern with a separate identity'. Dueñas Gonzalez (1977) notes that the vocabulary of the courtroom is so specialised that 'words used in simple hearings never appeared or appeared three times or less in a normal million words of print' (see also *Seltzer v Foley* 502 F. Supp. 600 [1980] @ 603, 606 n.4.). Research by Charrow and Charrow (1979) has demonstrated that standard jury instructions are often incomprehensible to jurors because of the esoteric vocabulary, special grammatical constructions and unusual discourse structures which constitute the distinct 'sub-language' of the courtroom.

Defendants whose utterances are transcribed by Harris could not always therefore be expected to comprehend such language. Consequently, their 'agreement' should be viewed with scepticism and evaluated with caution. Indeed, the Defendant's telling exchange with a Magistrate quoted at the beginning of Harris's chapter articulates (if that word correctly describes the Defendant's difficulty and dilemma) his incomprehension of court and court-related proceedings; his inability to understand and/or communicate with the Magistrate and a law enforcement officer/court official. Similarly the 'Case 1' Defendant's response: '. . . no I realise that' should not be understood to signify comprehension, in context, of a number of esoteric concepts.

The 'Case 2' Defendant is atypical. Despite limited formal education he is unabashed by the judicial process, unusually articulate, assertive and even aggressive. There is also an arguable level of 'congruence' between his and the Magistrate's/ Court Clerk's utterances. Despite those features of the exchange, I would hesitate to ascribe more than limited understanding to the 'Case 2' Defendant. The Defendant's response 'would you in my position' is in the form of a question but is probably a mere denial of the Defendant's intention 'to make an offer', an assertion that he is aggrieved. Similarly, the statement by that Defendant 'well I'll just pay the court a pound annually' is probably an assertion that he is dissatisfied or aggrieved. It is unlikely that he fully appreciated or should be understood to acknowledge the legal force of statements by or on behalf of the Bench (including the lengthy opening statement by the Court Clerk).

In summary, if Harris is correct in asserting that exemplified Defendants who represented themselves before certain British Magistrates exhibited 'perspectives of social reality' which differed widely from those of the Magistrates, it seems to me that those widely different perspectives of social reality derive from *in*comprehension rather than comprehension of lawyers'/ Magistrates' utterances.

As the chapters by Eades and Walsh in Part II illustrate, social disadvantage and culturally determined features of communication have been identified as reasons for Australian Aborigines' discomfiture, compliance, evasiveness, prompt (and often misleading) admission against interest, during court and police procedures. Harris's chapter suggests that the effects of limited education and social disadvantage upon non-indigenous defendants also merit wider recognition.

PART II

LANGUAGE AND DISADVANTAGE
BEFORE THE LAW

Language and disadvantage before the law

John Gibbons

In the introduction to Part I it was argued that the law is primarily designed to control behaviour through a system of penalties for acts of bad faith (through contract law) as well as theft and slander among many others. It follows that, as a system for controlling behaviour, law without justice is a mechanism of oppression, an instrument of power. Indeed by definition, the justice system should preclude this possibility. Nevertheless, the abuses that were perpetrated through the legal system in Eastern Europe during the Stalinist era, and under the Nazis, serve as a powerful reminder of what law without justice can become. Sometimes injustice is deliberately enacted by politicians, with the support of some or most of the population. In other cases it is the result of the way the legal system itself operates. In either case these injustices can involve language as it is used in the law. The price of justice, like freedom, is eternal vigilance. This second part of the collection is concerned with cases where the law is not providing just treatment because of the way it operates; it exposes areas where our vigilance must be exercised in order to prevent injustice.

The concept of justice is a difficult one however – too often it is equated with equal treatment. The difference can be illustrated by an example from education. If we have a class with some gifted children and some intellectually disabled children, we can teach lessons designed for the gifted to all the children. The children will then be receiving strictly equal treatment, because they are receiving the same treatment. The same can be said if we teach all the children lessons designed for the intellectually disabled. In both cases the children are receiving equal treatment, but in neither case are all the children receiving just treatment. In order for the education received by the children to be just, it must maximise their potential, in part by looking at what they bring to the classroom, their starting points. The same is true of just treatment within the law. Simply providing the **same** treatment for everyone within the legal system may not ensure true justice, particularly if that treatment has emerged from the culture and interests of a power élite. Within the language sphere it may be important to recognise that there are people who are disadvantaged by their lack of mastery of the language through which the law is accessed and applied, and/or by the discourse conventions of legal proceedings. The very definition of justice should of course preclude this.

The special characteristics of the legal register which distinguish it from everyday language were discussed in Part I, in particular its syntactic complexity and lexical specialisation. Labov and Harris's chapter in Part II includes an account of the US Steel Case. This case notes evidence from studies of both syntactic complexity and lexical frequency that a particular text produced for legal purposes was in some places very difficult to understand. Linguistic evidence of this sort is important, but it is also essential to demonstrate that the complexity of the text means that the actual readers of the text have difficulties with it. In this case the readers were Black steel workers with low skilled jobs, people who generally suffered from the triple disadvantages of their ethnicity, their limited education and their social class. Labov does a classic piece of applied linguistic work in which he demonstrates that Black working-class people genuinely misunderstood parts of the legal wording, in part as a result of dialect differences between their English and the legal English of the text. This is not a trivial issue since a misunderstanding of the text could have led to them failing to receive just compensation for alleged previous discrimination by their employer. Techniques for examining and demonstrating incomprehensibility of written texts are also demonstrated in the Thornfare Case, where Labov's genius in the development of appropriate methodologies is further illustrated.

In spoken interaction, particularly in the courtroom, the intrinsic difficulty of *understanding* legal language is compounded with the disparities of power discussed in Part I. The discourse conventions of a trial or hearing as a social event include the adversarial system (Maley's chapter also discusses this). In common law systems the prosecution and defence have the task of finding flaws in any evidence which contradicts the picture or 'story' (see Maley's chapter) that they are trying to construct. This involves cross-examination, which can be a most stressful and difficult form of interrogation for those on the receiving end. This adversarial approach, by its very nature, is likely to discredit those who are less articulate in legal language, or easily intimidated. We must remember that the adversarial system involves power disparities compounded with the intrinsic difficulties of legal language – see the chapters of Harris and O'Toole on this issue. In this context, those who are likely to be *less articulate* and to have problems with legal language include: those whose knowledge of the language of the courtroom or police station is less developed – most children and second language speakers; those who speak a different dialect – for example Black English or working-class speakers; and those who are in general less educated in formal registers. People likely to be *intimidated* include the psychologically traumatised, and those who are traditionally less powerful: children, women, recent migrants and oppressed minorities. The complex, power laden and adversarial language of the courtroom is archetypically male, middle class, adult and high proficiency. The chapters in this section and others such as Wodak-Engel (1984) demonstrate clearly that this can produce injustice for those who are traditionally disadvantaged in so many other social spheres – ethnic minorities, children, the deaf, the working class, women and the traumatised (the same could also be said to a lesser degree of police interrogation). A depressing picture, but also a strong call for action by legislators, legal professionals and legal educators.

Brennan's chapter shows very clearly how specific language taken from court interrogations of young children can disadvantage them. Brennan, like Labov does the linguistic analysis to show the sources of incomprehension, and then goes on to test this with young children and demonstrate that they simply do not understand this language. The chapters by Walsh and Eades discuss the manner in which Australian Aborigines are disadvantaged in court proceedings. Walsh's chapter looks at the differing interactive styles of Aborigines and white Australians. Having established possible sources of communicative clash, he uses quotations from the Bench which reveal the Judge's frustration with the breakdown – sufficient evidence of the damage that can be done, and its possible detrimental effect on the Aborigines' case. Walsh also describes 'knowledge economy' in Aboriginal culture – a theme that is picked up by Simpson in Part III, and by Eades. Eades shows that the entire discourse system centred around interrogation in the courtroom is alien to Aboriginal culture, since direct *questioning* of this type is not normally acceptable among Aborigines, and *answers* which contain certain types of information are frequently not permissible in their knowledge economy system. She also discusses intimidatory tactics in both courts and police stations, which may produce false confessions. Discovering the source of problems is the first step – actually addressing them is far more difficult. She suggests two main approaches – some modification in the court system itself, and various means of improving matters while working within the existing system. The main modifications include allowing a 'friend' or supporter to be present during both police and courtroom interrogation (addressing intimidation and fear), and imposing guidelines as to the manner in which interrogation should proceed (addressing the understanding/ articulateness issue). There may be a case for such procedures for other groups such as young children, rape victims and other ethnic minorities. Within the existing system, Eades suggests that there is a need for much more education of legal professionals and police, and the much more frequent use of interpreters, including interpreters of Aboriginal English. Again these prescriptions should apply to other groups that are disadvantaged before the law. The issue of legal interpreting is not a central concern of any of the chapters in this collection, but it is an important consideration in the prevention of disadvantage, as Carroll particularly indicates. Berk-Seligson (1990) provides a penetrating discussion of the need for and difficulties with the use of interpreters in the courtroom.

Labov in his conclusion articulates a basic principle of Applied Linguistics, one that is not always accepted by theoretical and descriptive linguists. This is that the true testing ground for the value of theory is the use to which it can be put. All the cases described by Labov, but in particular the final Prinzivalli case, exemplify forensic linguistics as well as issues of disadvantage before the law, and thus form a bridge into Part III.

EIGHT

Cross-examining children in criminal courts: child welfare under attack

Mark Brennan

THE CONCERN

The language used in criminal courtrooms is at best strange to the uninitiated. The armoury of language strategies deployed during cross-examination is formidable, so much so that participants and observers often comment: 'I can't remember what he said . . . but it didn't sound right.' To not 'get it right' when the witnesses are children, who themselves are the alleged victims of sexual assault, is to be missing something in the administration of justice.

The expressions of concern by professionals working in court and with children are often general and difficult to specify, and this is from people who are trained to listen for meaning. The following comments from an experienced counsellor illustrate this.

> I can't remember exactly the wording he used, but she just looked at him and she didn't know what he meant. I didn't either.

> He put instances to her that she related. Then he said 'Now you can't remember exactly whether he put his penis into your vagina or not, can you?' and then he went on with a similar question. It was almost a threefold question, but before he asked the question he said to her that she only needed to answer by saying 'Yes' or 'No', before he asked the question. The child said afterwards: 'I didn't know what to say. I had to say "Yes" or "No".'

In interviews with paediatricians, counsellors and police we did not achieve any more than these disconnected and general expressions of concern. Even close questioning elicited no more detail. This seemingly uninformed and undetailed information may in fact be a symptom of the pervasive strangeness of courtroom language. During cross-examination this strangeness can alienate the senses, so much so that observers of such court proceedings report incomprehensibility. It may be a symptom of 'feeling for the child'.

In spite of the fact that many workers in the field do not have the tools of linguistic analysis available to them which would make easier the task of describing the strange language of court, they are nevertheless able to cite examples of the inappropriate use of language with child victim witnesses. Their concerns for the alleged victims of child sexual abuse are based partly on their own reactions and partly on the need to pick up the pieces of a child's life after successive court appearances.

A child protection officer offered the following example of her frustration at the treatment of a child under her care. The cross-examining lawyer persisted, in her view, with a line of questioning phrased in strange language which was outside the capacity of the child.

> He kept asking her for dates before the 11th November. The 11th of November meant nothing to her. If he'd said 'after your birthday', which was the 4th of November she might have had a chance. Now, she knows when her birthday is. If he'd asked 'After your birthday did something happen to you?' She would have said 'Yes'. But he just kept on saying 'before the 11th of November'. Well the 11th November meant nothing, but he just kept on asking questions.

TESTING THE CONCERN

The problem becomes one of how to describe and display the distance between the child's language capacities and the language of the courtroom, a distance which, during cross-examination of the child victim witness, inevitably becomes most pronounced. In order to display this distance a testing programme using children unconnected with court was created. These children were asked to repeat a variety of questions.

The basic premise of the test is that if a person can repeat a piece of language (text) then the language, its structure, vocabulary and length are manageable and within the linguistic repertoire of the respondent. If they fail to repeat the text it indicates that there is a mismatch between the speaker and the listener. It is a rare situation to find complete understanding existing between speakers and listeners. However, in the courtroom this difference becomes a critical problem particularly when children are involved as witnesses. Language can be used which makes little or no reference to the developmental and linguistic characteristics of the person being cross-examined. Indeed, it often appears that this language barrier is being exploited for the benefit of the defendant rather than safeguarding the means through which children can best express their knowledge and understanding of what has happened to them.

The graphs in the four figures below represent the responses which children made when asked to reproduce questions presented as a mixed list. Nine children aged between 6 and 15 years are represented, three each of high, middle and low general language ability. The questions they were asked to reproduce were chosen according to the following functions:

1. *Counsellor*: questions from counsellors in counselling situations to children of specifiable ages.
2. *Teacher*: questions from teachers in teaching situations to children of specifiable ages.
3. *Random lawyer*: questions chosen from transcripts of cross-examinations of children, according to a random set of numbers. 200 out of a possible 5,654 were so chosen.
4. *Selective lawyer*: questions chosen from transcripts of cross-examination of children by lawyers according to our own subjective views of what might constitute strange language.

The outstanding features of the graphic summaries here are as follows:

1. *Counsellor* questions in all but one instance were reproduced with *the sense* left intact. Some element of challenge is obvious however, indicated by several instances of single element changes, but which nevertheless were reproduced with the original sense of the question. This is not surprising and indeed is an expected kind of result from an activity designed to include the sensitivities of the respondents to the fullest possible extent. It should be noted here though that we are

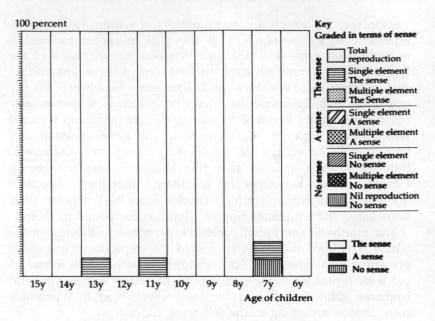

Figure 8.1 Question type – Counsellor

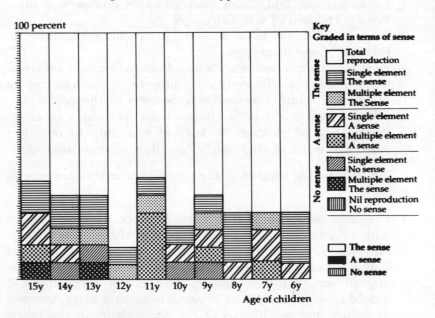

Figure 8.2 Question type – Teacher

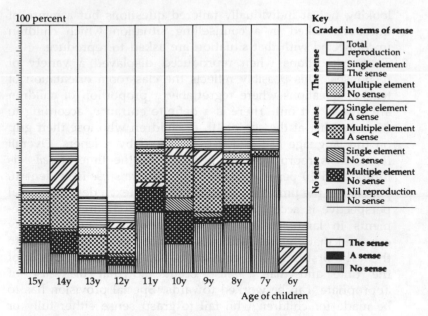

Figure 8.3 Question type – Random lawyer

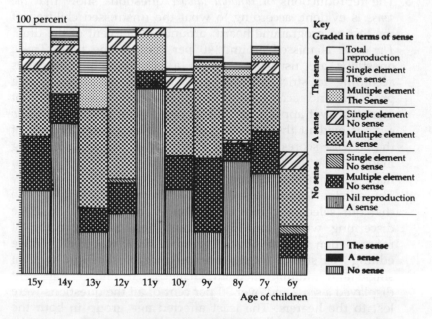

Figure 8.4 Question type – Selective lawyer

looking not at individually tailored questions but a genre of questions asked in a counselling situation which children unconnected with that situation are asked to reproduce.

2. *Teacher* questions when reproduced displayed a variety of responses. This possibly reflects the classroom orientation of teacher questions where regrettably a proportion of children are always left out. There is a definite entrance, according to these results, at the age of 10, of children who lose their grip on the language of the questions asked by teachers. Overall *the sense* is reproduced 80 per cent of the time, *a sense* is reproduced 10 per cent of the time and *no sense* is evident 10 per cent of the time. In an educational context a developmental perspective is acceptable when reviewing children's achievements in language and learning, and it is not generally expected that children will make *the sense* of all that is said to them the first time. It is enough that *the sense* is made most of the time and that *a sense* occurs so that *the sense*, if appropriate, can be worked towards. Special provision has to be made for children who fail to grasp sense either fully or partially.

3. The reproductions of *random lawyer* questions show that *the sense* is evident, according to what the unstressed children of the testing programme heard, around 60 per cent of the time. *The sense* is missed around 40 per cent of the time. These questions are usually asked in a context which operates according to strict rules of procedure aimed at generating precision and accuracy. *A sense*, however sensible, is not acceptable yet appears around 20 per cent of instances and *no sense* is evident the other 20 per cent. The greater amount of the *no sense* scores is due to no attempt at reproduction being made. These questions were not heard well enough to even make a stab at reproducing them.

4. The *selective lawyer* questions show more than anything else that our selective choice of the questions was by and large discerning with some 15 per cent only being capable of reproduction with *the sense*. A third of these required 'creative editing', as shown by the maintenance of sense in spite of single and multiple element changes. Around 30 per cent displayed *a sense* and over 30 per cent of all the questions were lost to the hearers. The least affected age group in both the lawyer selections, it should be noted, were the 6 year olds.

Possibly this indicates an echoic response . . . where their hearing was not impaired by a search for meaning. If nothing else this differential shows clearly the fraility of interpreting in only one way, in only one situation, childrens' responses to questions.

Notwithstanding this, the overall results here, across ages and ability groups, clearly show that the tested children failed to hear certain questions which were chosen from courtroom transcripts, with offensive material edited, in terms of *the sense*, 85 per cent of the time. Across all ages and responding to questions chosen at random from the transcripts *children failed to hear what was said to them 43 per cent of the time*. There is also no clear evidence of any adjustments being made for the age of the children. We shall consider in detail some of the features of these questions in a following section. The actual reasons for a failure to respond can of course be various, ranging from being offended, to being confused, to not being in total possession of the information. Alienation from the language forms where people simply do not comprehend the communicative and message making conventions around them can also define the inability to respond, because they do not hear. We can now move to substantiate the case that in an unacceptably large number of instances a child's inability to hear is because of the strangeness of words and situations. The strangeness is used in cross-examination to deliberate effect and capitalises well on the predispositions of the child victim.

SOME EFFECTS OF QUESTIONS

It is time to recognize that child sexual abuse is not comparable to other types of adult crimes, and should not be investigated as though it were. Children who have been frightened into silence about things they do not comprehend, and may not even have the language to describe, represent a special population that demands specialized approaches.

Questioning a young child about sexual abuse is not comparable to asking a burglary victim to enumerate items that were taken from his or her home. Asking a child what, if anything, unpleasant or unusual happened to him or her during a certain period of time may be an acceptably neutral way of framing a question, but if a young child has been molested and told not to tell, it is unlikely that the abuse will be revealed. Such a child might then become one of the thousands of adults who have reported that they never told anyone as a child because no one ever asked them

(McFarlane et al. 1986)

Questions asked in a way that preclude all but one or two responses are not questions which recognise the condition of the child victim. Questions which require 'Yes' or 'No' in response are insufficient for diagnosis and evaluation in other arenas yet in court, credibility can rise or fall on a series of Yes/No responses. Back in the counselling context Kee McFarlane states '. . . one wants to feel assured that the information is coming from the experience of the child, not from the influence of the interviewer'. Questions asked in cross-examination are aimed at not admitting the experience of the child and attempt to influence the child's response quite deliberately. Whatever the rationalisation for the court procedures they are generally not recognising the needs of the child, or the admissibility of evidence gathered and cross-referenced outside the combative, interrogating context of the courtroom.

What kinds of questions and procedures would enable this to happen? What are the features which distinguish between answerable as opposed to non-answerable questions? A clue to these queries lies in the responses which are less than answers; responses which neither confirm nor deny a proposition and which contain little information. One very common response to questions asked of children during cross-examination is 'I don't know'. This response is not usually acceptable as an answer, as a Yes/No response or one containing information might be. The effect of the response, however, goes beyond a supposed lack of knowledge to create an impression of an unreliable witness, a subtle but profound difference when credibility is at stake. This is illustrated in these two extracts from a transcript.

Q. And where was your mother.
A. I don't know.
Q. You do not know, but she was in the house when you went to bed was she not?
A. I think so.

Q. Yes. Sorry, you think so.
A. Yes.
Q. Can you not remember?
A. Yes.
Q. Where would she have been if she was not in the house?
A. I don't know.
Q. Now can you remember the first incident that something, that you
   say Uncle David interfered with you at Horsley.
A. It was at the Commission house.
Q. Yes, and was, that was in the morning was it not?
A. No.
Q. It was not in the morning?
A. No.
Q. When was it?
A. In the night.
Q. And what time of night?
A. I don't know.
Q. You do not know?
A. No.

The response 'I don't know' can stand for a variety of states of
knowledge but the purpose of cross-examination is well served
as it reduces the credibility of the witnesses: 'learners have
different thresholds for uncertainty and frequent users of "I don't
know" express uncertainty only when they have no idea at all . . .
some learners may tolerate great levels of risk and guess when
the likelihood of a correct response is 50%. Others may choose a
response only if the likelihood is 90%' (Linn 1987). Although
these assertions are in the context of a discussion about
educational testing the point is clearly made that the response 'I
don't know' can be provoked from different people under a
variety of conditions. The conditions of court suggest precision
and total accuracy. Given the language and propositional
conditions of expressions used in court it remains an athletic
exercise to force 'I don't know' or its companion 'I can't
remember' on witnesses.

The following questions come from the cross-examination of a
fifteen year old boy about something which allegedly happened
three years previously.

Just to be clear there is no doubt in your mind, you were assaulted the
first time on the first night on the first occasion? What were you doing

this first night? On the night what were you doing? If I asked you as I have, were you asked to stay at the Patton's you would understand what I ask would you not?

These questions are followed in this particular case with enquiries about details of the behaviour of the witness when he was nine years old. He said 'I can't remember' 53 times. The 'I don't know' or 'I can't remember' response tells us about the style of the question and about the general level of confidence of the respondent who has been instructed to tell only 'the complete truth'. 'I don't know' is often an indicator of uncertainty about the question rather than a total admission of a lack of knowledge about an incident. This concept is compounded by the companion assertion that 'females admit negative feelings such as anxiety more readily than males do.' Also 'An unwillingness to take risks may also lead females to avoid giving definite answers. Not giving an answer has the advantage that it avoids being "right" or "wrong" . . . thus saying "I don't know" provides an alternative to two unpleasant choices' (Linn 1987).

When the situation requires total certainty about multifaceted questions, and where the respondent is vulnerable for a number of reasons, saying 'I don't know' and 'I can't remember' are expected responses. We should not equate this, however, with not knowing and not remembering. The uncertainty many witnesses feel, but which child victims manifest more than most, can be increased in a number of ways, thus increasing their tendency to appear either misinformed or uninformed. Pressure is applied, not upon their evidence, but upon their ability to withstand the volume and style of interrogation. The requirements of what constitutes a good witness for the prosecution are increased for children so that only the most resilient and articulate will be called. The rest of the child population remain as victims. Some of the general characteristics of questions which cross-examination capitalises upon are as follows:

Complexity

Questions can be asked in a variety of ways with some being more difficult to process for the hearer than others. The complexity of any given utterance will depend on the number of connections that have to be made and how those connections are cued. Simple questions can be asked in a complex way. Complex questions make the listener work hard.

Connections

Questions are rarely asked in isolation and, in cross-examination, come one after the other. Ordinary conversation is in part driven by cues and clues about what is coming next and how what we are talking about now is related to something before. The connections between utterances are as vital to their sense as the utterances themselves. Unconnected utterances require constant reorientation.

Volume

Questions require responses and anyone's ability to respond coherently is limited. The sheer volume of questions can make a witness acquiescent and likely to respond in the easiest way possible. The responses may or may not be adequate answers.

Significance

Questions have their own significance depending on what kind of response is required and in what context they are asked. To answer in a variety of ways is a normal predisposition as well as more informative. The singular responses of cross-examination leave a lot of information unsaid.

Questions also have a significance in accordance with what the hearer thinks they are being used for. Questions can be used to search for information. They can indicate the questioner's need to know. They can be used as a format to display evidence. They can also be used as a means of discipline or punishment.

There is a wealth of information available to counsellors and educators about questions and questioning. The tools are available and accessible for the evincing of information. By and large the evidence so gathered is not displayed in court. If the prosecution fails to understand and use such evidence, however, and the Bench does not encourage its use, then the most available avenue for the promotion of a child's welfare in court has been blocked. The maintenance of existing language practices will do nothing to alleviate this.

USING THE POWER OF QUESTIONS

Lawyers are masterful language users. They may not be aware of the intricacies of their language usage at a conscious or descriptive level but they have at their disposal the benefits of fine training in the use and abuse of words, phrases, and structures. Their careers are built on words since these are the currency of the law. They know how to choose their words and structures to gain maximum effect, and they are skilled at using the words of others for their own benefit. In few other contexts are words and their meanings so tightly prescribed. To the child, a relative novice on the continuum of language usage, the distance between the language of the court and their own experiences of how and why language is used must appear immense.

> When do you get a chance to say something . . . I'm only 15 and it's hard for me to try and match their level of talking when you want to put something across. Some of the words they use, the long words that they might use and they (other children) might not even know the meaning of. And yet they sit there and they don't tell you and they expect you to answer.
>
> (15 year old male witness)

There are three conditions which surround the asking of questions in the courtroom. First, the fact that all interactions within the court are conducted on an adversarial basis for often lengthy periods of time will be disconcerting for the child witness. Their past experience of the world of language does not equip them well for this experience. Normal conversations contain a huge array of different language forms, including questions, explanations, expositions, descriptions, and narratives. The court allows only one of these forms, and that is strictly controlled by an established set of procedures. The lawyer asks the questions and the child is expected to respond. There is no provision, as there is in every other facet of communication, for the child to express their concerns, their possible lack of comprehension about the questions, or to negotiate in any way the content or direction of the line of questioning.

Second, because the cross-examiner is a skilled language user, he or she has a keenly developed ability to swap from one style of questioning to another at an often hectic pace. This movement often involves using terms which the child has previously included in her evidence, for instance words related to anatomical parts and descriptions of the details of the assault. This can then be juxtaposed with long, involved and highly formalised questions. The expectation that the child witness can keep in step with these quick changes of language register is unreasonable given their relatively short exposure to the world of language and its subtleties. They simply cannot keep up with the language pace and experience that characterises cross-examination. However, in a more open context or when a child is allowed to move between contexts, children show themselves to be masterful linguists.

Third, questions asked in a courtroom are not asked for the same reasons that questions are asked in the rest of society. Children are generally used to the idea that if someone asks them a question then that person is genuinely interested in hearing their answer. They are not used to questions being asked with the idea in mind that their responses can be manipulated for someone else's benefit, and that the someone else is the alleged offender. The major types of questions which children are asked in court in cases of child sexual assault are aggressively closed in terms of possible responses.

Goody (1987) classifies questions according to two dimensions; whether they seek information or supply it themselves (rhetorical questions), and whether they offer deference or seek to exercise control. Questions that not only seek information but also exercise control include interrogation, riddles, direct examination in the courtroom and school exams. The last two share the characteristic that the examiner knows the answer; but in the courtroom the lawyer wishes to display that answer to the decision maker, whereas in the schoolroom the teacher wants to learn what 'the student knows'.

In cross examination however, the order of the speakers is fixed in advance and whatever else is accomplished interactionally, their discourse must be fitted into the mould of the question answer sequences. This means that in contrast with spontaneous conversation, there is no negotiation over the right to speak or over what may be said.

(Danet 1980)

The results of the testing programme undertaken with thirty children of different language abilities showed that all children had difficulty in hearing certain kinds of lawyer questions and that the degree of the mismatch depended on the type of question asked.

TACTICS AND STRATEGY

The list of language features which are specifically court related is a long one. They are departures from common usage and pose the greatest degree of difficulty for unsophisticated and young language users. The following thirteen features are a sample of a more extensive list.

Use of the negative

Q. Now you had a bruise, **did you not**, near one of your breasts, do you remember that?
A. No.

(Transcript: 12 years)

Juxtaposition (of topics that are not overtly related)

> Q. And then you said he tried to put his finger in your vagina. Did he
>   put his finger on your vagina or in your vagina?
> A. In my vagina, in my vagina.
> Q. Inside, you felt it inside did you?
> A. (No verbal answer.)
> Q. Did he do anything else to you?
> A. No.
> Q. Do you know Frank Murphy?
>
> (Transcript: 14 years)

Frank Murphy has not been mentioned previously, and his identity in the case is not established subsequently.

Nominalisations

> Q. How many times did it happen this **tickling** of the vagina?
>
> (Transcript: 10 years)

Multifaceted questions

> Q. And did your mother ever say to you that if somebody asks you
>   the questions I am asking you, you should say that we didn't say
>   what was going to be said?
>
> (Transcript: 10 years)

Unclear or confused questions

> Q. Well I know, I understand what you say you have been talking to
>   her today but you see what I am asking you is this, that statement
>   suggests that you said those things that you now say are wrong to
>   the police. Now did you say it to the police or did you not?

214 LANGUAGE AND DISADVANTAGE BEFORE THE LAW

A. I don't know.

(Transcript: 10 years)

Specific and difficult vocabulary

Q. You went to, went and got into the car outside your home, I **withdraw** that, **whereabouts in relation to** your home, did you get into the car on this morning?
A. Well on the, when?

(Transcript: 10 years)

Unclear anaphora

Q. Well you are not sure whether you said **those things** to the police which are wrong?
A. Mmm.

(Transcript: 11 years)

It is very difficult, even with the advantage of time for reflection and the printed transcript, to establish exactly what the 'those things', anaphorically referred to in this question, relate to.

Use of police statements

Q. Did you say this that you did not tell that to the police?
A. Yes I told it to her before 'cause I didn't have a chance to tell it to her, I told her . . .
Q. Now just stop there . . .

(Transcript: 11 years)

Quoting of children's words

Q. Remember that you told us before the lunch break that you had never been out with Martin before this particular day, 8th of

November, do you remember saying that, before lunch, do you
remember or do you not?

A. No.

(Transcript: 10 years)

Children frequently have difficulties when they are asked to
comment on what can be termed a metalinguistic assertion.

Quoting of other people's words

Q. I put it to you that those conversations on the Monday and
Tuesday that I have spoken to you about he said to you 'I am
working'. What do you say to that?

(Transcript: 11 years)

Repetition of previous response

Q. And is that because of what you have told us that he threatened
to, not just bash you but bash, I think your words, all of you?

A. The family.

Q. The family?

(Transcript: 12 years)

Q. December last year, and was that a weekend or a weekday?

A. I can't remember.

Q. Cannot remember. Were the circumstances much the same then as
they were on this last occasion can you remember?

A. Yes, it was the same just about every time.

(Transcript: 8 years)

Time, space and location questions in cases of multiple assault

Q. I'm sorry, you might not understand me, the first time and then
it's finished, **how long until the next time** that your father put his
penis in your vagina?

(Transcript: 7 years)

Embeddings

> Q. Would it be incorrect to suggest that it was not so much a tripping but because of the state of inebriation of yourself, that you fell over?
>
> (Transcript: 15 years)

ABUSED AGAIN

In a combative arena where the format for questions is determined solely by the questioner who is also the more sophisticated and skilled language user, inequalities in language usage and expertise must confer lower status on the respondent. Any confused responses given by the child, the inevitable tearful and emotional breakdowns, and any examples of conflicting information offered, all confirm the child's lack of credibility within the corporate mind of the court. The fact that this credibility gap has been partially created by a language mismatch between the lawyer and the child witness is either tacitly acknowledged as acceptable practice, since it is permitted to perpetuate itself, or it is an issue which has fallen outside the province of those concerned with the administration of justice.

Whatever the reason, the fact remains that the credibility of the child witness is systematically destroyed by a combination of language devices and questioning styles. For the child who has asked for help and protection, to allow lawyers to use the full weight of the role of 'accuser', and thereby make the child fair game for attack, is not an acceptable construction for either welfare or justice.

NOTE

This material is based on a larger working paper, Brennan and Brennan (1988), available from the Centre for Teaching and Research in Literacy, Charles Sturt University, Wagga Wagga, New South Wales, Australia.

NINE

Interactional styles in the courtroom: an example from northern Australia

Michael Walsh

INTRODUCTION

My intention here is to indicate that differing interactional styles provide a basis for understanding the disadvantage that Australian Aborigines can suffer in Australian legal settings. I want to draw out two sets of features and show how these can be used to characterise some of the differences between the interactional styles of Aborigines in remote Aboriginal communities and of certain non-Aborigines. I will treat this latter group as being Anglo white middle class (henceforth AWMC). I make no apologies for restricting the group in this way: for better or worse it is the group that has come to exercise the greatest influence on remote Aboriginal communities and, as a member of it, it is the group I am most familiar with.

My understanding of interactional styles is based on fieldwork[1] I have carried out in various communities in Aboriginal Australia. With the exception of a brief period in South Australia my research has been confined to northern Australia and the bulk of that focused on Aboriginal groups on the west coast of the Northern Territory.

My conclusions about interactional styles draw mostly on long-term exposure to these particular groups but I feel reasonably confident that those results can be extended to other traditionally orientated Aboriginal people. In the next section I briefly lay out the background to interactional styles at Wadeye, the Aboriginal community I know best and one that I would argue is representative of most others in northern Australia. In the third section I propose a framework for comparing interactional styles. I then briefly sketch the differing ideologies held by the two

217

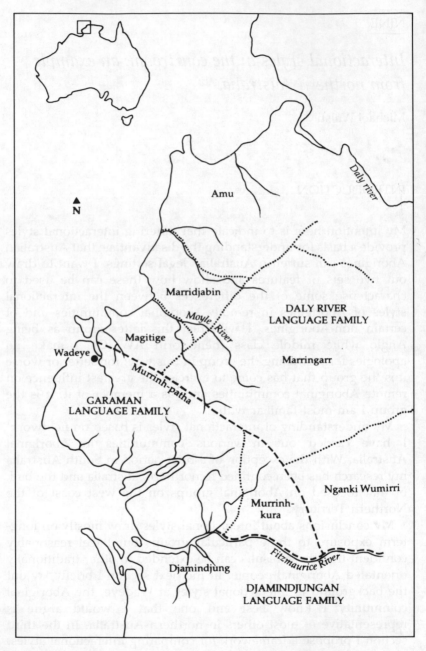

Figure 9.1 Languages and language families
(*Source:* from Street 1987)

cultures with regard to knowledge. The implications of these differences for legal situations are put forward in the section on 'Consequences in the courtroom'. In 'Solutions and prospects' I point out some of the difficulties in extending this framework to other situations in Aboriginal Australia and suggest how it might be related to situations elsewhere in the world.

INTERACTIONAL STYLES AT WADEYE

Background

Wadeye is a township of around 1500 people located on the west coast of the Northern territory. Apart from a small number of European support staff the population is entirely Aboriginal. Wadeye (formerly known as Port Keats) was set up as a Catholic mission in 1935 and became a township governed by its own Aboriginal Council in the 1970s. Like most such 'Aboriginal towns' in northern Australia, multilingualism is the norm (see, for example, Brandl and Walsh 1981). The most prominent Aboriginal language spoken there is Murrinh-Patha, which has become the local *lingua franca*. (For details of the language situation at Wadeye, see Walsh forthcoming.)

Styles of verbal interaction

Newcomers to Wadeye are often puzzled by the frequent lack of eye contact in conversations. 'How can you talk to someone without looking at them?' Of course Aboriginal people at Wadeye do have one-on-one conversations in which the interlocutors are facing each other but what impresses the newcomer is what seems so obviously different. People not only have conversations in which they do not look at each other – they do not even face each other.

As a starting point for considering interactional styles let me picture a few scenes from a remote Aboriginal community.

1. A group of men is sitting on a beach facing the sea. They are there for some hours and little is said. After a long period of silence someone says: 'Tide's coming in.' Some of the group murmur 'Yes' but most remain silent. After another very long pause someone says 'Tide's coming in'. And there is some scattered response. This happens many times until someone says: 'Must be tide's going out.'

2. A group of adults is sitting near a campfire while small children are present. The adults talk from time to time but for the most part are silent. The children chatter and yell almost continuously talking over the top of the adult conversation. One child throws a tantrum and yells so loudly that the adults have to raise their voices to be heard. Another child is banging the side of a nearby car with a stick while a number of adults say numerous times 'Leave it alone', 'Go away' . . .; the child doesn't stop. An old man sitting a little distance off playing with a kitten has been silent most of the time but responds to a joke made by one of the adults by laughing and saying 'Oh yes'.

3. A town meeting has been called. A government AWMC has flown in from Darwin and is addressing the crowd. While he talks for about twenty minutes some members of the audience are also conversing. Their talk is sporadic and only partly related to what the AWMC has to say. At the end of his address the AWMC asks for an opinion of his proposal. Some people say 'Yes'.

In each scene there are many potential participants in talk but only a few actually choose to verbalise. For the most part people do not face each other directly: the group of men at the beach sits in a row side by side; in the town meeting some of the people are turned away from the 'main' speaker. In each scene talk will overlap: the children talk over the adults' conversation; at the town meeting the local people talk occasionally at the same time as the AWMC is talking continuously. At the beach and in the camp talk is sporadic, there are relatively long periods of silence between snatches of talk. It is only the AWMC at the town meeting who talks 'non-stop' for twenty minutes.

Characterising talk

To characterise this talk we need to consider (at least) two factors: the relationship between the participants and the way in which the communication channel (talk) is used.

Regarding the relationship between participants I would say that the overwhelming tendency is for AWMC to 'talk in twos' while for Aborigines in remote communities this requirement is relaxed. When I say 'talk in twos' I do not mean that all conversations are one-on-one but that there is an AWMC ideology that one should direct one's talk to another specific individual. Public speakers are advised to let their eyes rove over the audience and to make eye contact with as many people as possible. A public speaker's success is measured, in part, by the extent to which each member of the audience feels that the speaker is talking directly to him/her. It is also a part of AWMC conversational strategy that each individual should be 'included' in the conversation; it is a failed conversation or even a rebuff if someone has been 'left out' of the talk.

By contrast in an Aboriginal conversation people will sometimes project bits of talk to no particular individual and there need not be any direct response. None of the men at the beach are even facing each other when they occasionally pronounce on the movements of the tide. In this situation bits of talk are 'broadcast' and it is up to the hearers whether they react to it explicitly. The old man playing with the kitten was 'tuned in' to the 'broadcast' talk at the camp in that he was able to react to one part of it: the joke. But for the most part this old man exercised his rights as a listener to say nothing at all. In an AWMC conversation it is a matter of comment and even concern for a member of the group not to join in at all. In AWMC conversations it is the speaker who exercises most control while in the Aboriginal conversation it is the listener who has more control in that he/she can take up the option to talk at will. Collectively I will refer to these differences as dyadic (for AWMC) vs non-dyadic (for remote Aboriginal communities). In summary:

dyadic   (an ideology of talking in twos)
           talk is directed to a particular individual
           people should face each other
           eye contact is important
           control by the speaker

non-dyadic   talk is broadcast
people need not face each other
eye contact not important
control by the hearer

Of course AWMC interactions *can* involve lack of eye contact and people do not *always* face each other. Usually this is because of high intimacy (e.g. between spouses) or because one or other of the interlocutors is involved in an activity that 'excuses' their otherwise strange behaviour (e.g. talking to someone while facing a computer screen, while in another room or while rummaging through the innards of an engine). But it is clear that this kind of interaction is regarded as some kind of 'abnormality'. People will say: 'Leave what you're doing and let's talk'; 'If you want to talk let's get so we can see each other.'

The other crucial factor in characterising talk is the way in which the communication channel is used. In my understanding the strong tendency in Aboriginal conversations is to turn the communication channel (talk) on and leave it on; it is *continuous*. By contrast AWMC conversation is relatively non-continuous: talk is packaged into discontinuous bits. For an AWMC the only (polite) way to disengage oneself from a conversation is to terminate the whole conversation (Look I can't talk now; I've got to go, etc.) or to suspend it temporarily (Hang on, that's the kettle; I've just got to take a . . .). In the Aboriginal setting where the listener has more control, members of the group can tune in and tune out of the ongoing (continuous) communication at will.

This conversational strategy in remote Aboriginal communities is determined in part by the built environment. Life in most remote Aboriginal communities is lived in full public view. Until the arrival of the whites there were scarcely any buildings and therefore no rooms to retreat to in order to gain privacy.[2] Even the most intimate bodily functions could be guessed at if not actually witnessed. One person going off into the nearby bush suggests one activity; a man and his wife, another. But for an individual to spend long periods of time alone is almost inconceivable. 'That person would be too lonely!'

The very notion of privacy is fundamentally different. For an AWMC person it makes sense to say 'I want to be alone'; 'I'm going to go off by myself now' because AWMC puts a high value on personal privacy. The built environment reflects this concern with spaces which can be closed off to anyone else and which can be specialised for particular functions: the study; the euphemistically named bathroom; the bedroom, and so on. Indeed, the value placed on personal privacy among AWMC seems to be escalating. Why should such a system evolve? The particular pattern of interaction can be viewed as a coping strategy: it enables an individual to opt for privacy but preserve the option to re-engage at any time. Since there are no suitable means of using the built environment to ensure personal privacy the members of the remote Aboriginal community manipulate the pragmatic environment keeping the communication channel continually open but only directly engaging when it is appropriate or when they choose to. For AWMC by contrast the communication channel is 'switched off' explicitly: 'I can't talk now; I've got to go now; we'll talk about this later'. When it is 'switched back on' it is typically in a one-on-one interaction. It is the non-dyadic, broadcast technique which allows an individual to engage: not at all; minimally ('Mmm', 'Yeah', etc.); or with more or less directness.

A FRAMEWORK FOR COMPARING INTERACTIONAL STYLES

The variables I have proposed (dyadic v. non-dyadic; continuous v. non-continuous) intersect. In applying these distinctions I think one can generalise to most remote Aboriginal communities from the specific communities with which I am familiar.

The intersection of these variables provides four possibilities:

dyadic and continuous
dyadic and non-continuous
non-dyadic and continuous
non-dyadic and non-continuous

Two of these possible combinations characterise the situations outlined above where there is a particular kind of community which is associated with a particular language:

dyadic and non-continuous   AWMC (English)
non-dyadic and continuous   Wadeye (Murrinh-Patha)

The other two possible combinations characterise situations that I would regard as marginal in relation to whole communities:

dyadic and continuous
non-dyadic and non-continuous

The first of these suggests a conversational style where the communication channel is 'switched on' and left on (continuous) and at the same time talk is one-on-one. This might happen in situations of high intimacy as between spouses but it is hard to see how it could be maintained across the community. On the other hand, a conversational style which is non-dyadic and non-continuous means that the speaker is not directing his/her talk to anyone in particular (non-dyadic) but at the same time the talk is compartmentalised into discrete chunks (non-continuous). To me this suggests extreme remoteness even to the extent of indicating some kind of conversational pathology. In summary:

	continuous	non-continuous
dyadic	EXTREME INTIMACY	LOW REMOTENESS English
non-dyadic	LOW INTIMACY Murrinh-Patha	EXTREME REMOTENESS

I am suggesting that these variables complement each other in such a way that only certain combinations are suitable for the communicative requirements of whole communities. The other combinations are in a sense marginal. An intersection of variables in which the conversational style is both dyadic and continuous is too intense while a conversational style which is neither dyadic nor continuous does not provide sufficient opportunity for members of the community to engage with each other. What is needed, I suggest, is a mixture of these variables and these mixtures involve opposing values of the variables. The particular combinations of the variables I have proposed are at once opposing and complementary and this has significant implications for cross-cultural communication.

KNOWLEDGE ECONOMY IN ABORIGINAL AUSTRALIA

Within a society one of the most important features of the economy is the view of property. For AWMC the focus is usually on material property of some kind. In Aboriginal Australia the predominant emphasis is on intellectual property. Let me give one example: within any culture there will be particular words/ key concepts which are multi-layered in meaning. What is particular to an Aboriginal society is the gradual admission to the innermost layers of knowledge about these words. This is unlike AWMC where sufficient persistence and access to appropriate library resources will enable one to uncover just about all there is to know about a word. By contrast some notions only become clear after a lifetime of gradual progression through ritual and this hard-won knowledge is jealously guarded. Von Sturmer 1987: 11–12 explains that access to knowledge is restricted as is the right to divulge it:

> The gender, age and other specifications of knowledge in Aboriginal societies are well-attested. For example, one scholar Michaels (1985). . ., calls Aboriginal societies 'information societies' by which he means that the dissemination of information is tightly controlled and hedged about with restrictions. This creates an 'information economy'.
> This perspective tends to focus on the information as such, and on the controls to which it is subject. It pays less attention to the modes and contexts of its appearances; that is, on how and when it is performed – as narrative performance, song performance, ritual performance, and so on. We are aware of divisions between 'women's business' and 'men's business'; and between the old men 'who know' and the young men who do not. But it would be naive to assume, on the basis of these classifications, that men are entirely ignorant of women's business, and so on. It is not a question of knowing; it is a question of who is entitled to display or perform the knowledge. Such entitlements are culturally determined (though in more complex ways than classifications of knowledge into male/female, old/young, etc., would suggest) and legitimated.

In order to assess responses properly both in day-to-day interaction and courtroom situations it is clearly necessary to understand this knowledge system in advance. Hesitancy, awkwardness, embarrassment, even unwillingness to respond cannot be taken as evidence necessarily of ignorance.

CONSEQUENCES IN THE COURTROOM

The courtroom imposes strict rules on the use of talk. When the judge arrives everyone is expected to stop talking. This expectation is sometimes made explicit by the ritualistic cry of the bailiff: 'Silence in the court!' Otherwise talk is to be kept to a minimum and should be carried out as quietly as possible. The sanctioned talk belongs to the main players: the judge and the lawyers, and, whoever is directed by them: court staff and witnesses. Perhaps more so than any other speech situation which is not inherently repetitious (like a religious ceremony or a play) talk is strictly regimented. Only one person may talk at any one time and turntaking is strictly hierarchical. Interjections do not detract from this summary position. Interjections have to conform to particular rules and are in sharp contrast to interruptions which are policed by court staff and, if regarded as sufficiently serious, penalised.

Of course a number of people have commented on the problems that can arise when Aborigines appear in a courtroom setting. Some have been legal practitioners like Kriewaldt 1960–62, Coldrey and Vincent 1980 or Neate 1981 (see also Neate 1989). Others have drawn on their immersion in Aboriginal culture over many years, for example, Elkin 1947; Liberman 1981; Eades 1982, (forthcoming) and this volume, Koch 1985, 1991; and McKay 1985. Inevitably there is a tendency to focus on features of grammar, vocabulary and pronunciation as areas where communication problems may arise. While these matters are important, pragmatic features create more insidious problems precisely because they are often less obvious. Eades 1982, in looking at information seeking among certain Aborigines in and around Brisbane, and Liberman 1981, 1985, and Eades this volume in considering such issues as 'gratuitous concurrence' among Western Desert Aborigines, have gone some way toward making these issues more explicit. In this chapter I want to develop a pragmatic framework which can be generalised from one Aboriginal group to another, have relevance for a wide range of communication problems and have implications for cross-cultural communication in general. The framework proposed above can be illustrated by looking at problems of interaction for legal purposes in the context of a traditional Aboriginal land claim.

In the Northern Territory of Australia, traditional Aboriginal land claims provide a relatively new setting in which Aborigines interact with the law. Over the last fifteen years a series of hearings have been held to determine which Aboriginal people should be found to be 'traditional Aboriginal owners' of certain areas of land in the Northern Territory. Aboriginal groups may put forward a claim under the terms of the *Aboriginal Land Rights (Northern Territory) Act 1976* to areas of unalienated Crown land. Land claims are prepared on behalf of the Aboriginal claimants by Land Councils set up under the Act. Researchers prepare extensive documentation on the details of how the claimant group relates to the land in question: the extent and composition of the group; the nature of their rights to the land; their knowledge of the land in terms of named locales and their spiritual significance and so on. Lawyers then present the case for the claimants in a hearing before the Aboriginal Land Commissioner taking evidence from the Aboriginal witnesses as well as arguing points of law. There are other parties who have interests in the land under claim and they are usually represented by lawyers, one of the chief protagonists being the Northern Territory Government. Evidence is taken from these other parties and from the claim researchers.

The hearing differs in a number of ways from the usual encounters that Aborigines in northern Australia have with the law. Most often Aboriginal people will deal with the local police whom they know quite well or with a magistrate in the local community courts that are held from time to time. The land claim hearing differs from such encounters in that it is more informal and less focused on just one individual.

At the same time it introduces into the local community a sizeable addition of new people. The judge arrives with a Counsel Assisting, a consultant anthropologist, an Associate and a sound recordist. The Northern Territory Government is represented by a number of lawyers (a solicitor and at least one barrister), anthropologists and observers. The Northern Land Council team includes a number of lawyers, anthropologists and general staff to handle the considerable logistical problems of mounting a claim. The community is likely to be small, perhaps a couple of hundred people, and quite isolated so that ordinary necessities of life like food and shelter must be brought along. It is part of the hearing process that all the interested parties should go to places in the claim area and take evidence *in situ*. This entails convoys of vehicles proceeding along rough bush tracks to remote areas with the attendant difficulties of frequent flat tyres and the occasional breakdown. It is a far cry from the relatively straightforward process of a single police prosecutor charging an individual of drunk and disorderly behaviour before a magistrate.

The context of the hearing introduces much more ambiguity into the respective roles of the parties concerned. The Aboriginal people are not always aware who is the judge, who are the lawyers or even why the questions are being asked! In other legal contexts the range of players is much reduced and the interaction unfolds in a specialised place: the courtroom. Ironically the attempt to make the setting of the hearing more informal may result in a clash of interactional styles.

Examples of this kind of clash can be provided from the Kenbi Land Claim which concerns land close to Darwin and was heard in 1989–90. Early in the proceedings there were some complaints from barristers representing non-claimants' interests because those lawyers felt that Aboriginal witnesses were not following appropriate procedure. A number of Aboriginal people had responded simultaneously to a question put by the barrister representing their interests. The judge commented:

> I do not think taking evidence ought to be conducted as a public meeting, and if the evidence is to be meaningful at all, it ought to be precise and attributed to particular witnesses.
> (Australia. Aboriginal Land Commissioner. 1989 – Kenbi Transcript
> p. 149)

As a result each of many Aboriginal witnesses had to be asked the same question in turn. This approach satisfied the conventions of the hearing but seemed quite strange to the Aboriginal people involved.

Accommodating to Aboriginal preferences was also less than straightforward. The standard procedure in a courtroom is to call on an individual, take that person's evidence in full (if possible) and then move on to the next witness. In a land claim hearing there are visits to sites which require a modified procedure. It is simply impractical to provide the usual arrangements to be found in a courtroom: judge's bench; bar tables; witness box, fixed microphones and so on. It was important to the Aboriginal people involved to talk about the places while they were there. On the other hand, members of the legal profession may have preferred to keep this kind of evidence taking to a minimum:

> HIS HONOUR: I appreciate that some witnesses feel more comfortable sitting on the ground, and talking and shouting from a distance. *I find that less than satisfactory* [my emphasis], and that it is not so easy for those of us who have to listen to, understand and comprehend what is being said. And I would have thought that after having obtained a little bit of familiarity with the people concerned and the sort of questions that are going to be asked, that the evidence which is not specifically site related ought to perhaps be deferred until we are back at the main hearing place.
>
> In saying that *I do not, in any way, wish to interfere with the presentation of the case by the claimants* [my emphasis], I have always adopted the view that the claimants' counsel is in charge of how he wishes to present the case. But from the point of view of the comfort and general facility of the rest of us involved, if perhaps those points can be taken into consideration.
> (Australia. Aboriginal Land Commissioner. 1989 – Kenbi Transcript
> p. 246)

There is a genuine difficulty here. On the one hand, the judge wants to see that the claimants' case is put in a way that suits them and their counsel. On the other hand, particular conduct may stand in the way of a full understanding of the case.

A land claim hearing can also bring out the particular stance taken by Aboriginals in divulging information. During cross-examination one Aboriginal witness was extremely reluctant to reveal information restricted in Aboriginal law (referred to locally as 'inside stuff'):

> I am in a position where I prefer not to talk about the insight [sic] stuff that I was talking about at Bakamanadjing. I prefer not to talk about that. I would rather somebody like Johnny B. [a senior ceremonial authority in this area] do the speaking if anything had to be said. That is my position now.
> (Australia. Aboriginal Land Commissioner. 1990 – Kenbi Transcript
> p. 2436)

He believed that he and his family could become seriously ill if certain information were revealed. His statement followed on from fairly extensive cross-examination during which the barrister for the Northern Territory Government pressed the point time and again:

Well, you might prefer not to, but I would ask you to tell me, please?
(Kenbi Transcript p. 2428)

and the judge became frustrated with the witness's failure to respond:

HIS HONOUR: Well, can I just say this, Mr B__, that – all this mystery that is associated with this particular item does not add to the credibility of your witness – your evidence. If – if there is something you have said – there is something that should not have been heard by – did not want to be heard by certain people – you are not prepared to identify the people – the only conclusion I can take – make – is that I ought not to give that evidence any weight. . . . If you wish to – your evidence – that aspect of your evidence to be given any weight and taken notice of, I think you are going to have to identify who it is. So, it is your choice. I am not going to order you to give the names, but if you do not we will just go on with the next point and ignore what you have said. . . . Mr B__, I must just say to you that what you have said today, and what you have said on other occasions, that I am inclined to the opinion that you have made up your own rules as you have gone along with this information. Now, you have told us there was – somebody told you something, someone else told you something, and you are inclined to add some mystical element to it by making your own determination as to who should hear it and who should not, and I must say that that sort of approach is completely unhelpful from my point of view, in that I have to come to certain conclusions after the hearing of this – this material, and your reluctance to be frank about an issue that you raised yourself, is completely unhelpful to the case that you are trying to support. But, anyhow, I am not going to make any order that you disclose the evidence – the names – if – if for some reason you do not want to, but it certainly is not helping your case by taking that attitude.
(Kenbi Transcript pp. 2429–30)

It is just one example of 'knowledge economy' and it's consequences in a legal setting.

The legal practitioners involved in land claim hearings are

often quite experienced in dealing with people from remote Aboriginal communities. For example, one of the Aboriginal Land Commissioners has remarked (Maurice 1988: para. 2.21.2):

> The witnesses from several Groups . . . suffered, at least so far as the evidence they gave in open hearing was concerned, from a number of communication difficulties engendered by the questioner's unfamiliarity (my own included) with the non-standard English spoken by them, by situational difficulties such as the structured (though informal) conduct of the hearing – particularly the question-and-answer format – and by socially and culturally dictated constraints on their behaviour, e.g. knowing the answer to a question but not having the right to know it or not having the right to say so in front of someone senior to them.

But there is a strong tendency to revert to the interactional style with which one is most familiar. Aboriginal witnesses are wont to launch into a monologue when the barrister wants to chop the discourse up into a linked series of questions and answers in which the questions have been carefully pre-arranged. From the Aboriginal perspective this approach jars: they are more comfortable with a non-dyadic continuous delivery. There is also a desire on the part of the barrister to ask much the same questions of a series of witnesses in order to establish that the witnesses share certain knowledge. This approach proceeds from the fundamentally different 'knowledge economy' that underlies the interactants.

SOLUTIONS AND PROSPECTS

One of the fundamental prerequisites in solving problems is to understand more fully the nature of the problem. In this chapter I have indicated that a significant reason for communication problems in a courtroom setting is a fundamental difference in interactional styles between Aborigines from remote communities and AWMC. Added to this a difference in the 'knowledge economy' of the two groups such that AWMC courts can mistakenly assume ignorance on the part of an Aboriginal person when it may be that the person simply does not have the right to divulge the information. Both factors contribute to disadvantage for Aboriginal people in legal settings.

These factors have a broader application. The arena of education is an obvious one in that AWMC teachers rely, even if unconsciously, on a dyadic, non-continuous approach in the classroom while their Aboriginal pupils have been socialised into a non-dyadic, continuous interactional style. Not surprisingly traditional Aboriginal education adopted this format and the opposing style used by AWMC teachers (and assumed as being appropriate in teacher training) creates considerable difficulties in the classroom. The jarring of interactional styles has unfortunate consequences, too, for the numerous meetings and negotiations which Aborigines must now participate in to gain access to AWMC goods and services. Having identified some of the problems the next step is to design some kind of intervention which can alleviate it.

More generally, the framework to distinguish the interactional styles of remote Aboriginal communities and AWMC can presumably be extended to other parts of Australia and to other parts of the world. There are a number of questions to be considered within Australia. One is the extent to which the speakers of the widespread English-based creoles used over vast areas of northern Australia by Aboriginal and Torres Strait Islander people use one or the other interactional style. Given that the creoles are a linguistic amalgam of English and local languages in terms of linguistic form it is intriguing to consider whether the pragmatic features are also an amalgam. This in turn leads to the question of whether the framework I have set up should be viewed in terms of continua rather than as categorical features. Finally,[3] consideration should be given to the applicability of the framework to Aboriginal people in urban settings.

NOTES

1. The bulk of my fieldwork experience in Aboriginal Australia has been focused on the west coast of the Northern Territory, mainly at Wadeye, Belyuen and the town camps of Darwin. I have also carried out shorter periods of fieldwork in northern Queensland, the Kimberleys, rural New South Wales and South Australia. For

financial assistance for some of this fieldwork my thanks to the
Australian Institute of Aboriginal Studies. For my limited under-
standing of Aboriginal Australia my sincere gratitude to my
Aboriginal teachers for their diligence and patience.

2. The Aboriginal handling of privacy has been referred to by a number
of observers, in particular Eades 1988: especially 105–6.
3. I gratefully acknowledge the help of the following people who read
earlier drafts of this chapter or responded to the ideas contained in it
and offered advice and suggestions: Diana Eades, Bill Foley, John
Gibbons, Nerida Jarkey and Jeff Siegel.

TEN

A case of communicative clash:
Aboriginal English and the legal system

Diana Eades

INTRODUCTION

Police and courtroom interviews are highly structured speech
events, in which *questions* and their *answers* are fundamental.
⎡Any chance of equality before the law requires specific communicative competence in understanding and answering questions.⎦ But not all speakers of English use questions in the same
way. In fact, most Aboriginal speakers of English are seriously
disadvantaged by the legal communicative system, because of
important and on-going differences between modern Aboriginal
and non-Aboriginal societies in Australia. This chapter examines
these cultural and linguistic differences, and their role in the
Aboriginal experience of the criminal justice system. Examples
from current fieldwork in this area are used to highlight
communicative clash, and the resulting difficulties in effective
delivery of justice for Aboriginal people. The chapter goes on to
examine a number of developments which seek to address this
communicative disadvantage and consequent legal inequality. In
conclusion, this chapter raises suggestions for changes and opens
discussion for further developments.

The situation of Aboriginal people in Australian law has
received considerable attention in the last few years, and with
the release of the final report of the Royal Commission into
Aboriginal Deaths in Custody in 1991, it will undoubtedly be
placed further under the spotlight. The extreme overrepresentation of Aboriginal people in the courts and the prisons is well
known (see for example Hazlehurst 1987; RCADC 1988, 1991).
Figures released by the Royal Commission in June 1989 indicate
that Aboriginal people are jailed at twenty times the rate of non-
Aboriginal Australians (*The Australian*, 29.6.89). It is now

painfully clear that there is something very wrong in the relationship between Aboriginal people and the legal system.

It would be naive of me, and outside my expertise, to attempt to address this question in any comprehensive way. A few of the areas which are outside of my scope here are racism towards Aboriginal people by the community generally, and by people within the police force and the judiciary specifically. My own observations in two states in recent years reveal a number of instances including the following (see also Foley 1984; McCorquodale 1987; RCADC 1991):

> In a NSW country town, during a hearing which did not involve any Aboriginal people, a magistrate talking about the difficulties and fear experienced by a taxidriver, said: 'He took four people in his cab, from the hotel late at night – including three Aborigines – out of town.' The magistrate made it clear that it was a braver deed to take Aboriginal passengers than non-Aboriginal passengers, when picking up people from a hotel.

> During an informal conversation I was having with a North Queensland magistrate about Aborigines and the law, the magistrate summed up his view: the real problem now with Aboriginal people in the north is that people from Brisbane tell them their rights.

Racism is only one of a number of factors contributing to the current tragedy of the relationship between Aboriginal people and the law. But more than this, as Bird points out (1987: 62), 'until [the] fundamental problem [of the legacy of the dispossession and colonisation of Aboriginal people] is addressed . . . Aborigines will continue to be overrepresented in the criminal justice system.'

This chapter, however, will focus on one area which I argue is central to this whole issue of the experience of Aborigines in the Australian system of law – namely the area of language and communication. A brief explanation of this scope is required: I use language in the sociolinguistic and anthropological sense to mean not just the utterances spoken, but also their meanings. To examine utterances involves studying sounds, as well as words, and the structure of sentences and larger chunks of discourse. To examine their meanings necessarily involves studying the relationship between utterances and their speakers, as well as the culture of speakers. [Culture can be defined as the knowledge which individuals need to function as members of their society, and as this chapter will show, to understand language it is necessary to understand culture.] It is also important to realise that different groups of people who seem to speak the same language in terms of utterances may differ in terms of culture, and thus in terms of certain meanings.

This chapter examines aspects of the communicative clash between Aboriginal and non-Aboriginal Australians which occurs daily in police stations, lawyers' offices, and courtrooms, even where all participants are speakers of varieties of English. I will show how this fundamental clash is between two very different cultures – contemporary Aboriginal culture, and non-Aboriginal Australian culture, specifically the subculture of the law. We will see that Aboriginal speakers of English are disadvantaged before the law because of significant differences in language use. My most detailed studies are on courtroom interaction, but other aspects of the legal process are also involved, and will be referred to where possible.

The complexity of legal language has long been recognised and discussed (see Maley, Bhatia this volume). Recent work by linguists and discourse analysts points to some of the specific linguistic and discourse features of the language of the law, such as unusual prepositional phrases (Charrow and Charrow 1979), unclear anaphora[1] (Brennan, this volume), and the specific turn-taking conventions in court (Atkinson and Drew 1979).

A number of writers have shown that witnesses are frequently disadvantaged by their lack of experience in dealing with this register or dialect of the law. [Wodak-Engel (1984)] goes further than this with a pilot study of courtrooms in Vienna, which concludes that ['justice relates to class and that language is evidently a significant factor in establishing or verifying class-related prejudices'] (p. 97). But this paper addresses a more fundamental area of the language of the court, and its effect on Aboriginal English speaking participants. Because, before we look at linguistic strategies specific to the courtroom (such as unclear anaphora, or specialised vocabulary), we must address basic communication strategies underlying any interaction, which differ between Aboriginal and non-Aboriginal speakers of English today.

Aboriginal English

Aboriginal English is the name given to varieties of English, spoken by Aboriginal people, which are largely mutually intelligible with Standard English. The differences are systematic and rule-governed, and they occur in all areas of the language: phonology (sound system), morphology and syntax (grammar), lexicon (vocabulary), semantics (the meanings of words and sentences), and pragmatics (the use and meaning of language in context).

Exact numbers of speakers of Aboriginal English are not available, but it is clear from the 1986 Census that the great majority of Aboriginal people speak some variety of English. In the census, only 3.4 per cent reported that they spoke no English at all, while over 76 per cent of Aborigines in Australia reported that they spoke only English. We have no information on how many of these people spoke varieties of Aboriginal English, rather than Standard Australian English, or other non-Standard non-Aboriginal varieties of Australian English. However, my belief is that the great majority of Aboriginal speakers who reportedly speak English, in fact speak a variety of Aboriginal English.

Recent studies (e.g. Kaldor and Malcolm 1991) have described Aboriginal English as consisting of a number of continua, which range from near-Standard English at what is termed the acrolectal end, to a number of more creole-like varieties at what is termed the basilectal end. Most studies of Aboriginal English have focused on features of language form (phonology, morphology and syntax), largely divorced from studies of the sociocultural context of speakers. Thus, in the instances where people working with Aboriginal speakers of English are aware of their distinctive language variety, most often it is one or more of these aspects of language form which they recognise as distinctively Aboriginal.

Differences of form between Aboriginal English and Standard English can cause problems of communication. For example, in basilectal forms of Aboriginal English there is no gender distinction in the third person pronoun, and thus 'he' is used to mean either 'he' or 'she'. Clearly such differences in English can have serious consequences for understanding in the legal interview. But they are relevant mostly to remote areas of Australia where these basilectal forms of Aboriginal English are spoken. It will not be possible to deal with these differences of form, that is grammar, sound and vocabulary in this chapter, but they are discussed by Koch (1985, 1991), and McKay (1985).

I have shown elsewhere that even where speakers of Aboriginal English share identical grammatical forms with speakers of Standard English, there may be significant *pragmatic differences* – that is, areas where *language meaning and use are not shared because of socio-cultural differences* (Eades 1982, 1984, 1988, 1991, forthcoming; Walsh, this volume). It is these pragmatic differences which will be the focus of this chapter, as they have great significance in the experience of the legal system by a large number of Aboriginal people. Many of these differences are also quite likely to be shared with speakers of traditional Aboriginal languages.

Contemporary culture of Aboriginal English speakers

There are many different types of Aboriginal societies or groups in Australia today. Nevertheless, there are a number of central aspects of culture which are shared across Aboriginal communities throughout Australia, regardless of the language spoken. Regardless of differences in lifestyle and socio-economic situation, Aboriginal people in Australia today belong to overlapping kin-based networks sharing social life, responsibilities and rights, a common history and culture, and experience of racism and ethnic consciousness (Eades 1988: 98).

One of the key features of Aboriginal society throughout Australia, regardless of the language being spoken, is the importance of indirectness. This has been raised in a number of anthropological studies (e.g. Sansom 1980; Hamilton 1981; Von Sturmer 1981; Liberman 1985). A summary of this indirectness in Aboriginal interpersonal interactions is in Eades 1988: 104–6. Very briefly, this indirectness involves giving other people interactional privacy, and it is a crucial social mechanism in societies where there is frequently little physical privacy (for more detail see Walsh, this volume). In fact this is an area of extremely important communicative difference when we are looking at Aboriginal people and the law, as we shall see. Other relevant aspects of contemporary culture are also introduced below.

Bicultural competence

There can be no doubt that some speakers of Aboriginal English can communicate very successfully with non-Aboriginal speakers of English. The large majority of these particular Aboriginal people are biculturally competent – that is, they can communicate in an Aboriginal way in Aboriginal interactions, and in a non-Aboriginal way in non-Aboriginal interactions. However, the number of Aboriginal English speakers who are truly biculturally competent is very small. The extent of bicultural competence, and the ability to switch (consciously or unconsciously) between Aboriginal and non-Aboriginal ways of interacting, depends to a significant extent on the individual's experience in mainstream domains, such as education and employment. My experience with Aboriginal students in tertiary education indicates that many of these people lack significant bicultural competence. It is thought that most of the Aboriginal English speakers who come before the courts have had marginal and/or largely unsuccessful participation in mainstream Australian education and employment. Hence they have had little chance to develop this bicultural competence.

THE CLASH

(While this work is based primarily on detailed studies carried out in Queensland, there is considerable reason at this stage to believe that the clash reported in this chapter occurs widely throughout Australia.)

Aboriginal ways of seeking information

One of the most obvious differences between Aboriginal and non-Aboriginal ways of seeking information is in *the use of questions*. While questions are frequently used in Aboriginal conversations in certain contexts and functions, there are constraints on their use which serve to protect individual privacy.

[*Direct questions*] are used to seek orientation information – namely clarification of a topic, often by way of background details about people especially, but also about the time, place and setting of some event. [Where direct questions are used in Aboriginal English, their linguistic form is usually that of a statement with rising intonation, e.g. 'You were at the pub?', 'Janey came home?', 'That's his brother?' This linguistic form is consistent with the indirectness typical of much Aboriginal conversation.] [Rather than directly ask for information, the questioner presents some proposition for confirmation or correction.] Of course this linguistic strategy is sometimes used by Standard English speakers. But the most common linguistic question (or interrogative) form in Standard English involves word order inversion with rising intonation (e.g. 'Were you at the pub?').

But the differences beween Aboriginal and non-Aboriginal ways of using English to seek information are not simply matters of linguistic structure. [There are fundamental socio-cultural differences in expectations and patterns of social interactions. It is significant that these differences are both reflected in, and continually created by, fundamental differences in linguistic patterns, and cannot be separated from them.]

Most importantly, where Aboriginal speakers seek [*substantial information*,] such as important personal details or reasons, *questions are not used.* [The process of seeking information in these situations is much less direct and involves the person who is seeking information contributing some of their own knowledge on the topic, followed often by silence. For example, rather than ask 'What happened at the pub last night?', an Aboriginal speaker would seek information indirectly with a statement like 'I heard there was the biggest row at the pub last night'. Of course these strategies used by Aboriginal people to seek information are sometimes used by Anglo Australians, particularly in sensitive situations. But for Aboriginal people these strategies do not signal a sensitive situation – these are the *everyday* ways of seeking information.]

Thus information seeking is part of an exchange between

individuals who have an on-going reciprocal relationship. There is no obligation on a knowledgeable person to provide the information, and there is no expectation that information sought will necessarily be provided. [Unlike non-Aboriginal Australian society where much information is freely accessible, in Aboriginal societies there are controls on many types of knowledge, and information is given only to those who have rights to the information (see particularly Walsh, this volume on 'knowledge economy'; also Keen 1978, Sansom 1980, Simpson, this volume). Many of the restrictions, on either secret or personal knowledge, are gender specific.]

[This cultural difference in information seeking strategies is fundamental, and it is a major factor in the classic Aboriginal failure to handle interviews successfully, and in the hesitation, silence and dysfluency which typifies much Aboriginal participation in interviews.] It is not just Australian Aboriginal societies which seek information as part of a two-way exchange. It is relevant here to briefly quote the work of [Roger Abrahams]with Black Americans, for whom information seeking strategies involve necessary reciprocity. Abrahams says: ['simply by asking questions (any questions) . . . we have committed an unconsidered ethnocentric act, for we have assumed that all people pass on information as we do'](Abrahams 1976: 3).

Aboriginal answers to legal questions

Unfortunately the whole legal process in Australia, as throughout the Western world, is centred around questions and answers – right from the police interview through all stages of the judicial process. Not only are questions central to obtaining information, and establishing facts in dispute, but as Harris (1984a) shows, they are used frequently to make accusations.[In the courtroom, it is not always easy to establish whether a particular question is being used with information-seeking function or accusation function, or both.] Further, the witness is prohibited from asking questions, and the majority of questions asked require only short answers, and they often contain already completed propositions. [Thus, as Harris has clearly shown, questions asked in the courtroom are a powerful means of control over the discourse.]

Thus all witnesses are disadvantaged in some way by courtroom questioning, in which the power rests with the legal professionals. But Aboriginal people in all parts of Australia are seriously disadvantaged by the question-answer method of establishing the truth in the following specific ways:

1. As it is not their usual way of giving important information, they do not have the same experience and competence in this conversational strategy as other Australians.

   Perhaps it could be argued that the school classroom, which is also founded in question-answer discourse patterns, prepares Aboriginal people for the legal system. But in fact Aboriginal people have overall been spectacularly marginal to, and unsuccessful in, the education system. Further, the questions addressed to school children are largely about matters which are not at all personally related to the student, unlike the questioning in the legal process.

2. Typical responses to legal questions may be misinterpreted, especially where the questioner does not recognise aspects of Aboriginal culture and mistakenly assumes that the Aborigine is speaking Standard English. For example a common Aboriginal response to inappropriate non-Aboriginal questioning is 'I don't know', or 'I don't remember'. Often this is not a statement concerning the speaker's knowledge or memory, but it is a comment on the communicative strategy, and would translate into Standard English as something like: 'This is not an appropriate way for me to provide information of this nature'. This cross-cultural misinterpretation can have serious implications for an Aboriginal person's admissions concerning the seriousness of a crime.

3. Silence is an important and positively valued part of many Aboriginal conversations. This is a difficult matter for most non-Aboriginal people to recognise and learn, because in Western societies silence is so often negatively valued in conversations. For example, between people who are not close friends or family, silence in conversations, or interviews, is frequently an indication of some kind of communication breakdown. On the contrary, in Aboriginal societies silence indicates a participant's desire to think, or simply to enjoy the presence of others in a non-verbal way.[2] This difference has serious implications for police, lawyer, and courtroom inter-

views of Aboriginal people. Aboriginal silence in these settings can easily be interpreted as evasion, ignorance, confusion, insolence, or even guilt. Note that according to law, silence should not be taken as admission of guilt, but it is difficult for police officers, legal professionals or jurors to set aside strong cultural intuitions about the meaning of silence, especially where one is not aware of cultural differences in the use and interpretation of silence.

4. [Another well-known difficulty which Aboriginal people experience in many interviews concerns the use of questions which ask for the respondent to choose one of two alternatives. These questions are known as 'either-or' questions,[3] and are rarely found in the linguistic structure of traditional Aboriginal languages or Aboriginal varieties of English.] Liberman (1981) is one writer who has drawn attention to the difficulties in using this structure in asking questions of Aboriginal people. Liberman rightly points out that Aboriginal answers to 'either-or' questions usually refer to the last alternative proffered.

5. [A further disadvantage suffered by Aboriginal people in legal questioning, concerns cultural difference in the use of eye contact.] It is widely recognised throughout Australia that direct eye contact is frequently avoided in Aboriginal interactions, where it is seen as threatening or rude.

Conversely, in much non-Aboriginal interaction in Australia, the avoidance of eye contact, especially when asking or answering questions, is interpreted as rudeness, evasion or dishonesty. [This cultural difference in use and interpretation of eye communication can be very important in police or courtroom interviews, especially as it has been pointed out that 'It is common for barristers to look witnesses directly in the eye at the most aggressive moments'] (Liberman 1981: 248).

6. [Official legal transcripts (of police interviews or court hearings) do not record hesitations, or dysfluencies.] Thus where further legal proceedings, such as appeals, use earlier transcripts as evidence, there is no recorded evidence of the extent to which the witness had difficulty in handling the earlier interview. Clearly, this omission can disadvantage any witness, but it is particularly relevant to Aboriginal witnesses, many of whom lack basic communicative competence in the interview process, for reasons explained in this section.

7. [Possibly the most serious disadvantage experienced by
Aboriginal English speakers is caused by the very common
Aboriginal conversational pattern of agreeing with whatever
is being asked, even if the speaker does not understand the
question.] This interactional feature of Aboriginal conversations throughout Australia, of which many non-Aborigines in
a wide range of professional and para-professional areas are
aware, is aptly named ['gratuitous concurrence'] by Liberman
(1981, 1985). [Liberman,] whose work on this has considerable
relevance to the law, explains gratuitous concurrence as

> a strategy of accommodation [that Aboriginal people have
> developed] to protect themselves in their interaction with Anglo
> Australians [Aborigines have found that the easiest method to deal
> with White people is to agree with whatever it is that the Anglo-
> Australians want and then to continue on with their own business]
> Frequently, one will find Aboriginal people agreeing with Anglo
> Australians even when they do not comprehend what it is they are
> agreeing with.
>
> (Liberman 1981: 248–9)

This phenomenon has long been recognised by people
working with Aborigines. More than fifty years ago, the linguist
Strehlow (1936: 334) remarked: 'the White man putting the
questions will usually receive answers which are calculated either
to avoid trouble or to excite his pleasure: he will be given the
information which he desires to get'. A decade later, the
anthropologist Elkin (1947: 176) observed: 'For here [in the court],
too, their fundamental aim is to satisfy the questioner, to tell him
what they think he wants to be told.' And more recently, the
Central Australian Aboriginal leader, Lester (1973) said that
'[Aboriginal] people who are frightened of the court will often
plead guilty, even when they are innocent, so as to get finished
and out of court quickly'. (See also Coldrey 1987: 83–5 for an
excellent example of gratuitous concurrence in a police interview
of an Aboriginal man in the Northern Territory.)

While the examples cited in the literature have been primarily
with traditionally oriented Aborigines, who speak traditional
Aboriginal languages, the phenomenon of gratuitous concurrence
is also widely recognised by people working with Aboriginal
English speaking people in non-traditionally oriented societies.

In my experience this strategy is particularly common where a considerable number of questions are being asked, the situation with both police and courtroom interviews.

⌈Thus a very common strategy for Aborigines being asked a number of questions by non-Aborigines is to agree, regardless of either their understanding of the question, or their belief about the truth or falsity of the proposition being questioned⌉ A number of the questions in a police interview particularly would lend themselves ideally to this pattern of gratuitous concurrence answers, for example questions asked at the end of the police interview which start with words such as 'do you agree that. . .?'

⌈One experienced Aboriginal Legal Aid solicitor expressed the view to me that this is *the* major problem in effective communication with Aboriginal clients⌉ This is particularly so with police interviewing of Aboriginal people where the tendency to use gratuitous concurrence is escalated by physical or verbal intimidation, no matter how slight. Many Aboriginal people in Queensland have told me of such intimidatory experiences, not all of them slight.[4]

Undoubtedly, there are now a number of legal professionals who are aware of this Aboriginal strategy of 'gratuitous concurrence', and who exploit this strategy in their questioning of Aboriginal witnesses. Thus it is possible for this strategy to work even more strongly, either in favour of, or against, the Aboriginal witness.

There is a tragic irony here for many Aboriginal people. Although they use much silence in their own interactions with other Aboriginal people, they frequently experience difficulty in exercising their legal right to remain silent – in the sense of not answering questions. Here the crucial factors of police power and intimidation combine with the Aboriginal person's fear, and desire for gratuitous concurrence, often with disastrous consequences.

An example of gratuitous concurrence was discussed with me by an Aboriginal Field Officer in North Queensland. Four youths in a country town had stolen a car, and then picked up a fifth youth, who did not realise that the car was stolen. The first four youths instructed their solicitor that they would plead guilty to the charge of stealing a motor vehicle. The fifth youth was not guilty, and was advised by the solicitor to plead not guilty. The not guilty charge was to be heard one month after the four pleas of guilty. But the fifth youth explained to his solicitor that he did not want to go through the court hearing without his mates. So he insisted on pleading guilty along with his mates.

Is it possible that many Aboriginal people, when charged with an offence would rather plead guilty and accept the consequences, even jail, than face the seemingly endless barrage of questions, which accompany a plea of not guilty? Is it possible that for some Aboriginal people jail is a less traumatic option than the legal questions, so alien to Aboriginal ways of interacting? And to take another angle, is jail preferable to the difficult and squalid living conditions experienced by Aboriginal people in some areas? (This frightening choice has been suggested as a possible explanation by some Aboriginal people I have spoken to.) But even if this is possible, the horrendous picture of Aboriginal deaths in custody which has emerged in the last few years, points to the possible tragic consequences of such a choice.

While there is certainly much evidence of Aboriginal people using this strategy of gratuitous concurrence to agree to propositions which they either do not understand, or which they know to be false, we must not ignore the other possibility – namely of an Aboriginal person's denial to a charge, being changed and untruthfully represented as a confession. This practice, known as 'verballing', was rife in the Queensland police force until 1988 (Fitzgerald 1989). (See also the material on police 'verbals' in Gibbons 1990.)

Being specific in Aboriginal English

Another relevant aspect of Aboriginal communication concerns the way in which speakers talk about time, size, quantity and distance, which in Standard uses of English tend frequently to be expressed by [quantifiable specification – that is, either the use of a numeral, or the naming of one of a series, such as days of the week or months of the year. Aboriginal speakers tend not to use expressions of quantifiable specification.]

[Counting systems in Aboriginal 'traditional' languages are often less complex than that of English. Items, people and places are often listed or named rather than counted.) This way of indicating number is also common with Aboriginal speakers of English today. For example, if asked 'how many people were there?', an Aboriginal speaker would frequently reply by naming the people present. Further, the difficulty which Aboriginal people typically experience with Western mathematics is commonly seen to be a result of this difference between Aboriginal and non-Aboriginal ways of being specific.

Thus Aboriginal speakers (of traditional languages and English varieties) tend not to use numbers or other means of quantifiable specification (such as days of the week). [Specification in statements (including replies to questions) often refers to physical, social, geographical, and climatic events and states of affairs] For example, time reference for past or future events usually involves reference to a social event or situation, rather than clocktime or calendar time. This is part of a wider Aboriginal worldview, which has been characterised by the anthropologist Bain (1979), writing about a traditional Aboriginal society in the Northern Territory, as one in which quantification is 'not only irrelevant, but contrary' (quoted in Christie 1984: 7).

Giving specific answers in court

So, in addition to all of the disadvantages discussed above which are faced by Aboriginal people in legal interviews, there are further disadvantages in answer to the [How-where-when-type questions which seek specific information (known linguistically as WH-questions). [In answer to such questions seeking quantifiable specification asked by non-Aboriginal speakers, (e.g. 'how many drinks did you have?') Aboriginal speakers of English are frequently either non-specific or vague, (e.g. 'oh, must have been quite a few'), or else they are specific in relation to another situation (e.g. 'must be more than Freddie')]

[This difference in the use of English has serious implications for the police and courtroom interviewing of Aboriginal people, where precision is vital to the functioning of the law] For example, an Aboriginal witness could easily provide quite different answers at different times to the same WH question. For example, in a police interview, an answer to the question 'what time?' might be 'not long before dark'. In the subsequent trial, the same witness might answer 'yes' to the question 'was it about 5 o'clock?' But later in cross-examination, the witness might also say 'yes' to a question of the same event 'was it 7 o'clock?' [Such differences in answers to the question seeking specific information should not be interpreted as indicative of an unreliable witness. Rather, these disparities indicate a dialectal difference between Aboriginal English and Standard English as well as a common unfamiliarity with, and lack of competence, among Aboriginal people in handling precise quantification.]

The legal system – a ritual which excludes Aborigines?

In the last few years I have observed a number of Aboriginal speakers of English in various judicial hearings throughout Australia. [To observe such events is to observe participants who appear to be non-participants] Magistrates often talk in a low, even unclear tone, and use the specialised register of the court which is unnecessarily obscure to many participants, not just Aboriginal witnesses (e.g. addressing the person as 'defendant'). [Many Aboriginal people clearly see the process of law as a ritual in which they are observers. Even the words which will bear so much weight in the judicial decisions affecting the individual's future seem to be fixed ritual expressions, as in the following example, reported to me by a solicitor]

> A few years ago, an Aboriginal English-speaking man in north Queensland was the uninvolved witness in a traffic accident. He was called to give evidence in court, and was asked something like 'Can you tell us in your own words what happened?' To which the Aboriginal witness replied: 'I plead guilty, eh?'

And Liberman (1981: 252) provides a similar example of the ritual nature of proceedings from Carnarvon in Western Australia. Aboriginal people in this area had been advised of their right to seek delayed payment of a fine, rather than serve a prison sentence. Liberman tells of an elderly Aboriginal man giving evidence, who was asked just before the conclusion of his evidence, if he had anything further to say before the court. He replied with the ritual phrase: 'Time to pay'.

This ritual nature of Aboriginal participation (if it can be called participation), has been recognised for some time by many professionals in the legal system. For example, Justice Kriewaldt of the Northern Territory Supreme Court said: ['The plain fact is that in the Northern Territory the trial of an aborigine in most cases proceeds, and as far as I could gather, has always proceeded, as if the accused were not present. If he were physically absent no-one would notice this fact'] (Kriewaldt 1960: 23; see also Parker 1987: 144).[5] Kriewaldt was pessimistic about whether this could be overcome, but I do not think we need to be as pessimistic now in the 1990s.

ADDRESSING THE CLASH

In the last ten or so years, a number of initiatives have been taken to address the disadvantage experienced by Aboriginal people in the law (see also Carroll, this volume). But since so little has been written or explained specifically about the language and communication problems faced by Aboriginal English speakers, it is hardly surprising that many of the initiatives within the legal profession have not really addressed these particular issues. However, as we will see in this section, some of the general initiatives already taken have been able to assist Aboriginal English speakers in some ways with their language and communication disadvantage in the law. With greater understanding of the nature of these disadvantages, further assistance should develop in the future.

Aboriginal Legal Services

Undoubtedly, the first major breakthrough came with the establishment of legal aid services specifically for Aboriginal people. Following the establishment of the first Aboriginal Legal Service (ALS) in 1970 in Redfern (an inner Sydney suburb), ALS offices spread throughout Australia in the 1970s. These regional services, which are run by elected local Councils, provide solicitors and Aboriginal field officers. These Aboriginal field officers, who frequently act as cross-cultural interpreters, are undoubtedly the 'crucial link' (Lyons 1984: 143) between Aboriginal clients and legal professionals.

However, the specific matters about Aboriginal English which have been raised in this chapter are not widely known, and ALS staff are not provided with formal education about communication differences between Aboriginal and non-Aboriginal people. Often, members of the Aboriginal community are able to assist, but such assistance could clearly be enhanced by specific documentation of these differences.

In relation to the language differences discussed in this chapter, one of the main achievements of ALS staff in many areas is to advise and persuade Aboriginal people not to talk to the police, or to commence a police record of interview, without a field officer or solicitor present. This advice is particularly important given the the danger of using gratuitous concurrence, and thus making a false confession. While the presence of a solicitor or field officer will not automatically prevent the disastrous use of gratuitous concurrence, it does serve to make the police interview less intimidating for the Aboriginal suspect, and thus lessen its likelihood. Of course, the presence of a solicitor or field officer is also important in addressing police racism and intimidation, experienced so often by Aboriginal suspects.

Specific legal provisions

Specific legal provisions addressing the communicative needs of Aboriginal people in the law have mainly focused on speakers of traditional languages, who may speak English as a second language. The most significant ruling is that of Justice Forster in *R* v. *Anunga* (NT Supreme Court 1976). Known as the Anunga Rules, these nine guidelines for the police interviewing of Aboriginal suspects, seek to protect the rights of the Aboriginal suspect through a number of basic provisions.[6] In introducing these guidelines, Justice Forster drew attention to the phenomenon now known as 'gratuitous concurrence', which has been discussed above. Three of the guidelines specifically address some of the linguistic and communication disadvantages experi-

enced by Aboriginal suspects. Thus, there is specific provision
for care needed in formulating questions, as well as in relation to
the Aboriginal suspect's understanding of the police caution.]

The guidelines also indicate the requirement of an interpreter
unless the suspect 'is as fluent in English as the average White
man of English descent'. But while so many people, both
Aboriginal and non-Aboriginal, are unaware of the extent of the
difference between Standard English and Aboriginal varieties of
English, such guidelines are bound to be inadequately observed.
(The question of interpreters of Aboriginal English is raised
below.)

Nevertheless, the Anunga Rules are a positive step in
recognising and accommodating communication disadvantage
for Aboriginal suspects, and they do function to protect
Aboriginal suspects. Although these guidelines are not obligatory
and they are not always followed, legal counsel for Aboriginal
clients can use the Anunga Rules to rule as inadmissible police
evidence which has not been taken in accordance with these
rules. Furthermore, the Anunga Rules do not protect speakers of
'light' varieties of Aboriginal English, and they have no
application outside of the Northern Territory.[7]

Queensland, South Australia and the Australian Capital
Territory all have some guidelines for the police interviewing of
Aboriginal suspects, mainly requiring the presence of an
independent third party (see Foley 1984). Such provisions aim
mainly to ensure that Aboriginal confessions are made voluntarily, and they do not address the more complex issues of
linguistic and cultural misunderstanding. But as with the
Anunga rules in the Northern Territory, the Queensland and
South Australian provisions are not applicable if the suspect is
considered to be fluent in the English language. The dialectal
differences raised in this chapter reveal the inadequacy of such
provisions.

The Royal Commission into Aboriginal Deaths in Custody

The Royal Commission into Aboriginal Deaths in Custody was
established in 1987 to investigate the deaths of Aboriginal people
in police custody, prison or in any other place of detention, since

1970. Over one hundred deaths were investigated, and the Commission examined the circumstances of the deaths, as well as taking account of 'social, cultural and legal factors'. The Interim Report of this Royal Commission (RCADC 1988) made 56 recommendations ranging from the decriminalisation of public drunkenness to the training of police and prison officers in first aid and resuscitation techniques. Recommendation 32 states that

> All personnel of police, prison, social welfare or other departments whose work will bring them into contact with Aboriginal people should receive appropriate training or re-training to ensure that they have an understanding and appreciation of Aboriginal history, culture and social behaviour and the abilities to effectively communicate and work with Aboriginal people
>
> (RCADC 1988: 70)

The *National Report* (1991) added to this recommendation, stating that judicial officers and others whose work in probation and parole services bring them into contact with Aboriginal people, should also 'wherever possible participate in discussion with members of the Aboriginal community in an informal way in order to improve cross-cultural understanding' (Recommendation 96).

FUTURE POSSIBILITIES

But does equity in the law entail more than enabling Aboriginal people to participate in non-Aboriginal structures using non-Aboriginal ways of interaction? Does it also entail a recognition of the fundamental right of Aboriginal people to use Aboriginal ways of interacting? How might it be possible to incorporate Aboriginal ways of communicating in the delivery of justice to Aboriginal English speakers?

We can provide answers to the last of these questions in two different ways: first, by accommodating Aboriginal English ways of communicating within the existing legal system, and second, by making changes to the legal system which enable Aboriginal English speakers to use their ways of communicating where possible.

Accommodating differences within the existing system

Education

The obvious first step in accommodating the language and communication differences of Aboriginal English speakers involves the education of all non-Aboriginal personnel with whom they have dealings: police officers, legal professionals, and jurors.

To be effective, such a process of education must have an input in many directions; such as training of police recruits, courses in the law in Universities and Colleges, in-service training of police and lawyers already qualified, and articles in professional newsletters and journals. A growing number of police and legal professionals recognise this need, and the Queensland Law Society recently published a handbook for lawyers on effective communication with Aboriginal speakers of English (Eades 1992). This handbook explains the pragmatic differences which have been the focus of this chapter, as well as differences in all other areas of language – sound system, grammar, and vocabulary – all of which must be covered in the education of legal personnel. (See also recommendation No. 32 of the Interim Report of the Royal Commission into Aboriginal Deaths in Custody, RCADC 1988: 70.)

The education of jurors is more difficult, as there is no specific training for jury service. However, a set of guidelines could be prepared to advise on significant communication differences between non-Aboriginal and Aboriginal speakers of English.

It is also important that Aboriginal English speakers be educated about the language of the law, and advised about how their use of language, for example silence, may be interpreted.

The need for interpreters of Aboriginal English

The need for Aboriginal speakers of traditional languages to have access to interpreters has been raised in numerous reports, such as RCADC 1988: 23: 'the availability of trained interpreters in court proceedings is essential to the proper administration of justice'. However, it is evident from the discussion above that there is a need for many Aboriginal English speakers to have access to cross-cultural interpreters in the legal system.

Perhaps the most significant statement on interpreters generally comes from the Australian Law Reform Commission in its report *Evidence* (No. 38), which recommends that 'A witness may give evidence about a fact through an interpreter unless the witness can understand and speak the English language sufficiently to enable the witness to understand fully, and to make an adequate reply to, questions that may be put about the fact' (ALRC 1987: 156). This recommendation, which recognises the multilingual nature of Australian society, effectively changes the onus, so that a person is 'entitled to an interpreter unless the court orders otherwise' (ALRC 1985: 339). And this is one of a number of recommendations in the new Evidence Bill, which was introduced into Federal Parliament in 1991. In this recommendation a witness's competence in English is rightly the decisive factor in the use of an interpreter.

It is often thought that interpreters translate words or sentences from one language to another. In fact, interpreting involves more than this. The interpreter must translate the concepts or ideas expressed in one language to those expressed in another. Where the two speakers are from similar cultural backgrounds, there may be many words with almost exactly equivalent meanings. But where the two speakers have rather different cultures, then the process of interpretation necessitates much paraphrasing and explaining of the concepts and ideas being translated. It is this aspect of interpreting which is particularly important in the question of interpreters of Aboriginal English in the legal system, and for this reason perhaps we should use the term 'cross-cultural interpreter' here.

This chapter has shown some of the ways in which many Aboriginal English speakers are disadvantaged in police interviews, lawyer interviews, and courtroom hearings, because of the miscommunications arising from the differences between their dialect of English and Standard English. But the need for interpreters has been largely unrecognised, primarily because the majority of non-Aboriginal people in Australia do not understand that Aboriginal English dialects are valid, distinct dialects of English which differ significantly from Standard English. Further, in areas where the Aboriginal English does not sound very different from Standard English, both Aboriginal and non-Aboriginal speakers are often unaware of the subtle, but crucial differences between the two dialects.

Not all dialectal differences between Aboriginal English and Standard English necessarily cause miscommunication. Just as an Australian can usually understand a Scottish speaker of English, so too many non-Aboriginal speakers of English can frequently understand Aboriginal English speakers. But this chapter has shown why there is a need for interpreters of Aboriginal English in the legal system. Because of the considerable cultural differences between Aboriginal and non-Aboriginal societies, some of the dialectal differences are significant, and they do cause miscommunications. This fact, combined with the extremely high overrepresentation of Aboriginal people in Australian courts and jails, make it important for speakers of dialects of Aboriginal English to have access to cross-cultural interpreters in the legal system.

Changes to the system

The following tentative suggestions are made in the knowledge that change to the law is a very complex proposition. Thus this section contains a number of questions, which can only be answered after wide-ranging discussions in a number of forums, in order to establish any possible avenues of change.

Changes to the role and structure of interviews

Given that Aboriginal people are culturally disadvantaged by the interview format (as discussed above), is it possible to develop different ways of taking evidence from Aboriginal witnesses, so as to lessen the centrality of the interview?

Is it possible for Aboriginal witnesses to be questioned in

police stations, lawyers' offices and courtrooms in an open-ended interview? This would entail a number of Aboriginal English type of strategies for seeking substantial information. For example, 'we're trying to find out all we can about the fight at the hotel on the night of x'. This change would also necessitate a patient and positive use of silence, in accordance with Aboriginal uses of silence.

Such an open-ended interview style would allow Aboriginal witnesses to make use of narratives rather than answering seemingly endless questions. This is exactly what the Royal Commission into Aboriginal Deaths in Custody in Queensland did, as part of its information gathering from Aboriginal witnesses. Using open-ended interviews, field officers or solicitors spoke to witnesses before the hearing, to gain sufficient information for a statement, which served to answer many of the relevant questions. Then during the hearing, the witness, or a friend of the witness, read the statement to the Commission. Following this, the witness was examined and cross-examined. In this process, the interview was not totally avoided, but its use was mitigated, and with some witnesses, almost avoided.

The replacement of formal interviews with open-ended interviews may be useful to some extent in the tendering of statements. It is important too that these narratives be video-recorded, so that details of Aboriginal English pronunciations, and other aspects of language could be studied later, if necessary with an interpreter, to gain a full understanding of the narrative, and check for any possible confusion.

[The greater use of narratives, or free reports, in the courtroom, has been recommended *for all witnesses*, by the Australian Law Reform Commission in its report *Evidence* (No. 38).] The Commission studied a number of reports of psychological research, which gave support to the claim 'that being tied to answering designated questions tends to result in the distortion of [witnesses] testimony' (ALRC 1986: 337). But even if the police record of interview could be transformed into a video-taped police eliciting of narrative, and if witnesses in court could give evidence in free report or narrative form, it would undoubtedly still be necessary to use traditional interviews in the courtroom. Apart from clarification of details, one of the major functions of questioning in the courtroom appears to be 'harassment' of the witness, in order to try to show inconsistencies in the evidence.

So, an important question here is: What other strategies can be used to seek possible inconsistencies in a witness's story?

And how useful would this change be, if the Aboriginal suspect or witness did not answer certain questions at all? This is quite likely, given the norm in Aboriginal interactions that questions do not necessarily have to be answered. Making the interview more like an Aboriginal process of information seeking would presumably lead to greater use of Aboriginal norms of information seeking, including the expectation that questions do not necessarily have to be answered. Would this situation lead to unmanageable impracticalities in the delivery of justice? Would the presumed greater use of Aboriginal silences be acceptable, as all suspects and witnesses have the right to remain silent (and this silence can not legally be taken as an admission)? But would this open the possibility of greater misinterpretation of Aboriginal silences by police, jurors and legal professionals? How effective would education and advice given to all police and legal professionals about cultural differences in the interpretation of silence be, in setting aside strong cultural intuitions about the meaning of silence?

If Aboriginal witnesses in court can narrate their evidence in an Aboriginal way, then there is a possibility that the evidence could be misinterpreted by non-Aboriginal lawyers, magistrates, judges and jury. This would depend on how close the speaker's Aboriginal English is to Standard English in such aspects as grammar, accent, and vocabulary. For example, use of expressions to refer to individuals differs between Aboriginal and non-Aboriginal English. An example is the use of 'one' in Aboriginal English as an indefinite article, corresponding to Standard English 'a'. 'One' is also used to mean 'person', so the Aboriginal English phrase 'this one here' would translate into Standard English as 'the person I have just referred to'. Aboriginal phrases such as this would occur more frequently in narrative than in answers to questions. This points further to the need in many instances for an interpreter of Aboriginal English, an issue raised above.

If the ways in which Aboriginal people give evidence could be changed to lessen the centrality of the interview, then the overwhelming problems with interpreting 'I don't know' answers, and the use of gratuitous concurrence should be considerably lessened. It seems clear that 'either-or' questions should not be used with Aboriginal witnesses, and their answers to such questions should be ruled inadmissible as evidence.

Can legal provision be made that direct eye contact should not be used with Aboriginal suspects or witnesses? And if so, how can this be checked for police interviews which have not been video-taped?[8] Is it possible or advisable to interview Aboriginal witnesses in court hearings on closed-circuit television. Such systems are used in several overseas courts, and in January 1990, the NSW Attorney-General announced a decision to allow child victims of sexual assault to give evidence on closed-circuit television.

Taking all of these suggestions for changes together, perhaps we need a new trial system for Aboriginal people. (While this chapter is examining Aboriginal English speakers, it is most likely that such changes would be found to be necessary also for more traditionally orientated Aboriginal people, who still speak 'traditional' Aboriginal languages.) Such a new trial system would implement these different ways of seeking required information, and would use cross-cultural interpreters or advisers to provide magistrates and judges with necessary cultural and linguistic explanations to interpret the evidence of Aboriginal people.

A fundamental issue

[If there is to be a new trial system, or changes to ways in which Aboriginal people give evidence (not necessarily those proposed above), then who is entitled to give evidence in these different ways? This raises two questions, first who is an Aborigine, and second what about an Aboriginal person who is biculturally competent, that is, able to communicate using non-Aboriginal norms of communication? Who should decide, and what criteria should they use, to test an Aboriginal English speaker's suitability to give evidence in a different way?]

Perhaps one of the most basic, and at the same time the most crucial, problems in the delivery of justice to many Aboriginal people today is the failure of many Australians, including legal professionals, to recognise the former's rightful claim to

Aboriginality, and the cultural and linguistic differences which are involved. Many of the latter are unaware of the Commonwealth definition, which is also widely accepted by Aboriginal people:

> An Aboriginal or Torres Strait Islander is a person of Aboriginal or Torres Strait Islander descent who identifies as an Aboriginal or Torres Strait Islander and is accepted as such by the community in which he or she lives
> (ALRC 1986: 8)

[This definition makes no reference to the physical characteristics of the Aboriginal or Torres Strait Islander person; it is based on the three factors of descent, self-identification and community acceptance of this self-identification, thereby avoiding the mistaken assumption that behaviour or ways of acting, and resulting identity and rights must be proportional to biological characteristics.]

In fact any scientific study of human social behaviour will show that it is our socialisation and experiences which most effect our ways of acting, including our ways of speaking. To take a very simple example – if a child of two English speaking Anglo-Australian parents is adopted at a very young age by a Samoan family, and grows up in a Samoan village, then this child will speak the language, and share the beliefs, values, expectations and ways of acting of the Samoan villagers. That is, regardless of the child's biological inheritance, it will be socialised as a Samoan. So it is with any person –[features such as skin colour are largely irrelevant to our culture, to our beliefs, values and ways of acting.]

The second question was – how to identify biculturally competent Aborigines who do not need a new trial system. Probably the best resolution of this issue is to follow the recommendation of the Law Reform Commission in its report on Aboriginal customary laws (ALRC 1986). This Report recommended that the applicability of provisions for 'traditional Aborigines' be worked out on a case-by-case basis. In the case of proposals for change affecting Aboriginal English speakers, this would be more complex, suggesting the need for an independent adviser who can assess the bicultural competence of the English-speaking Aboriginal witness.

Further questions

Comparable research on cultural and communication patterns has not been done for other minority groups in Australia, some of whom may be affected by similar (or different) communicative disadvantage. Should they have these ways open to them? or other ways? Or is reform for Aborigines urgent and crucial because of their dramatic overimprisonment and its tragic consequences?

Could some of the changes suggested be uniform? Could all Australian suspects be questioned, and witnesses be examined and cross-examined in the same, new ways? But if we advocate more sensitivity to Aboriginal communication patterns would non-Aboriginal witnesses be disadvantaged? As I have pointed out above, the strategies used by Aboriginal people to seek information are sometimes used by Anglo-Australians, particularly in sensitive situations. It could be that the use of less direct questioning strategies in the law will be welcomed by many who see police, lawyer and courtroom interviews as sensitive situations.

Insurmountable aspects of the clash

Despite any solutions to the communicative differences discussed above, there will always remain areas of insurmountable clash. [There is a fundamental, and to a considerable extent irresolvable, cultural difference involving what might be called the 'forced communication' in the legal process] The basic process of law in Australia assumes the right to information about an individual suspect or witness. But in Aboriginal societies, as I have explained above, only certain people have rights to certain knowledge – these people must be in some kind of relationship with the person with the knowledge (often a kin relationship). But for Australian justice to work, suspects and witnesses must be called to give information or knowledge to designated police and legal personnel. It is just not practical in a large-scale society such as Australia, to always have the right environment for the Aboriginal exchange of serious information. However, there are some positive steps which can be taken:

1. It is important that more Aboriginal people be recruited into the police force and the legal profession. (See also recommendation no 26 of the Interim Report of the Royal Commission into Aboriginal Deaths in Custody, RCADC 1988: 70.) However, in the foreseeable future it may not be practically possible to have sufficient numbers. (Furthermore, even if a police officer is Aboriginal, it may not necessarily be easier for him or her to interview an Aboriginal suspect – for example, they may come from different family groups, and the required information may be impossible to share in that relationship.)

2. In view of the gender restriction on much Aboriginal information exchange, Aboriginal witnesses should be interviewed by a police officer, or lawyer, of the same sex, particularly on personal matters, especially relating to sexual and health areas. But in an open court, this knowledge is still heard by people of both sexes, so the problem can not be fully resolved.

Other areas of clash

An examination of the charge of using obscene language (or swearing) reveals an area of cultural clash between contemporary, non-traditional Aboriginal and mainstream Australian societies. Simply put, what is widely considered to be obscene language in many sectors of mainstream Australian society, is much less likely to be offensive in Aboriginal societies. Langton (1988) shows that 'swearing and fighting in contemporary Aboriginal society constitute processing and social ordering devices derived from traditional Aboriginal patterns' (p. 202). But, as Langton continues: 'The extraordinary arrest and imprisonment rates for swearing and fighting are major contributors to the overall arrest rate and imprisonment rates of Aborigines nationally – the highest recorded in the world' (p. 221). (Similar culture clash exists on the charges of drunkenness, described by Eggleston (1976: 14) as the 'Aboriginal offence par excellence', and assault, which are outside the scope of this chapter.)

Further, although the situation in mainstream Australian society is undoubtedly changing, there is still a greater social prohibition on the use of obscene language by women than by men. However, this gender distinction is not significant within Aboriginal culture, as Langton (1988: 208) points out: 'there is no public sanction on swearing by women in Aboriginal Australia'. [The second matter, which I can only mention briefly, concerns the Aboriginal cultural value of family loyalty, which contrasts, sometimes seriously, with the legal requirement of individual responsibility. I am aware of at least one case where an Aboriginal man confessed to his brother's crime, and there are numerous cases where Aboriginal victims of assault refuse to give evidence against relatives. Such loyalty to the family can appear as the telling of lies, and as directly obstructing the course of justice. From the Aboriginal cultural perspective, however, such loyalty may be far more important than individual accountability.]

CONCLUSION

This chapter has illustrated and explained some of the factors involved in the communicative clash which occurs daily when Aboriginal speakers of varieties of English are involved in 'forced communication' with the law, in police stations, in lawyers' offices and in courtrooms. There can be no doubt that there are significant differences in the way in which Aboriginal and non-Aboriginal people use English, and further, that these differences are a part of the current crisis in the effective delivery of justice to Aboriginal people. Some initiatives have already been taken in addressing the disadvantages faced by Aboriginal people in the law. But it is time to address specifically the language and communication disadvantages faced by Aboriginal speakers of varieties of English. At the least this necessitates widespread and on-going education of all parties concerned, about cultural and linguistic differences which affect communication in the legal system. It also necessitates the recognition of the need for cross-cultural interpreters in many legal interviews with Aboriginal English speakers. But beyond these measures which enhance cross-cultural communication within the existing system, we need to look at changes which can enable Aboriginal speakers of English to use important aspects of their own language and communication patterns in their dealings with the law. To this end, this chapter has raised some possibilities, but much more detailed investigation of the issue is warranted.

ACKNOWLEDGEMENTS

I am indebted to a considerable number of people who have assisted in various ways in the development of this chapter. Many Aboriginal people and legal professionals have provided time, interviews, transcripts and comments on the study; particularly Jeanie Bell, Peter Bevan, Mandy Brazier, Pat Cranitch, Gary Davey, Frank Deemal, Graham Evans, Carol Fewquandie, Jacob George, Rob Hulls, Hilda Johnson, Cathy McKinstry, Ron Neemo, Mark Plunkett and Sue Sheppard. For detailed comments on drafts of this chapter I am grateful to Cliff Goddard, Jeff Siegel and Lew Wyvill. Of course, all material not otherwise acknowledged is my own, and I accept full responsibility for it.

NOTES

1. 'Anaphora' is the linguistic term to describe references we make in language to something which we have already said, such as the word 'them' in the sentence: 'When you saw them, what time was it?'
2. Some similarities can be noted with the use of silence in American Indian societies (Basso 1970; Philips 1976).
3. Note that the actual words 'either' and/'or' need not be used in this question type. Any question which asks the respondent to choose one of two (or more) alternatives is known as an 'either-or' question.
4. Liberman points out (1985: 198) that gratuitous concurrence is a frequent strategy of oppressed peoples. It appears to be relevant to the situation in Britain, recently discussed by Cohen (1990), who believes that fear and police coercion frequently cause suspects to make false confessions.
5. Again, the published accounts refer mainly to traditionally oriented Aborigines, who may not speak English as their first language. But this reflects research focus, rather than actual occurrence of this phenomenon, which I have frequently observed and been told about in my work with Aboriginal English speakers.
6. Some of these provisions appear to be rights basic to all detainees,

e.g. 'If it is necessary to remove the prisoner's clothing for forensic examination, steps must be taken to supply substitute clothing' (reported in McCorquodale 1987: 372).

7. For further discussion of the Anunga Rules see Coldrey 1987, Foley 1984, McKay 1985. For cases in which the Anunga Rules have been discussed see McCorquodale 1987 and Simpson (this volume).

8. The Northern Territory uses video-taping of police records of interview, which is also currently being introduced in Queensland, New South Wales and Tasmania. However, in Victoria it has been compulsory since early 1989 for police to tape record interviews which relate to charges on indictable matters.

ELEVEN

Addressing social issues through linguistic evidence

William Labov and Wendell A. Harris[1]

INTRODUCTION

In many recent meetings of linguistic societies, the feeling has been expressed that linguists should be able to apply their knowledge outside of the university and the classroom, and contribute towards the solution of social problems. This is not just wishful thinking on the part of linguists. In a number of legal cases over the past ten years, linguistic evidence has been brought to bear on social issues, sometimes with positive results.

The discussion to follow will consider three cases where linguistic testimony played an important part in a judicial decision. They cover only a small fraction of the range of issues on language and the law that have been brought to linguists' attention in recent years. In these three cases, linguistic data and theory were introduced to support an expert opinion on the facts of the matter under consideration.

It is true enough that almost all linguistic testimony comes in the form of expert opinion, with a system of advocacy where one can expect to find an opposing expert opinion. This can happen in civil suits, automobile accidents, or criminal cases of various kinds. But in the cases we will report here, there is a more serious issue of taking sides on matters of right and wrong. In each of these cases, the facts are part of a larger situation involving justice and injustice, and the linguistic testimony has been used in the search for justice – at least as the linguist sees it.

The first example is a report of a use of linguistics in a case involving basic human needs for food, shelter and medical care.

THE THORNFARE CASE

On 8 April 1982, Governor Thornburgh signed into law Act 75, a major amendment to Pennsylvania's Public Welfare Code. Before then, Pennsylvania had a unified program that provided benefits to all needy individuals who were not receiving some other form of assistance. This General Assistance (GA) amounts to $US172 a month. The new law, passed in the legislature by a small majority, divided people into two groups: those classified as 'chronically needy' would continue to receive assistance, but those classified as 'transitionally needy' would receive assistance for only 90 days in any given year.

In September, the Department of Public Welfare (DPW) began re-classifying people by a 'desk review' as transitionally needy or chronically needy. They sent out termination notices to a first group of 17,000 people, who were told that they would receive only 90 days worth of assistance from that date. These people would then have exhausted their assistance in December or early January.

Community Legal Services of Philadelphia (CLS) was monitoring this process on behalf of clients who received GA. They had consulted with one of us (WL) on an earlier case involving repossession notices. At that time he had argued that linguistic testimony did not have to be limited to opinions, but could be based on surveys and experiments that showed how people actually interpreted such notices. CLS sent the termination notice for us to examine: they were concerned that people might not understand their rights of appeal or how to qualify for ongoing aid.

The termination letter is given as Appendix A. We found that it was written in a very complicated language and might be hard for anyone to understand, particularly those paragraphs that dealt with the definitions of 'chronically needy' and 'transitionally needy':

> Chronically needy persons are those who because of age, physical or mental handicap or other limited circumstances are less likely to be able to provide for themselves through employment . . .

> Transitionally needy persons are those who are not limited in employability by their circumstances and should be able to support themselves without public assistance . . .

Two phrases in particular seemed hard for anyone to understand. 'Not limited in employability by their circumstances' is a very involved way of saying 'able to work'. In the first paragraph, 'other limited circumstances' is even harder to understand. What is 'limited'? the number of such circumstances? It was quite possible that many people would not be able to figure out the difference between the two classifications and what they could do about it.

At that time we were engaged in research on the influence of race and ethnicity on language change. Many of the several hundred people interviewed by one of us (WAH) were members of the black and Puerto Rican communities of North Philadelphia, and they had received or were receiving GA. Many of them were in the group who would receive such letters, and did receive them during this period. We thought that we were in a good position to find out how people reacted when they received such letters, and do a comparative survey that would provide hard evidence on the interpretation of the letter.

Preliminary inquiries

We first tried to see what kind of information people would receive who were trying to understand the letter and appealed to district offices of DPW. WAH telephoned several district supervisors for information on behalf of a welfare client, a Spanish speaker who was a friend of his. This person had in fact received the letter, and since he had a great deal of trouble reading English, he did need help.

In responding to this request, the first district supervisor said that there were in fact no 'other limited circumstances'. He implied that this phrase was put in simply to give the impression that there were grounds for appeal when there were none. A second supervisor told us that someone on active treatment for a drug or alcohol problem would qualify under 'other limited circumstances', or someone who was caring for another adult.

We then designed an exploratory interview to get at people's attitudes and interpretations of the letter. They were asked to read it aloud if they could; if not WAH read it to them. They were then asked to explain the difference between chronically and transitionally needy, and to explain what they thought 'other limited circumstances' might be. WAH interviewed a dozen people in the social networks he had been studying before, and he also interviewed people waiting in welfare offices. He found that people were not confused by the meaning of 'chronically needy' and 'transitionally needy', but they were confused by 'other limited circumstances'. Many thought that they would want to appeal but they had no clear idea of how to go about it. They were particularly concerned with the fact that they would have nothing to eat, nowhere to live, and that if they got sick, they would not be able to afford a doctor's care or a hospital. In North Philadelphia, public emergency clinics are open only between 8 am and 4 or 5 pm. If a person has a Medicaid card, they can go to any hospital emergency room; otherwise, they have to wait until the clinics are open.

People's reactions to this letter were strong. Some became almost hysterical: even though they had not received the letter yet, they were terribly distressed at the thought of receiving it.

We slowly found out more about who would receive the letter. Those with small children would not, since they were in the class of Aid to Families with Dependent Children rather than GA. The reference to age in the termination of the letter turned out to have surprising interpretation: anyone over 45 would be classed as chronically needy, and only those 18 to 45 would receive the letter. But as long as we were acting in the position of someone who had no special resources, we were still missing a great deal of information.

WAH then made a trip to Harrisburg to get an interpretation of the termination notice from the policy-makers themselves in the state office of DPW. He interviewed welfare recipients in the waiting room, as he waited to speak to the supervisory personnel. He then had an interview with the Director of the Harrisburg Regional Office, who refused to give an interpretation, but offered to assist by calling her superior. Eventually WAH obtained a telephone interview with the Deputy Secretary of Public Welfare.

From these interviews, some surprising facts came to light. 'Other limited circumstances' included more than we had been led to believe at the beginning. People who had worked for 48 months out of the past eight years, and had used up their unemployment benefits would be classed as chronically needy. Anyone over 45 years old or under 18 and was unemployed would have that classification, or someone who was 18, going to school, and would graduate before becoming 19. The caretaker provisions applied to people taking care of a disabled person of any age as well as children under 6. In testimony given later by representatives of DPW, it was said that these provisions of the law had been posted in district offices as early as September, but we did not find that supervisors, case workers or clients knew about them.

It was even more surprising to discover that people would be able to use Medicaid cards and get food stamps even after they were terminated from the general assistance program. The letter said that people to be classified as transitionally needy 'should be able to support themselves without public assistance'. The term 'public assistance' is not a legal term but is generally understood to include any form of help from the state government. We had not found anyone in Philadelphia who knew – or was willing to tell us – that food stamps and Medicaid cards would be available on request from the people who would be terminated.

The questionnaire

In November, we met with Jonathan Stein, Richard Weisshaupt and Niles Schorre of CLS, and presented what we had found out so far. They planned a class action in federal court, asking for an injunction against the state's procedures on behalf of the 50–100,000 people involved. We proposed to do a survey of GA recipients that would provide hard evidence as to how people understood the notice and what conclusions they drew from it. We designed a short interview (Appendix B) that took 15–20 minutes to administer. Subjects were first asked to read the termination letter.[2] They were then asked a number of questions on the meaning of the letter and what actions they would take if they received it. We particularly wanted to know what they would infer from the absence of information on 'limited circumstances'. We included questions on Medicaid and food stamps to find out what they would conclude from the absence of information on those benefits.

We aimed at a judgment sample of the population most likely to get the termination letter: adults 18–45 years old in areas of high unemployment. We had about two weeks to do the job, since the hearing for the preliminary injunction was scheduled for 2 December. We planned to get 30–40 subjects on a first round: we would then judge how many more we needed by the results.

WAH was able to draw on the social networks in North Philadelphia that he had already studied for a large part of this sample. In one week he used the Thornfare questionnaire with 32 people: 21 blacks and 11 Puerto Ricans. Table 11.1 shows the age range, education, and public assistance record of this 'North Philadelphia' sample. Eighteen of the 32 were then getting General Assistance, and 28 had received General Assistance at some time. Sixteen had less than a high school education, 11 graduated from high school, and 5 had some college. The most important fact about this sample is that it strongly represented the group that is weakest in most surveys of inner city areas: working-class Black men from 20 to 35 years old.

The results of this survey were so consistent that we decided we did not need any more interviews in North Philadelphia. They were not obvious results: in some respects they were the opposite of what we might have expected. We decided to survey another group of people likely to receive GA but as different as possible in social background. Teresa Labov, a sociologist familiar with West Philadelphia, suggested that the Ecology Coop would be an excellent place to locate people in this category. Many of the workers and customers of the Coop had high educational levels but low income, and could qualify for assistance at one time or another. She applied the Thornfare questionnaire to 13 Whites at the Coop. As Table 11.1 shows, this 'West Philadelphia' group is similar in age and sex distribution to the North Philadelphia group, but has more education: 12 had some college or more. Six of the 13 had received some form of public assistance: either General Assistance or food stamps.

The testimony

On 9 December, WL testified before Judge Norma L. Shapiro in the US District Court for the Eastern District of Pennsylvania, as an expert witness on behalf of the plaintiffs. Results are summarised in Tables 11.2–11.5 from the written report submitted.[3]

Table 11.1 Distribution of subjects surveyed

| | Age range | | | | | | |
	18–19	20–24	25–29	30–34	35–40	41–45	Total
Male	3	6	4	6	4	3	26
Female	2	4	5	5	0	3	19
Total	5	10	9	11	4	6	45

Education

	Less than High School	High School	Some College or higher
N. Philadelphia	16	11	5
W. Philadelphia	0	1	12
Total	16	12	17

Public Assistance

	Receiving GA	Received GA	Food Stamps	None
N. Philadelphia	18	10		
W. Philadelphia	2	1	3	7

Table 11.2 shows the results for Part I of the questionnaire, which dealt with subjects' understanding of the main effect of the termination letter. As far as the primary distinction between 'traditionally needy' and 'chronically needy' was concerned, there was no problem. Only one person of the 45 subjects did not clearly understand that being classified as transitionally needy meant being cut off from General Assistance after 90 days.

On the other hand, people had almost no luck at all in trying to guess what 'other limited circumstances' would be. One person from North Philadelphia and one from West Philadelphia rightly thought that if someone broke his leg on the job, he could be classified as 'chronically needy'. One person from West Philadelphia guessed the caretaker provision, and another the provision for drug treatment. The rest simply did not know or guessed that having small children would qualify someone for assistance. This is irrelevant, since they would then qualify under Aid to Families with Dependent Children instead of GA.[4]

People were also wide of the mark on the age provision. Most thought that you would have to be over 65 to qualify as chronically needy. Only one person out of 45 knew the right answer: that those over 45 years old would continue to get GA.

Table 11.2 Definition of chronically and transitionally needy

What's the difference between transitionally needy v. chronically needy?
Understood basic distinction   44
Did not clearly understand   1

'What could "limited circumstances" be?'

	N. Philadelphia	W. Philadelphia
No jobs available	11	2
Children, no baby-sitter	8	3
Don't know, term is vague	13	5
Health	1	
Broken leg, hurt on job	1	1
Responsible for older family		1
Drug problems		1
Criminal record		1

'What do you think they mean by age?'
65 and over   26
55 and over   14
50 and over   4
45 and over   1

'Would "limited circumstances" be . . .'

	Yes	Should	Maybe	No	Don't know
Drug and alcohol treatment	25	2	7	9	2
Working for 4/8 years	21	7	2	12	3
Mother sick	29	5	3	7	1
Broken leg	28	2	4	9	2

The interviewer than suggested four of the provisions that were written into the law, asking the subject to judge whether these would be 'limited circumstances'. As the last section of Table 11.2 shows, most people responded positively to these suggestions, but the overall picture (particularly the responses to question two) shows that they thought these provisions *should* be included, not that they in fact were.

In Part II of the questionnaire, we quoted the sentence from the letter that read, 'according to the information we have about your situation, you must be considered transitionally needy'. We asked, 'Did you ever give information about your physical or mental health?' and 'Where do you think they would get this information?' Table 11.3 shows the answers to this question. No one in North Philadelphia said that they had supplied any

Table 11.3 Source of the information used

'Did you supply the information?'	N. Philadelphia	W. Philadelphia
Yes	0	7
No	31	6
Not sure	1	0
'Where did they get the information?'		
Don't know	21	0
They don't have it	11	0
From subject	0	7
From institutions	0	6

information and 11 people were sure that the welfare office did not have it: 'they're bull-shitting . . . making it up . . .' On the other hand, the more educated West Philadelphia subjects were split on this point.

Many thought that they had supplied the information, or that the state had gotten it from military records, voting records, or some other source. Testimony at the trial from income maintenance workers showed that the North Philadelphians were probably right in their suspicion of the authorities. The only information in the dossiers was on the forms that had been filled out at the time of application, and much of the information needed for an accurate classification simply was not there.

In the third part of the questionnaire, we asked about the alternatives that people would have if they could not get GA. The purpose of this question was to see if people would think of the possibility that food stamps and medical cards would remain as benefits, even though they were not mentioned in the letter. We asked people how would they eat? What would they do if they got sick? The North Philadelphia subjects saw themselves in a desperate situation, as Table 11.4 shows. People said they would 'beg, borrow or steal'; go to the clinic but refuse to pay their bills. The West Philadelphia group was calmer: they put more reliance on family and five thought they could help themselves by appealing. Nobody mentioned that they might be able to use food stamps to eat or use a medical card if they got sick: they assumed that these benefits would be gone along with GA.

We then inquired directly on these points. The interviewer said, 'Somebody told me that "transitionally needy" people

Table 11.4 What would you do?

What would you do after 90 days?	*N. Philadelphia*	*W. Philadelphia*
borrow	4	0
beg	6	0
steal	5	0
go to clinic	9	0
die	2	0
don't pay bills	9	0
food bank	1	0
try to find work	2	0
appeal to a doctor	2	1
go to another institution	1	2
rely on friends	10	4
rely on relatives	8	7
make welfare appeal	0	5
don't know	10	4

would still receive food stamps and a medical card. If that's true, do you think it would be in the letter?' As Table 11.5 shows, only one person answered 'no'; three said, 'no, but it should be'. The rest expressed the idea that the information would be in the letter if it was true. We then asked 'Since it's not in the letter, and they say that transitionally needy persons "are entitled to only up to 90 days worth of assistance per year", is it likely true that after that you will be able to get food stamps and use a medical card?'

The results are shown in the second half of Table 11.5. Of the 32 North Philadelphia people, 30 said simply 'no', two said

Table 11.5 Food stamps and Medicaid

'(Somebody told me that "transitionally needy" people would still receive food stamps and a medical card.) If that's true, do you think it would be in the letter?'

yes	29
should be	12
no – but should be	3
no	1

'Since it's not in the letter, is it likely to be true . . .'

	N. Philadelphia	*W. Philadelphia*
no	30	8
maybe	2	3

'maybe'. No one thought it really might be so. While Table 11.4 shows that people did not think of food stamps or medical cards as possible resources, Table 11.5 shows that on the basis of the absence of the information in the letter, they refused to consider the possibility. There was a significantly greater proportion of people in West Philadelphia who expressed doubt, but only one response that suggested that it could really be so.

The question on food stamps and medical cards was not relevant to an appeal, though it was surprising to find that the state did not see fit to tell desperate people that they would still have these resources. We interpreted the responses to this last question as evidence that those who received the letter accepted it as a complete and reliable guide for deciding on a future course of action. They also believed, like our first district supervisor, that if 'other limited circumstances' included anything so relevant as being treated for drug or alcohol problems, it would have been mentioned.

In cross-examination, the state district attorney asked WL how it could be that people from North Philadelphia showed such strong suspicion of the state's claim to have information on them, and yet had such confidence in the letter as a source of information. It is an apparent paradox. The fact that people's conscious resentment against DPW does not match their unconscious trust in the document indicates that there are presuppositions about the letter that lie well below conscious awareness. Under what conditions do people conclude from the absence of information that certain possibilities do not exist?

There is no doubt that the North Philadelphia people regard the DPW as an agency acting in a hostile manner, that is, as an adversary. Yet they interpreted the letter as basically fair, that is, one that gave them all the information they needed. Why should they believe that an adversary is fair? The interpretation of the letter apparently depends on a principle that hearers do not attribute mixed intentions to speakers, leading to the following Rule of Mixed Communication:

If an adversary A gives information to B that is favourable to B, B will interpret that action as involuntary.

The letter did say 'if you disagree with this finding, you have the right to appeal' and there were four paragraphs on how to make an appeal. We can infer that the recipients of the letter regarded DPW's action in notifying them of the right to appeal as an involuntary one, under control of some unspecified legal authority, and the letter was then considered as an instruction from a neutral or favourable source. We can infer the operation of a second Rule for Interpreting Instructions:

> If B receives information on how to perform an action from a neutral or favorable source A, B will assume that the instruction contains all the information necessary to perform that action.[5]

In the course of the preliminary hearing, it became increasingly clear that the phrase 'other limited circumstances' was not an adequate instruction. The memorandum submitted in support of the complaint by CLS argued that it was certainly DPW's duty to inform recipients of GA as to the 'rules of the game'. The complaint continues:

> Contrary to the most basic notions of fair play, the termination notice not only fails to give the specific rules that govern how eligibility for GA is now being determined, but it also actively misleads the recipient into thinking that h/er case and all the facts s/he may have divulged to the caseworker have been considered.

The decision

On 15 December, Judge Shapiro enjoined the state from reducing or terminating welfare benefits. She instructed the state to send out a new and more adequate notice, stating clearly the provision of Act 75 and the categories of eligibility for continued benefits. Persons already terminated were to be located and a new notice with more information sent to them; if they appealed, their benefits were to continue until the appeal was decided.

Judge Shapiro's opinion of 24 December agreed with the plaintiffs that the class had a substantial private interest; that the notice did not give adequate information and that there was a substantial risk of erroneous deprivation; that the government had shown no reason why a more adequate notice had not been sent; and that class members would suffer irreparable injury if injunctive relief was not granted.

The first wave of termination notices went out to 17,000 persons. Though most of the people we asked told us that they would fight the notice, fewer than 300 appeals were actually received after the first notification. A new and more adequate notice was enlarged and all eight special provisions were listed. In addition, information was given on continued rights to medical benefits and food stamps. By the end of January, more than 4,000 appeals had already been received. Those who appealed continued to receive benefits until their cases were resolved. By May, the DPW estimated that 68,000 new termination letters had been sent out. At that time, the department had received about 10,000 appeals.

More general legal challenges were made to the Thornfare legislation in the months that followed, but they were not successful. The CLS success was in the long run only a delaying action. As one attorney put it, 'we helped quite a few people get through the winter'. For nine years, the Thornfare distinction between 'chronically needy' and 'transitionally needy' has been the law of Pennsylvania. During this period, the number of homeless people on the streets of Philadelphia has increased dramatically. Surveys of the homeless show that a good percentage of them would have been eligible for general assistance if they had not been classified as 'transitionally needy'. CLS has continued its work against the Thornfare legislation.

THE US STEEL CASE

In the 1960s the American steel industry was the focus of a number of federal actions to eliminate practices that discriminated against minorities and women. One of these class action suits was located in Pittsburgh, on behalf of Black steel workers in the city. The linguistic issues concerned the fairness of a legal notice that informed the steel workers that they would have to give up their claims in the local suit to accept a partial settlement of a national suit.

The Pittsburgh case was rooted in the history of Black steel workers over the previous two decades. Blacks had come from the South to work in the steel industries of Chicago, Gary, Cleveland, and Pittsburgh during the war years and after. Some had been brought as strike breakers, but almost all had come as lower-paid workers, in janitorial and furnace-type jobs that were considered less desirable and paid less than others. A complex system of tracking made it difficult for them to move upward, since if they moved to a better-paying track they would lose the seniority they had gained in the lower-paying one.

In the late 1960s a number of federal suits were brought under Title VII of the Civil Rights Act of 1964, to correct such practices and establish equal pay for Blacks and Whites, men and women. The Equal Employment Opportunity Commission and the legislation that established it made possible the creation of class action suits, where a single attorney could obtain corrective action for a very large number of clients. One such suit was brought on a national basis against the nine major steel corporations, and settled by a consent decree under Federal judge Pointer in Birmingham in 1974. A certain amount of money was to be paid to Black and women steel workers as compensation for lower salaries they had received, and corrective action was to be taken to eliminate many of the practices considered unfair by the courts (though the steel industries never admitted that they had discriminated).[6]

In Pittsburgh, attorney Bernard Marcus had worked over many years to establish a class action suit representing some 600 Black steel workers at the local Homestead works against US Steel and the union. He hoped this suit would bring considerably more profit to the steel workers than the national settlement was likely to do.[7] He had experienced many difficulties in getting the class action established, and had carried an appeal as far as the Supreme Court to obtain permission to communicate with his clients. He had joined forces with the NAACP Legal Defence Fund to pursue the case. The linguistic issue arose at a moment where it seemed that new action by all the other parties involved might reduce the class he was representing to almost nil.

An 'Audit and Review Committee', representing the steel union, the companies, and the government, was about to send out cheques in the settlement of the national case. To accept the cheque, local steel workers would have to give up their claim in the local case. Marcus felt that the letter the committee was sending out explaining the issues, along with the legal notice of waiver, was biased in favour of accepting the cheque and against continuing the local case.[8]

In the fall of 1975, Marcus called Labov (WL) and asked if he could, as a linguist, examine the letter for objectivity and comprehensibility. He assembled a group of four who might be able to throw light on the matter. Two would be concerned with the comprehensibility of the document. Mort Botel of the University of Pennsylvania Graduate School of Education was one of the country's leading experts on readability, and the author of one of the widely used indices of readability. Jeff van den Broek was then engaged in a dissertation on sociolinguistic variation in syntactic complexity in the Flemish of Maaseik, and had done extensive work on measure of syntactic complexity.[9] Two would be concerned with possible bias in the document. Kroch's dissertation (1979) dealt with the semantics of quantifier scope, and he examined the text for semantic bias of quantifiers and other grammatical features. WL's contribution centred on the empirical question as to whether the formulations of the letter actually did produce a semantic bias in those who had to make the decision.

The notice was a twelve-page document, under the authorship of the joint committee representing the steel companies, the steelworkers' union, and the government agency. It introduced the consent decree and the local case (the *Rodgers* case), and notified readers that they were members of both classes. It urged the steel workers to read the notice carefully, and to get help if they did not understand it. It explained the relations of the two cases, and the consequences of signing the waiver or not signing it. The last page was the legal notice of waiver itself, which was one long sentence in technical legal language. This sentence was also to be printed in small type on the back of the cheque to be signed.

Our group testified in Pittsburgh February 17–18, 1976, before Judge Hubert Teitelbaum in a hearing on the comprehensibility and objectivity of this notice of rights. Botel was qualified as an expert on readability, and made a strongly favourable impression on the judge. We presented the data on readability by half-pages of the letter, as shown in Fig. 11.1. At the top of the diagram are general titles that give some idea of the content of the pages concerned. The vertical axis on the left shows the Botel readability measure, based on word-frequency as registered in

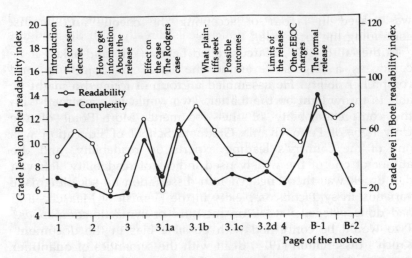

Figure 11.1 Readability and syntactic complexity of the notice

the Lorge–Thorndike list. The measure is in terms of grade-level: it can be seen to vary widely from one section of the document to the other. The index falls to a low level – that is, readability is high – in the section on 'How to get information', which begins:

[1] You should read this letter carefully. If you have any questions which are not answered by this letter, representatives of the Implementation Committee at your plant will be available to answer such questions at the times and place shown on the sheet which you have received along with this letter.

The grade level index is also quite low in the discussion of possible outcomes, where on page 3.3c we read:

[2] Whichever of the parties in *Rodgers* (either plaintiffs or the defendants) are successful, the unsuccessful parties would be entitled to appeal to a Court of appeals and possibly could appeal to the United States Supreme Court. Such appeals could result in affirmance or reversal of any judgment entered by the District court. Accordingly, it is likely that it will be at least several years even after trial of this case until it is finally known whether plaintiffs or the plaintiff class will receive any back pay or injunctive relief in the *Rodgers* case. Consequently, it is unlikely that there would be any final resolution of the *Rodgers* case, including appeals, before 1979.

On the other hand, the grade level is quite high, and readability low, when the notice deals directly with the Rodgers case, as on p. 3.1b:

[3] The *Rodgers* plaintiffs seek an injunction prohibiting defendant Company and defendant Unions from continuing such alleged discriminatory policies or practices, as well as back pay, punitive damages, attorneys' fees, and any other relief which the District Court may deem appropriate.

Van den Broek had also examined the text with eight different measures of syntactic complexity, which were all highly correlated. He selected the Hunt Measure for display in court, based on the mean length of T-Units (independent clauses and all clauses dependent on them). It is superimposed on the readability measure in Fig. 11.1, using the vertical index on the right, to show that in general, there is a good agreement between the two measures. The sections that show the lowest grade levels for readability also show the lowest syntactic complexity, and vice versa. Both measures reach a climax with the formal release, which begins with the sentence:

[4] I, the undersigned, acknowledge receipt of the gross sum shown on the face of this check, in consideration of which I irrevocably and unconditionally release United States Steel Corporation, the United Steelworkers of America, the past and present parents, subsidiaries, divisions, offices, directors, agents, local unions, members, employees, successors and assigns of either of them (severally and collectively 'Releasees') jointly and individually, from any and all claims known or unknown which I, my heirs, successors and assigns have or may have against Releasees and any and all liability which Releasees may have to me or them; (1) resulting from any actual or alleged violations occurring on or before April 12, 1974, based upon race, color, sex or national origin, of any federal, state or local equal employment opportunity laws, ordinances, regulations, orders, the duty of fair representation or other applicable constitutional or statutory provisions, orders or regulations; and/or (2) resulting at any time from the continued effects of any such violations by Releasees of any such laws, etc.

The readability and complexity measures diverge at the end of the release, where the language shows complex arrangements of fairly ordinary words as in

[5] This release is the sole and entire agreement between me and Releasees and there are no other written or oral agreements regarding the subject matter hereof.

Kroch was qualified as an expert in linguistics, and testified on the semantic bias introduced by words like EVEN, AT LEAST, and ANY. He explained to the court that in passages like [2], it was always possible to characterise a length of time by either a least lower bound – WILL BE AT LEAST THREE YEARS – or a most upper bound – WILL BE FINISHED IN LESS THAN FOUR YEARS, and the consistent choice of the former showed a clear bias. He showed that EVEN and ANY introduce further bias toward the writer's point of view that no progress towards the resolution of the case is likely. The multiplication of these presuppositions and negative implications all led to the idea that one should accept the offer and abandon further action.

Judge Teitelbaum carefully followed Kroch's testimony on what the sources of bias were and how they might be eliminated. Here, for example, is an extract from Kroch's discussion of the third sentence in [2] above, as he applied arguments based on Gricean implicatures and his own work on the semantics of time adverbials:

[6] KROCH: Beginning with the words 'Accordingly, it is likely that it will be at least several years even after trial of this case before it is finally known whether plaintiffs or the plaintiff class will receive any back pay . . .' When you indicate only the lower bounds of a time period and not the upper bounds there is a strong suggestion by the reader that it may well drag on indefinitely. Now, I understand that lawyers want to be careful not to make promises that they can't fulfil and that things often go on longer than you might think. However, this document is addressed to laymen who will read it as ordinary English. They won't read these qualifications as being particularly lawyer's qualifications; they will read them as ordinary English and a speaker of ordinary English

at least assumes that when a phrase like 'at least' is used that the author is using it because he cannot say something more clear and helpful to him. That, on the other hand, it could have said something like, 'It is likely that within three or so years this case will be settled'. Now, that is slanted the other way . . .

THE COURT: Would it be perfectly unslanted if it said, 'You should be advised that it may be three years before this matter is settled'. Is that in the middle?

KROCH: Well, frankly, I would take that as in the middle, but whether it is perfectly unbiased is not a question that I can judge immediately.

Throughout the trial, the courtroom was quite full, and several benches were occupied by steel workers from the Homestead plant. We noticed that they paid a great deal of attention to Kroch's testimony, and enjoyed particularly his exchanges with the judge and the defence attorneys.

My own testimony had two parts. One concerned the distribution of elements with semantic bias as against the distribution of readability and complexity. Fig. 11.2 shows the biasing elements that we identified by the half-page, against the background established by Fig. 11.1. It is immediately evident that these biasing elements – ANY, EVEN, AT LEAST, etc. – were not scattered randomly throughout the text. Instead, they are

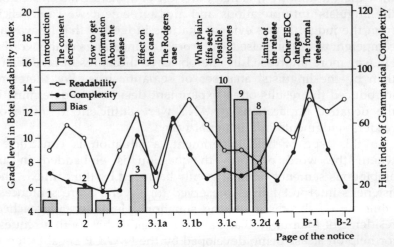

Figure 11.2 Distribution of biasing elements in the notice

concentrated at just those points where the text is simplest: first, in the section on 'How to get information', and then in 'Possible outcomes'. Our answer to both questions – 'is the letter comprehensible? is it objective?' – were therefore 'Yes'. But where the document was comprehensible, it was not objective: and where it was objective, it was not comprehensible. We need not think of such a distribution of bias as the result of deliberate manipulation. Where the authors of the letter tried most earnestly to simplify their language and help the reader decide what to do, they naturally introduced their own way of looking at things – that the Pittsburgh steel workers should take the money and run.

So far, our testimony rested in part on accepted techniques of measurement, in part on linguistic theory, and in part on the specific organisation of the document. We emphasised the negative implications of ANY in passages like (2). ANY is a negative polarity element and demands negative contexts in sentences like 'I don't think anything about it'. There is a further implication that the occurrence of ANY in neutral contexts strengthens negative interpretations of the existential situation. In (2) the repeated use of this quantifier leads to the implication that even if a judgment is arrived at, there may not be any parties found injured; and even if parties are found to be injured, there may not be any pay awarded. The weakest point in the expert testimony was that our view of semantic bias rested on the linguists' interpretations and any agreement we could elicit from the judge. It was evident that the judge felt that he was as competent as anyone else to interpret the meanings of the words. He was more impressed by the objective measures of readability than by the linguists' analyses of semantic bias. We therefore introduced the results of an experiment designed to determine if the negative implications of ANY were sufficient to influence readers' judgments in a material way.

In this type of field experiment, a situation is constructed where the word or form in question is embedded in an ambiguous sentence, almost evenly balanced by the context. The listener's interpretation is preserved for several more sentences, while he or she discusses the situation. Here, we approached residents of Mantua, a Black area of Philadelphia, with a request for help on a case being developed by the NAACP Legal Defense Fund:

[7] This is about a guy in Pittsburgh. He worked for US Steel, for
quite a few years. There was a group that was suing the steel
companies for back pay, on account of discrimination in hiring
policies, so that there were a lot of black people who were earning
less money for a long time. So one day he got a letter from the
company with a check for $700. If he signed the check within 30
days he could cash it; but he had to sign a release, giving up any
claim or connection with this suit for back pay. He had to figure
out what were the chances: if there was a good chance of collecting
on the suit, to let the check go; if the chances weren't so good, to
cash the check and forget about the back pay. So he went to a
lawyer. And the lawyer told him *there was no question about his
getting any back pay.* Now how would you deal with that? Would
you take his advice?

The semantic question revolves around the interpretation of the
italicised clause, which was alternatively delivered in two forms
to subjects:

[8a] there was no question about his getting **any** back pay.
[8b] there was no question about his getting **the** back pay.

Answers to the questions did not always reveal the interpretations made by listeners, but in 16 out of 22 cases, there was a
clear indication as to whether people thought the advice was
positive – that he would get the back pay, and he should wait for
it; or negative – that he would not get the back pay, and should
not wait. The effect of *any* was clear.

Table 11.6 Negative implications of *any* v. *the* in US Steel experiment

	Interpretation of lawyer's statement on chances of suit	
	any back pay	the back pay
positive	2	8
negative	5	1
undetermined	4	2
Totals	11	11
(Probability by Fisher's Exact Test, p = 0.036)		

This result supports our analysis of the negative implications
of ANY in these contexts: the use of ANY can effectively alter

listeners' interpretation of a situation and their probable course of action.

The outcome

The judge was at first most favourably inclined towards our testimony, and in fact asked Mort Botel if he would act as AMICUS CURIAE and rewrite the notice:

> [9] THE COURT: Do you want to do something for history and do it in this case?
>
> BOTEL: Well, I agree with Mr Marcus when he said before that this is worth doing.
>
> THE COURT: Doctor, it is only worth doing as far as I am concerned if it is done by the experts totally independent of counsel and without the interjection of any legal concepts in it, but really stating what is there.

Unfortunately, the judge was not willing to accept the delay that Botel estimated would be necessary to produce a revised notice in truly neutral and readable form. He did ask for a brief on the law concerning the responsibility to communicate to the public, and found none. The judge finally decided to rewrite the notice himself, taking officially into account the existence of these biasing elements. Actually, he changed it very little, and we can consider the case lost.

Judge Tietelbaum ruled against the plaintiffs, arguing that 'any benefits which might theoretically be gained by such a revision are far outweighed by the detriments that would attend a lengthy delay'.[10] Nevertheless, he entered into the opinion the following appreciation of the new issues raised:

> [10] In support of their position, plaintiffs have offered the testimony of various experts in the fields of linguistics and (for want of a better term), 'readability'. I have listened attentively to that testimony and, candidly, cannot say that I find it to be utterly devoid of merit. Indeed, I am inclined to believe that the general question of the 'readability' level of class and other legal notices

is one which might well require serious judicial consideration at an appropriate time.

He added a footnote that neither the parties nor the Court had been able to find a case which addresses the 'readability' level argument advanced by plaintiffs.

Although the US Steel case was not won, it introduced into federal courts the issue of the responsibility of the judicial system to communicate its instructions clearly to the public that must act on them. Since that time, considerable progress has been made in that respect. Our participation in this case convinced us that the federal courts did offer a forum that would attend to and assess objective evidence on these issues.

THE PRINZIVALLI CASE

In October 1984 Labov received two tape recordings from attorney Ronald Ziff of Los Angeles. The first tape contained excerpts from a series of telephoned bomb threats made to Pan American Airlines at the Los Angeles Airport. They included such phrases as:

[11] uh, it's gonna be planted on that plane by (a majority) Communist group and I hope you die on it. It's gonna be a bomb, a nuclear bomb that's gonna be able to kill you and everybody on that plane, and I hope you know it by now.

[12] there's gonna be a bomb going off on the flight to L.A. . . . . It's in their luggage. Yes, and I hope you die with it and I hope you're on that.

[13] It's like gonna be a big shoot out tonight up in the air when that plane takes off. On 815 there's gonna be a big shoot out tonight up there.

[14] At eleven when it takes off at 11.15 tonight we're gonna shoot it down. They will shoot it down up in the air after it takes off for tonight.

The second tape had recordings of Paul Prinzivalli speaking the same words. He had been accused of making these telephone calls and was awaiting trial under a series of felony charges. The recording was made by Sandra Disner of the UCLA Phonetics Laboratory, who with Peter Ladefoged was working for the defence, particularly on sound spectrograph identification data (see Nolan, this volume) that showed that the two recordings had different voice qualities. They had referred Ziff to me because the defendant was from the New York metropolitan area of Long Island, and apparently people thought that the bomb threat caller was also from New York. I was asked to contribute my knowledge of the New York City dialect to bear on the case.

As soon as I played the tapes I was sure Prinzivalli was innocent. He obviously was a New Yorker; every detail of his speech fitted the New York City pattern. But it was equally clear that the bomb threat caller was from Eastern New England. In any phrase, one could hear the distinctive features of the Boston area. Every phonetician familiar with the area who heard the tapes came to the same conclusion within a sentence or two, and non-phoneticians who knew the Boston area had the same reaction. In the course of my work for the case, I made recordings of several Bostonians: they all recognised the bomb threat caller as coming from their area without any question.

There's gonna be a bomb going off on the flight to L.A.	
Bomb Threat	dɛˇz gənə bi ə bɔᵖm goɪn ɒf ɒn ðə flaˤɪt tu ɛl eⁱ
Defendant	dɛˆz gɔna bi ə bɒm goɪŋ oˀf an ð flaɪt tuˤ ɛl ɛˆⁱ

Figure 11.3   IPA transcriptions of the bomb threat caller and the defendant's pronunciations of BOMB and OFF

There was therefore no doubt about the guilt or innocence of Prinzivalli. The problem was how to convey this linguistic knowledge to a judge in the Los Angeles area who, like many other West Coast people involved, heard the two speech patterns as very similar. One could of course testify on the basis of an expert phonetician's opinion that the two dialects were different. But it seemed that unless that opinion could be supported by objective evidence that would bring home the reality of the situation to others, there was a serious danger than an innocent person would be convicted of a major crime, with a heavy prison sentence. It is well known that Americans are not sensitive to dialect differences, and from the standpoint of the West Coast, the difference between New York and Boston is hardly notice-able. The differences might appear great to a phonetician attuned to sound patterns, but not necessarily to an untrained listener raised on the West Coast.

Until I arrived in Los Angeles, I knew nothing more about the case than what was on the tapes, and that this was evidence being used to accuse a man of felony charges carrying heavy prison sentences. Here I will present the background facts that were given me after the trial: some have been reported in recent newspaper accounts.

The defendant was a cargo handler for Pan American, the airline involved. He was said to have a grudge against the airlines, because of their handling of shift schedules, among other things, and had been heard to say that he would 'get even' with the company. Several executives of Pan American thought the bomb threat calls sounded like Prinzivalli, though others who had worked closely with him thought they did not. He was arrested and released on bail. The bomb threats continued and his bail was increased to $US50,000 which he could not raise. When he was returned to jail, the bomb threat calls stopped. A month later the district attorney offered to release Prinzivalli on time served if he would plead guilty to three felony counts. He refused, and spent the next eight months in the Los Angeles County jail, awaiting trial.

To prepare for the trial, I first made detailed phonetic transcriptions of the two sets of recordings. I then made instrumental measurements of the formant positions, using the linear predictive coding algorithm at the Linguistics Laboratory of the University of Pennsylvania, and the various charting programmes which we use for displaying vowel systems. All of this measurement was done by WL, though the other phoneti-cians at the laboratory – Franz Seitz, Sharon Ash and David Graff – all contributed their critical thinking to the investigation. Since WL was to present the testimony, it was important that I be able to answer for the continuity of the data and the procedures used throughout by personal knowledge.

WL also made recordings of several Bostonians speaking the same words, and was able to confirm the similarity of the Boston pattern to the phonetic features of the tape. Several new and remarkable characteristics of the Boston dialect appeared in these investigations, which were not introduced into the testimony, but lend further certainty to our conclusions.

The trial was held in Los Angeles on the week of 6 May, without a jury, before Judge Gordon Ringer.[11] The defence had been willing to wait for an opening in Ringer's calendar, since they shared the general high opinion of his intelligence and ability. The prosecution presented evidence from ticket-reservation clerks who had given descriptions of the bomb threat voice at the time, from executives at Pan American who believed that the voice on the recorded bomb threat calls was Prinzivalli's, and evidence that he was a disgruntled employee.

The defence began with efforts to introduce evidence from voice-print (or sound spectrograph) identification by Disner and Ladefoged. Although Ladefoged opposed the free use of voice-prints to identify voices as the same, he has since concluded that voice-print identification is more evidentiary than we thought, and can be used to argue that two voices are different (see also Nolan, this volume). Disner's analysis showed that the individual voices on the tapes had different qualities. However, there was considerable legal argument on the admissibility and reliability of voice-print identification.

WL testified on 10 Friday May. He was qualified as an expert on linguistics on the basis of phonetic studies of New York City and other areas, of sound changes in progress and dialect diversity in the United States. The testimony was divided into four parts: auditory comparison of the dialect features; differences in phonological structure; relation to established knowledge of the dialect areas; and instrumental measurements of the vowel systems. As an expert witness, WL's role was to present an opinion, along with an account of the various steps that he had taken to reach that opinion, and the evidence that was the basis of it. The aim was to present that evidence clearly enough so that Prinzivalli's innocence would appear to the judge as a matter of fact, rather than a matter of opinion.

In the first part, WL played the tape recordings submitted to show the steps he had gone through to form an opinion. The most effective instrument here was the Nagra DSM loudspeaker, which projected to the four corners of the courtroom a clear and flat reproduction of the voices. Several people who had thought the voices sounded similar were suddenly struck with the differences that they now heard when the sound was projected through the Nagra.

He first called attention to the contrast in the pronunciation of the words BOMB and OFF in the phrase, AND A BOMB GOING OFF, as spoken by the bomb threat caller and the defendant, so that it would be immediately apparent that the vowel quality of BOMB and OFF was the same for the bomb threat caller, but different for the defendant. All of the tokens of short *o* and long open *o* words spoken by the bomb threat caller are low back-rounded vowels. But the defendant shows the characteristic New York City distinction between low central /a/ in POSITIVE, lower back /ah/ in BOMB, and the high, over-rounded and ingliding /oh/ in OFF.

The second part of the testimony introduced the theoretical basis of the argument: the concepts of phoneme, phonemic inventory, and phonemic merger. The notion of word class and phonemic identity are difficult enough to establish among linguists, but much more so for the non-linguist who thinks about language in terms of words and sound rather than structure. The major emphasis was put on the merger of COT and CAUGHT in the Eastern New England area (as in Pittsburgh and throughout the Western United States), and on the structural difference between dialects that make such a distinction and those that do not. WL also drew attention to some diagnostic phonetic features in the tape recordings, such as the tense front vowel in AIR as spoken by the bomb threat caller, with a following /j/: [ejə].

At this point the judge remarked that the tape of the bomb threat caller did sound to him like Robert Kennedy. But for reasons to appear later, it was important to draw attention away from such direct impressions, and focus instead on abstract structural features of the two recordings. In addition to the merger in the low back vowels, the bomb threat caller showed a consistently fronted nucleus of /ay/ in DIE and FIVE. It was evident that this nucleus was structurally identified with short /a/, while the defendant's New York City pattern showed the expected coincidence of the nucleus of /ay/ with the low central vowel /ah/ of ON.

Most significant was the vowel in THAT in the phrase, 'I hope you're on that' in [12] above. In New York City, this is always and absolutely a lax /æ/, and never shows the tensed and fronted phoneme /æh/. But in Eastern New England, THAT can have the tensed, raised and fronted vowel, at roughly the same position as New York City THERE. In fact, the sentence 'I hope you're on that' was mistranscribed in the text originally submitted to the court as 'I hope you're on there'. Most people still heard it as 'there' until it was replayed through the Nagra loudspeaker and pointed out the unreleased /t/ at the end which was clearly audible. Such a pronunciation of THAT is not a real possibility for a New Yorker: of the thousands of short A words measured in our New York City studies, not one ever showed tensed /æh/ or /eh/ before voiceless stops.

The third part of WL's testimony introduced evidence from American dialectology, to show that the phonological differences between Eastern New England and New York City were established facts in linguistic scholarship. A copy of Kurath and McDavid's *The Pronunciation of English in the Atlantic States* (1961: 12) was introduced into evidence, and the data shown in Table 11.7 was displayed from the table of low back phonemes of each dialect region. The first column shown in Table 11.7 shows for Eastern New England a single phoneme for three word classes: short *o* words ending in voiced stops, which are low central unrounded in New York City, and short *o* words ending in voiceless fricatives, which merge in New York City with the third class of original long open *o* words in the phoneme /o/.

WL added to this evidence the figures from 'The three dialects of English' (Labov in press), which include the distribution of the COT-CAUGHT merger for the United States as a whole. These data are drawn from a 1966 study of the speech of long-distance telephone operators, and include information on the perception of speech as well as production.[12] They show the merger located in Eastern New England, an expanding area around Western Pennsylvania, Canada, and most of the western United States. There is no sign of this merger in the New York region or the surrounding mid-Atlantic states.

Table 11.7 Low back vowel phonemes in ENE and NYC

Word class	Eastern New England	New York City
Cot, crop, stock, etc.	ɒ	ɑ
loss, frost, off, etc.	ɒ	ɔ
law, salt, talk, hawk, etc.	ɒ	ɔ

The last part of the testimony introduced instrumental measurements of the vowel systems of the bomb threat caller and the defendant, providing confirmation of the auditory impressions and the structural analyses.

The vowel system of the bomb threat caller is shown in Fig. 11.4a. This is a two-formant chart, with the first formant on the vertical axis, and the logarithm of the second formant – approximating the perceptual relations – on the horizontal axis. Though we had measured the entire trajectory, and had evidence on differences in trajectories, the patterns appear most clearly in the distribution of vowel nuclei, as shown by the single point for each word selected to represent the nucleus in a systematic way.

Figure 11.4b showed a comparable analysis for the defendant. To support such displays, it was necessary to present to the court the theoretical concept of formant, and its relation to vowel quality, with some of the limitations involved. It was also necessary to explain the differences between linear predictive coding analysis of the digital signal and spectrographic analysis, which had become involved with the problem of the admissibility of voice print evidence. Since we had not used spectrographic techniques in our analysis of the vowel system, our evidence was free of the legal challenges that had been made to voice-print evidence, which uses the electro-mechanical spectrograph.

The significant features of Figs 11.4a and 11.4b were presented through a series of simpler displays. Figure 11.5a showed the single low-back phoneme of the bomb threat caller, with the vowels of BOMB, OFF, ON, POSITIVE and COMMUNIST all in the same low-back range.

Figure 11.5b showed the corresponding date for the defendant, with the three distinct phonemes characteristic of the New York City system. Most short *o* words like ON, POSITIVE and COMMUNIST have a low central vowel that is represented by the phoneme /a/. A small number of short *o* words are lengthened and backed, and join other long *a* words like FATHER in the phoneme /ah/: BOMB is a member of this class (Cohen 1970).

Figures 11.6a and 11.6b dealt with the fronting of /ay/ which marks the Eastern New England dialect; in this system, the nucleus of /ay/ is identified with the nucleus of the /ah/ phoneme that merges traditional long *a* words like FATHER and HALF with words where post-vocalic /r/ is vocalised as in CAR

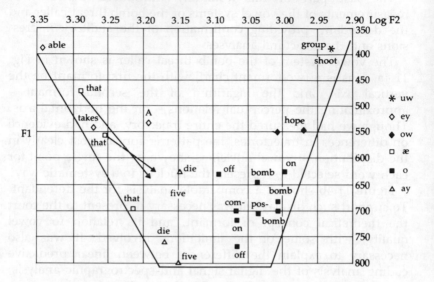

Figure 11.4a Vowel system of the bomb threat caller

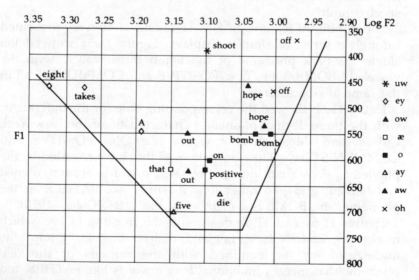

Figure 11.4b Vowel system of the defendant

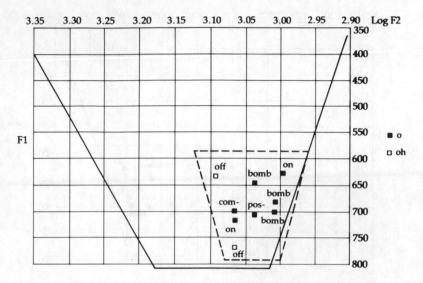

Figure 11.5a /o/ phoneme of the bomb threat caller

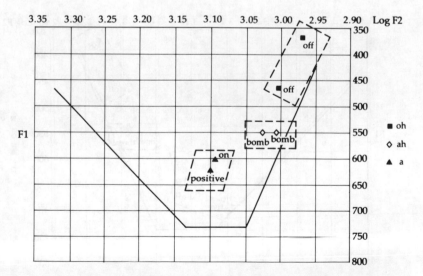

Figure 11.5b /a,ah,oh/ phonemes of the defendant

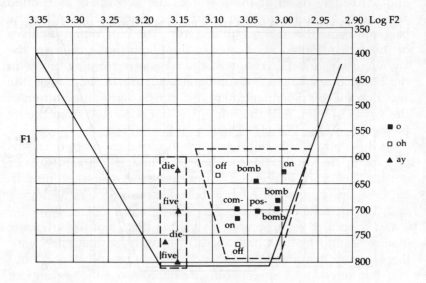

Figure 11.6a

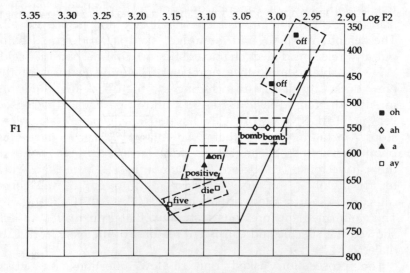

Figure 11.6b

and MARKET. In all of these words, the /a/ nucleus is fronted and shows a good margin of security separating it from the low back phoneme that merges /o/ and /oh/. The only representatives of these two-fronted phonemes in the bomb threat calls are the /ay/ words. Figure 11.6a showed the consistent fronting of /ay/ in the bomb threat calls. The comparable Figure 11.6b showed the situation for the defendant: here /ay/ ranges across the bottom of the vowel system, and the nucleus is not separated from the /a/ phoneme in ON, POSITIVE and COMMUNIST.

At this point it was not necessary to introduce more diagrams or explain the implications of the instrumental data in greater detail. The judge intervened to interpret the diagrams himself, since he saw clearly the relation between the previous testimony and the instrumental display.

WL concluded his testimony by stating that all of the linguistic features found in the bomb threat call could be identified with the linguistic features of the Eastern New England dialect, and that the defendant's speech consistently showed the features of the New York City dialect. In answer to the defence attorney's final question, WL stated that the two recordings were spoken by different people.

Judge Ringer then asked the defendant to rise and recite the pledge of allegiance to the flag: 'I pledge allegiance to the flag of the United States of America and to the Republic for which it stands, one nation, indivisible, with liberty and justice for all.' The defendant did so, and the judge asked WL if he could point out any relevant dialect characteristics in what he had just said. WL was able to indicate a number of defining features of the New York City dialect in including the high back ingliding /oh/ in ALL, the tensed /æh/ in STAND, and in particular the tensed /æh/ in FLAG. New York City has tense /æh/ before all voiced stops, including /g/. Other Mid-Atlantic dialects have the phonemic split between lax /æ/ and tense /æh/, but none of them have tense /æh/ before /g/. As one passes from New York to Philadelphia, the first sub-class to drop out of the tense category is short *a* the words before /g/: FLAG, BAG, RAG, etc. This confirmed the previous testimony that Prinzivalli's speech showed the specific and consistent features of the New York City dialect.

The prosecution asked only a few questions on cross-examination. Most of the questions concerned the identification of individuals, and whether WL could say if a given speech sample belonged to a given person. In response WL tried to point out that he had no expertise in the identification of individuals, but that his knowledge concerned speech communities. Though sociolinguistic studies have found from the outset that communities were more consistent objects of description than individuals, there are limits on the range of variation for any individual who belongs to that community.

The question that naturally followed was whether an individual New Yorker could imitate a Boston dialect – whether Prinzivalli could have disguised himself as a Bostonian. WL's reply was that when people imitate or acquire other dialects, they focus on the socially relevant features: the marked words and sounds, but not on the phonological structures. He was able to cite Payne's work in King of Prussia (1980), which shows that all children acquire the low level sound rules of the Philadelphia area in a few years, but only those with parents raised in Philadelphia reproduce the phonological distribution of Philadelphia lax /æ/ and tense /æh/. If it could be shown that the defendant had had a long familiarity with the Boston dialect, and a great talent for imitation, then one could not rule out the possibility that he had done a perfect reproduction of the Boston system. But if so, he would have accomplished a feat that had not yet been reported for anyone else.

On the following Monday morning, Judge Ringer called the attorneys to the bench and asked them if they wanted to continue the case. Since the prosecuting attorney did not consent to dismiss the charges, additional testimony was submitted on voice-print identification. The following morning the prosecuting attorney summarised his case. When the defence attorney rose to present his final argument, Judge Ringer said that there was no need for him to do so. He acquitted the defendant, finding on the basis of the linguistic testimony evidence of a reasonable doubt that Prinzivalli had committed the crime. In discussion in chambers and to the press, he stressed the clarity and objectivity of the linguistic evidence, a point on which all the attorneys agreed.

Prinzivalli was offered his job back at Pan American, on condition that he did not sue for damages or back pay. He filed suit for damages; the case has not yet been resolved, but he has been reinstated at Pan American and is now working in Long

Island. In a letter of thanks to WL he said that he had waited fifteen months for someone to separate fact from fiction, and when he heard it done in the courtroom he was much moved.

CONCLUSION

These cases are taken from a larger set where linguistic evidence was used to testify in the search for a just interpretation of the facts of the matter. We have chosen them to illustrate the possibilities open to a science of linguistics which draws on observation and experiment to establish its conclusions. All our efforts were not equally successful. But in each case, the objectivity of this approach to linguistics was favourably received by those who are quite removed from the academic issues that determine success or failure within our field.

The objectivity and reliability of our linguistic evidence produced intense interest among both attorneys and judges. In our legal system it is assumed that there will be advocates and experts on each side. It is assumed that each side will use every rhetorical device to strengthen its case. There is no claim for impartiality in argument. Therefore all the more value is put on the solidity and objectivity of evidence that is inserted into this system of advocacy, which creates belief and justifies decisions in the face of contending parties. It has been pointed out to me that judges in particular are grateful for evidence that allows them to decide a case with confidence, and commit themselves to sleep at night without wondering if they have sentenced an innocent person to jail or let a criminal go free.

The bridge between the facts of a case and the conclusion cannot be made without the help of linguistic theory. No web of inferences and deductions can be made without general principles that rest on a long history of observation and testing. Here we have illustrated the application of the theory of negative polarity, and the association of negative polarity with distinctive meaning. We have also dealt with the theory of the phoneme, intimately connected with the fundamental concept of the arbitrary character of the linguistic sign.

When we contrast linguistic theory with linguistic practice, we usually conjure up a theory that builds models out of introspective judgments, extracting principles that are remote from observation and experiment. This is not the kind of theory we have in mind when we search for a way to establish the facts of a matter.

We are, of course, interested in theories of the greatest generality. But are these theories the end-product of linguistic activity? Do we gather facts to serve the theory, or do we create theories to resolve questions about the real world? We would challenge the common understanding of our academic linguistics that we are in the business of producing theories: that linguistic theories are our major product. We find such a notion utterly wrong.

A sober look at the world around us shows that matters of importance are matters of fact. There are some very large matters of fact: the origin of the universe, the direction of continental drift, the evolution of the human species. There are also specific matters of fact: the innocence or guilt of a particular individual. These are the questions to answer if we would achieve our fullest potential as thinking beings. General theory is useful, and the more general the theory, the more useful it is, just as any tool is more useful if it can be used for more jobs. But it is still the application of the theory that determines its value. A very general theory can be thought of as a missile that attains considerable altitude, and so it has much greater range than other missiles. But the value of any missile depends on whether it hits the target.

NOTES

1. The introduction and Thornfare case were co-authored by Labov and Harris. The US Steel and Prinzivalli cases are drawn from Labov (1988). We have received help from many people in doing the work described in this chapter. In particular, we would like to thank Teresa Labov, who carried out the West Philadelphia survey, and to Carmen Rivera and Dalia Rodrigues, who helped with Hispanic subjects for the North Philadelphia survey.
2. For two Hispanic subjects whose reading ability was limited, Harris read the letter aloud.

3. The report was read by the judge and attorneys, but the state objected to the motion to introduce it as evidence on the grounds that survey data was hearsay. It was used as the basis for the expert opinion, and Labov read extensively from the tables in his testimony.

4. People over 45 were not supposed to get a letter, but in the hasty reclassification there were many mistakes. If someone over 45 got the letter, they would have no way of knowing that they could and should appeal.

5. These two rules, drawn in the format of Labov and Fanshel (1977), are constructed here for the first time on the basis of this situation. Whether they will apply to a wider range of situations remains to be seen.

6. Consent decrees I and II issued by Judge Sam C. Pointer, Jr. on 12 April 1974, signed by representatives of the Department of Justice, the Department of Labor, the Equal Employment Opportunity Commission, Armco Steel, Bethlehem Steel, Jones & Laughlin, National Steel, Republic Steel, US Steel, Wheeling-Pittsburgh Steel, Youngstown Sheet & Tube, and the United Steelworkers of America.

7. Jimmie L. Rodgers and John A. Turner vs. United States Steel Corp., Local 1397, AFL-CIO and United Steelworkers of America, AFL-CIO, Civil Action 71–793 in the US District Court for the Western District of Pennsylvania.

8. Notice of rights to back pay under Consent Decree I, US et al. v. Allegheny Ludlum Industries, Inc. et al., Basic Steel Industry Audit and Review Committee.

9. See Van den Broek (1977) for other uses of these measures.

10. Opinion of 8 March 1976, in the case of Rodgers v. United States Steel Corp., No. 71–92.

11. The account of the trial that presented below is limited to WL's testimony, the preparation for it, and information received from the defence attorneys on what happened immediately after. There was other important testimony that WL did not hear, in particular the statements of Disner and Ladefoged, since he was not allowed to be in the courtroom while they were testifying.

12. In this study, operators were asked for the telephone number of a Mr [həri hak], spoken with a low front central vowel. Operators from a one-phoneme area first looked up the spelling H-A-W-K, since it is more common than H-O-C-K. In the course of the discussion that followed, they also gave their own pronunciations of these two words, as well as COT and CAUGHT, reacted to my own two-phoneme pronunciation, and were led to give some information on their own geographical background. Though the mechanisation and centralisation of telephone information makes it impossible to

pursue this approach, it gave a fairly fine-grained view of the status of the merger at that time.

APPENDIX A: THE TERMINATION OF ASSISTANCE LETTER

Commonwealth of Pennsylvania
Department of Public Welfare

PHILADELPHIA COUNTY BOARD OF ASSISTANCE
Tioga District
Germantown & Sedgeley Avenues,
Philadelphia, Pennsylvania 19133

Dear ____

According to a new law enacted on April 8, 1982, persons who qualify for General Assistance must be classified as either chronically needy or transitionally needy, depending on their circumstances.

Chronically needy persons are those who because of age, physical or mental handicap or other limited circumstances are less likely to be able to provide for themselves through employment. These people are entitled to receive General Assistance for as long as they need it, if they meet all conditions of eligibility.

Transitionally needy persons are those who are not limited in employability by their circumstance and should be able to support themselves without public assistance. These persons, therefore, are entitled to only up to 90 days worth of assistance per year.

According to the information we have about your situation, you must be considered transitionally needy. (See PAEM 141.61 (d) (2).) This means that, unless your circumstances change, you may receive General Assistance only until Dec 31, 1982. You will receive seven (7) checks in the amount of $131.00 with the last check being in the amount of $131.00 on 12/22/82.

If you disagree with our finding that you are transitionally needy and have not had an opportunity to provide medical verification of any serious physical or mental handicap which you have, please get in touch with me promptly, and I will give you the proper form on which you can submit this verification.

In addition, if you disagree with this decision, you have the right to appeal and may ask for a hearing to challenge it. However, you must request the hearing within 30 days of the date of this letter.

At the hearing you can present to the Hearing Officer the reasons why you think the decision of the County Assistance Office is incorrect and present evidence or witnesses on your own behalf. You have the right to represent yourself or to have anyone represent you. A staff member of the County Assistance Office will refer you for legal help, if you request them to do so.

If you wish to appeal, you may make an oral request by calling the Office of Hearings and Appeals at their toll-free number, 800–932–0580 or you may call your worker and complete the following and send this letter back to the Office of Hearings and Appeals at P.O. Box 8326, Harrisburg, PA 17105.

1. I want to appeal because:

2. My telephone number is:

APPENDIX B: THE QUESTIONNAIRE

1.   Understanding the letter.
1.1 What's the difference between transitionally needy vs. chronically needy? Which do you think is better?
1.2 If you got this letter, how would you fight it?
1.3 It says that 'Chronically needy persons are those who because of age, physical or mental handicap or other limited circumstances are less likely to provide for themselves.'
   1.3.1 What do you think they mean by age? If somebody was 50 years old, would they qualify?
   1.3.2 It says 'other limited circumstances'. What could 'limited circumstances' be?
   1. If somebody was being treated for drug or alcohol problems, do you think they would qualify under 'limited circumstances'?
   2. If somebody had been working for years, say four years, and used up all their unemployment compensation, would they qualify under 'limited circumstances'?
   3. If your mother was real sick, and you have to stay home and watch her, would that be 'limited circumstances'?
   4. If you were decided to be 'transitionally needy', used up your 90 days, and then you broke your leg, could you expect to be re-classified as 'chronically needy'?

2.   Information.
2.1 It says, 'according to the information we have about your

situation, you must be considered transitionally needy'. Did you ever give information about your physical or mental health?

2.2 Where do you think they'd get this information?

3. Public assistance.
   If they decide that you are 'transitionally needy' and you have to support yourself 'without public assistance' after your 90 days, how would you get along?

3.1 What if you got sick? What would you do?

3.2 How would you eat?

3.3 Somebody told me that 'transitionally needy' people would still receive food stamps and a medical card. If that's true, do you think it would be in the letter?

3.4 Since it's not in the letter, and they say that transitionally needy persons 'are entitled to only up to 90 days worth of assistance per year', is it likely true that after that you will be able to get food stamps and use a medical card?

APPENDIX C: EXTRACTS FROM NOTICE TO BE SENT TO CLIENTS WHO HAD ALREADY RECEIVED TERMINATION LETTERS IN ACCORDANCE WITH PRELIMINARY INJUNCTION OF 15 DECEMBER, 1982

Dear

In September or October we told you that you were transitionally, not chronically needy, and that your General Assistance would end some time in December or January. This notice is to give you more information so that you can decide whether you now want to request a hearing.

You may be chronically needy, and eligible for continuing assistance because:

A. You are under age 18.

B. You are 18 and in school and expect to finish school before age 19.

C. You are over 45 years of age.

D. You have a serious physical or mental problem that prevents you from working.

E. You are needed at home to care for a child under age 6 or a disabled person of any age.

F. You are getting treatment in a drug or alcohol program.

G. You are working at least 30 hours a week but are not earning enough to support yourself or your family.

H. Your income has been reduced because of natural disaster but you can't get unemployment benefits.

I. You worked 30 hours a week for at least 48 months in the last 8 years and had no unemployment benefits left when you applied for assistance . . .

Also, on the same day your General Assistance ends, the Medical Assistance you now have will end. You will get a different kind of Medical Assistance that has fewer benefits. The ending of your General Assistance will not make you lose your food stamps . . .

TWELVE

Lawyer's response to language and disadvantage before the law

John Carroll

A SEARCH FOR 'TRUTH'

Lord Maugham said 'I think it will be conceded by all that the object of the legal trial is the ascertainment of truth.' The language used by judges in the course of trials, and the rules used to control trial procedure and the giving of evidence are often expressed in terms requiring the revelation of truth. Witnesses are required to take an oath to tell the truth. They are subjected to examination and cross-examination so that the facts can be verified as far as possible.

Leaving aside the difficulty of defining or establishing 'the truth' it is clear from the chapters assembled in this part and elsewhere that the Australian trial system (based on the English model) falls well short of this. For the adversary system to work, there must be a genuine contest between more or less equally placed forces rather than a one-sided affair.

The chapter by Brennan highlights problems inherent in the criminal justice system. [The credibility of a criminal trial depends upon a genuine effort being made to establish the facts. A criminal trial, however, is not directed to resolving a dispute between the parties.] The trial is accusatorial and the accused is regarded as innocent until proven guilty. [The central issue is not whether the accused is guilty or did certain things but whether the prosecution has proven the guilt of the accused beyond reasonable doubt.] The balance is struck in favour of the accused. There are elaborate rules governing the evidence of prosecution witnesses for example with respect to child victims of sexual assault.

As highlighted by Brennan's chapter, the rules are much less concerned with protecting the interests of other participants in the trial process such as witnesses. The primary focus is on allowing the accused to probe or challenge the evidence of others. This is understandable given the serious consequences for the accused, in say, a child sexual abuse case.

This may have the consequence of putting a child witness, who has already suffered, through further abuse through the legal system for nought. Courts have developed some mechanisms for reducing unnecessary attacks on witnesses. For example, the rules relating to the questioning of witnesses forbid unnecessarily insulting, harassing, offensive or annoying questioning. Reforms on presentation of evidence of child witnesses have in Australia concentrated on removing some of the confrontation from the process, such as through the use of closed circuit television, but have not directly addressed the need for effective communication.

The absence of protection would appear to reflect indifference to, or a lack of appreciation of, the importance of language and the need to ensure that communication breakdowns are minimised.

One response to the chapters in this part is to replace the adversarial system with one in which the primary focus is the search for truth. In arguing for the use of inquisitorial methods, Mr Leroy Certoma then of Australia's Immigration Review Tribunal states (Certoma, 1990):

> Truth in adversarial systems is merely a procedural truth and the Court is only concerned with declaring a winner in an area which is characterised by procedural tactics, including skilful and selective manipulation of questions and answers, extreme standpoints dictated by an object to win rather than to reveal the truth, and elaborate rules of evidence such as hearsay and other evidentiary rules which are complex, and even contradictory, and often operate to exclude relevant evidence.

However inquisitorial systems are not necessarily more likely to unravel the truth than adversarial systems. They too are subject to problems with respect to the protection of the most disadvantaged. More significantly, the precepts of the adversarial system are well accepted in Australia and elsewhere and it is extremely unlikely that there will be radical changes in the nature of the legal system.

It is therefore important to consider the measures which may be tacked on to the trial system to make it fairer and to remove language and other communication barriers. These barriers are not restricted to children and people with inadequate English language skills. As demonstrated in Labov and Harris's chapter, there are many people whose primary language is English who have real difficulty in understanding what goes on in legal proceedings in which they are involved and in making themselves understood in those proceedings.

Part of the problem lies in the complex language of the law and of the jargon used by lawyers and by the Courts. Courtroom English is recognised as a register of English which would be confusing to those whose education or vocabulary is limited. Indifference is often exhibited by judicial officers and court officials to non-professional (and those who may be perceived by them to be non-professional, such as interpreters) participants in the legal process. The example given by Eades of the witness pleading guilty in civil proceedings in which he was not involved is not completely atypical. To a fairly typical defendant in a criminal case the exchanges between the prosecutor, magistrate and defence counsel may appear as a series of indistinguishable mumbles, apart from the pronouncement of the penalty on the defendant. As demonstrated in the chapter by Walsh, the structure of the discourse has the capacity to further block communication between interested parties.

MEASURES TO ADDRESS DISADVANTAGE BEFORE THE LAW

What then can be done? As a starting point there must be an appreciation of the need for effective communication with all of the participants in the proceedings. For a trial to be fair, all of those affected by its outcome must have, or be provided with, the faculty to adequately understand the proceedings. Procedures should be in place to ensure that prior to this stage, communication barriers do not prejudice the interests of those involved. For example, cultural differences and inadequate language skills are likely to place a police suspect at considerable disadvantage in the criminal investigation process. The use of abstract language, police jargon and the intricacy of grammatical relations between clauses in police warnings make it necessary for protection for those with inadequate language skills at the stage prior to any hearing of the case.

The chapter by Eades sets out a number of possible or partial means by which disadvantage for aboriginals and other groups can be minimised.

Relevant measures include:

1. changing the composition of the judiciary, so that they come from a range of ethnic backgrounds and have a knowledge of language issues and not from a narrow class of society with a background as practicing lawyers;
2. changing the nature of legal discourse;
3. greater emphasis on plain language in the law;
4. simplifying legal procedures so that they are less threatening to those with insufficient language skills; and
5. increased training of lawyers and judges with respect to effective communication, although this can be counter-productive.

I shall now deal in more detail with some of the possible responses.

Specific legal provisions addressing the communicative needs of Aboriginal people in the law

The Eades chapter refers to the protections provided by the so-called Anunga Rules. These guidelines were formulated in the Northern Territory in the case of *R* v. *Anunga* for police officers to follow when interrogating aboriginal suspects. The guidelines are not rules of law. Compliance with the guidelines would generally result in the admission of the evidence thereby obtained. Non-compliance will not necessarily result in the exclusion of evidence.

The rules stated in *R* v. *Anunga* do not apply to every instance where aboriginals make confessions, for many aboriginals in the Northern Territory are not subject to the disadvantages of language and education which the rules have in mind.

The rules have been added to and included in Commonwealth legislation. The *Commonwealth Crimes (Investigation of Commonwealth Offences) Act 1991*:

1. provides an entitlement to an interpreter where the investigating official has reasonable grounds for believing that a person in custody is unable because of inadequate knowledge of the English language to communicate with reasonable fluency in that language;
2. gives an accused a right to communicate with a friend or a relative or a legal practitioner;
3. requires tape recording or videotaping of cautions, interviews, confessions and admissions;
4. limits the time in which suspects can be held in police custody before charging to four hours.

There are also specific provisions for Aboriginals, such as:

1. a requirement to notify a representative of the Aboriginal Legal Service that the person is under arrest for that offence;
2. the police must not question the person unless an interview friend (which includes friends, relatives, lawyers, representatives of Aboriginal Legal Aid advisory bodies) is present or that the person has voluntarily waived the right to an interview friend being present;
3. and the Minister for Justice is required to maintain and publish a list of suitable interview friends and interpreters.

The use of interpreters

The Commonwealth Government has introduced an Evidence Bill into Parliament. It provides that the right to an interpreter in civil proceedings will only be displaced if it can be established that the person has an adequate command of the English language. Such a provision represents a considerable advance in Australian law.

Victoria and South Australia have enacted legislation entitling non-English speaking persons to an interpreter in court in particular circumstances and in the criminal investigation process. In other jurisdictions judges have a discretion at common law to regulate the provision and use of interpreters. The material consideration is whether, without an interpreter, a witness is likely to be unfairly handicapped in giving evidence. For a party, the question will also arise whether he or she can sufficiently understand what others are saying without the assistance of an interpreter.

The adoption of such a provision was recommended by the Australian Law Reform Commission and the Commonwealth Attorney-General's Department in its report *Access to Interpreters in the Australian Legal System*.

However it does not address the concern of Diana Eades with respect to those who speak aboriginal English dialects and still leaves the discretion as to whether a person should be entitled to an interpreter to a judge who is likely to be a monolingual, white Anglo-Saxon male. There was considerable evidence presented to the Attorney-General's Department that such judges, as non-linguists, were often misled by an appearance of fluency concealing a quite deficient command of the language. Without an interpreter, persons with inadequate English language skills are deprived of the opportunity to communicate their evidence with accuracy and to adequately put their side of a case.

The Department was advised that in applying the common law there was a strong tendency in all courts to deny the use of an interpreter unless the judge was virtually unable to understand the witness's English. This reflects concerns that a witness with some understanding of English should not obtain an unfair advantage and the need to minimise the barriers to communication caused by the use of interpreters. Less attention was given to the real risk that a witness with insufficient knowledge of English may not be able to adequately understand the questions put and convey the meanings he or she wishes to express. Often the assessment by the Court of an individual's language skills was extremely superficial and inaccurate, not going beyond questions relating to name, address, occupation and length of residence in Australia. The statistics which were collected with respect to the use of interpreters in various courts and tribunals showed a surprisingly low usage of interpreters.

Given the expertise required to assess a person's English language skills, it may well be that for a judge to be properly satisfied that a person can communicate adequately in English, this could only be done after the calling of expert evidence concerning the language competence of the person seeking to use an interpreter.

The Report found that the major difficulty with respect to the use of interpreters in the Australian Legal System was the use of

untested or incompetent interpreters. As stated by Mr L W
Roberts Smith QC (1989)

> Untrained interpreters, far from facilitating communication, can cause
> many problems. Their language skills may be deficient; they may not
> have the necessary appreciation of relevant cross-cultural differences;
> they may not have interpreting skills (as opposed to conversational
> abilities); their choice of words may be imprecise and consequently
> misleading and they may have a tendency to flavour the interpretation
> with their own views and perception of the facts.

There is plenty of evidence that the role of the court interpreter
is vital in shaping impressions that listeners form of witnesses.
Incompetent interpreting or that which does not follow proper
standards and procedures can have a significant impact on the
course of legal proceedings. Laster (1990) refers to a study of
proceedings which were interpreted into Spanish. It was found
that the way in which the interpreter translated the witness's
evidence had a marked effect on the perceptions of jurors with
respect to the witness. When the interpreters added politeness
markers such as 'sir' or 'madam', jurors were likely to consider
the witness considerably more convincing, competent, intelligent
and trustworthy than those who heard the same witness when
the politeness markers were taken out.

Witnesses with some but inadequate English language skills
face a difficult decision. Do they continue in English or do they
use an interpreter and risk being regarded as devious, evasive or
running for cover? Sir James Gobbo of the Victorian Supreme
Court argues that whilst judges often found particular witnesses
were truthful and impressive, this was rarely said of witnesses
whose evidence was given through an interpreter, as such
evidence often lost all impact.

The Attorney-General's Report found that the development of a
registration system for interpreters, together with the means of
enforcing professional standards, was of primary importance in
addressing the availability of competent interpreters in the legal
system. It proposed that, except in exceptional circumstances, the
use of registered interpreters should be compulsory. Evidence
given through unregistered interpreters should be taped, so that
the accuracy of the interpreters can be checked in appropriate
circumstances.

That report did not deal with the particular needs of Aboriginals in depth. The main demand for interpreters in Aboriginal languages is in central and remote Australia. Typically, Aboriginal languages have very small speaking populations, which coupled with remoteness and kinship factors, limit the availability of competent interpreters. The systems for achieving the availability of competent interpreters in the legal system are less developed than for most other languages.

Given the low levels of education of most Aboriginals who live in the desert areas, the pool of competent interpreters is very limited. The training required to achieve command of Aboriginal languages and English has been recognised by the Commonwealth government in its response to the Royal Commission into Black Deaths in Custody.

Method of giving evidence

There is evidence to support the contention that tying witnesses to answering designated questions results in the distortion of their testimony. A free report often gives a more accurate version of the events in dispute. This is particularly likely to be so given aboriginal patterns of discourse described by Walsh and Eades. However many legal practitioners find a free report to be sketchy or incomplete.

Free narration of evidence should be encouraged. To this end the Court should have the power to direct that a witness give the whole or part of his evidence freely and without questioning. This should minimise some of the disadvantage suffered by those with different patterns of speech and those who are less articulate. Provision to this effect has been included in the Australian *Evidence Bill*, 1991.

Training of participants in the legal system

Lawyers who deal with people of a non-English-speaking background and in fact, clients from all backgrounds, need to be aware about the processes of communication, what is involved in interpreting, the risks of misunderstanding due to linguistic and cultural differences and the means by which communication can be maximised, including the use of qualified interpreters and development of skills for effective use of interpreters, including examination and cross-examination of witnesses requiring an interpreter. The Eades chapter highlights, however, how this increased awareness can be manipulated to the disadvantage of aboriginal witnesses.

In Australia these issues are being addressed in various random and *ad hoc* ways such as:

1. inclusion of curriculum materials for cross-cultural awareness for undergraduate law schools;
2. inclusion of short courses on cross-cultural communication and the effective use of interpreters in practical legal training for students prior to admission as lawyers;
3. seminars and workshops on communication skills and the use of interpreters as part of continuing legal education for practising lawyers;
4. continuing judicial education with respect to communication skills (for example as part of the response to the Royal Commission into Aboriginal Deaths in custody, the Commonwealth Government and the Australian Institute of Judicial Administration are collaborating on a project to develop awareness of communication difficulties with aboriginal people); and
5. training of police on cross cultural communication, particularly with aboriginals.

CONCLUSION

Lawyers are students of language by profession. Their role is to manipulate the opinions of others, through highly developed language skills. The basis of the Australian adversarial system is the question and answer process between the lawyer and the witness. This is designed to ensure, through the language tools available to lawyers and interested parties, that the truth is discovered. Yet very little emphasis is placed on analysing that process to ensure that the interests of all parties, particularly those most disadvantaged in the community, are protected. The manipulation of children, Aboriginal and non-English-speaking witnesses suggests a lack of concern for the interests of those who are already least able to look after their own interests.

In Australia over the last decade there have been many reports which have highlighted language barriers in the legal system, particularly for non-English speakers. In the last few years there have been some concrete steps taken to reduce communication barriers in the legal system. I have described some of them in this chapter. However, to date measures taken to ensure that barriers to communication are minimised have not significantly improved the right of disadvantaged Australians to be heard.

The challenge with legislative entitlements is to create the means necessary to exercise the right to be heard and to a fair go in the legal system and not merely the illusion of a right.

PART III

FORENSIC LINGUISTICS

INTRODUCTION

Forensic linguistics

John Gibbons

Forensic linguistics is concerned with the provision of expert linguistic evidence, usually in court. Before continuing it is necessary to give a very simple language model for the classification of types of linguistic evidence. It should be noted that this model makes no theoretical claims, and that the boundaries between categories are indistinct. One basic classification much used in applied linguistics is the following:

	Spoken language	Written language
Comprehension	*listening*	*reading*
Production	*speaking*	*writing*

This model is hopefully self-explanatory – spoken language is accessed through the ear, written through the eye. (The model is too simple to include other channels such as Braille or semaphore.)

Another classification is that of language levels. These are:

1. *Grapho-phonic*: for *spoken* language, speech sounds, including single sounds, and stress, rhythm and intonation/tone/pitch; for *written* language – handwriting/typeface, spelling, punctuation, etc.
2. *Lexical*: words, their use, frequency, the company they keep (collocation), etc.
3. *Grammatical*: both morphology (word changes, such as adding 's for possession in English, and structure words such as *the*) and syntax (word order and sentence structure).
4. *Discoursal*: the structure and nature of spoken and written texts (genres) including the patterning of spoken interaction; and the cohesive links between sentences.

319

The chapters in Part III are ordered roughly according to these levels, so that chapters deal with increasingly large linguistic units.

Using the distinction between comprehension and production, we can categorise forensic linguistic evidence into two main classes. First, there is evidence as to whether a specific person, persons or a class of people could *comprehend* certain language. Second, there is evidence as to whether a specific person, persons or class of people could *produce* certain language. Most forensic evidence, including many of the papers in this collection, is concerned with the latter category, sometimes referred to as the issue of disputed authorship. Nevertheless, as the Thornfare and US Steel Cases in Labov and Harris's chapter illustrate, forensic evidence as to comprehension can also be of considerable significance.

Forensic evidence concerning *comprehension* has three logical stages. The first is the determination of the degree of internal complexity of a corpus of language. The second stage is to determine the extent to which this complexity affects comprehension by the intended audience – i.e. can they understand the corpus? The third stage, of social action rather than forensic linguistics, is to modify the corpus, so that it is comprehensible to its intended audience. Labov and Harris in the Thornfare and US Steel Cases illustrates all three stages for written texts. In Gibbons (1990) I have done the same for oral texts (police cautions), and have given these findings as evidence in court on several occasions.

The language levels provide a framework within which comprehensibility can be examined. At the *graphophonic* level, the clarity of speech, handwriting and print can be assessed. Labov and Harris discuss the clarity of tape-recordings in the Prinzivalli case. Handwriting can be legible or illegible, print can be muddy or sharp, small or large, simple or elaborate in typeface, etc. At the level of the *lexicon*, words can be specialist or non-specialist, common or uncommon – Smith discusses word frequency, as do Labov and Harris in the US Steel Case. *Grammatical* structure can be complex or simple, and sentences short or long – such features may be handled through readability measures (see Labov and Harris, US Steel Case) or through direct syntactic analysis (see Gibbons 1990). At the *discoursal* level, written or spoken texts can be organised and coherent, or disorganised and incoherent](see Coulthard's chapter on this issue). The text type or genre may be specialised or common. Any or all of these levels may be analysed for its effects on comprehension.

Turning now to *production*, forensic linguistics is most often concerned with demonstrating similarity or difference between language corpora. So if we have language corpus A, language corpus B and language corpus C, the forensic linguist may be attempting to demonstrate that language corpus B is similar to language corpus A, and/or that language corpus B is different from language corpus C. While this is discussed in most of the chapters which follow, it is demonstrated most clearly and overtly in Eagleson's chapter. A language corpus may be spoken or written. The linguist's evidence is typically concerned with the form of the language, rather than its content (for example its truthfulness).

[The purpose of this process of demonstrating similarity or difference is normally to establish *authorship* (written or spoken) of one corpus or more. Often there is a comparison corpus whose authorship is not in dispute. This is compared with a language corpus that *is* in question to prove or disprove the authorship of the disputed text.]

[A major issue in this process of determining authorship is the variation in the language behaviour of individuals produced by changes in context.] (Context is used in a very broad sense here, following for example Giles and Coupland 1991.) This has been well established by Labov (1972) and others.[People have a repertoire of language forms from which they select (consciously or unconsciously) according to the situation in which they find themselves, and their purposes within that situation.] If we take the graphophonic level for example, it is now well attested that speakers usually produce more non-standard pronunciations in casual settings than they do in formal ones. Looking at purposes, people may accommodate their speech towards that of their interlocutor if they are trying to reduce social distance, or they may attempt to use language that is as different as possible from that of an interlocutor they dislike, in order to increase social distance (Giles and Coupland 1991: 60–93). Similarly in writing, a writer's level of non-standard spelling and punctuation may be higher in private or informal writing than it is in a more carefully attended and monitored piece of writing (although there is an attendant possibility of hyper-correction). Context may be highly constraining in some cases. To give an extreme case, the wording that one person uses in completing a tax form may be very similar to that of another person completing the form. Here the context constrains the possibility of variation to a high degree.

This role of context and purpose is very important for forensic linguistics. In the tax form example it would be very difficult to establish authorship on the basis of wording (rather than handwriting). A question frequently asked in court is whether a person could have simulated the language style of another person or class of persons, in other words whether their repertoire includes that style. Indeed it may appear that variability in context means that the type of comparison described in a preceding paragraph is impossible to perform. This is clearly not the case, as the chapters which follow clearly demonstrate. It is, however, an issue that almost all the authors address in some way. Sometimes it is possible to establish that certain language is not within a person's repertoire – for example in Gibbons (1986) I indicated that it was not possible for a low proficiency, second-language speaker to suddenly begin to speak like a native speaker. Labov and Harris make a similar point concerning regional accents in the Prinzivalli case. In these cases we have features which vary between individuals rather than within an individual, and such features are often useful in constructing a case. If we take handwriting as an example, there will be characteristics that differentiate a person's 'best' handwriting from their rushed handwriting. On the other hand, there will be many features that remain constant for that individual whatever the circumstances, and distinguish that individual's handwriting from that of another person – features which vary by user rather than use. Another approach is to control for the effects of context and purpose, usually by ensuring that corpora for comparison are taken from contexts that are as similar as possible, especially on such parameters as formality and topic (see also Smith's section on 'A Proposed Method'). Complete identity of situation is not always possible, so the likely influence of contextual differences must be taken into account when discussing similarities and differences between language corpora.

Two of the best known forensic linguistic approaches are voice-printing and stylometry. Both are machine based, using a spectrogram and a computer respectively, which gives them a scientific appearance that can be of help in gaining acceptance as evidence. Nolan, and to a lesser degree Jones, examine voice-prints, and Smith's chapter is a critique of stylometry. In both cases the conclusion is that these techniques do have evidentiary potential, but that both have been abused and their certainty over-stated.

Sometimes it is possible to make absolute statements in court. Very often, however, one is compelled to make probabilistic statements. Jones's chapter, for example, discusses methods for calculating probabilities and expressing them in statistical form. This is of course normal scientific method, but as Eades's chapter notes, it is often very difficult to persuade judges and lawyers of this – they sometimes insist on deterministic statements – the 'yes–no' question beloved of barristers. This should of course be resisted – and lawyers should be aware that in some cir-cumstances an expert witness who produces an absolute and certain judgment on the basis of probabilistic evidence is either a fool or a charlatan. It is also odd that lawyers have such difficulty in accepting probabilistic statements, since many legal judgments are made 'on the balance of the probabilities'.

The uses to which such forensic evidence is put are varied. The most common is to prove or disprove that a certain incriminating piece of language presented as evidence was produced by a certain person. Jones's chapter discusses a number of such cases, and there are other examples in Eagleson's, Coulthard's, and Labov and Harris's chapters. Another use can be illustrated by a case of plagiarism in which I was involved, where evidence was required as to whether a person had simply copied a question-naire, or whether the similar purpose, identical text type and similar target audience had resulted in an almost identical text – a tricky question involving the role of context, and the role of intertextuality – i.e. the use of other questionnaires as the same model for both the questionnaires involved in the case.

The chapters in Part III cover the full gamut of language levels, and both spoken and written language. Nolan and Jones both examine the use of phonological evidence, in particular how speech sounds can form a basis for speaker identification. Nolan carefully argues for the complementary roles that can be played by the expert ear and by machine analysis of speech sounds. Jones expands on several of the issues raised by Nolan, and illustrates them with data from real cases in which he has been involved. Importantly, Jones gives the statistical basis on which calculations can be made of the probabilities of two speech samples coming from the same or different speakers. Nolan, Jones and Labov and Harris all mention problems in using tape-recorded material, because of the loss of sound quality that recording can produce, especially when recorded in less than ideal conditions.

With regard to the written language, this is the topic of Eagleson's chapter. By analysing various linguistic features, particularly spelling, punctuation and grammar, he arrives at an archetypical forensic account. Smith's chapter is a critical discussion of a well-known but tendentious form of forensic linguistics, namely stylometry, which consists of analysing corpora for the comparative frequency of occurrence of certain structure words. He looks at the work of the major figure in this movement, Morton, and traces the development of stylometry from its origins in literary and biblical studies, to its current use in forensic linguistics. Smith challenges stylometry on statistical and theoretical grounds, so the discussion by its very nature is somewhat technical. The very accessible conclusions are of considerable interest to legal professionals who are faced with or who are contemplating the use of stylometric evidence.

The interest of Coulthard's chapter comes not only from the discussion of discourse by a pre-eminent discourse analyst, but also from the infamous nature of the 'Birmingham Six' case which it discusses. He shows how features of spoken discourse such as elipsis of previously mentioned information, terms of address, and normal variation in accounts of events can be used as evidence that a transcript of a spoken text has been concocted or tampered with.

Heydon, in his role as an international figure in the field of evidence, finishes the book on a cautionary note concerning the admissibility of linguistic evidence. While he sees it as having some evidentiary value, he questions the adequacy of both its intelligibility and its certainty. There is a gentle irony in the fact that linguists have such difficulty in communicating their message.

Before this, Simpson's chapter, which also deals with disad-vantage before the law, is included because it contains an important warning to all those involved in forensic linguistics. It is often desirable if not essential for the forensic linguist to discuss with the client (often the accused) the case or crime at issue, particularly when attempting to obtain a substantial language sample for comparison with other accounts of a crime – see Coulthard's chapter, for example. This type of sampling is important in controlling for the effects of context discussed earlier, and in collecting less consciously monitored language where the client is strongly engaged with the content of the account rather than being concerned with its form. Simpson's chapter makes it clear that such data are not protected by any right to confidentiality. To prevent the recording of potentially self-incriminating statements forensic linguists may be forced to collect less appropriate data or to collect samples only in the presence of a solicitor. Precautions may also be required when linguists are doing fieldwork and gather information that is either culturally sensitive or has a criminal aspect. The linguist may feel it is necessary to destroy important cultural archival material in order to protect sensitive information from being demanded in court at some future date. As Simpson points out, it seems unlikely that the law will be changed to accommodate the need for confidentiality. To finish on a cautionary note, it is important that forensic and other linguists are aware of the possibility that they can be compelled to betray the trust or damage the case of people that they are trying to help.

THIRTEEN

Auditory and acoustic analysis in speaker recognition

Francis Nolan

INTRODUCTION

No automatic speech recognition system exists which anywhere near rivals the ability of the human ear and brain to extract the linguistic content of the acoustic speech signal. Faced, in the forensic context, with deciphering what was said in a recording it is unlikely that machine analysis would often give much additional help to the ear of a speaker of the language involved.

Surely we would expect the situation with *speaker* recognition to be the same. We are, after all, very experienced at recognising speakers in everyday life, just as we are at understanding speech. It would be reasonable to assume that no more appropriate instrument exists for speaker recognition than the human ear, and furthermore that if the ear in question has been phonetically trained, it will be even better.

In this chapter I shall argue that the ear cannot be relied on for speaker recognition. Specifically, I shall explore some of the reasons why, in principle, the ear may not be as good at recognising speakers as it is at recognising speech, and why, in many forensic circumstances, auditory analysis should be supplemented by analysis using acoustic instrumentation.

The meaning of 'auditory' and 'acoustic' in phonetics

In popular usage the distinction between the terms *auditory* and *acoustic* may not be as clearly drawn as it is in phonetics. The related term 'audio-' is used, for instance, in contexts such as 'audio tape-recorder', to indicate a device which records the speech signal (in order that it can be heard again, of course). In phonetics, however, *auditory* is used to describe specifically the reception and processing of the speech signal by the ear and brain. When reference is made to the physical sound signal itself, the rapid pressure variations in the air which in the case of speech form the link between speaker and hearer(s), the term *acoustic* is used.

It follows from this restriction of the term acoustic to the physical signal that *acoustic analysis* involves the application of techniques from physics. The principles involved are those of wave analysis and resonance, and in practical terms acoustic analysis is carried out either by specially designed electronic hardware, or, after conversion of the acoustic signal into a digital form, by computer. This much is common to all acoustic analysis, whether of music, aircraft noise, or speech. Acoustic phonetics, the acoustic analysis of speech, brings to bear some specific methods and concepts stemming from our knowledge of how speech is produced in the vocal tract, and how it is perceived, but the approach is still in essence that of the physicist examining a phenomenon in the natural world.

Auditory analysis of the speech signal, on the other hand, is performed by the ear of a hearer. We must be careful, however, to understand by 'ear' not merely the mechanical parts of the outer, middle, and inner ear on either side of the head, but rather a hierarchy of levels of processing in which, ultimately, the linguistic knowledge of the hearer is drawn on in a mental process of interpretation. In one sense we carry out auditory analysis every time we interpret an utterance (or indeed any sound), even though we cannot bring the process to conscious awareness, or have explicit intuitions about how it works. But in the context of phonetics, auditory analysis does refer, at least in part, to the application of techniques about which the phonetician can be explicit.

Phoneticians traditionally receive a detailed training in a system of description for (in particular) vowels and consonants. The descriptive framework relies partly on how speech sounds are produced – for instance there is a class of sounds including [p] and [m] which are made at the lips, and another class including [k] and [g] which are made by the back of the tongue against the roof of the mouth; and it relies partly on defined reference qualities of sound to which other sounds can be compared – for instance there is a reference or cardinal vowel [u] rather like that of the English word *food*, and another [ɑ] rather like that of *palm*, but they are specified closely enough that it is possible to use the references as invariant landmarks in comparing the way different accents of English would pronounce those words, or to compare similar vowels in other languages. The basis of the descriptive framework is thus partly articulatory, that is, to do with how speech sounds are made or 'articulated', and partly purely auditory, that is, how they are heard using learnt reference qualities. In applying the framework a phonetician takes note of what can be seen of articulation (lip movements, for instance), but relies mainly on listening, inferring articulations where necessary. In analysing tape-recorded speech, of course, the process can only involve listening. Because of this, I shall refer in the rest of this chapter to auditory phonetic analysis, or simply auditory analysis.

Details of the traditional framework for classifying speech sounds can be found in textbooks such as O'Connor (1973), Ladefoged (1982) and Catford (1988).

Terminology in speaker recognition

As far as terminology to do with speaker recognition is concerned, a possible set of distinctions is as follows (cf. Nolan 1983: 1.1.2). *Speaker recognition* is the most general term, referring to any activity whereby a speech sample is attributed to a person on the basis of its phonetic-acoustic properties. The process of speaker recognition may be *casual* or *technical*. *Casual* speaker recognition is familiar in everyday life, for instance over the telephone or when we hear an acquaintance outside the room. It involves making a judgment about identity without invoking any explicit technique of analysis, either auditory or machine-based – we just make a global, snap judgment. *Technical* speaker recognition, on the other hand, does involve explicit techniques of analysis. It may be performed by a phonetician applying the traditional method of describing vowels and consonants on the basis of listening, or at the other extreme by a computer making physical acoustic measurements and reaching a statistically based decision.

A separate distinction is that between two classes of task under the heading of speaker recognition, namely *speaker verification* and *speaker identification*. In *verification*, the truth of an identity claim has to be judged. Telephone access to a bank account, or to other private information, might be controlled by checking the claimed identity of the caller. This of course might be done casually, by a human recipient of the phonecall. Normally, however, discussion of speaker verification concerns techniques by which a computer automatically compares the voice of the caller to a stored reference sample of the speech of the person whose identity is being claimed. In speaker verification we are dealing with a cooperative speaker, willing to produce, and if necessary repeat, a chosen utterance for comparison. The caller is unlikely to be adopting any voice disguise, although day-to-day variation in a voice will have to be accommodated. Impostors, however, need to be excluded. The criterion used for accepting or rejecting a claim has to be made stringent enough that the risk of accepting false claims is low, but not so stringent that true claims are rejected more than occasionally.

In speaker *identification*, on the other hand, which includes the usual forensic situation, the circumstances are rather different. Two samples (or sets of samples) have to be compared, it is true – one from the crime and one from the suspect – but otherwise things are more difficult. It will be hard to obtain from the suspect, even if he or she is cooperative, a sample of speech which is genuinely equivalent to the one which occurred during the crime, since freely spoken speech is not well imitated by reading, and many factors including stress levels may be different. The criminal sample may involve disguise. Artefacts may have been introduced in the criminal sample by distortions in transmission (e.g. poor quality telephone lines) or recording (e.g. a tape recorder running at the wrong speed). Although there may sometimes be a question of comparing the criminal sample to a number of suspect samples to see which it is most like, ultimately a criterion has to be applied to identify or reject one of the suspect samples as being from the same speaker as the criminal sample.

It is taken as uncontroversial in this chapter that identifying a person on the basis of speech samples is a matter of likelihood rather than certainty. Voice samples are not on a par with fingerprints; the former bear too indirect a relationship to the organism which produces them. The case against overestimating the voice as a clue to identity has been argued in detail elsewhere, e.g. Jones (this volume), Nolan (1990: section 3, and 1991).

AUDITORY AND ACOUSTIC ANALYSIS IN FORENSIC SPEAKER IDENTIFICATION

It seems intuitively sensible that, given we can all to some extent perform casual speaker identification, someone properly trained in auditory phonetic analysis should be well able to make reliable judgments on whether two speech samples come from the same individual, or not. This appears to be the view taken by courts in the UK, which for many years have accepted auditory phoneticians and dialectologists as expert witnesses. It is, however, far from being the unanimous view of phoneticians themselves. The controversy surfaced, for instance, at the 1980 meeting of the Colloquium of British Academic Phoneticians, a body of which the majority of professional phoneticians in the British Isles are members. A resolution was framed to the effect that 'phoneticians should not consider themselves expert in speaker identification until they have demonstrated themselves to be so', and was passed by 30 votes to 12.

This resolution focused on the lack of experimental assessment of how well phoneticians can perform speaker identification under forensic conditions. The situation is little different today – only one experiment, to my knowledge, has specifically addressed the issue. This is reported in Shirt (1984), and it found that on average a group of phoneticians did more or less the same as a control group of music students on a number of speaker identification tasks. It can be argued that the experiment did not give phoneticians sufficient chance to apply their specific skills, since the samples of speech used were too short to contain enough examples of different vowels and consonants. None the less, there is still an absence of experimental evidence backing up those who believe that phoneticians have special abilities in speaker identification. Another issue is the probabilistic nature of forensic evidence – see the introduction to this section of the book.

The auditory phonetic technique of speaker identification

Little appears to have been published concerning the auditory technique as applied in forensic investigation, but see Jones, this volume and particularly Baldwin (1977, 1979) and Baldwin and French (1990). Baldwin's (1979) main emphasis is on the notion of idiolect. Any group of people speaks with an accent or dialect, even if it is one which is normally regarded a 'standard' variety of the language. The population can thus be subdivided or partitioned by their particular combinations of regional and social dialect. A person can speak like an educated Scot, or like a working-class Liverpudlian, and so on. This much is well established in linguistics. The notion of idiolect takes this partitioning further, so that it is suggested by Baldwin that, even within a narrowly defined dialect-community, individuals will have their own preferred detailed pronunciations of particular words. The combination of a number of such preferred alternative pronunciations of words yields an overall pronunciation which is idiosyncratic – that is, an individual's idiolect.

In addition to this clearly linguistic individuality, a person will also be characterised by a voice quality and pitch range (see Jones, this volume, for a detailed discussion). On the assumption that voice quality and pitch, on the one hand, and idiolect, on the other, define an individual, the auditory phonetic analysis concentrates on both the overall impression made by the speech samples and on individual sounds. Judgments are made as to whether the overall voice quality and pitch of the two samples are similar enough that the samples might originate from the same vocal tract. Comparisons are also made, using the phonetic descriptive framework described briefly in the second section above ('Auditory and acoustic analysis'), of the pronunciation of (ideally) all the vowels and consonants of the language as they occur in the two samples. If voice quality and pitch range match well, and if there are (simplifying somewhat) no audible differences in the vowels and consonants between the two samples, it seems that practitioners of the technique arrive at the conclusion, often quite boldly stated, that the two samples are from the same speaker.

There are two main points to be made here. The first is that phonetics does not provide a framework for judgments of individual overall voice quality, nor are phoneticians trained in perceiving it. In fact, in a sense, they are trained to ignore it. This may seem paradoxical, but it is merely an extension of the fact that all language users have to set aside physique-determined differences in speech if they are to regard others as able to say the same word, the same sentence, and so on, as themselves. In a traditional phonetics class, the teacher produces unfamiliar speech sounds, and each student learns to discriminate them auditorily and to produce them, getting progressively nearer the teacher's model until the teacher is satisfied that the student's production is the same. But of course the student is imitating the linguistic aspect of the sound only, not the particularities of the teacher's vocal tract; he or she will not be required to sound indistinguishable from the teacher in all respects. I would certainly not want to claim that a traditional phonetics training makes phoneticians worse at perceiving individual quality; my point is rather that there is no *a priori* reason to assume that it will make them better. In fact there now exists a framework for the phonetic description of voice quality (see Laver 1980), but it is not clear how far its scope extends beyond those aspects of voice quality that a speaker can control to those which are physique-determined. Nor is this framework usually a part of a phonetician's training.

The second point to be made concerns idiolect. Although Baldwin (1977, 1979) presents the concept of idiolect as a fact, it is really only a hypothesis. It has not, to my knowledge, been demonstrated that every speaker of a homogeneous dialect has a reliably unique pronunciation. Furthermore, given the role of pronunciation as a marker of group identity, I suspect it is unlikely to be the case.

The position is further complicated by the fact that most individuals' pronunciation varies. It varies according to the formality of the setting in which they are speaking, the accent of the person they are speaking to, and in ways which may turn out to be essentially random – see Jones, this volume, and the discussion of 'context' in the introduction to this section.

The auditory phonetic technique has been used forensically to make definite assertions that two samples were spoken by the same speaker. However, as I have detailed elsewhere (Nolan 1983: ch. 2), the way in which identity is encoded in speech is extremely complex, and the speech production mechanism exhibits considerable plasticity. The relation between a speech sample and the identity of the individual producing it is thus far from being a direct one. I would argue therefore that absolute assertions about identity based on speech may in principle never be justified, whatever techniques are used. But apart from that, I have suggested that the two main strands of the auditory technique may be open to criticism. When phoneticians judge similarity of overall voice quality, they are operating purely impressionistically in a domain for which phonetics has not provided them with a specific technique of analysis. And when they infer identity from an absence of audible differences in the pronunciation of the vowels and consonants of the language, they are relying on an undemonstrated hypothesis that each person has a distinct idiolect.

Where the auditory-phonetic technique is appropriate

The foregoing section paints a somewhat gloomy picture of what the auditory phonetician, working without the aid of machines, can contribute to the forensic process. In fact there is an important role for traditional (exclusively auditory) phonetic analysis, provided its limitations are clearly recognised. This is in the elimination of a sample which, although superficially similar to (say) a criminal recording, nevertheless manifests some minor but consistent differences of accent.

Auditory phonetic analysis, properly carried out, can then assess whether the phonetic properties of the two samples are in fact the same or not in detail. A phonetician might notice, for instance, given two samples of standard Southern British English, that only in one sample did the first and last vowels in the word *decided* (and in other words with the same affixes) contain an [i] sound like that of *pit* – the other speaker might use a vowel more like [ə] in the first syllable of *banana*. Perhaps in the first sample the consonant [t] is never accompanied by a glottal stop, whereas in the second sample it is consistently accompanied by a glottal stop when it occurs before another consonant. And the first sample might have a vowel in words with [a], such as *bad*, which sounds more like the vowel of *bed* than the equivalent vowel in the second sample. In fact from these minor differences alone, it would be clear to the phonetician that the first sample represented a more 'old-fashioned' version of standard Southern British English.

Depending on the number and consistency of such differences between the two samples, a reasonable conclusion would range from 'more likely than not two different speakers' to, maybe, 'almost certainly two different speakers'. In discovering fine but consistent phonetic differences – differences which to the untrained listener might be submerged by a general similarity – the auditory phonetic technique, properly applied, can yield a reliable elimination. The reliability is not absolute, since there may be individuals who have a perfect command of two accents (the equivalent within a language of bilinguals), and in principle variation determined by social setting might mislead; but *elimination* by purely auditory phonetic analysis remains, in my opinion, a valid enterprise.

On finding no pronunciation differences between the samples it is, however, a fallacious leap if the auditory phonetician concludes that one and the same speaker is responsible for both samples. In other words, on the basis of an auditory analysis it may be possible to say that two samples are produced by different speakers (see for example Labov and Harris, this volume). However, to say that two samples are produced by the *same* speaker can be questionable.

The leap would not be fallacious if it had been established beyond doubt that every individual really does have a unique idiolect, and if it were also known what the minimum size of sample were from which the speaker-defining idiolect would emerge. But neither of these conditions have been established, as far as I know. Properly, then, the auditory phonetician who encounters two samples between which he cannot hear any differences can say no more than that he has failed, on the basis of trained listening, to eliminate the possibility that they were spoken by the same speaker. The question should then be posed as to whether there are further tests which can be carried out which would potentially eliminate this possibility.

Since the development in this century of acoustic analysis of speech, and the progressively increasing availability of machines of various kinds to perform that analysis, it would seem perverse to ignore this line of attack. We must consider first why some have argued against acoustic analysis in speaker recognition, and then why in principle it should yield information complementary to auditory analysis.

Arguments against acoustic analysis in forensic speaker identification

Baldwin (1979: 231) cites the rejection by acoustic phoneticians of *voice-prints* as a means of identifying speakers, and uses this as an argument against the use of acoustic analysis. The criticisms of 'voice-printing' were certainly well founded, but their implied extension to all possible roles of acoustic analysis in speaker identification is not warranted.

Briefly, a voice-print is a visual representation of a spectral analysis of speech, showing how the balance of energy at different pitches or frequencies changes through time. In most areas of speech research it is called a (speech) *spectrogram*. As such, it has proven an extremely useful tool in understanding the nature of speech. Its application to speaker identification, however, was marred by an exaggeration of its reliability for that purpose (see Nolan 1983: 1.1.8), reflected in the term 'voice-print' with its implicit analogy to fingerprints. It was the overconfidence in what could be achieved with voice-prints, together with courtroom evidence from individuals lacking adequate knowledge of speech science, which led the technique into disrepute and provoked widespread opposition to it from the academic speech community. The strictures against the voice-print technique cannot properly be interpreted as a general rejection of acoustic analysis for speaker recognition.

A separate argument which I have heard in court against acoustic analysis concerns the variability which will appear in the acoustic signal because of extraneous factors such as background noise, the quality of the recording, and distortions introduced in transmission (for instance by different telephone lines). These are indeed reasons why it is not sensible to present, say, the visual record of an acoustic analysis (such as a spectrogram) to an untutored audience, and invite judgments on the similarity or otherwise of two samples. The same person saying the same sentence in the same way would look strikingly different in spectrograms if one sample were a high quality recording, and the other were taken from the telephone, where a lot of high frequency energy is lost; and indeed the first might have much greater overall similarity to a high quality recording of a different speaker, even though the untutored audience would have had no difficulty telling the difference by listening.

But acoustic analysis should not be seen as consisting merely of the output of a machine. Integral to the process is skilled interpretation. The interpretation of the acoustic pattern needs to be done by someone who is familiar with the ways in which such patterns are affected by factors extraneous to speech, and who fully understands the relationship between a vocal tract and the continuously varying, but coherent, pattern of acoustic energy it creates in speech – including the kinds of variation which any voice undergoes according to time and circumstance. If these requirements on interpretation are satisfied, useful information can be gleaned even from samples with different recording characteristics.

The real question is whether differences in recording characteristics can mislead; whether, for instance, two recordings from different speakers will sound more similar in overall quality – maybe overwhelmingly so – when one or both have undergone distortion. It would not be surprising if this were the case, particularly in the case of telephone speech, since the main criteria of adequacy for telephones have concerned the intelligibility of the message rather than the identity of the speaker. The effect of common distortions on auditory speaker recognition clearly needs experimental quantification.

In my view, then, the arguments against acoustic analysis as one component in speaker recognition are largely ill-conceived; and, insofar as they are valid, apply equally to auditory analysis.

WHY THE EAR CAN MISLEAD

The relation between the acoustic speech signal and our perception of it is a complex one. Two acoustic signals can differ, and yet give rise to the same percept – we hear them as the same. Information, in the technical sense, is thus lost, and at first sight this would appear to be a shortcoming in our perceptual abilities.

But in most cases it turns out that such perceptual 'distortion' either has no effect on, or else actually enhances, our efficiency in the main task of speech perception, namely the decoding of the linguistic content of the signal.

This section will focus on two well-established phenomena discovered by experiments on speech perception, and argue that, in principle at least, they have a bearing on auditory speaker identification. (The following account of the phenomena aims to be accessible to non-phoneticians, and therefore omits many technicalities.)

Perceptual integration of formants

Early on, acoustic analysis of speech revealed that speech sounds can be regarded as the combination of a number of resonances at different frequencies. A vowel, such as that of the word *hid*, phonetically [i], provides an example of this. The vibration of the vocal cords during the vowel's utterance produces acoustic energy, and the air in the vocal tract vibrates, or resonates, in sympathy with part of that energy. For [i], the tongue is pushed rather high in the mouth towards the palate, leaving a relatively small air space between the tongue and lips, a large air space from the tongue back to the larynx. A large object, or enclosed body of air, has a low natural frequency of vibration or *resonant frequency*, and a small one a high resonant frequency. Roughly speaking, for [i], the air in the vocal tract resonates both at a relatively low frequency (around 400 Hz or cycles per second) and a high one (around 2000 Hz), and acoustic energy in the signal is enhanced at those frequencies.

The resonant frequencies of the air in the vocal tract are called *formants*. Each vowel has formants at characteristically different frequencies, determined by the different vocal tract shapes made by moving the tongue and lips. In fact, each formant depends to some extent on the vocal tract as a whole, and there are as many as half a dozen in the frequency range on which perception relies. Formants can be seen on spectrograms as dark bands, indicating the greater energy in the vicinity of a resonant frequency, and Fig. 13.1 shows a spectrogram of five English words.

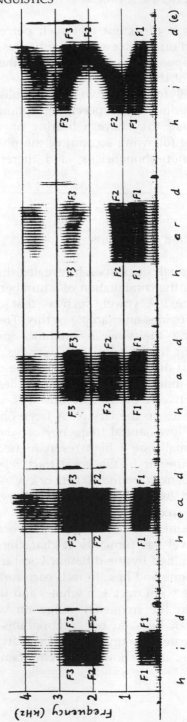

Figure 13.1 Example spectrogram: hid, head, had, hard, hide

Notice how in the last one, *hide*, the first formant lowers in frequency and the second formant rises as the mouth closes during the diphthong (phonetically [ai]), and how each vowel in the preceding four words has its own characteristic pattern reflecting the shape of the vocal tract used in its production.

It was found that adequate approximations to most vowels could be made on a speech synthesiser by replicating their lowest three, or even two, formants. But it also emerged that human perception did not work by straightforwardly identifying each formant individually. Rather, when two (or more) formants occur close together in frequency, they are integrated into a single percept. To put this another way, two close formants have the same effect, in terms of phonetic quality, as one formant placed at an intermediate frequency.

This effect is seen, for instance, in experiments such as that of Carlson et al. (1975). Their experimental subjects had to adjust the frequency of the upper formant of two-formant synthetic vowels so that their phonetic quality best matched that of four-formant (synthetic) reference vowels.

Figure 13.2 is not a plot of experimental data, but is an illustration. It is, however, closely modelled on the data of Carlson et al. (1975) for similar vowels of Swedish. It shows the kind of results which might be obtained for the vowels of the first four English words in Fig. 13.1. Notice how, in the first three vowels of Fig. 13.2, the second formant (unfilled bar) of the two-formant stimulus is positioned not at the frequency of the second formant of the four-formant reference, but at a frequency intermediate between its second and third formant. In some

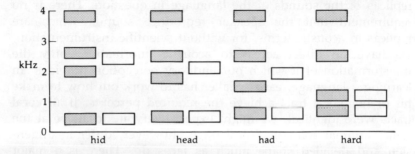

Figure 13.2 Schematic illustration of the matching of two-formant (unfilled bars) and four-formant (filled bars) synthetic vowels

sense, these two formants are close enough together to be heard as equivalent to one intermediate formant. In the vowel of *hard*, the interval between the second and third formant has become great enough that the second formant of the two-formant stimulus is matched directly to the second formant of the four-formant reference. The relative lack of energy in the third formant of this vowel (not schematised in Fig. 13.2, but see the relatively pale bar in Fig. 13.1) will contribute to its lack of effect. The fourth formant of all these vowels is also weak and probably contributes little.

The fact that a two-formant stimulus can fall into the same phonetic category as a four-formant vowel does not mean that it sounds identical to it. There may remain differences of tonality, and indeed the two-formant version may not in some sense be as 'good' a representative of the category. But it is worth remembering that the two-formant stimuli are absolutely minimal syntheses of vowel quality. If a similar experiment were carried out matching three-, or even five-formant vowels to the references, then it is likely that phonetically equivalent patterns could be found which were nearer to being perceptually identical in all respects.

The above account only scratches the surface of a phenomenon which is highly complex, and whose details are still being investigated. The important and well-established gist of the matter, however, is that a similar or even identical phonetic quality may result from acoustically different formant patterns.

Why is this important for speaker recognition? Let us consider what the requirements are on a speaker of a language. Basically, each speaker has to be able to achieve perceptually acceptable replicas of the sounds of the language in question. There is no requirement that the speaker reproduce sounds which are replicas in acoustic terms, for without scientific instrumentation, we have no direct access to acoustic information, only the transformation of it which our auditory perception provides. In learning a language, each speaker has to work out how to make his or her vocal tract achieve the required percepts. If all vocal tracts were identical, we might expect everyone to arrive at the same, optimal solution. Vocal tracts, however, differ in dimension and detailed shape much as faces do. There is a major difference of size and proportions between an average male and an average female vocal tract, and wide variation within each of those categories. This makes it more likely that a variety of solutions will exist to achieving a particular phonetic percept, for instance a different tuning of the various resonances of the vocal tract to achieve the required overall distribution of energy.

This appears indeed to be the case. Nolan (1990) reports a case where two forensic samples of speech exhibited very similar auditory phonetic quality for a number of sounds, including the [a] of *that*. Acoustic analysis, however, revealed that where one sample consistently showed a strong third formant around 2500 Hz for examples of this vowel, the other sample showed weak third and fourth formants close together below and above this frequency. A consistent difference of this kind is strongly suggestive of different source vocal tracts, hence different individuals, and yet two purely auditory analyses had previously come to the conclusion that the samples were by the same speaker. Since this was a real-world case, the 'right' answer is not known, but other evidence pointed strongly to the conclusion that the two samples were spoken by different individuals.

In principle, then, the ear may be inherently ill-equipped to pick up some differences between speakers which show up clearly in acoustic analysis. A 'design-feature' of auditory perception, which is of benefit in speech communication because it may contribute to a tolerance of variation in the acoustic signals produced by differing vocal tracts, is potentially a handicap in the auditory identification of speakers.

Trading relations among phonetic cues

The perceptual integration of formants, discussed above, is partly a reflection of the frequency resolution of the ear, and thus not a phenomenon peculiar to the perception of speech. There are, however, interactions in the auditory processing of speech which are closely tied to the structure of speech. It is to a specific subset of these that we now turn.

It has long been recognised that a given speech sound will be associated with more than one cue in the acoustic signal. Thus the *sh* sound of English (a single sound, phonetically [ʃ], despite the spelling) is recognised not only by its hissy noise, or *friction*, extending over a specific range of frequencies, but also by effects in the adjacent vowels. In particular, the second formant of the adjacent vowel will tend to be raised near the consonant. This *formant transition* is simply the acoustic consequence of the tongue moving to, or from, the articulation of the [ʃ].

It turns out that listeners do not need exact, invariant values for the friction noise, and the formant transition, to perceive a [ʃ]. In an experiment which synthesised a variety of friction noises ranging along a continuum from clearly [ʃ]-like to clearly [s]-like, and attached them to following vowels with a formant transition appropriate either to [s] or to [ʃ], Mann and Repp (1980) showed that a correct formant transition was not essential to produce the [ʃ] percept. In its absence, however, the friction noise had to be more clearly [ʃ]-like than when the transition was present. The lack of appropriate transition could thus apparently be compensated for by the clearly [ʃ]-like friction; or, looking at it the other way, some of the [ʃ]-ness of the friction was *traded* for the lack of [ʃ]-ness in the vowel transition.

Other experimentally demonstrated instances of *trading relations* among acoustic cues to phonetic distinctions (mainly among consonants) abound. Repp (1982) provides a useful summary. One of the most complicated and best researched is the voicing contrast in initial stops. In each of the pairs *bay-pay*, *day-Tay*, and *gay-Kay*, the consonant beginning the first member of the pair (e.g. [b]) is often referred to as *voiced*, whereas that in the second member (e.g. [p]) is *voiceless*. This implies that voicing, or vocal cord vibration, is present for the first one but not the second. For English this is a useful approximation from the point of view of the overall pattern of the sounds, but it does not realistically reflect the perceptual cues to the distinction, particularly since often there will not, in fact, be any vocal cord vibration in the [b], [d], or [g].

Crucial for the perception of the initial voiceless stops in English is a delay in the onset of vocal cord vibration, during which time a brief [h]-like sound or *aspiration* is produced – hence phonetic transcriptions such as [pʰei] for *pay*. Generally, aspiration lasting longer than around 30 milliseconds will be needed to cue the voiceless member of a pair. It transpires from experiments with synthetic speech, however, that for stimuli near that boundary the duration of the aspiration can be traded for its amplitude (roughly, its loudness). For instance, if the aspiration of a [p]-like sound is shortened to the point where it begins to be categorised perceptually as [b], the [p] percept can be restored by increasing the amplitude of the aspiration.

Further trading relations can be demonstrated between these cues and at least two further cues, the onset frequency of the first formant, and the onset frequency of vocal cord vibration (the latter known as the fundamental frequency, abbreviated to F_0). After a voiced stop, such as [b], the first formant tends to be low; and so does F_0. Lowering either of these frequencies can shift an otherwise borderline stimulus into the voiced category, and raising them will shift it into the voiceless category.

These various cues to the distinction are not an arbitrary grouping of acoustic properties; rather, they all follow naturally from the different way in which a voiced stop and a voiceless stop are produced. However it is likely that individuals have some latitude in the control of the fine detail of the productive gesture, and may arrive at alternative solutions which, because of the ability of perception to 'trade' among cues, all satisfy the perceptual targets of the language.

If it is indeed the case that speakers exploit the latitude allowed by perceptual trading relations, the possibility arises that the same sound produced by two individuals might be identical auditorily, yet exhibit under acoustic analysis a clearly different weighting of the tradable cues. The implications of this for auditory speaker identification are clear, and similar to those to be drawn from the perceptual integration of formants discussed earlier. The ear is flexible in its handling of acoustic variation in speech, in a way which promotes robust decoding of the linguistic content of the signal. But this very flexibility may make it inherently less reliable in detecting potentially important between-speaker differences.

The above suggestion that trading relations are a problem for auditory speaker identification is, at this stage, merely a suggestion. A number of objections might be raised, of which two are dealt with below.

The first is the question of whether stimuli which are categorised in the same way (e.g. 'heard as a [b]'), but have a different balance of traded cues, are in fact auditorily identical. In most experiments, the task is to *label* each stimulus as one sound (or word) or the other. It is possible that the listener experiences a variety of percepts, but knows that they all function as [b] (or whatever). The lay subject, furthermore, would have no vocabulary with which to describe fine, within-category, phonetic differences. Perhaps the phonetician would be able to analyse these explicitly, and use the information in distinguishing speech samples. Experiments where the task is labelling leave this question open. Another type of experiment, however, has the potential to provide an answer. In *discrimination* experiments the task is not to label a stimulus, but merely to report, in effect, whether a given pair of stimuli presented together are 'same' or 'different'. For some phonetic distinctions, discrimination experiments have suggested that listeners are not in fact able to hear any difference between stimuli which are within the same category but differ in the balance of their traded cues. Findings of this kind are to be found, for instance, in Best et al. (1981), who dealt with trading between the length of stop closure for [t] in a *stay-say* continuum and the onset frequency of the first formant of the following vowel. So whilst it has not been demonstrated that all trading relations may result in auditory equivalence, it seems probable that some do.

The second objection is that (to my knowledge) it has not been widely established that speakers do in fact vary in the way potentially allowed for by perceptual trading relations; and, if there is variation, that it serves to discriminate speakers, rather than merely constituting a range within which all individuals exhibit similar variation. An oblique answer to the first point is that it would be surprising if the flexibility exhibited by perception in its trading of cues were not matched by variation in real speech – it would be a sophisticated cognitive solution to a non-existent problem. A straight answer to the first point, and any answer to the second point, will require extensive research. This research could make use of existing, as well as new, data on production, but the research would have to be structured specifically from the point of view of auditory speaker identification.

CONCLUSIONS

Auditory phonetic speaker identification has been a pragmatic application of an existing skill to a largely new problem. It is not a problem-specific technique worked out from first principles;

nor has it been adequately tested. What I hope to have shown in this second section is that there are facts about speech perception which make it likely, in principle, that the ear will be insensitive to some types of distinctions between the speech of different individuals. This is a hypothesis which is susceptible of empirical refutation, but unless that refutation is forthcoming, the hypothesis should be borne in mind when assessing the validity of the auditory phonetic technique in forensics.

From the belief that the ear actually obscures potential speaker-specific cues it follows that listening should always be supplemented by acoustic analysis unless there are clear differences of accent, or voice quality. The information yielded by the two analyses is not the same, and the picture of speaker identity provided by a combined approach will be more complete than that from either technique alone. Of course sometimes acoustic analysis may be impossible for technical reasons, and in this case the greater uncertainty of any conclusion should be made clear.

What should the balance be between auditory and acoustic analysis? What are the limitations of auditory analysis by itself? These are questions which can only be answered by properly structured experimental research. The experiments should be of two kinds. The first would replicate typical forensic cases in all relevant respects, except that the 'answer' would be known. This type of experiment permits a general assessment of reliability in practical circumstances. The second type would be driven by findings in phonetic and psychoacoustic research. Experiments on formant integration, or trading relations, and the perception of speaker identity would be of this type. No doubt many others would arise. Such experiments would gradually contribute to an understanding of how perception deals with speaker characteristics, and allow for a principled understanding of performance in the task of speaker identification.

FOURTEEN

The limitations of voice identification

Alex Jones

INTRODUCTION

The identification of voices is an everyday activity. It happens when we are greeted by telephone callers who plunge into conversation without bothering to announce their names, or in many of the other cases when we hear a voice and the speaker is for the moment out of sight. It is part of a whole repertoire of methods of identification available to us, from visual identification of a person's features to recognising the characteristic cough or even footstep of a close friend or family member. Some of these kinds of identification are more reliable than others, as common experience confirms. It is considered normal to be able to recognise the face of a person after a single meeting, whereas one normally only recognises the footsteps of people that one hears constantly and knows very well. The face, of course, is dense with information: there are innumerable ways in which faces differ from one another, and they are differences which we are attuned to paying attention to, for everyday life involves dealing with numbers of people and knowing who they are. Footsteps, on the other hand, differ from one another in pulse frequency and in pulse amplitude, but probably in few other ways. The information in a set of footsteps is sparse, and there is no reason to suppose that the human ability to discriminate between them is highly developed, for in the general course of things very little hangs on being able to tell one set of footsteps from another. Like many things, the characteristics of one person's tread can be learnt from sufficient repetition, but the set that anyone can learn to discriminate is probably small. Somewhere in this continuum between the face and the footsteps

346

falls the voice. The sound signal that constitutes the human voice is produced from one or more sources between and including the vocal cords of the speaker and the lips, and its quality is affected by individual habits in sound production and by the configuration and volume of the cavities that make up and are connected with the speaker's vocal tract. So in principle, just as the unique sound of a particular violin depends on the materials it is made of and the structure of its resonating cavities, human voices will derive from the unique apparatus used to produce them, qualities that distinguish them from every other voice.

To admit that this may be the case does not necessarily mean that it is going to be possible to identify a speaker from his or her voice in any particular situation, nor does it mean that these unique characteristics are what the ordinary person is acting on when an everyday identification is made.

PROBLEMS OF EVERYDAY VOICE IDENTIFICATION

The story of John and Julie provides a warning (the names and some details here and in other cases have been changed in the interests of anonymity).

John and Julie got to know one another at their local church. John was a handyman, while Julie conducted a real estate business. This frequently took her out of the office, and would-be clients would leave messages on her answering machine. Julie employed John to do some restoration work for her and agreed on one occasion when John asked if he could store some of his materials in a garage on one of her properties. Some time after the work was completed, Julie asked John to remove the materials from the garage, using words at which John took offence. A quarrel ensued, after which John went to the garage while Julie was out and removed the materials. When Julie next returned to the office she found on her answering machine a message in a male voice describing her genital organs and saying what the caller was proposing to do to them. Julie came to the conclusion that John was the caller. Her conclusion was reinforced when she played the tape over the phone to her boyfriend who was away in the country and asked him if it sounded like John to him. The boyfriend was furious and threatened to attack John. The dispute soon got around, and split the church into pro-John and pro-Julie factions. The minister was asked to mediate, and sought expert advice.

A close examination of the tapes in this case showed no rational grounds for identifying one voice with the other. John had a voice of a general Australian type with some sporadic exotic features (he had spent some years in another country), none which were displayed by the voice on the answering machine. That voice, on the other hand, used broad Australian vowels and less careful articulation, and, either voluntarily or otherwise, had a sustained breathy or panted quality not characteristic of any normal speech but quite in keeping with the content of the message. About all the two voices had in common was that they were from mature male speakers.

What was clear was that in making the identification Julie was responding to the interpersonal content of the message. John was the only person with whom she had engaged in hostile communication, and so the message which was interpreted as hostile was attributed to John. The boyfriend's corroboration was suggested to him by Julie and was more a demonstration of solidarity with Julie than any independent judgment that the caller was likely to be John.

Similar elements were present in the case of Ngaire and Nick:

> A musician told a journalist that when playing idly with some sound equipment he had discovered that a record made by the Australian singer Ngaire when played at two thirds the speed turned out to be by Nick, an English male vocalist. The newspaper was interested in the story, but with the defamation laws in mind decided to consult an expert before printing it.

The musician's statement, though apparently made in good faith, did not survive a close examination of the tapes. Slowing Ngaire's voice down did give some approximation to the male singer's voice, though clear difference remained between the Australian and the English vowel sounds and spectrographic measurements made it clear that slowing had shifted components of the vowels significantly away from their normal positions. The rest of the identification depended on a mixture of scepticism about Ngaire's ability, wishful thinking, and perhaps envy. What Julie, her boyfriend and the musician did in these cases is precisely what we do so much of the time when we identify a voice.

The human voice signal is very rich in information, but it is not primarily information of an identificatory sort. The main function of the voice is to convey linguistic content – meanings – and emotional and attitudinal content; the *identificatory* content that it carries as well, though inevitable, is largely irrelevant to the individual's communicative desires. In everyday identification what the speaker is talking about, in the most general sense, has a large effect on judgments about who the speaker is. Everyone has probably had the experience of conversing with an unknown voice on the telephone which is gradually identified from the content as the conversation takes shape: conversely a caller who claims to be a particular person may very well get away with it if the content is appropriate and the conversation is not prolonged. It can be very hard in the absence of other clues to tell a voice, even a well known one, apart from that of an impersonator.

Australian radio stations at election times have had the experience both of offending listeners by having their impersonations of politicians taken for the real thing, and by having the real thing mistaken for an impersonation. In the everyday sense identification of a voice involves drawing a conclusion which is shaped very much by the limits of what one expects to hear and which takes the content of the message into account at least as much as the form. There is no reason to think that subtle individual characteristics that make each voice unique play a large part in everyday judgment: voices are perhaps much more like footsteps to the untutored ear than we might at first suppose. A 1984 study of the ability of persons without special training to recognise famous voices (well-known television personalities, etc.) showed a success rate of only 26.6 per cent when the possible responses were unlimited: when the subjects were asked to match the voices with the people's names however, the success rate was very high. The success of matching relies on a limited context, and its validity depends, as with John and Julie, on how appropriately the context has been limited.

Equally, a strong familiarity with the voice is an important element in recognition (see *R. v. Smith* 1984 NSWLR 463 for a review of the kind of familiarity that the courts require). McGeehee (1937 and 1944), presented subjects with a number of voices and then asked after various intervals of time whether or not voices then presented to them were among those they had heard before. He found an increase in errors from 17 per cent after one day to 87 per cent after five months. It would seem that the familiarity of a voice would need to be refreshed by repeated contact, and that non-specialist evidence about the similarity of a voice heard at the time of an offence and the voice of a person not otherwise known to the witness who is charged after a lapse of some time is probably worth very little. This is not surprising: there is no reason to suppose that the untutored human ear has any great powers of discriminating between voices except in the crudest way, for no particular advantage would have been gained by being able to do so. The ear when listening to speech is best at discriminating those differences in sound which distinguish conventionally coded messages from one another in the speaker's own linguistic community. What is idiosyncratic in the speech, the indicia of personal identity, is what remains when its systematic content is removed, and from the point of view of that content it is noise that has to be ignored.

EXPERT VOICE IDENTIFICATION

The expert approaches the speech signal from a different direction. A phonetician is trained to examine the form of the signal rather than its content, and so is less likely to make Julie's kind of mistake. The problem for the expert is in weighing the importance of observations and in being alert to the fact that their significance may change in different situations.

The speech of the individual, as mentioned above, is potentially stamped with an individual character by the fact that no two vocal tracts are precisely the same. In addition it may, however, be distinguished in other ways. First, there are the idiosyncratic features that distinguish an individual, *idiolectal* peculiarities in the use of sound – pronouncing 'r' as 'w' for example. Second, there are *sociolectal* features, which characterise the person's social grouping, whatever it may be. A third kind of feature is *accent*, either foreign or regional. Fourth, there is the *fundamental frequency* or pitch of the speaker's voice. Finally, there is the combination of idiolectal habits and the physiology of the vocal tract that produce the *sound spectra* of a person's utterances which can be measured in various ways.

Idiolectal peculiarities are the hardest features to deal with, because little or nothing is known about their distribution. A peculiarity of this kind is often something that speakers are unaware of and hence which they will not modify to disguise their voice. For example, a person convicted of having made a number of telephone calls claimed that the voice in question could not be his because of a speech peculiarity recorded in those calls involving the use of uvular r in certain positions. Study of extended samples of his own speech, however, showed the sporadic occurrence of an identical usage, although most of the time his r sounds were of the normal type. However, without knowing how many people share the characteristic, it is impossible to assess how likely it is that the presence of the characteristic in an unknown voice will establish that the voice is that of a person known to have that characteristic. Without an assessment of the frequency of the characteristic in the population at large the presence of the characteristic is corroborative rather than probative. It is also difficult to separate this type of feature from sociolinguistic features: any feature which is a peculiarity in one linguistic community could characterize a whole group in another.

It is with *sociolectal* groupings that one of the main problems in the use of the overt features of speech for identification is encountered. Speech is part of the social face that we present to the world, and as we do not always wish to display the same social face, speech is liable to alter from situation to situation. Among other areas which will be affected is the sociolectal classification of speech, and different conclusions will flow from different situations. The voice in which a threat is delivered, for example, may well be modified sociolectally as well as in other ways by the speaker's desire to avoid detection, whereas one might assume that the speech of a person talking at ease to a friend on the telephone would reveal the speaker's native sociolect. Australian English speech has been divided by Mitchell and Delbridge (1965) into the sociolectal groups Broad, General and Cultivated, containing, in the case of the adolescents they studied, about 34, 55 and 11 per cent of the population respectively. These categories, however, are very labile: a speaker may move from one to the other over time (Gunn 1963) or simply in response to a situation (Labov 1972). Bernard (1967) has this to say about the problem as it complicates research in sociolectal phonetics.

A most glaring example of this was provided by a Sydney Teachers' College student who had been described by the lecturer as having the broadest accent in the College. He was an older student and had worked for many years as a boiler-maker. At the first meeting he did indeed seem to be a broad speaker and arrangements were made to have him cine-X-rayed at the Royal Alexandra Hospital for Children.

On the journey there he began to apologise for his 'bad speech'. Despite warm assurances that it was not 'bad', and that it was in any case just the sort of speech that we were interested in, he continued to be doubtful. When the cameras turned he was no longer broad. By an effort of will, perhaps in an attempt to please or to acquit himself well, he produced vocalic nuclei which were general.

(Bernard 1967: 64f)

Equally speakers will vary in the other direction, from cultivated to general to broad if they wish to or if the context seems to require it. The courts by their decisions have certainly endorsed the perception that sociolectal grouping is a variable. Raymond Gilmore, a general Australian speaker as extensive interviews with him showed, was convicted of making telephoned bomb threats under the name of Mosman in a voice whose vowels were not so much cultivated as modified (*R.* v. *Gilmore* 1977 2NSWLR 935). This being the case, there is little to be gained from a sociolectal comparison of the voice of a suspect with a voice used under such circumstances as to make its user conscious of, or likely to have reason to modify, his way of speech. On the other hand, comparison of recordings made in situations likely to call forth the same response from the speaker could be of some use in identification. If an unknown voice is that of a broad Australian speaker and a suspect is also broad the chance that such a coincidence has occurred at random is 34 per cent. This is not a particularly impressive statistic in itself, but may be combined with other independent measurements to produce a significant judgment.

Much the same comments apply to *accents*, though there are at least some grounds for discriminating between genuine and bogus accents. On the one hand, a *foreign accent* which shows no consistent difficulty with any English sound is likely to be assumed. On the other hand, no one over the long term is likely to be capable of producing an entirely consistent accent unless it is genuine. McHardie was one of two men charged with making and carrying out bomb threats against Woolworths Ltd. (An appeal which reviews some of the principles is reported at 1983 2NSWLR 733. The whole facts of the case may be found in Anderson 1985.) McHardie had the majority of the phone calls involved attributed to him on the grounds that the foreign accent in which the calls were made was inconsistent and that he was known to talk in a foreign accent as a party trick. McHardie, perhaps wisely, remained silent from the time of his arrest until his conviction. With regard to *regional accents*, Peter Chedzey, charged with attempted extortion against Qantas, was held to have made the threatening calls in what may have been a provincial British accent although his accent, while British, was of a quite different type (*R.* v. *Chedzey*, a 1987 Western Australian case, unreported as far as I know). The courts in these cases have carried into judgment the ordinary perception that people can and do alter their accent as well as their sociolect, and there is little that the expert can contribute to that judgment other than offering an opinion on whether an accent is likely to be genuine.

The *fundamental frequency*, or pitch, of the voice is a variable of a different kind that does offer real identificatory possibilities, though it must be used with a cautious appreciation of the limits that have to be placed on the information it provides. The fundamental frequency of a voice depends on the mass and the tension of a speaker's vocal cords. There is little a speaker can do about the mass of the vocal cords, but the tension varies during speech and from one occasion to another. In any particular instance of speech, depending on the amount of emotion expressed, the voice may rise or fall over quite a wide range: the differences between the highest and the lowest values of fundamental frequency recorded may be as much as an octave or more. The mean value of a speaker's fundamental frequency also varies from occasion to occasion. It reflects the amount of tension in the vocal cords, which no doubt in turn is related to the speaker's mental state, or how s/he wishes to appear. The fundamental frequency of the voice of a prominent Sydney sporting identity measured over sixteen conversations with different people was seen to vary significantly with the fundamental frequency of the person he was talking to. This is perhaps what we would expect of an extrovert in a relaxed situation – it is part of the way he relates to other people and puts them at their ease. In a tenser situation, or for a more introverted person, variation may be driven by internal states. Whatever the cause of the variation, the long-term mean fundamental frequency of any one speaker, that is the fundamental frequency measured over multiple conversations, has a standard deviation of about a semitone. For convenience the abbreviation LTMFF will be used for this quality in what follows.

Beyond this there is the variation between speakers. Fry (1979) says that the mean fundamental frequency for mature male speakers is 120 Hz, and for mature female speakers 225 Hz. My own figure for mature Australian males is 116.4 Hz (about the B flat two below middle C) with a standard deviation of 18.8 Hz. This mean is not necessarily significantly different from Fry's, though it could be that criminals and suspected criminals have lower pitched voices than the general population, just as they apparently contain a disproportionate number of people with the chromosome pattern XYY. It is clear, though, that the genetics of the population will affect the mean figure: small samples suggest that the mean figure for Hong Kong Cantonese speakers is higher.

When it is a case of comparing measurements with a view to identification all these sources of variation must be borne in mind. Some examples will illustrate how these affect the possible results:

> Peter, an architect was one of a number of persons charged with conspiracy to defraud. He was recorded in the witness box and the fundamental frequency of his voice measured as 84.7 Hz. George, one of his co-defendants wished to demonstrate that his evidence was malicious by proving that Peter had made an intercepted telephone call in which the speaker threatened to 'get' George. The mean fundamental frequency of the voice in the telephone call was 83.7 Hz.

In this case each speaker was represented by a single conversation, and so each of the measurements had associated with it the same variance as characterises the range of variation in a speaker's fundamental frequency from occasion to occasion, i.e. giving a standard deviation of about a semitone. Now for any band of frequencies, the likelihood that the LTMFF falls within that band for both speakers is the product of the probabilities that each individual speaker's LTMFF falls within that band. The total probability that the two speakers coincide is the sum of these products over all frequency bands. The probability that this coincidence is random is the sum over all frequency bands of the triple product of the previously mentioned probabilities for the individual speakers and the proportion of all speakers that fall into that band. In Peter's case, dividing the spectrum into bands of 22.5 Hz centred on the mean of the two observations, the probability that both LTMFFs would fall into the same band was 0.9666. Because the voices of both Peter and the unknown were a relatively long way below the mean for speakers of Australian English the likelihood of this coincidence occurring at random was relatively small – 0.1185 – leaving the probability of a non-random coincidence as 0.8481. The probability of the null hypothesis being true, that is that the LTMFFs did not coincide, was therefore 0.1519, or rather less than one in six. Confronted with this and other measures of similarity Peter subsequently admitted to having made the call.

In Peter's case the fact that each measurement was based on a single observation was counterbalanced by the fact that both diverged substantially from the mean, enabling a result with a reasonable probative value to be derived. The case of Chen and Chan stands in contrast to this:

A Cantonese speaker calling himself Chen made two phone calls which lured police into a situation where several of them were severely injured. The mean of the mean fundamental frequencies of the two calls was 130.5 Hz. A man named Chan who had a grudge against the police was arrested. The mean of his fundamental frequencies over three interviews was 131.3 Hz.

In this case the variance associated with the estimates of LTMFF was divided by two and three respectively, because multiple conversations were available from which to derive the two estimates. However, for lack of a database the population mean had to be estimated as the mean of the two estimates, namely 130.9 Hz. This meant that if the two LTMFFs did correspond it would be in a region of the spectrum containing a large proportion of the population. For bands 17.5 Hz in width centred on 130.9 Hz the likelihood that the two LTMFFs coincided was found to be 0.8798, but the probability of this occurring at random was 0.3141, leaving the probability that the null hypothesis was true at 0.4343 – just less than half. This result could only have probative value in combination with other tests of much greater significance. So even though the variance associated with the elements had been reduced their location in a popular part of the spectrum made it difficult to draw a conclusion from their similarity.

Fred's case shows the dangers of using insufficient evidence very clearly.

Fred was charged with assault on the basis of an intercepted telephone conversation in which a person alleged to be him described the crime. The mean fundamental frequency of the telephone conversation was 124.1 Hz. A recording made of Fred giving evidence during other proceedings was in general too noisy for the fundamental frequency to be measured, but a measurement of 130 Hz was made at one point. The prosecution sought to tender evidence that this measurement was consistent with the two voices being the same.

In this case the variance associated with estimating the LTMFF from the voice in the telephone conversations was the same as in Peter's case. The variance associated with the measurement of 130 Hz, however, was much greater, as it was a single sample taken from a conversation in which the fundamental frequency could well range over an octave and more: the resultant standard deviation was almost three semitones. For a spectrum divided into 30 Hz bands centred on 127.1 Hz, the probability that the two LTMFFs coincided was 0.5156, and the probability that this was due to chance was 0.2588, leaving the probability that the null hypothesis was true at 0.7432: there were three chances out of four that the two voices were not the same. The prosecution's contention, though true, was extremely misleading.

Measurement of the fundamental frequency is therefore a means of identification which though potentially powerful, must be used with caution and with awareness of the range of variation that the fundamental frequency can undergo. Being one of the variables in the voice that is at least partly under voluntary control it is likely to be most useful when the recordings used are of more or less spontaneous speech, and least so when a deliberate attempt to disguise the voice is being made.

Probably the most controversial area of voice identification is in seeking to measure those characteristics of the voice that derive from the combination of individual physiology and individual habits of speech. These methods depend upon the interpretation of *sound spectra*, often in the form of sound spectrograms, which are records that show over a specified range of frequencies how the energy present at a particular frequency changes with time. The human speaking voice may contain components up to about 12000 Hz and no doubt information upon which identification might be based is disseminated throughout that range. In forensic investigation, however, most of the information to be studied comes via the telephone, which transmits a band of frequencies between about 300 and 3300 Hz, and many microphones have little high frequency response. The investigator who would use sound spectra for identification must therefore be content with the telephone bandwidth: what cannot be detected within that bandwidth will not be of practical importance.

In the interpretation of sound spectrograms, one form of which is the 'voice-print', the name of Tosi is probably the best known. Tosi's (1979) contention is that the same speaker saying the same words will produce a unique three-dimensional pattern of energy density mapped against frequency and time. His practice has been to have suspects say the words that they are charged with having uttered, and to compare spectrograms of these utterances with spectrograms of the original threats or whatever the test may be. This approach has obvious difficulties, both practical and theoretical. The attraction is that it works with the text as it is given: it can be used whatever the message happens to say. The chief practical problem is a correlative of this: that it is impossible to establish a prior confidence limit for the similarity of two signals when the content of the signal is not known in advance. If the voice producing the words in evidence is similar to that of the accused person saying the same words then what of that? What degree of similarity measured over those words is sufficient to establish identity? And to what confidence level? These are basic questions to answer which is going to require quantitative research in each case, and research which must be sure that it is comparing like with like – that conditions of accentuation for example are allowed for or held constant. Certainly observation makes clear that the same speaker may produce patterns that differ strikingly from one occasion to another, and that different speakers may produce strikingly similar patterns. The experience of the Independent Commission Against Corruption (NSW) investigation of harassing telephone calls made to Mr Edgar Azzopardi is instructive here (for full details see ICAC 1990).

> A voice, which subsequently turned out to belong to a member of the police force, had been recorded using threatening words identical to those used by a known person about ten years previously. A point by point comparison of sound spectrograms showed a correspondence greater than that between the voice under investigation and the voices of others then suspected of making the call. However it turned out that the caller of ten years before had been in prison and under surveillance at the time the later call was made, and that when he was persuaded to record the words in question spectrograms of his voice, which had matured in the interim, showed no more than a general similarity with that used in the call in question.

A practical difficulty in such cases is likely to be obtaining the cooperation of the suspect, and the view that a court may take as to the genuineness of any consent obtained. This is not to say that Tosi's illustrations are not persuasive, but that to assign a probative value to them may be problematical.

For these reasons it is desirable to seek for methods which, while retaining the advantage of operating with the data which happen to be available, extract quantities that characterise the speaker in a general way from those data. If such quantities can be derived, the way is open for comparing any two samples of speech whatever their content and for setting up confidence limits to apply to such comparisons. One way of doing this is to model the vocal tract of the speaker from the recorded signal. A more abstract approach, taken by Sambur (1976), breaks up the sample of speech into successive segments for each of which a spectrum is calculated showing for that segment how much energy is present at each frequency or in each band of frequencies. A two-dimensional pattern is produced for each point, and the data are reduced to a set of such patterns, the number in the set corresponding to the number of data points selected. Using a fourteen-channel representation of the frequency spectrum Sambur claims that the ten most significant underlying patterns provide the possibility of discrimination with a confidence level of 95 per cent or better (see also Nolan, this volume).

Theoretical considerations suggest that better discrimination could be achieved by limiting the set of sounds considered. The vowel system in any language has few linguistically significant dimensions of variation, thus making more room, as it were, for the identifying information; vowels are likely to be sounds primarily relied on for identification because of their greater average sonority, and their energy lies substantially within the telephone bandwidth. Experience with such a reduced set of sounds tends to lead to conclusions consonant with those of Sambur, but suggests that the location of the identificatory characteristics depends partly on the linguistic community within which the identification is made and partly on the individual: one must judge the similarity of two patterns with respect to some feature by comparing it with the observed similarity of individuals with respect to that feature in the community from which the speaker comes. It follows from this that a similarity sufficient to establish an identity in one linguistic community will not necessarily lead to the same conclusion in another. This is not an unexpected result: it would not be surprising if a facial feature common among Chinese, for instance, had great discriminatory power among Europeans, and it is reasonable that the same should be true of voices. So any characteristics derived from the spectrum and used for identification, whether they take the form of vocal tract models or more abstract quantities, need to be supported by a database which allows the significance of degrees of similarity in the characteristics measured to be computed.

By using such a procedure – comparing the value of some property of the underlying structure of the spectrogram with the value found for that property in comparison of different speakers – it is possible to quantify spectrographic similarity. For example in the case of Danielson, one of the convicted 'Woolworths Bombers', and 'Bridge', the alias used by a person who made some telephone calls concerning the collection of the ransom in that case, spectra of vowel peaks used by the two voices were reduced to six underlying components in each case. A comparison of these sets of components found that the second most important variable common to the two accounted for 20.2 per cent of the variance of the two sets of components compared with a value for unrelated speakers of 17.5 per cent with a standard deviation of 0.9 per cent. The likelihood of this value arising by chance was therefore 0.0015, from which it could be concluded beyond reasonable doubt that Bridge and Danielson were the same person. For Wayne, the conclusion was less clear:

Wayne offered a young woman a lift home in his car. When she arrived home she claimed that Wayne had raped her. The police took possession of a tape recorded in the car which appeared to contain a recording of conversation between the two people before and during the rape. Wayne denied that the voice was his.

A comparison between underlying features of the two voices showed the most important variable common to the two accounting for 30.8 per cent of the variance compared with 29.2 per cent with a standard deviation of 1.2 per cent for unrelated speakers. This gave a probability of 0.0929 that the two voices were different, not small enough to convict Wayne on that evidence alone, but hardly evidence that could be used by Wayne's defence, which was not keen to acknowledge a 91 per cent probability that the voices were the same.

All of these approaches depend on the quality of the signal available. In real situations noise is omnipresent, and the original itself is likely to be degraded by the use of low fidelity equipment such as answering machines. Such losses of information can be compensated for only partly, if at all. It is not unknown for battery operated recorders to be used which later prove to have been running at ever decreasing speed as the batteries ran down. All of these things destroy information. In suitable cases the effects of loss of information from the signal can be counteracted by the use of independent tests. For example, combining a spectral envelope based test which puts the similarity between two voices at 90 per cent with a fundamental frequency test which does the same, one reduces to 1 per cent (0.1×0.1) the probability that both of these similarities arose by chance.

CONCLUSION

The reliability of voice identification depends directly on the amount that is known about the characteristics of speech and the way they vary. As our knowledge in this area increases, reliability will improve, but claims made on this basis will always be statistical rather than definitive, a form of evidence not always welcomed or understood in court. As discussed at the beginning of this chapter, identification in the everyday situation depends crucially on variables of content as well as those of form, and when seeking to rely on form alone one must be content with many verdicts of not proven. At their best, experimental techniques can be used to establish identity, but they must be used with an awareness of the variability of the factors that are measured, and must be associated with estimates of the degree of reliability that can be attached to the results.

FIFTEEN

Forensic analysis of personal written texts: a case study

Robert Eagleson

INTRODUCTION

The case

In 1981, a Sydney husband was arrested on a charge of homicide. When originally interviewed by the police, he had produced a six-page letter which he claimed had been written by his wife as a farewell to the children. Among other things the letter explained that the wife was leaving home to live with another man elsewhere. As the police could not find the wife's body, the authenticity of the letter became critical. Although the police were suspicious, any possibility of arguing for its genuineness would have seriously undermined the other evidence.

Because the letter had been typed on the family typewriter, and because the husband insisted that the wife had written it, the likely authorship was reduced to either the wife or the husband. As the letter was completely typewritten without even a signature, it could not be subjected to the usual handwriting tests. However, the police were able to obtain a reasonable amount of material that had been written by both the husband and the wife in the months preceding the event. It became a question of comparing the disputed letter with other writings of the husband and wife to see which one was the likely author.

Texts

The texts available for investigation were:

F (the 'farewell' letter in dispute): 2551 words – all typewritten.

H (a letter and other writings of the husband): 3725 words – all typewritten.
W (a letter and other writings of the wife): 3294 words – all handwritten.

H and W especially were fairly comparable in size. Moreover, they were similar in level of formality. Though the size of each was not large, this quantity was balanced by the fact that at least two of the sets had quite distinctive characteristics in context-independent, objective elements of language, and in particular by the fact that certain divergent forms arose in relatively large numbers. The range of the types of dissimilarity that could be found and the persistent uniformity in the results of their application offset any theoretical reservations that might have been felt about the size of the sample texts – they had qualities which established their adequacy. Examples drawn from these texts are referenced as follows: (W14.4) – meaning line 4 of page 14 of the wife's material.

Procedures

The procedures start from the premise that writers have many constant features in their practice springing from ingrained habits of using language, so that the writings of one author will resemble each other in numerous ways. These are features which are not affected by variations in subject matter or 'field', such as the vocabulary differences produced by a shift from law to cricket. Nor are they features that are affected by variations in formality or 'tenor': grammatical and lexical choices will alter as we move from a casual to a formal situation. In comparing two texts we look for those features which are largely independent of context and which are likely to occur no matter what the writer is discussing and no matter what the circumstances. These context-independent linguistic characteristics are also objective, yielding to verification by anyone subjecting the material to scrutiny. They do not depend on personal interpretation to produce results.

More often than not, the difference between authors is a matter of the frequency with which a linguistic form is used rather than its absolute use or non-use in one of the authors. We look at the rate at which an author uses certain forms which are common to several pieces of writing. The assumption is that the rate of frequency for the occurrence of the selected forms is fairly constant in the texts of the one writer (see Smith, this volume). Any fluctuations should have an explanation. Major categories for analysis are: syntactic structure, morphological inflections, vocabulary, spelling and punctuation.

It is essential that the agreement should involve several features and not just one or two items, and several instances of each feature. The greater the number of features and the more the features belong to different categories, the stronger the case for shared authorship. At the same time we seek to show that the unattested document disagrees with other documents in the same features and, possibly, in other points. In effect we work in two directions: to establish significant similarities with certain known sources and significant dissimilarities with others. Such procedures are well established: see particularly Ellegård (1962), Svartvik (1968), and Michaelson et al. (1978a, b). These procedures have been applied by the author and others in disputes over the reliability of police records of interview (police 'verbals') in recent years.

THE EVIDENCE

Spelling

Errors in individual words

The proportion of spelling errors in individual words, excluding faulty capitalisation, in the three sets was: F(1.7%), H(2.5%) and W(0.3%). The farewell letter and the husband's documents were much closer in the rate of spelling error; the wife's documents were markedly different. The authors of F and H are comparatively weak spellers, the author of W a reasonable one.

Even more telling, the F and H shared the same spelling mistakes, while W avoided them for example:

F	H	W
assult, assullt	assult (twice), assulted (twice)	assault
carring	carring (twice)	carrying
thier	thier	their
treat	treat (twice), treaten	threatened

F and H also had difficulty with derived forms of *sex*, whereas W coped successfully, for example, F: 'sex's remarks' (for 'sexist'); H: 'sex intercourse' (for 'sexual'); and W: 'sexually molest'. Again, F and W conflicted in the spelling of some words which did not occur in H:

F	W
eet (twice)	etc
Ughily (three times)	ugly (six times)

This series offered additional, separate confirmation that the writers F and W differed in spelling practice. 'Ugly' was particularly convincing as it could not be attributed to a typing error.

Capitals with common nouns

H showed a strong tendency to spell a common noun with a capital where normal practice expects a small letter. The practice was less frequent in F, though the number of instances in this letter might be reduced because it was typewritten. W very rarely committed this fault. There were some interesting contrasts:

F	H	W
Mother	Mother	mother
Old	Old	old
Solicitor	Solicitor	solicitor
You	You	you

As well, F and H were inconsistent in their behaviour here. *Mother*, *old*, and *you*, etc., were sometimes spelt with a capital and sometimes with a small letter. W maintained a consistency.

Small letters with proper nouns

The farewell letter (F) was inconsistent in its practice of spelling proper nouns. It has such pairs as:

Billy: Henry: Olga: Pam: Vicki:
billy: henry: olga: pam: vicki

It also has 'jim' (four times) but 'Don', 'Fred', 'Ian'. H has a similar inconsistency with such pairs as:

Chris: God: Joan: Tommy
chris: god: joan: tom

It also has 'pam' (twice) but 'Don', 'Vicki', and 'green' but 'Valley'. W did not show this trait, always spelling proper names used as nouns with a capital. There was one instance of a small letter in place of an unexpected capital, but then the item was being used as a modifier: 'the irish joke' (W14.4).

Intrusive apostrophe

In both F and H there were several occurrences of an apostrophe in noun, pronoun and verb endings where it is not normally required, for example:

F	H
(making me) offer's	(the poor little) kid's
(Beautiful) baby's	(my) trouble's
(it) hurts	(kids) saving's
(he) put's	(the only) one's
(he) want's	he's (fault)
wors't	(of) her's
wor'st	

There were no instances of this intrusive apostrophe in W. In quoting her husband, the wife inserted an apostrophe in the non-standard *you's*, but this could be rather a recognition of the irregularity of the form, just as many write 'the 3 R's'. The apostrophe here is certainly not of the same type as the intrusive ones found in F and H.

Grammatical morphology

The verb; present tense inflection

Both F and H were erratic in the use of the s inflection in the environment of the third person present singular, and there were several instances of omissions. There were none in W. The facts were:

F	H	W
–	believe	–
get	–	–
–	give	–
keep	–	–
–	think	–
want	want (4 times)	–

The verb: past tense forms

There were many instances of the use of the regular weak past tense ending in '-ed', in all three sets of documents. In F and H, however, it was also often omitted. There were some seven instances in F, and in H thirty-seven failures to attach the morpheme. Parallel examples are:

F6.4   He would get upset with them because they *believe* me.
H6.11   I never really *believe* her.
F6.2   He *threaten* me.
H12.6   She had a knife and *threaten* during argument.

W was quite accurate in the use of the past tense morphemes. With verbs which indicate the past tense through internal changes rather than the addition of an inflection, F and H showed a similar fluctuation in practice, choosing non-standard forms as frequently as standard ones:

F	H
come (1 out of 3)	come (2/6)
done (2/2)	done (2/3)
–	keep (1/1)
seen (1/2)	seen (5/7)
–	sware (1/1)

That is, F and H used the non-standard forms more frequently than the standard.

In W, there were only two instances of non-standard forms: *come* and *swang*. Both occur only once each, and the one instance of 'come' has to be set against fourteen occurrences of the standard form 'came', and *swang* is matched by one occurrence of 'swung'. That is, the non-standard forms must be regarded as random instances in W, a possible slip or error, whereas they have a more regular status in F and H. In the expression of the past tense, then, F and H had a strong non-standard component both in regular and irregular verbs, whereas W was definitely standard, with only two non-standard occurrences and those in irregular verbs.

Syntax

Sentence structure

In F many independent sentences were not clearly separated. Instead they were run together without any marking of their division with a full stop and a capital letter, for example, 'since his accident at work he's slowed down before that he wanted it everynight always woke up with a horn everymorning ready to go for it again' (F3.13–15). A full stop would have been in order after 'down', and 'before' should have begun with a capital letter. A similar arrangement might have applied after 'everynight'.

Alternatively, a comma was found inserted in place of the required full stop, for example, 'Alan look after helen, when she has the baby, look after it be proud of it like I am of you, never bad talk or run it down' (F1.14–15). A full stop, for example, would have been in place after 'helen', with 'when' being spelt with a capital letter.

The same weakness in sentence control characterised H, but did not appear in W. The total numbers of errors in sentence-division were: F(80), H(142), and W(4). The correlation between F and H is strong enough to point to a close similarity in linguistic practice. The correlation between F and W on the other hand appears quite weak.

In this part of the investigation two criteria were used to establish the division between sentences: the presence of a full stop at the end of one and the presence of a capital letter at the beginning of the next. I have left out of consideration those instances in which the writers failed to insert a full stop but commenced a segment, which was legitimately a fresh sentence, with a capital letter. It seemed reasonable to regard the capital letter as sufficient recognition of sentence division; for example, 'he would keep saying he wanted to go to Noosa Heads, just because you were there I was suppose to keep dropping my pants till he decided to take me, when tommy . . .' (F2.2–3); and 'the Oldman will look after the children He loves you very much' (F6.27). The details of such instances, with absence of stop but with presence of capital, were: F(6), H(44) and W(19).

The reasonable exclusion of these figures did not in any way affect the conclusion reached on control of sentence structure. Even if they had been included in the earlier totals, they would not have materially altered the strong correlation between F and H, and the distinction between them on the one hand, and W on the other.

Disrupted structures

In the farewell letter (F) there are nine instances of what might be termed disrupted structures, that is, sentences in which a structural element had been omitted. Six of these involved the word 'to': 'got you . . . paint' (F2.28); 'whether . . . start' (F4.1);

and 'try . . . help' (F6.28). One involves the omission of 'of': 'hundreds . . . dollars' (F2.18).

There is nothing difficult about the types of structures involved in these examples. On the contrary they are straightforward and fairly frequent. Moreover, the words 'of' and 'to' are simple and well known. Their use is almost automatic, and their absence could not be attributed to some stylistic intricacy in the pattern. Their relatively small number might lead to them being regarded as slips.

The same disrupted patterns, however, occurred in the husband's writing (H), though with greater frequency. There were forty-seven instances of the pattern with 'to' missing, and fourteen of those with 'of' missing.

Punctuation

Comma: omission at end of clauses

In F the practice of inserting a comma between clauses within sentences was not always followed, for example, 'Ian Henry to halfdrunk knocking at your door at all hours of the night trying to climb on top of you, telling me how beautiful I was wants his daughter to look . . .' (F2.10–11). A comma would have been in order both after 'night' and after 'was'. H exhibited the same type of omission but to a considerably greater degree, but this feature was almost absent in W. The details were: F(20), H(62), and W(5). For the document to share the feature in equal strength, taking F as the base, the figures should have read: F(20), H(29), and W(26). F and H clearly had much more in common than either of them had with W.

Comma: omission in series

A comma between items in a series was regularly omitted in F; for example, 'Meg Ruth Barbara Myself and others' (F2.23). The same sort of omission occurred in H. Moreover, the proportion of occurrences in F and H was the same. The feature never occurred in W. The details were: F(14), H(22), and W(0).

Asides

There were three occasions in which asides were indicated by the use of brackets or dashes in F. One was: 'he would run out and buy something to try to get me to love him, (poor old fool)' (F6.14). On the other hand, there were twelve occasions in which the asides were not marked. On three other occasions commas were used in place of brackets or dashes. On four other occasions brackets were used incorrectly. H also failed to signal asides appropriately on twelve occasions. W, however, was always accurate in this area.

Full-stops: influence on spelling

Punctuation has an influence on spelling inasmuch as a full-stop at the end of one sentence leads to the word beginning the next sentence being spelt with a capital letter, even though elsewhere the word would be spelt with a small letter. In F there were fifty-eight occasions a small letter appeared instead; for example, 'and what I have to offer them. you my babe . . .' (F3.5). In H there were seventy-one full-stops; twenty-two of them were followed by a small letter. In W in all 225 occasions where a full-stop occurred at the end of a sentence, the opening word of the next sentence began with a capital letter. The details were: F(15), H(23), and W(0). The accuracy of W in this matter is as significant, when compared with F and H, as is the fairly high correlation between F and H.

FINDINGS

There were many significant differences between the language of the farewell letter and the language of the wife's documents.

These had nothing to do with extraneous matters, such as variation in subject-matter or in level of formality, but reflected instead a marked divergence in underlying linguistic practice. The clear conclusion on the basis of this evidence was that the wife – the author of the documents labelled W – was not the author of the farewell letter.

On the other hand, there were many strong similarities between the language of the farewell letter and the language of the texts composed by the husband. The high correlation between the two indicated a strong probability that the husband was the author of the farewell letter. There was definitely nothing in F that would be inconsistent with his normal linguistic practice. On the contrary, the large degree of comparability pointed in his direction.

Equally to the point, it was not possible to find a feature in which F and W agreed to the exclusion of H. Where F and W agreed, for example in the order of subject and predicator or the forms of personal pronouns, so also did H. It was only F and H that matched up to the exclusion of W. Indeed, the style of writing in W stood apart quite dramatically from that of F and H, mainly because of the good control of sentence structure. The sentences in W were well constructed and properly delimited. Even when the wife was presenting notes, and so used truncated sequences, she observed the normal conventions for sentence construction. In addition to this feature, which has already been commented on in above (Syntax: sentence structure), there were such other niceties unique to W as:

1. The marking of a special word with inverted commas, e.g. 'He "rasberried" in my face' (W12.22) and 'snarling' (W14.12).
2. Varied sentence openings, e.g. 'Upon arriving home my husband . . .' (W16.5).
3. The exploitations of a wide range of punctuation marks. Not only did W have the full-stop and question-mark, but it alone employed the exclamation mark and quotation marks.

Not only did W not share many features with F and H, it was uniquely different from them in others. Table 15.1 summarises the findings of the linguistic investigation at points of significant comparison between F and W, and F and H.

Table 15.1 Summary of comparison of three sets of documents

	H	F	W
1. SPELLING			
1.1 Errors in individual words	+	+	−
1.2 Capitals with common nouns	+	+	−
1.3 Small letters with proper nouns	+	+	−
1.4 Intrusive apostrophe	+	+	−
2. GRAMMATICAL MORPHOLOGY			
2.1 The verb: present tense	+	+	−
2.2 The verb: past tense	+	+	−
3. SYNTAX			
3.1 Sentence structure	+	+	−
3.2 Disrupted structures	+	+	−
4. PUNCTUATION			
4.1 Comma: with clauses	+	+	−
4.2 Comma: in series	+	+	−
4.3 Asides	+	+	−
4.4 Capitals after full-stops	+	+	−

Notes: + = possession of a shared feature; − = absence of shared features.

This table demonstrates clearly that the language of the farewell letter was inconsistent with the language of the wife and that it was not reasonable to consider her as its author. The table also forcefully demonstrates that if only one of two persons was the writer of the farewell letter, then on the basis of the evidence coming from the investigation of the language it was legitimate to conclude with a high level of probability that the author of the texts, (H), was also the author of the farewell letter.

POSTSCRIPT

The husband pleaded his innocence at the committal proceedings and continued to affirm that the wife had written F. The linguistic evidence was subject to extensive cross-examination. After being committed for trial, the husband changed his plea to one of manslaughter for which he was subsequently found guilty. He admitted to writing the farewell letter F.

SIXTEEN

Computers, statistics and disputed authorship

Wilfrid Smith

INTRODUCTION

In 1851 Professor Augustus de Morgan of the University of London, writing to a friend at Cambridge, argued that the epistles of St Paul to the Greeks may be distinguished from those to the Hebrews on the basis of average word length. If so, de Morgan declared that he would be quite sure that the epistles to the Hebrews were not by Paul (Allen 1974). This may be the first recorded instance of a suggestion for a method completely independent of literary qualities to discriminate between authors.

Although much effort has been expended to derive and develop such methods, particularly since the advent of computers, more than 120 years later the judge presiding at the trial of Patricia Hearst decided against hearing psycholinguistic evidence essentially on the grounds that:

1. The jury was to decide whether she meant what she said rather than the question of her authorship of the utterances attributed to her.
2. Hearing expert testimony on authorship would be inordinately time-consuming.
3. The relative infancy of this area of scientific endeavour might well have created an unjustifiable aura of special reliability and trustworthiness around the testimony.

Subsequently the judge was said to have admitted privately that he was uncertain of the propriety of his ruling. Nevertheless, the Court of Appeal upheld his decision (Bailey 1979).

Gudjonsson and Haward (1983) relate somewhat similar legal cases of disputed authorship in which the Reverend Andrew Q. Morton acted as a psycholinguistic expert. Describing him as 'an acknowledged international authority of stylistics' and as 'the world's leading exponent of statistical stylistics', they recount that in one case, that of Ronald St Germain, Morton explained to the Court of Appeal that 'a human being writing eight hours a day for 300 days a year for a million years is still very unlikely to produce such differences' as those between the disputed and admitted statements. Gudjonsson and Haward report that other experts supported Morton's analysis and praised his expertise. Nevertheless, the appeal was refused. While recognising that Morton was a classical scholar of great renown, and that stylometry is now established as a science, the Court noted that Morton had been unable to advance his conclusion beyond that of hypothesis. The outcome was that the Court felt that the hypothesis did not merit hearing further evidence on this point. Gudjonsson and Haward comment that if the English Courts are to wait for scientific certainty they will be waiting for a long time. They consider that the rejection of a scientific hypothesis 'with such an infinitely small random probability' of error is inconsistent with the practice in relation to the evidence of other forensic scientists and they report that Lord Justice Scarman spoke favourably about the science of psycholinguists. Gudjonsson and Haward (1983) are unambiguous in their conclusion. They state,

> What can be said with assurance is that stylometry, with over 1000 scientific publications to its credit, is a psycholinguistic tool of increasingly recognised value, and that documentary evidence in Court, particularly confessions, can have a more accurate and scientific evaluation of their validity than ever before.

Accepting even the widest reasonable definition of stylometry, it seems improbable that there had been anything approaching 1000 publications.

The probability above, vividly illustrated by Morton, is so remote as to make the conclusion drawn from it to appear as a virtual certainty. Moreover, Morton's study had apparently won unqualified approval from other experts. Thus, *prima facie*, the Court would seem to have been ultra-conservative in its caution. Indeed, Gudjonsson and Haward appear to rationalise the judgment by assuming that the reasoning behind the decision was not doubt concerning stylometric evidence but that instead the Court decided that the differences between primary testimony and secondary hearsay evidence in this case were of greater importance.

Because Morton appears to have figured more in legal cases than any other stylometrist, his methods are examined critically in this chapter. The approach now is to investigate first the evidence Morton has presented to justify the claims he makes. Because his method is an *ad hoc* practical procedure, a theoretical framework is then deduced to describe it. The analysis is constructive in that techniques are derived to overcome many of the shortcomings of Morton's work.

MORTON'S STYLOMETRIC METHOD USED ON LITERARY TEXTS

Morton describes his techniques in the book, *Literary Detection* (1978). Although the method was originally developed for distinguishing authors of Greek texts, chapters 10 and 11 contain an adaptation for use when disputed material is in English. Morton entitles his work 'stylometry', although this term had been in use since before 1950, and maintains firmly that it is a science. (This section of the chapter has been abridged from M.W.A. Smith 1985.)

Literary Detection is written in three sections whose content may be summarised as:

1. background information, including illustrations of some practical statistical techniques required for the method;
2. the development of the method;
3. applications of the method.

The relevant part is the derivation of the method for English texts as described in chapters 10 and 11 of section 2. In these chapters Morton advances three types of tests, namely, comparisons of two or more samples of text by means of:

1. Positions of prescribed words in sentences. Such tests take the form of a comparison of the number of occurrences in each sample of, for example, *the* as the first word of a sentence related to the total number of its occurrences elsewhere.
2. Collocations – that is, the number of times a prescribed word is either followed by (fb) or preceded by (pb) another prescribed word related to the total number of times the first

word is used in other circumstances. A comparison of samples by means of the number of times *of* is followed by *the* related to the number of times *of* is not followed by *the* forms a typical test of this type.

3. 'Proportionate pairs' – that is – word-pairs. The number of occurrences in each sample of two specified words is compared. For example, the two forms of the indefinite article, *a* and *an*, are deemed suitable.

A pre-condition Morton imposes upon his technique is that 'in every type of problem the disputed material must be compared with similar material' (p. 131). Of course, such a restriction is not questioned, but it is curious to find him, in chapter 15, comparing the script of an Elizabethan play with Bacon's essays (see Smith 1984).

Chapter 10 can be regarded as consisting of four parts with chapter 11 contributing one further part. These are:

1. An investigation to reveal writers' habits suitable for tests using one sample of English prose from each of ten authors. The sources of the ten samples were published between 1909 and 1961.
2. An investigation of the stability of authors' habits under 'the maximum of internal change'. The texts used are from *The Antiquary* and *Castle Dangerous* by Walter Scott.
3. An investigation of the stability of authors' habits under 'the maximum of external change . . . likely to bear upon his writing'. The texts adopted are from *The American* and *The Ambassadors* by Henry James.
4. An investigation of the habits of an author, 'who prides himself in being able to write quite differently in different genres'. The texts used are from *The French Lieutenant's Woman*, *The Magus*, and *The Collector* by John Fowles.
5. An investigation of 'proportionate pairs' of words using the same samples of text as in (2), (3) and (4).

Tests on samples of texts (1909–61) by ten authors

The purpose of testing ten samples of texts, one per author, is to determine (a) the particular words occurring in which prescribed positions in sentences, and (b) which collocations, are suitable for tests of authorship. Morton's guiding principle is, 'Only if the occurrence was consistent within the sample and differed between samples was it accepted as being, *prima facie*, a test of authorship suitable for further investigation' (Morton 1978: 132).

A major deficiency is the size of the samples which varies between 1042 and 1164 words. This is very brief for any sort of testing. Morton gives a table of twenty-three frequently used words of which only sixteen occur often enough to provide an average number of actual occurrences of five per sample. Indeed, only nine of these words appear at least five times in every sample. Occurrences in prescribed positions and almost all collocations (that is, except collocations such as *to* fb verb) appear very much less frequently than the prescribed words themselves. Nevertheless, Morton declares:

> In both cases [that is, for position and for collocation] the testing
> followed the same pattern. The sample of each of the ten authors was
> divided into as many sub-samples as would leave an expectation of
> five occurrences per sub-sample. In most cases the conclusion was that
> the occurrence was consistent within the whole sample. But in a
> number of instances periodic effects were found to be present and a
> further investigation of these was undertaken.
>
> (p. 132)

(Periodic effects are multiple occurrences of a feature in close proximity, separated by relatively long sequences of text which do not contain that feature.) Unfortunately, nothing of the 'further investigation' is reported. However a second table containing eight of the original twenty-three words is provided, which, Morton states, 'may occur often enough in preferred positions to enable them to be used as tests of authorship involving samples of a thousand words or more' (p. 132). No figures for occurrences of any of these eight words in any position for any sample are quoted to substantiate his findings. Notwithstanding, evaluation of this statement is possible, because the *total* number of occurrences of four of the eight words is:

at – less than five occurrences in three of the ten samples,
but and *for* – less than five occurrences in four of the ten samples,
so – less than five occurrences in six of the ten samples.

With the number of occurrences in any prescribed position almost invariably very much less than the total usage of a word, it is difficult indeed to understand how differences between samples, and even more so, consistency within samples, could possibly have been demonstrated at all – never mind at a level of reliability appropriate to scientific investigation. Furthermore, data for an illustration of a positional test is taken instead from entirely different texts – those by Walter Scott which are used for the next part of the investigation.

Concerning the collocations, no data whatever is included. This is not at all surprising since these samples are far too brief for such tests. Such a failure to present comprehensively the data upon which the conclusions of this part of the investigation are based is an omission which alone would invite suspicion that the underlying investigation had not been rigorously undertaken. To be taken seriously, Morton's report should have presented, for example, full details of each subsample, occurrences of the various features in each subsample, data showing which tests demonstrated consistency under what criteria, those that illustrated differences, together with details of any tests which were deemed unsuitable for the determination of authorship and the reasons for their rejection.

(ii) Stability under extreme internal change

The report in *Literary Detection* of the work on the ten samples of English prose was completed without presenting, in the form of a short list, full details of all the habits which were deduced as possible tests of authorship. However, eight words were put forward (without evidence) as being suitable for tests of position, but no specific collocations at all were suggested. These features, Morton claims, had fulfilled 'the routine of testing' as explained in the following quotation, which also indicates the next step in the derivation of the method.

> The occurrences of each key word in a preferred position, or in a
> collocation with any other word which occurred often enough to form
> a useful basis for statistical testing, was [sic] listed in the ten samples.
> Only if the occurrence was consistent within the sample and differed
> between the samples was it accepted as being, prima facie, a test of

authorship suitable for further investigation. Before such habits could be accepted as tests of authorship two things had yet to be established. The first is that they were stable under extreme conditions. The second is that they are independent of each other.

(Morton 1978: 132)

Although the words 'such habits' in the quotation above may be understood to indicate that the purpose is to establish particular tests of position and collocation for general use to distinguish writers of English, the intention is clarified at the end of this chapter: 'So the examination does confirm the starting hypothesis that, for writers in an uninflected language, the placing of words in preferred positions or in collocations offers a range of tests of authorship' (p. 146). Clearly, no specific tests for general use are to be proposed.

To accomplish the objective of demonstrating stability under extreme internal change, samples from the works of Walter Scott were adopted. Chapters 14 to 45 of *The Antiquary* (1816) and chapters 1, 4, 5, 13, and 14 of *Castle Dangerous* (1831) provided texts. Between writing these works Scott suffered a number of strokes. Whether or not his habits, as quantified by Morton's method, would be likely to remain unaffected by such an internal change presumably depends upon which areas of Scott's brain had been damaged and also upon the extent and permanency of such damage.

The statistical measure Morton uses most frequently to establish consistency or otherwise of an author's writings is chi-square. As the value of chi-square increases, the corresponding probability that two works are by the same author becomes more remote. When the probability is 0.05 or less (the 5 per cent significance level), the interpretation for Morton's method is that the texts under comparison are the work of more than one author. On the other hand, if this value exceeds 0.05 no information is obtained. It is a one-way test pointing only to differences of authorship.

The homogeneity of *The Antiquary* is investigated first. Morton uses his table of eight words in prescribed positions, together with another table containing twenty-six collocations 'frequently occurring in writers of English' (p. 137) to provide nineteen words in all and to furnish a total of twenty-seven tests. Since no information is provided as to how these features were selected and since the background is formed only from experimentation on the ten brief samples of English texts, it would appear that the main criterion for the choice of tests was Morton's personal judgment of which words depend least on subject matter and context. Of these twenty-seven tests, Morton declares that five are significant at the 5 per cent level. Neither details of, nor figures for, the features which form the remaining twenty-one tests are presented. It is difficult to deduce any reliable information from such data. However, in the discussion arising from this table, the general approach is unaffected.

Morton first notes that one of the anomalies is due to the titular use of *the* followed by an adjective (for example, 'the old man', in place of a name). He contends that when cases of this specific type of usage are subtracted from the figures, the anomaly disappears. What is suggested could become a misuse of statistics: it is analogous to an experiment designed to investigate the effectiveness of a drug in which the experimenters, having acquired the data, are informed as to which animals received the drug and which were left untreated. If, then, they do not like the outcome they can decide which data ought to be reclassified upon whatever grounds they subsequently choose. Once the subjectivity of the investigator enters, the advantage of the objectivity of statistical interpretation departs.

Morton continues, 'If for any reason this procedure is not acceptable, the alternative is to look at another form of distribution . . . In the present case all the exceptional occurrences are examined as Poisson distributions and in every case the statistically significant differences vanish' (p. 140). He also notes: 'In extreme cases it may be that a negative binomial distribution alone will fit the observations' (p. 140). The discussion is concluded with the advice:

> The anomalies play a useful part in reminding the researcher that it is literary texts which are being examined. The evidence can only be fully understood and safely interpreted when the nature of the material is kept in mind. The examination starts from a text and it should always end with the text; the statistics are only a useful summary description of what an author is doing.
>
> (p. 141)

While it would appear at this stage that only those tests which give rise to results compatible with different authorship are afforded special scrutiny, at the end of chapter 10, Morton adds,

'What has not been described but has been done and should always be done, is the inspection of the data to confirm the converse proposition, that the absence of any statistically significant result is not due to some periodic effect or other factor' (p. 146). In chapters 10 and 11 only samples by the same author are compared by the tests. While all the tests in these two chapters give rise to about fifteen anomalous results, the large majority of values of chi-square falls within the 5 per cent level of significance. Almost every one of these fifteen significant values either has been explained by a special feature in the text or has been eliminated by applying an alternative statistical procedure. Yet of all the other tests, whose results are compatible with identical authorship, not one was apparently either perturbed by, or found to reveal, any peculiarity in any of the samples.

Having decided that the samples from *The Antiquary* show that Scott is consistent throughout his writings in these twenty-seven habits, Morton reports that, when the same set of tests is applied to compare samples from *Castle Dangerous* with *The Antiquary*, none showed a statistically significant difference. Apart from figures for the use of *but* as the first word of a sentence – figures which Morton substituted for numeric evidence from the ten samples in section (i) – no data whatever is provided to permit a check of this claim to be performed.

During the formulation of the method in chapter 10 and 11, the test of *but* as the first word of a sentence (fws) is one of only two comparisons of position based on data from more than a single literary work in English, for which the values of the counts are actually quoted. It is the only one which permits a number of comparisons and therefore assumes importance. Although Morton quotes the value of chi-square as 21.91 for *The Antiquary*, the value should read 15.15 as shown in Table 16.1. Such a result indicates a high degree of homogeneity of the samples. The other values for chi-square in Table 16.1 also appear to emphasise that homogeneity exists not only within but between the two works.

At this point an opportunity presents itself to perform some comparisons to check these conclusions by a different treatment of the data. The figures from *Castle Dangerous* establish the size of sample which Morton considers adequate for a reliable result. Therefore, for a more rigorous test, the chapters of *The Antiquary* are grouped consecutively in pairs to form samples containing a comparable number of occurrences. Each sample is now com-

Table 16.1 Morton's test of *but* as the first word of sentences (fws) for samples of Walter Scott's writings

Chapter of The Antiquary	Occurrence of but: total	fws	Contribution to chi-square
14	25	7	0.06
15	29	8	0.10
16	35	4	4.27
17	26	5	1.13
18	20	6	0.00
19	21	9	0.99
20	34	10	0.02
21	39	16	1.32
22	34	13	0.61
23	21	3	1.86
24	31	10	0.02
25	23	6	0.17
26	28	9	0.02
27	33	17	4.58
Total	399	123	$\chi^2 = 15.15$ for 13 df*

Chapters of Castle Dangerous			
1, 3, 5	14	55	
13, 14	6	35	
Total	20	90	$\chi^2 = 0.85$ for 1 df*

Samples of:			
The Antiquary	123	399	
Castle Dangerous	30	90	
Total	153	489	$\chi^2 = 2.62$ for 1 df*

Note: *df indicates degrees of freedom.

pared with every other sample, including that from *Castle Dangerous*. These results are shown in Table 16.2, in which the samples are identified by the initial letter(s) of the title of the work from which they were drawn and by subscripts indicating chapters. The figures in the table are values of chi-square for one degree of freedom calculated using Yates' correction. Only one

Table 16.2 An alternative test for consistency of *but* as fws in samples of Scott's writings. The figures are values of chi-square for 1 degree of freedom, calculated using Yates' correction

Sample	$A_{14,15}$	$A_{16,17}$	$A_{18,19}$	$A_{20,21}$	$A_{22,23}$	$A_{24,25}$	$A_{26,27}$
CD	0.30	0.87	2.28	2.94	0.53	0.63	6.21
$A_{26,27}$	2.14	10.26	0.16	0.42	1.74	1.56	
$A_{24,25}$	0.00	2.90	0.25	0.27	0.02		
$A_{22,23}$	0.00	2.72	0.31	0.35			
$A_{20,21}$	0.55	6.45	0.01				
$A_{18,19}$	0.48	5.34					
$A_{16,17}$	2.21						

sample – that is, chapters 16 and 17 of *The Antiquary* – appears decidedly different from the others. However, the magnitude of some of the values may be disturbing as is the occurrence of another large value for the comparison of $A_{26,27}$ with the sample from *Castle Dangerous*. Moreover, Morton points out that Scott paid very considerable sums to a Mr Cadell for emendations to the books *Count Robert of Paris* and *Castle Dangerous*. It can be inferred, therefore, that Mr Cadell's contribution to the phraseology might have been substantial. Thus a second unquantifiable influence is present: under such circumstances it would be imprudent to interpret the results of this test either as support or otherwise for the method, whether or not extreme internal change is accepted.

(iii) Stability under external change[1]

Henry James, according to *Literary Detection*, arrived in Europe in 1875. After writing *The American* (*Amer*) (1877), he 'settled in England and deliberately changed his cultural background'. In 1903 he published *The Ambassadors* (*Amb*). These two books were therefore chosen to exemplify any alteration which a major external change would induce in an author's habits. For purposes of testing, Morton used chapters 1 and 2 of each book in which he counted the number of occurrences of a variety of collocations. These are shown in Table 16.3. Unfortunately, without supporting evidence, Morton writes 'that some of them occur at very low

Table 16.3 Comparison of samples from two works by Henry James

Collocation	Amer			Amb			chi-square (df)	
a fb adj*	122	50		186	58		3.11	(1)
and fb the, adj	132	12	6	192	11	20	4.66	(2)
at fb the	47	12		70	20		0.13	(1)
in fb a, the	74	5	25	135	14	32	2.78	(2)
of fb a, the	100	6	15	296	16	50	0.23	(2)
the fb adj	214	62		383	93		1.57	(1)
to fb the, verb	130	11	70	249	14	127	1.84	(2)
was fb a, the	59	5	2	118	8	6	0.40	(2)
						Total	14.73	(13)

* adj is an abbreviation for 'adjective'.

rates and their consistency was confirmed by recording them in succeeding chapters of the text' (p. 143).

There are two differences in the statistical handling of the data between that in Table 16.3 and Morton's approach. Two collocations, namely, as followed by (fb) if and on fb the are eliminated due to their low number of occurrences which leads to expected values less than five in 2 × 2 contingency tables. In larger contingency tables a minimum total number of eight actual occurrences was accepted.[2] The second difference is that collocations such as to fb the and to fb verb are grouped together into a single 2 × 3 contingency table.

When the values of chi-square from the contingency tables are added, a total of 14.73 for 13 degrees of freedom is obtained. (Yates' correction is not used in any of the calculations.) This confirms Morton's conclusion that there is a high degree of homogeneity between the two samples.

Morton's account of the effect of John Fowles' attempts to change his own style suffer from similar methodological flaws – see Smith (1985). As these do not further the analysis they will not be discussed here.

A comparison of two authors by collocations

If the method is to function correctly, it must avoid producing an excessive number of large values of chi-square when samples

Table 16.4 Occurrences of collocations in samples of works by James and Fowles

Collocation	Amer	Amb	FLW	Mag	Coll
and fb the, adj	132 12 6	192 11 20	198 9 17	198 11 19	334 20 28
as fb if	42 2	143 18	78 15	59 13	70 7
at fb the	47 12	70 20	75 24	60 13	52 11
for fb the	27 4	98 12	56 7	33 3	48 6
in fb a, the	74 5 25	135 14 32	170 17 34	122 14 26	148 18 41
of fb a, the	100 6 15	296 16 50	247 2 52	177 6 27	137 2 23
the fb adj	214 62	383 93	439 *	325 101	400 34
to fb the	130 11	249 14	278 31	205 14	263 11
was fb a, the	59 5 2	118 8 6	165 20 12	126 12 6	212 11 11

Note: * value not given in *Literary Detection*.

written by the same person are compared, while not being so insensitive as to fail to distinguish different authors. It was shown in section (i) that, due to lack of information and the small size of each of the ten samples, there is severe doubt concerning the rigour of the tests Morton applied to ascertain the ability of collocations to distinguish authors. It is therefore appropriate to investigate as far as possible from the information provided whether their use can distinguish reliably the writings of Henry James from those of John Fowles. Collocations for which figures are available for both authors and which give rise to expected values greater than five when tested by 2 × 2 contingency tables, or provide a total of at least eight occurrences when tested by a larger contingency table, are listed in Table 16.4. The full values of chi-square, obtained when the samples from each work are compared with the samples from every other work, are in Smith (1985).

Table 16.5 contains the totals of the values of chi-square, with the corresponding number of degrees of freedom in parenthesis, for each comparison of the samples. However, due to some very large values obtained for tests involving *the* fb an adjective together with the possible effect of the missing figure, this test could have a disproportionately distorting effect on the totals. It is therefore excluded from the total in Table 16.5.

The results are collated into Table 16.6. The first of its two sections summarises the tests of samples which are of different authorship by showing the total number of values of chi-square together with the number which indicates the correct result. The criterion is the one Morton adopts – that is, a value exceeding the 5 per cent level of significance indicates that different authors are

Table 16.5 Total (omitting values for *the* fb adj.)

Sample	Coll	Mag	FLW	Amb
Amer	13.40(10)	15.97(11)	27.45(11)	9.32(10)
Amb	7.43(12)	6.25(11)	21.27(12)	
FLW	25.45(11)	12.23(11)		
Mag	10.65(11)			

Notes: Degrees of freedom (df) are in parentheses.
For significance at the 5 per cent level chi-square is 3.84 for 1df, 5.99 for 2df, 18.31 for 10df, 19.58 for 11df and 21.03 for 12df.

involved. In Table 16.6 values of extreme magnitude from an individual collocation cannot have an overriding effect upon totals. Thus, comparisons of *the* fb an adjective are included in the figures for the row labelled 'total'. This row shows that, of the forty-seven values of chi-square calculated when the authors are different, only eight (that is, 17 per cent) indicate the correct result. As the effect of Yates' correction is to decrease values of chi-square, its inclusion would tend to reduce even further the power of discrimination of the method. However, when samples by the same author are compared, the values of chi-square are consistent with one writer in about 90 per cent of the cases. It is ironic, therefore, that since only differences are significant, the worse outcome (at only 17 per cent correct) is the one which actually matters.

When the contents of Table 16.5 – the total values of chi-square for each comparison of samples – are similarly treated to form the bottom row of Table 16.6, it can be seen that these tests of collocation, taken together, also do not provide a reliable indicator of authorship.

While Morton discovered some anomalies when he tested

Table 16.6 Classification of the results from Table 16.5

Collocation	Number of comparisons			
	Different author		Same author	
	Total	Correct	Total	Correct
and fb the, adj	6	0	4	4
as fb if	5	2	3	3
at fb the	6	0	4	4
for fb the	2	0	1	1
in fb a, the	6	0	4	4
of fb a, the	6	2	4	4
the fb adj	4	3	2	1
to fb the	6	1	4	3
was fb a, the	6	0	4	3
Total	47	8 (17%)	30	27 (90%)
Overall	6	2	4	3

within the authors, had he decided to check if his method would detect differences between James and Fowles, he would have found first, that none of the individual tests (for which figures are available) and, second, the outcome when these tests are combined, were able to provide sufficiently reliable evidence to distinguish with confidence the works of these two writers.

Tests of word-pairs

From his own experience and that of others Morton recommends, as a test of authorship, a comparison of the rates at which pairs of words occur in the samples. The values of the counts for the tests chosen to illustrate the technique in chapter 11 of *Literary Detection* are given in Table 16.7. The abbreviations of the titles of the books are those used in previous tables, except that *The Antiquary* is now denoted by *Anti*. However, as suggested corrections for possible errors, the following figures have been changed:

Table 16.7 Counts for word-pairs

Word-pair	Scott		James		Fowles		
	Anti	CD	Amer	Amb	FLW	Mag	Coll
a	1333	511	122	186	316	219	318
an	226	98	16	29	41	27	31
all	222	76	19	23	28	32	78
any	77	46	7	8	7	5	21
in	1120	478	70	135	170	122	148
into	101	43	13	14	10	18	12
no	221	207	13	16	42	25	33
not	301	283	22	58	131	37	32
that	777	379	*	*	154	91	106
this	371	197	*	*	39	23	24

Note: * values not presented in *Literary Detection*.

1. The number of occurrences of *a* in *The Ambassadors* is altered from 183 to 186 to maintain compatibility with the figure given previously.
2. For the samples from James's works Morton may have inadvertently interchanged the figures for *in* and *into*. The values of *in* given as 13 and 14 are therefore replaced by 70 and 135.
3. The total of 216 occurrences of *a* for the samples from *The French Lieutenant's Woman* is replaced by 316.

The changes in (2) are justified by experience alone; it appears that *into* occurs very much less frequently in samples of text than *in*. In (3) if the suggested figure of 316 is assumed, a value for chi-square of 1.40 is obtained for the test in *Literary Detection* whereas if 216 is used the value of chi-square is about 120. However, if Morton's figure for chi-square of 1.32 is approximately correct, 316 is not only a reasonable value to assume but also brings the usage of *a* relative to *an* into line with that normally encountered.

While there are no rules for deducing appropriate pairs of words, *a* and *an* is a choice which is difficult to justify. The nature of Morton's approach is to test features which rely as little as possible upon the context. Consequently, such words as nouns and adjectives are normally shunned. The form of the indefinite article depends upon the following word and therefore its use indirectly depends, at least in part, upon its context. It follows that results from this test are unlikely to reflect sensitivity to differences of authorship. In contrast with the tests of *it* fb *a* and *it* fb *the* in the previous section, the test of the word-pair *a* and *an* is not eliminated because it is one of the most popular tests in Morton's method, and evidence concerning its use is therefore important. In any case, both *a* and *an* occur very much more frequently than either of the collocations above in the samples for which figures are available.

As is shown in Table 16.7 the comparisons are based on the two separate samples by each of Scott and James and the three samples by Fowles used previously to test collocations. Morton selects a total of five tests to illustrate behaviour typical of word-pairs. Unfortunately comparisons are restricted by his omission of the figures for *this* and *that* for the samples from the works by James.

Morton compares explicitly the occurrences of pairs of values only between the samples of works by the same author. He finds that two values of chi-square are significant beyond the 5 per cent level. These, he claims, do not show significance when fitted to a Poisson distribution. This would seem to be an arbitrary adjustment of technique, instigated by knowledge of the required result. Of much more moment, however, is Morton's comment: 'For tests of such a simple nature proportional pairs are remarkably effective, as may be judged by looking at the differences between the authors in the table' (p. 150). This time sufficient data is presented to enable a check to be made on one of his assertions.

A comparison of three authors by word-pairs

Tables 16.8(a) to 16.8(e) show the outcome of comparing each sample by Scott, James and Fowles with every other sample, for which data are available, for a test of each of the pairs of words. Even though the values of chi-square are for one degree of freedom, as in section (iv), to provide results as favourable as possible to Morton's assertion, Yates' correction is not adopted. Following normal practice when an expected value less than five is calculated, the figure for chi-square is not evaluated but is replaced by an asterisk in the Table. Table 16.8(f) shows the sum of the values of chi-square and (in parenthesis) the corresponding number of degrees of freedom. Table 16.9 summarises these results using a layout identical to that of Table 16.6. In all components of Table 16.8, the values of chi-square within the dotted line are for comparisons of samples of text by different authors. Of these, as can be seen from Table 16.9, only twenty-one of the sixty-nine values (that is, 30 per cent) are greater than the 5 per cent level of significance which Morton adopts as the criterion to infer different authorship. However, when the samples compared are by the same author, twenty out of twenty-four values are consistent with the known authorship of the works. The content of Table 16.8(f) is shown in a compatible form in Table 16.9, by the row labelled 'overall'. Even these composite values of chi-square do not reveal characteristics of authorship accurately. Indeed, as for the individual tests of collocations

Table 16.8 Details of tests of word-pairs. Values of chi-square are without Yates' correction

(a) *a* and *an*

Sample	Coll	Mag	FLW	Amb	Amer	CD
Anti	7.71	2.19	2.20	0.16	0.87	0.88
CD	9.90	3.67	3.88	0.83	1.76	
Amer	0.83	0.03	0.00	0.27		
Amb	2.97	0.68	0.50			
FLW	1.30	0.04				
Mag	0.72					

(b) *all* and *any*

Sample	Coll	Mag	FLW	Amb	Amer	CD
Anti	0.83	2.67	0.55	0.00	0.02	5.99
CD	7.04	7.63	3.81	1.53	1.08	
Amer	0.39	*	0.40	0.01		
Amb	0.29	1.65	0.32			
FLW	0.02	0.54				
Mag	1.03					

Note: * expected value less than 5.

(c) *in* and *into*

Sample	Coll	Mag	FLW	Amb	Amer	CD
Anti	0.11	3.31	1.59	0.22	5.32	0.00
CD	0.09	2.79	1.39	0.19	4.67	
Amer	3.95	0.34	7.27	2.04		
Amb	0.36	0.88	1.78			
FLW	0.53	5.26				
Mag	2.38					

Table 16.8 *continued*

(d) *no* and *not*

Sample	Coll	Mag	FLW	Amb	Amer	CD
Anti	1.67	0.09	18.02	11.61	0.36	0.00
CD	1.70	0.08	17.60	11.44	0.35	
Amer	1.70	0.09	2.48	2.93		
Amb	12.88	5.60	0.20			
FLW	15.36	5.77				
Mag	1.40					

(e) *this* and *that*

Sample	Coll	Mag	FLW	Amb	Amer	CD
Anti	10.50	7.12	11.41	*	*	0.62
CD	12.22	8.62	13.31	*	*	
Amer	*	*	*	*		
Amb	*	*	*			
FLW	0.15	0.00				
Mag	0.11					

Note: * values for *Amb* and *Amer* unavailable in *Literary Detection*.

(f) Total values of chi-square

Sample	Coll	Mag	FLW	Amb	Amer	CD
Anti	20.82(5)*	15.38(5)	33.77(5)	11.99(4)	6.57(4)	7.48(5)
CD	30.94(5)	22.80(5)	39.99(5)	13.99(4)	7.87(4)	
Amer	6.87(4)	0.47(3)	10.15(4)	5.25(4)		
Amb	16.50(4)	8.81(4)	2.80(4)			
FLW	17.37(5)	11.61(5)				
Mag	5.64(5)					

Notes: * Degrees of freedom (df) are in parentheses.
For significance at the 5 per cent level, chi-square is 3.84 for 1 df, 7.82 for 3 df, 9.49 for 4 df, and 11.07 for 5 df.

Table 16.9 Classification of the results from Table 16.8

	Number of comparisons			
Word pairs	Different author		Same author	
	Total	Correct	Total	Correct
a and *an*	16	3	5	5
all and *any*	15	2	5	4
in and *into*	16	4	5	4
no and *not*	16	6	5	3
this and *that*	6	6	4	4
Total	69	21 (30%)	24	20 (83%)
Overall	16	10	5	3

shown in Table 16.6, the comparisons of these word-pairs do not seem to be sufficiently sensitive to changes of authorship to permit attribution. Moreover, because the use of the words chosen by Morton is influenced by many factors, reliance on the 5 per cent level of significance for chi-square would appear to be particularly inappropriate, as a measure specifically of authorship.

Comment

Morton has insisted that his work is scientific and has made uncompromising claims for its accuracy. If such claims could be substantiated, the outcome of his research would be of benefit to the legal profession and to a variety of scholars.

From a scientific standpoint it has been disappointing to have demonstrated the scale of the inadequacy of documentation, the lack of systematic procedures for selecting data, the haphazard approach to statistical inference, and the limited number and incomplete nature of the tests for establishing the validity of the method. In short, no attempt is evident to conform to scientific standards. Even the aims and objectives for each section of his work are not stated with precision nor are their fulfilment, or otherwise, analysed critically (see also Herden 1965, Johnson 1974 and Kenny 1986).

Morton also fails to mention straightforward but important definitions. Those missing include sentences and collocations; for example, if a punctuation mark occurs between its two words is the collocation still valid? The specification of rules to determine which of the two words forming a collocation should be used as the reference (to distinguish a 'preceded by' from a 'followed by' type), and whether or not elided words (e.g. *wasn't*) are incorporated in the counts are likewise not divulged.

Nevertheless, the strength of Morton's work has been his recognition of *classes* of features which have potential for discriminating between writers. Because experience confirms such potential (Smith 1982a, 1982b, 1983a), a theoretical analysis is undertaken next with a view to establishing a more rigorous procedure.

FORENSIC USE OF STYLOMETRY

Background

Totty et al. (1987) have investigated the application of Morton's method to the authenticity of disputed statements. They consider that his work is worthy of more attention and study than it has received to date and express the hope that their findings will stimulate interest so that eventually there will be sufficient evidence to substantiate or refute his claims. While not detracting from the value of such practical demonstrations, the comments of Totty and colleagues exemplify the nagging doubts which remain as to whether the cases they tested are typical. Accordingly, a more analytical approach is developed in this section, and in Smith (1989a).

Implications of Morton's procedures

For illustrative purposes, data is taken from the tables provided by Totty et al. (1987). By adding the prefix T to their numbers, these tables are distinguished from those in the present chapter. In table T3 the authors quote a typical test of position, as used by Morton. It actually consists of two tests, comparing independently the occurrences of the word THE, in disputed and accepted utterances, as first word (*fws*) and penultimate word (*pws*) of sentences as shown in Table 16.10. The authors follow Morton's technique exactly and calculate a value of chi-square for each contingency table (18.7 for *fws*, 9.0 for *pws*). Because Morton depends on the number of tests for which the value of chi-square exceeds the 5 per cent level of significance as his criterion for detecting a difference of authorship, all tests must be independent. However, the tests of THE as used by Morton are not independent because THE *fws* includes THE *pws* and THE *pws* includes THE *fws*: the approximation is small, but unnecessary. If, instead, both tests were combined as a 3 × 2 contingency table (as in Table 16.3), this flaw would be eliminated and the value of chi-square would be calculated for two degrees of freedom (df).

By his dependence on the number of values of chi-square (usually for 1 df) which exceed the 5 per cent level of significance, Morton implicitly elevates the importance of Yates' correction. This adjustment is usually incorporated when chi-square is calculated for 1 df, but its inclusion does not command unanimous agreement. The effect of the correction generally

Table 16.10 Position test of the word THE in disputed and accepted utterances

	Disputed	Accepted
Morton's tests		
THE *fws*	10	22
THE $\overline{fws}$	64	691
THE *pws*	11	41
THE $\overline{pws}$	63	672
Amalgamation of Morton's tests		
THE *fws*	10	22
THE *pws*	11	41
THE *elsewhere*	53	650

Notes: *fws* = first word sentence; $\overline{fws}$ = not first word of sentence; *pws* = penultimate word of sentence; $\overline{pws}$ = not penultimate word of sentence.

diminishes with increasing sample size but because the numbers of occurrences of the features tested by Morton are often small, its use would tend to decrease the numbers of tests which are significant. Clearly the elimination of the uncertainty as to whether the corrected or uncorrected figure should be taken would be desirable.

In the test shown in Table 16.9, Morton assumes that the person responsible for the text used the word THE as fws and elsewhere according to a binomial distribution, and similarly for the occurrences of THE as pws and elsewhere. According to Totty and colleagues, these are two of 40 features which Morton examined. Typical of Morton's other tests of position are A, AND, AS, BUT, FOR, IF, IN, IT, NO, OF and THAT as fws and IT also as last word of sentence (lws). Each is assumed to occur according to its own independent binomial distribution. However, the words suitable for testing are among those which always occur most frequently. Combined they can therefore form a substantial fraction of the total number of words in the text. The validity of the assumption that these binomial distributions are independent is related to the number of such tests.

For applications such as Morton's, observance of statistical theory would dictate that values of chi-square, calculated for tests assumed independent, be added to obtain an overall figure from which to determine if statistical significance is present. However, Morton merely counts the number of tests significant at the 5 per cent level. Implicitly, then, he is selective in his belief that the probabilities corresponding to the values of chi-square relate exclusively to authorship. Another consequence is that, although Morton is content to depend on the 5 per cent level of significance as a reflection of authorship alone, he does not define a null hypothesis or provide a priori a precise criterion for its rejection.

An example of the consequences of adding the values of chi-square can be deduced from tables T4, T5, T6 and T7. In the first two of these tables, utterances by the same person are compared and total values of chi-square of 23.5 for 11 df and 84.8 for 54 df, respectively, are obtained. Both are significant at the 2 per cent level. In table T7, texts supplied by two different people are compared resulting in a value for chi-square of 42.2 for 16 df. This, at less than the 0.1 per cent level, is even more highly significant. When one person's disputed and accepted utterances are tested, in table T6, a value for chi-square of 36.34 for 15 df ensues. This is again highly significant, in fact, beyond the 0.5 per cent level. When confronted with a test returning an embarrassing result, Morton switches to fitting the data to a Poisson distribution (see subsection (ii) of the previous section). Adding chi-squares prevents such malpractice.

The results obtained from the data published in tables T4, T5 and T7 imply that information relating to authorship could be contained in the occurrences of the features Morton uses and might reveal itself in the relative magnitudes of the totals for chi-square. Nevertheless, in view of the haphazard nature of Morton's derivation and validation of his method, it would be rash to venture an opinion on the disputed statements from a comparison of the total value for chi-square for table T6 with those from tables T4, T5 and T7.

Morton's claim that n tests significant at the 5 per cent level would mislead only once in 20^n trials is incorrect. If random sampling is assumed, the probability of a test reaching the 5 per cent level of significance by chance is indeed $1/20 = 0.05$. Assume now that fifteen tests are performed – a figure compatible with the number of tests used in the comparison reported by Totty and colleagues. Then, if $P(r)$ is the probability of r tests showing significance at this level by chance,

$$P(r) = \begin{pmatrix} 15 \\ r \end{pmatrix} (0.95)^{15-r}(0.05)^r.$$

The probability of three or more of the fifteen tests being significant by chance is therefore

$$1 - \sum_{r=0}^{2} P(r) = 0.036.$$

This is equivalent to a probability of 1 in about 28, whereas Morton claims 1 in 8000 (Morton 1978: 73).

Turning now to the possibility of a difference of authorship passing undetected, Morton, referring to his 'standard' tests, states that there will usually be 'no statistically significant difference in anything from two-thirds to three-quarters of the habits' (Morton and Michaelson 1984). Because of the vagueness of this information, a figure of 0.3 can be taken for the probability of a test revealing a known difference of authorship, where all tests are assumed to be of equal power. The probability of less than three of fifteen tests reflecting this difference is then obtained from

$$\sum_{r=0}^{2} \binom{15}{r} (0.7)^{15-r}(0.3)^r = 0.130.$$

Consequently, using the criterion of less than three tests significant at the 5 per cent level for lack of evidence to reject an implicit null hypothesis of identical authorship, there is an approximate one in eight chance that a difference of authorship will pass undetected.

Thus, setting aside considerations as to whether the textual aspects of Morton's stylometry are valid, from statistical considerations alone and incorporating only information provided by Morton himself, the verdict of Totty et al. (1987) that 'a significant difference in 2 or 3 habits between accepted and disputed texts could occur by chance and should be ignored' is upheld and consequently cannot be attributed to any peculiarities of the particular samples they tested.

The multinomial distribution

How authors write is influenced by literary and other experiences, the subject matter and a host of other factors. If each author were to write so that the features selected for the tests occur in his texts as if they were random samples generated in accordance with his own (not necessarily unique) probability vector, a statistical explanation would be at hand for Morton's tests, from which his treatment of the data could be regularised. A basis would thereby be provided from which to deduce alternative more systematic methods. The multinomial distribution can be introduced to replace the separate binomial distributions of Morton's tests by a framework which collects together the tests in coherent groups.

With respect to the features selected for testing, a text of undisputed authorship is assumed analogous to a known sample. Sampling is by replacement because when an author uses a feature, he does not decrease his available stock of that feature. The author's use of features is assumed to be constrained by his own hypothetical probability vector (HPV) at the time of writing and the associated probabilities could be estimated from the known sample. Because an author's HPV of the features selected for testing is not necessarily unique, a positive ascription can only be possible when the disputed text is known to be by one of a given set of authors and an adequate supply of appropriate text by each is available.

Application of hypothetical probability vectors to tests of position

Morton's individual tests of position may be combined in accordance with the assumption that authors write as if choosing words according to their probability vector. The tests are not altered by this step; instead, they are given coherence by unifying them in a theoretical framework. The main advantage is that once an understanding has been gained, development of the method can be (at least partly) by deduction. Simultaneously, both uncertainty about the inclusion of Yates' correction and doubts concerning the degree of independence of Morton's tests are removed. The null hypothesis is that the texts are by the same author and can be tested by contingency tables and chi-square. Imponderables are therefore confined mainly to whether the results can be taken to reflect authorship alone, or whether other factors can influence the outcome, and if so, to what extent.

To begin, assume that authors write or speak each word as if it were a ball drawn randomly from a bag and that no distinction is made between positions in sentences. For explanatory purposes the words prescribed are the twelve already quoted and are among those Morton uses for tests of position. The author's corresponding HPV is then the left-hand column of Fig. 16.1. Adjectives, nouns, verbs, etc., i.e., the words most dependent on subject matter, are grouped in this vector into a single category, denoted by the subscript 'all other words'. The vector gives the probability that each word produced by the author will be a particular prescribed word (indicated by the subscript of p) or some other word. To model the composition of text as a random sample governed by such probabilities is, of course, at best an approximation; for instance, THE cannot normally be followed by THE, but in this model no sequence of words is precluded. Once a word has been generated it may occur in a prescribed position or elsewhere in sentences. Such joint probabilities are accommodated by subdividing the probabilities for each word to obtain the enlarged probability vector on the right-hand of Figure 16.1.

On the basis of Fig. 16.1, to test the null hypothesis that these

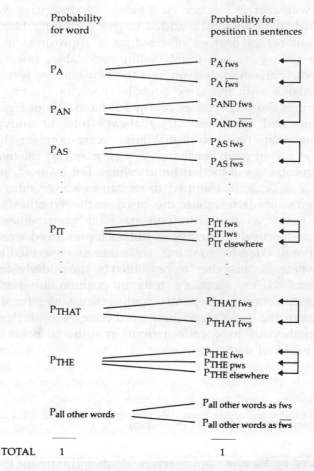

Probability for word		Probability for position in sentences
P_A		$P_{A \text{ fws}}$
		$P_{A \overline{\text{fws}}}$
P_{AN}		$P_{AND \text{ fws}}$
		$P_{AND \overline{\text{fws}}}$
P_{AS}		$P_{AS \text{ fws}}$
		$P_{AS \overline{\text{fws}}}$
$\vdots$		$\vdots$
P_{IT}		$P_{IT \text{ fws}}$
		$P_{IT \text{ lws}}$
		$P_{IT \text{ elsewhere}}$
$\vdots$		$\vdots$
P_{THAT}		$P_{THAT \text{ fws}}$
		$P_{THAT \overline{\text{fws}}}$
P_{THE}		$P_{THE \text{ fws}}$
		$P_{THE \text{ pws}}$
		$P_{THE \text{ elsewhere}}$
$P_{\text{all other words}}$		$P_{\text{all other words as fws}}$
		$P_{\text{all other words as } \overline{\text{fws}}}$
TOTAL 1		1

Figure 16.1 The probability vector which forms implicitly the basis for Morton's tests of position

two sets of figures are samples generated by the same probability vector, a 2 × 28 contingency table would be formed using counts from the author's known work and the disputed text. A value of chi-square for 27 degrees of freedom would be calculated and its significance determined. Morton, however, uses 2 × 2 contingency tables. (In cases where these tables should be combined into a table of increased dimensions, such as for THE *fws* and THE *pws* described previously (Table 16.10), this step is assumed.) These small tables, one for each prescribed word, are indicated by the groupings on the right-hand side of Fig. 16.1. To accord with correct practice, the values of chi-square from the individual tables should be added to give a total for 14 df.

The number of degrees of freedom is approximately halved because testing by individual contingency tables offers only a limited comparison to determine if the two samples were drawn in accordance with the same probability vector. Testing in this way permits the probabilities on the left-hand side of Fig. 16.1 to vary (provided, of course, they always total to unity) while assuming that the sub-probabilities corresponding to each remain in a fixed ratio. For instance, p_{THE} may vary relative to the other probabilities in the left-hand column but $p_{THE\ fws}$, $p_{THE\ pws}$ and $p_{THE\ elsewhere}$ are assumed to remain in a fixed ratio.

Morton's approach is therefore based on the hypothesis that an author writes as if constrained by joint probabilities which govern, respectively, whether or not each prescribed word, after the author has decided to use it, will occur in a specified position or elsewhere. Because they were unified by the underlying theory of authors' HPVs, Morton's tests of position are statistically independent once any separate contingency tables for different positions of the same prescribed word have been amalgamated. Whether they are independent from an authorial point of view will be explored next.

An alternative approach to test of position

Influenced by Morton's approach, O'Brien and Darnell (1982) also first consider 2 × 2 contingency tables to test position, but form each contingency table from the number of sentences beginning with a prescribed word and the number beginning with all other words. Noting that such tables cannot provide statistically independent results, they perform comparisons by referring occurrences of prescribed words first in sentences to the total number of sentences beginning with other words. Nevertheless, Stiger (1983) points out weaknesses in other aspects of their approach so severe as to render the conclusions invalid.

There is another reason for exploring the possibility of an alternative to Morton's type of tests of position. If an author were told that his text was rather involved he might respond by shortening sentences. The relative numbers of occurrences of prescribed words in particular positions and elsewhere very probably would then be altered. Thus many, if not all, of Morton's tests of position could be affected. Although independent from a statistical point of view, one factor could influence all of them. For instance, a police officer could express a well-educated person's statement in a less elegant but syntactically simpler form of English. Such a statement could then appear unlike other examples of the latter's writing. It is hoped that the approach described in the next section will prove to be less sensitive to such interference.

The form of the probability vector on which the alternative procedure is founded is that of the left-hand side of Fig. 16.1. In this case, however, '$p_{all\ other\ words}$' is replaced by '$p_{all\ other\ first\ words}$'. Therefore, to test the null hypothesis that a sample of $n - 1$ prescribed words in N_2 sentences of the disputed text has been generated by random sampling governed by the same HPV as that giving rise to the sample of known text containing N_1 sentences, the data in Fig. 16.2 is treated as an $n \times 2$ contingency table.

The author of this chapter had independently derived and extended this approach to other positions, namely, second, penultimate and last words of sentences (Smith 1982a). Because the first word of a sentence constrains the choice of the second, and the penultimate and last words are likewise dependent, if most sentences are much longer than, say, six words, it may be reasonable to reduce the number of results to two by adding the value of chi-square for *fws* to that for either *pws* or *lws* and likewise for the remaining two positions. Rules are, of course, essential to define sentences and the prescribed positions in sentences of less than four words (Smith 1983b).

fws	Known text	Disputed text
A	a_1	b_1
THE	a_2	b_2
TO	a_3	b_3
.	.	.
.	.	.
.	.	.
Other words	a_n	b_n
Total no of sentences	N_1	N_2

Figure 16.2 The nature of data for test of first words

Authors, it may be assumed, do not write or speak the features chosen for testing so that they occur like random samples governed by a probability vector. Accordingly, significance levels and probabilities corresponding to values of chi-square cannot be translated into odds for authorship; their values contain the effect of all the influences to which an author is subjected. Thus a method which relies on relative magnitudes of chi-square, normalised to nullify the effects of different sample size, would avoid spurious significances and ridiculous probabilities, and would emphasise the uncertainties inherent in such investigations.

An analysis of tests of collocations

Morton's method for distinguishing authors depends on collocations mainly of the form AND fb THE; AND fb A; AS fb THE; AS fb IF; AS fb A; BEEN pb HAVE. Referring to the tables in the chapter by Totty and colleagues, it can be seen that Morton also includes collocations such as A fb X fb OF, THE fb X fb AND, THE fb X fb X fb THE, where X is any word and, presumably, in the third example the second X cannot be AND. As far as the present author is aware, there is no evidence that these types of collocations discriminate between authors. In fact, four such tests combine to provide a value for chi-square of 5.3 in table T7 which compares utterances known to be by two different people. This is considerably less than the 5 per cent level of significance, which is 9.5. Because such a result does not augur well, these tests are omitted from the analysis which follows.

The numbers of occurrences of certain prescribed words in a given text may be regarded as a random sample drawn with replacement (or drawn from an infinite population) according to its author's appropriate HPV. Such a vector could be expressed as in the left-hand side of Fig. 16.3. The probabilities forming the left-hand column of Fig. 16.3 are subdivided to define the occurrences of prescribed collocations as conditional probabilities, e.g. $p(\text{AND fb A}) = p(\text{AND})p(\text{A}|\text{AND})$. A number of points now arise from this expansion.

As in Table 16.12 for a test of position, Morton's contingency tables of size 2×2 are not suitable in cases such as AND above. This is because, for the test of AND fb THE, AND $\overline{\text{fb}}$ THE (where $\overline{\text{fb}}$ means 'not followed by') includes A, and vice-versa for the test of AND fb A. Such a lack of independence is overcome as before by incorporating both in a 3×2 contingency table. If the previous word of the text had been, for example, AND used in the prescribed collocation AND fb THE, then the present word (THE) is not probabilistic but already fixed. Accordingly,

$$P_{\text{THE fb adjective}} + P_{\text{THE fb others}} = 1.$$

The probability vector in Fig. 16.3 therefore can be assumed to apply only if the previous word was selected under p_{OTHERS}. This statistical description, then, can only be a reasonable approximation if p_{OTHERS} is close to unity. But if a large number of collocations of frequently occurring words is prescribed, this condition will not be satisfied.

The order of the collocation is not predefined. For instance, is AND fb THE more appropriate than THE pb AND? The values obtained for chi-square calculated for a 2×2 contingency table can differ considerably, depending on which of the totals for the other occurrences of the two words the number of appearances of the collocation is referred to.

Comparisons typified by the groupings marked on the right of

Fig. 16.3 indicate a partial test of homogeneity similar to that described previously for tests of position.

It is difficult to envisage a mechanism by which authors could subconsciously relate the number of occurrences of a collocation directly to the total usage of either of its two constituent words. If authors write collocations as if governed by an HPV, such as that in Fig. 16.4, an alternative method of testing is suggested. If Fig. 16.4 contains m entries, comparison is by an $m \times 2$ contingency table as in the case of Figure 16.2. Provided the number of prescribed collocations is very much less than the total number in the text, the approximations inherent in this model are small.

Finally, if a test of position were performed by means of one large contingency table containing two columns based on the right-hand probability vector of Fig. 16.1, and if a test of collocations on the same text were undertaken similarly, on the basis of the right-hand column of Fig. 16.3, it would not be valid to consider the two tests to be independent if both distributions had words in common in the left-hand columns. However, Morton's partial tests of the samples, using separate small contingency tables as indicated on the right-hand sides of Figs 16.1 and 16.3, can be taken as independent.

Word-pairs and authors' hypothetical probability vectors

The third class of test in the applications reported by Totty et al. (1987) is that which Morton termed 'proportional pairs' (see the first part of this chapter).

To resolve a problem of authorship Morton usually combines tests of positions, collocations and word-pairs. These tests are assumed to be independent but when written with individual probabilities as in Fig. 16.5, because of possible repetition of key-words (such as A and TO) they cannot be considered to originate from an author's single HPV: the total probability would exceed unity.

If HPVs for tests of positions and collocations are separated, and any additional words required for comparisons by proportional pairs are included, two distributions as illustrated in Fig. 16.6 are obtained. Because A is already included in a position test, the pair A/AN (setting aside questions as to its validity) would be assumed to be in the left-hand probability vector.

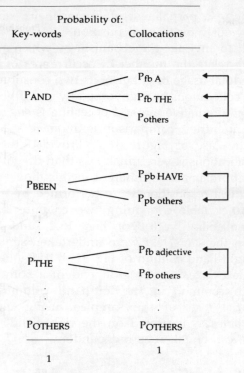

Figure 16.3 A probability vector expanded to include prescribed collocations

Probability
$P_{AND THE}$
$P_{AND A/AN}$
.
.
$P_{TO THE}$
$P_{TO A/AN}$
.
.
$P_{other collocations}$
1

Figure 16.4 A probability vector of collocations

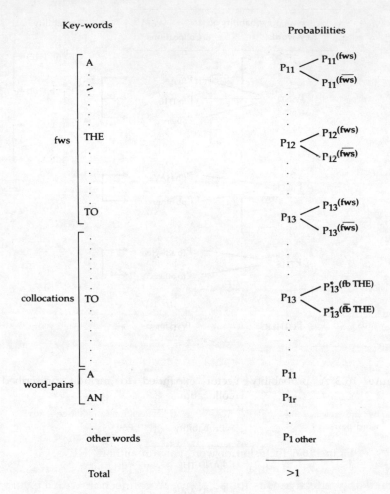

Figure 16.5 Individual probabilities for Morton's tests

Since neither of the components of the other pair in Fig. 16.6 are used in tests of positions or collocations, ALL and ANY could be inserted in either vector. The probability vectors in Fig. 16.6, taken together, provide a statistical framework for Morton's three classes of test. It follows that a comparison by a set of word-pairs alone is an incomplete or restricted test of whether samples were generated according to an underlying HPV of the form of the left-hand side of Figure 16.1.

Morton's conclusion (1978: 150) that proportional pairs are

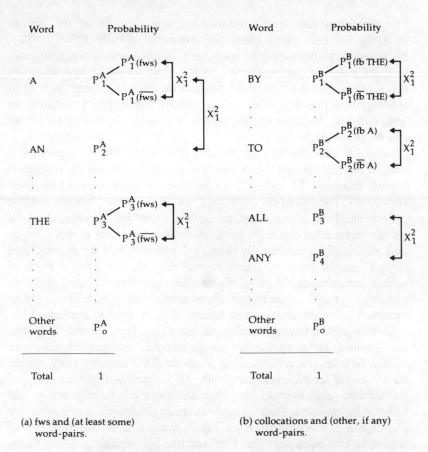

Figure 16.6 Inclusion of word-pairs in authors' HPVs

remarkably effective was found above in connection with *Literary Detection* not to be consistent with an investigation of the data on which he based his claim. Yet single words have been used successfully to distinguish authors, provided they have been rigorously screened for the purpose (Mosteller and Wallace 1964).

A PROPOSED METHOD

Arising from the preceding theoretical analysis, a practical method to resolve problems of authorship has been proposed.

The technique has been validated on, and applied to, the scripts of early English plays (see, for example, Smith 1989b, 1991). Because the punctuation of such texts is not necessarily authorial, tests of position are restricted to the first word of speeches. In this section, the term 'words', should be taken to mean 'words in a prescribed position', 'all words not in prescribed positions' or 'collocations', because the procedure is essentially the same for all three classes of test.

Before examining any of the disputed texts, the stylometrician should decide on the classes of word which should be relegated to the category of 'others', regardless of how frequently they appear – for example, proper nouns, some verbs and/or pronouns. Using computer programs, lists are generated of all words in each of the texts both in descending rate of occurrence and arranged alphabetically. For each class of test an appropriate cut-off rate is chosen; those above that figure form a pool of words for subsequent tests. From the alphabetical lists, absolute numbers of occurrence are determined to which are added inflected variants and related forms (e.g. A should include AN).

Ideally at least two samples of the same type as the disputed text should be available by each possible author. If they are relatively brief (each consisting of about 3000 words), they would have to be combined for tests of prescribed positions and collocations and a check for each author's own variation would have to be omitted. Each sample is compared with every other by forming a $2 \times n$ contingency table, where n is the number of words in the pool plus the total for the other words. Only those words which occur sufficiently frequently to give expected values of at least five are retained. Chi-square is calculated for the reduced table but only its components (corresponding to the remaining words) form the basis for the next stage in the procedure.

To determine which words distinguish between each pair of authors, the components of chi-square obtained from the initial comparisons of their texts are examined. For example, if two specimens of text are available by each of two authors, six sets of values of components of chi-square are available to determine the words which distinguish them.

Two rules define the discriminatory words. First, when any of the four possible comparisons of texts, one by each author, give rise to a value, chosen arbitrarily, of 3.841 or greater *and* for the same word both comparisons of texts by the same author give rise to a value of less than 3.841, the corresponding word is accepted. Second, let author A write samples a_1 and a_2 and author B write samples b_1 and b_2. Assume that for a particular word w, in a comparison of a_1 with a_2 and/or b_1 with b_2, a value v of 3.841 or more is computed. Then, if in all possible comparisons of a_1 and a_2 with b_1 and b_2 no value corresponding to w is less than v, and at least one is not less than 3v, w is selected as a word to discriminate between these two authors.

These rules are, of course, arbitrary and were devised to be suited to studies of early English plays. They can therefore be altered, provided any such change is not made in the light of known counts of features in the disputed texts during a particular investigation. Any such statistical malpractice would be reminiscent of Morton's subjective manoeuvres and would render the outcome invalid.

The test for an author's own variation cannot, of course, be performed when only one sample of his writing is available. Use of components of chi-square, rather than a simple differential ratio, ensures that low frequency words are eliminated and that as frequency of occurrence increases, the percentage difference in the author's rates of use decreases for a word to be classed as discriminatory. The second rule is only invoked when an author's own internal variation is large but still less than that between his own writing and that of the other author. A separate but not necessarily unique subgroup of words is thereby deduced to differentiate between each pair of authors.

To assign a disputed text, it is compared with specimens by possible authors, taken in pairs, using the corresponding lists of discriminatory words. The discriminatory words which occur more frequently in one author are placed in a group, the remaining such words in a second group and all other words in a third group. This means that words which occur more frequently have greater influence. The disputed text is then compared in turn with the four texts by these two possible authors, using a 2×3 contingency table. In each case the resulting value of chi-square is normalised by multiplying by K/N where N is the combined number of words in the two texts under comparison and K is a constant to provide figures of suitable magnitude. Both values thus obtained when the disputed text is compared with the two samples by an author are averaged and whichever average is the smaller indicates the writer more likely to be responsible for the disputed text.

If, in all comparisons, the disputed text is closer to the work of one possible candidate than any of the others, that person can be suspected of writing it.

CONCLUSIONS

When the probability of error in studies of attribution is stated to be an infinitesimal figure, suspicion is immediately aroused. For instance, D J Lake (1975: 156), using Ellegård's (1962) method to find an author for the anonymous play *The Revenger's Tragedy*, claimed that a conservative estimate 'for the fraction of the population of Jacobean dramatists who write as much like *The Revenger's Tragedy* as Middleton does [is] one hundred-millionth or one-fifteen-thousand-millionth', depending upon which variant of the method is chosen. Such a powerful technique, apparently capable of pinpointing one person beyond even the most unreasonable doubt from an incompletely defined set of contemporaneous playwrights would seem ideal for many forensic applications. Regrettably, such remote odds are the consequence of unsubstantiated assumptions inherent in the method combining to mislead (Smith 1987a).

A thorough investigation of Morton's method has been presented and has substantiated theoretically the poor performance which Totty and colleagues experienced. In addition, a major weakness of Morton's procedure is the influence that the experimenter can exert on the results; in practice, what to test is chosen in full knowledge of the data. Nevertheless, the present author's previous experience led him to believe that the types of features Morton used are capable of distinguishing authors. The fundamental problem is to determine which specific features discriminate between any two authors. Thus by deducing a separate distinguishing set of features for each pair of authors the new approach, outlined above, was devised.

Morton has continued his activities and has published alternative procedures (e.g. Morton 1986) which combine some of his earlier methods with words which occur once only (hapax legomena). Unfortunately a theoretical and experimental study (Smith 1987b) revealed that his claims for these new suggestions are even less well-founded than those for his original techniques.

Undeterred, Morton has announced yet another technique (the Qsum Method) for distinguishing authorship, which 'works down to a limit of under ten sentences, . . . is unaffected by the differences between spoken and written sentences and . . . can be used in any language' (Morton 1991). According to a press correspondent, Morton's help has been enlisted in a number of high-publicity legal cases but a report by Professor David Canter for the Crown Prosecution Service has subsequently termed the new method 'pseudo-scientific nonsense' (Matthews 1993). The tenor of this news item is substantiated by Hilton and Holmes (1993) who described Morton's approach as 'either subjective or arbitrary, without a firm statistical basis' and by Hardcastle (1993) who found the method 'to be ill-defined and its application amateurish. In its present form it cannot be accepted as providing reliable evidence of authorship when applied either to the written or spoken word'. Thus it would appear that Morton's most recent proposal is meeting the same unfortunate fate as his previous procedures.

However, a great variety of procedures for the resolution of problems of authorship in literary studies has been advanced by numerous investigators since average word-length first made an appearance. The main problem facing a person with a case of disputed authorship is not the availability of possible methods but a dearth of in-depth investigations of their efficacy. When books attract reviewers' attention, limited time and space can induce rather superficial comment – and the merits of articles are usually less well explored, or even ignored. Similarly at law, the mere expression of experts' opinions is not a substitute for rigorous analysis. In the light of the extolment of the virtues of Morton's work, as reported in the article by Gudjonsson and Haward, it is indeed comforting that the subject of stylolinguistics has, by and large, been treated so soberly by the law.

NOTES

1. *Literary Detection* (p. 136) uses the words 'internal change' in connection with Henry James. It is asumed that this should read 'external change'.
2. The minimum expected value is empirical. For 2×2 contingency tables the accepted minimum is currently considered to be five. Some sources quote a minimum expected value of ten and/or a minimum total number of occurrences of twenty to fifty. For larger contingency tables some expected values as low as unity (or even less) are thought to be satisfactory. Very low rates of occurrence of features in texts may be unrepresentative of an author's habits. To accommodate both considerations, a minimum of eight actual occurrences was arbitrarily chosen as the minimum for $2 \times c$, $c > 2$, contingency tables.

SEVENTEEN

Powerful evidence for the defence: an exercise in forensic discourse analysis

Malcolm Coulthard

INTRODUCTION

Until recently most forensic linguists, at least in Britain, worked with graphetic and phonetic data, that is, making comparisons of samples of handwriting (Davis 1986) and of tape-recorded voices (Nolan 1983, and this volume, Hollien 1990 and Baldwin and French 1990). In this area the methodology is already well developed. By contrast forensic discourse analysis is a very new area and this article is intended as a contribution to a methodology which is still being developed *ad casum*.

I propose to focus on one case, that of William Power, one of the so-called Birmingham Six, all of them Irishmen arrested in 1974 after two public houses were blown up by the IRA. All of them were beaten up by both police and prison warders and convicted some nine months later, partly on dubious forensic evidence and partly on their disputed confessions. (For a detailed presentation of the background to the case, the trial and the first two appeals see Mullin 1990.) They were released seventeen years later, in March 1991, after their third appeal when, finally, the police evidence was judged to be at best 'unsafe'. This chapter is based on a report that I was asked to make on William Power's confession.

THE DATA

All the quotations are taken from publicly available documents presented at William Power's trial. The texts referred to in the analysis are as follows:

1. INT: The typed police records of the interview and of the statement-taking session with William Power as presented to the court at his trial.
2. STAT: The typed police record of William Power's confession statement as presented to the court at his trial.
3. TWT   (Trial within the trial): The court transcript of William Power's evidence given during the trial within the trial at Lancaster Crown Court. At one point the defence challenged the admissibility of some of the prosecution evidence and this evidence was therefore presented to the judge in the absence of the jury. After three days the judge decided to admit the evidence, so virtually the same ground was covered again in the presence of the jury.
4. TBJ   (Trial before jury): The court transcript of William Power's evidence given before the jury at his trial at Lancaster Crown Court.

[Usually in cases of disputed statements one is faced with the problem of trying to distinguish utterances which the accused claims to have made from utterances which he claims not to have made.] [The Power confession is a much more complicated document because it has four potentially different types of utterance: those Power claims not to have made, those he admits having made and claims to be true, those he admits having made but claims to be untrue, and one utterance he claims to have repeated under duress: 'Jesus, I am sorry . . .']

Obviously the linguist has no way of evaluating the truth of what was said *in* a text but fortunately can, at times, evaluate the truth of claims made *about* a text. Thus, let us begin with the conflicting assertions made about Power's confession.

The police version

The police claimed to have interviewed Power twice, on the first occasion for forty minutes, during which time he was said to have admitted his own guilt, involved the other five and described in some detail how and where he had planted his bombs. They then left Power to think about what he had said for about an hour and on their return asked him to make a statement. They offered to write the statement down, Power agreed and one of the officers 'then took down a statement at his dictation, which he read over to him and which he then read, signed and captioned' (STAT: 15).

Power's version

According to Power information was elicited from him over a much longer period. He distinguishes *three* separate occasions: (i) when giving evidence in court (TBJ: 51, 53) he refers to these interactions as 'interrogation' – a time when he says he was also being beaten; (ii) 'notes' – when the police were interviewing him; and (iii) 'statement' when he claims the police constructed the text that he would later sign as his confession.

Power was always adamant that he did not dictate this statement

> Mr Skinner . . . do you remember before you dictated that statement
> Power   I never dictated this.
>
> (TWT: 106)

Instead Power claimed that the statement was a compilation of what he had said during the 'interrogation' and 'notes' stages, plus answers to supplementary and clarificatory questions put to him at the time the police were constructing the 'statement'.

DISCUSSION

In my analysis I worked on the assumption that Power's statement was, as the police claimed in the witness box, governed by normal statement-taking rules which would have required first, that the police took down all and only the words uttered by Power on the occasion of making the statement and second, that no questions were asked.

[I will present my observations under four headings, *coherence, over-specificity, terms of address* and *repetition*.]

Coherence

Given the circumstances, one might reasonably have expected Power to be under considerable strain. He had been arrested late at night, accused of the worst murder ever perpetrated in Britain and had been very badly abused. Thus he might also have found the task of reconstructing a coherent report of past events difficult. However, even a cursory glance is sufficient to confirm that there is no sign in the statement that Power is an unwilling or hesitant dictater. Indeed, the text is surprisingly detailed, well formed and well organised. There are, for instance, no examples of the doubt, occasional lack of specificity and breaking of temporal sequence that usually characterise personal reports and all of which occurred during Power's evidence:

Power   . . . [he] shouted something at me I can't remember sir . . .
Power   . . . he made some reference to the heavy mob or something
Power   . . . I had better mention now, [that] before that happened . . .
(TBJ: 2–3)

Over-specificity

One oddity of the language of the statement is the description of the bags which contained the bombs (forensic evidence was later to indicate that the bombs were not left in plastic bags at all):

Walker was carrying . . . two white plastic carrier bags . . .
Hunter was carrying three white plastic carrier bags . . .
Richard was carrying one white plastic carrier bag . . .
Walker gave me one of the white plastic bags . . .
Hughie gave . . . Walker his white plastic bag . . .

It is, in fact, highly unlikely that Power would have used the complex nominal group, 'numeral + white + plastic + carrier + bag(s)' even once. First, this represents a degree of detail we do not see in the rest of his statement. Second, the detail does not seem to have any importance in the story he tells and it is very unusual for narrators to provide detail which has no relevance to their story.]Third, it is a noted feature of speech that speakers do not normally produce long noun phrases of this kind; rather they assemble complex information in two or three bits or bites. As a comparison we can notice how the same information came out in the 'interview', which has a ring of authenticity:]

> Power   He'd got a holdall and *two bags*
> Watson   What kind of bags?
> Power   They were *white*, I think they were *carrier* bags

Even then there was nothing about 'plastic'.

[Fourth, as it is unlikely that Power would have used the full phrase even once in his statement, it is exceedingly unlikely that he would have repeated it twice and then gone on to use 'white plastic bags' twice more.] As we can see from the extract below, once a full form of a referring expression has been used a speaker's normal habit is to employ a shortened version on subsequent occasions.

> Mr Evans   And did you say '*two white plastic carrier bags*?'
> Power   Yes sir.
> Mr Evans   Whose idea was it that Walker was carrying *two white carrier bags*? Were those your words or the Police Officers' words?
> Power   They were the Police Officers'. They kept insisting that I had told them that they carried *plastic bags* into the station.
> Mr Evans   Does the same apply to what Hunter was carrying?
> Power   I don't know what you mean sir.
> Mr Evans   I am sorry. Whose idea was it that you should say that Hunter was carrying *three white plastic bags*?
> Power   Well, sir, I said that.
> Mr Evans   But was it your idea?
> Power   No. They kept saying that I had already told them that they were carrying *plastic bags* into the station. When I said that, they said 'who was carrying them? who was carrying them?' They threatened me. I said 'They were all carrying them.' They asked me how many were they carrying and I just said *one, two, three, one and one*.
> Mr Evans   You say that Hughie gave Johnny Walker his *plastic bag* and then walked away . . .
>
> (TWT: 60)

Thus the linguistic evidence of normal speaker usage supports the claim made by Power in the above quotation, i.e. that it was the police officers who were interested in the detailed description of the bags and that it was they who put these details into the statement.

Terms of address

It is a feature of forensic language – the language of policemen, lawyers and expert witnesses – that participants are usually referred to by surname alone. By contrast, it is a marked feature of Power's authenticated usage that he refers to his friends by first name or by first name plus surname. One can exemplify this usage from almost any page of his trial evidence chosen at random:

> Power Sir, he asked me who had arrived, and I told him *John Walker, Gerard Hunter, Hughie and Richard*.
>
> (TWT: 44)

Indeed, he frequently 'corrects' the professional and replies with his own labels for his friends:

> Mr Skinner Did you make any arrangements with any of the other accused?
> Power Yes sir.
> Mr Skinner With Walker and Hunter?
> Power *Gerry* Hunter and *John* Walker.
>
> (TWT: 92)

> Mr Skinner Callaghan was whimpering away and half out of his mind?
> Power *Hughie* lay down on the bench, if I can remember right.
>
> (TBJ: 36)

Speakers do not change the habits of a lifetime on a single occasion. It is not oversurprising that there are occurrences of just surname usage in some of the utterances attributed to Power in the *interview*, because in that context it is possible for the police to transcribe 'negotiated' utterances. However, the confession statement, which should be in Power's own words, contains nineteen occurrences of Power apparently referring to his companions by surname alone – this is exceedingly unlikely. A much more reasonable explanation is that there was police collaboration in the wording of the statement. Indeed we can see two occasions where police editing apparently occurred in the transfer stage between 'notes' and statement:

> Watson   Who came back next?
> Power   Richard and *Paddy* Hill

(INT: 4)

becomes

> Then Richard and *Hill* came back

and

> *Paddy* had a small case

becomes

> *Hill* was carrying a small case

(INT: 14)

Repetition

[A close textual comparison shows that parts of the 'interview' and the 'statement' are verbally identical.] The police, when cross-examined, saw this as unremarkable – Power had simply retold the same events in the same words; Power's explanation is equally simple, that the second telling was in fact in part copied from the written record of the first.

[It is a common misconception that people can remember verbatim what they and others have said.] Every day we hear people report conversations in direct speech: 'and then I said . . . and then she said . . .'

[In fact memory, even of verbal events, is not normally stored in verbal form. What people remember is the gist of what was said, which means that each retelling requires a re-coding in verbal form, with the result that slight differences occur each time (see Hjelmquist 1984).] Power himself, interestingly, kept reminding the barristers of this fact at his trial:

> Power   Yes sir, some words to that effect . . .
> I don't know the exact words, sir.
>
> (TBJ: 4)

We can see the phenomenon of re-coding demonstrated quite clearly in the following examples from Power's trial when, by fortunate chance, he was questioned twice, once in closed session (TWT), and once before the jury (TBJ), about the same events. As is evident sometimes the verbal differences are small, as in the first two examples and sometimes they are more marked as in the third. These differences are usually insignificant in terms of content, but from our point of view they are crucial indications of re-coding:

> Power   One of them shouted 'who is the sixth man?' . . . I said 'what sixth man?'
>
> (TWT: 54)

> Power   *Somebody was* shouting 'Who *was* the sixth man, *who was the sixth man?*' . . . I asked 'what sixth man, *what sixth man?*'
>
> (TBJ: 6)

* * * * * *

> Power   [he said] you'll never have sex with your wife again
>
> (TWT: 53)

> Power   [he said] you will never have sex *in your life* again
>
> (TBJ: 6)

* * * * * *

> Power   They told me there was a mob outside the house and my wife and children would be lynched, only for the Police who were inside ragging it, searching it.
>
> (TWT: 49)

> Power   *He* told me there was a mob outside *my* house and *they were ready to lynch my wife and children and the only thing that was stopping them was because the Police were outside my house.*
>
> (TBJ: 4)

As these examples show – and there are many many others, see Appendix 1 – even when 'saying the same thing' speakers tend to verbalise it in a slightly different form. Therefore, what is very noticeable when we compare the 'notes' and the 'statement', two other texts which purport to be separate recountings of the same events, is that there are many utterances which are actually *identical*; (in each case the interview version comes first and the statement second):

> and then he told Richard to give me one as well
> and then told Richard to give me one as well
>
> Hughie said 'You're going to take them it's not only you that you've got to worry about.'
> Hughie said 'You're going to take them it's not only you that you've got to worry about.'
>
> Hughie came back . . . said to me 'You have to take them to the pub at the side of the Rotunda.'
> Hughie came back and said to me 'You have to take them to the pub at the side of the Rotunda.'
>
> he said, 'It will be easy you've got half an hour or more and by then you'll be on the train.'
> he said, 'It will be easy you've got half an hour or more and by then you'll be on the train.'

One could go on for several pages. There are too many identical passages for these two texts to be records of two separate tellings – no one has this degree of accurate verbal recall. Thus in so far as these texts are identical, the only reasonable explanation seemed to be that one of them was based on the other.

As mentioned above, Power claimed in court that his statement was based directly on the interview. I therefore set out to replicate what the police must have done, if Power's claim were true – that is to turn the final and incriminating third of the interview text, pages 11–15, from a question and answer sequence into a monologue, by adding only essential linking items and omitting anything that seemed redundant to the narrative. Appendix 2 presents my 'composition' side-by-side with Power's alleged confession. The similarities between the two texts are sufficiently striking to suggest that this indeed is the way in which at least that part of the statement was created. Thus, here again the evidence seems to support Power's version of events rather than that of the police officers.

CONCLUSIONS

First, it appears that the weight of linguistic evidence does support Power's claim that his alleged statement is in fact a collaborative document, that it is a compilation of what was said on at least two different occasions and that some of it is in the words of the police officers.

Second, the methodology looks promising for use in other similar cases; I am currently working on another confession claimed to be a collaborative document – that of William Bentley, hanged 40 years ago for the murder of a policeman. In this case there is no interview record for comparison, but the first three approaches illustrated above are yielding results, and in addition I am using a corpus-based comparison of police and lay usage to show the oddity of one feature of the narrative grammar.

APPENDIX 1: COMPARATIVE EXTRACTS FROM POWER'S EVIDENCE

Q: Did they close [the doors] completely?
Power: No they kept them open about six or eight inches TWT:50

Power: They were being held open about six inches TBJ:5

* * *

Power: and someone said "the one with the glasses and the green coat" . . . I said there was nobody with glasses TWT:54

Power: and they shouted at me "the man with the glasses and the green coat" or it might have been "green car" . . . I says "sure it was none of us with glasses; there was nobody with glasses" TBJ:7

* * *

Power: I pointed at French and I said "you were right, you were right" TWT:55

Power: I started pointing to French and Watson and said "you are right, you are right" TBJ:7

*   *   *

Power: here was a blackboard in it [large room] and our names were written upon it. There was like a map of Birmingham drawn on it with chalk TWT:56

Power: there was a blackboard in it, sir, with a map of Birmingham drawn on it and our names on the board TBJ:7

*   *   *

Power: French put his hands to his back pocket as if to take out the handcuffs again TWT:59

Power: French motioned to take his handcuffs out of his back pocket again TBJ:10

APPENDIX 2

A comparison of Power's alleged statement, the left-hand column, with the text I created from pages 11–15 of the police account of the interview. I have underlined in my version all the phrases which are identical with those in the alleged statement.

Power's alleged statement	*Coulthard's version*
Walker gave me the overcoat to put on and then gave me one of the white	Walker <u>gave me one of the</u>

plastic bags he had been carrying and then told Richard to give me one as well. So he gave me one. Hughie gave Johnny Walker his white plastic bag and then walked away with Richard leaving me Walker and Hunter together. I think we all had two bags each. I certainly had two. Hill then joined us he was carrying a suit case. Hughie then came back and we were	carrier bags and then he told Richard to give me one as well Then I saw Hughie give Walker his bag and then he and Richard walked away from us. It was about then that Hill joined us. He was carrying a small case. Then Richard and Hughie came back and we were
standing all in a group. I said to them all 'I'm not taking these.' I just knew what they were. There were bombs and I didn't want to take them. Hughie said, 'You're going to take them it's not only you that you've got to worry about.' Richard then came back and called Hughie over to the side. They talked together then Hughie came back and said to me 'You have to take them to the pub at the side of the Rotunda.' He just said, to go round and put them in the pub. He said, 'It will be easy you've got half an hour or more and by then you'll be on the train.' He told me to go straight round and do it so I started to walk away. I went out of the station and passed the Taxi Rank. I looked back	all in a group together. I said to Hughie 'I'm not taking these'; I knew what they were, I just knew, bombs. But Hughie said 'You're going to take them, it's not only you you've got to worry about.' Then Richard (and Hughie walked away) then Hughie came back and said to me 'You've got to take the bags to the pub at the side of the Rotunda 'It'll be easy, you've got half an hour or more and by then you'll be on the train. Go and do it straight away.' So I went out of the station past the taxi ranks alone. When I looked

and saw Hunter and Walker coming out behind me carrying two bags each. I walked straight round to the Rotunda to the Mulberry Bush. I walked in from the left-hand side as I came to it. I turned right inside and down a couple of steps there were quite a few people in so I walked over to the bar and put the bags down at my feet because I was going to have a drink.	back I saw Hunter and Walker walking along behind me carrying two bags each. I walked round to the Rotunda, into the Mulberry Bush through the door on the left-hand side
	and down a couple of steps (into the bar.) I walked over to the bar and put the bags down. I was going to have a drink but it was a bit crowded and I was afraid.
I changed my mind and picked the bags up again because I panicked and was going to take them out. I started to walk out and then I put the two bags down by the Juke Box and then I walked straight back through the other door and went straight back to the station the way I came. When I got back there the others weren't there. A few minutes later Walker and Hunter came back again. They weren't carrying anything this time. Then Richard and Hill came back in from the other entrance. Richard was carrying the holdall and suitcase and Hill was carrying a small case. Hughie didn't come back at all we all went to platform nine together and got on the train that was	So I picked the bags up
	and then I put them down again and walked straight out through the other door and went straight back to the station. When I got back to the station the others weren't there. After a while Walker and Hunter turned up. They weren't carrying anything this time. Richard and Paddy Hill came back next. Richard had a holdall and a suitcase and Paddy a small case. Hughie didn't come back at all. Then we all went to platform nine and got on the train.

already there. Soon afterwards
it moved out. There were
other people in the carriage
so we couldn't talk much.

We just had a game of
cards. I was in a daze and . . .

After a while
it moved

We didn't talk much
as it was quite crowded.
We just played
cards.

EIGHTEEN

Confidentiality of linguistic material: the case of Aboriginal land claims

Jane Simpson

INTRODUCTION

Since the passing of the *Aboriginal Land Rights (Northern Territory) Act 1976*, many groups of Australian Aborigines have, with the help of the Northern and Central Land Councils, made claim to unalienated Crown land in court hearings before an Aboriginal Land Commissioner. The lawyers helping these people prepare their cases have often called ethnographers (linguists and anthropologists) to act as expert witnesses in court, providing evidence relating to land tenure. These researchers usually (but not always) have worked with the claimants before, as part of gathering ethnographic material.

In the course of such court hearings, a number of important issues about the role of the expert witness have surfaced. In one such hearing (a hearing by the Aboriginal Land Commissioner, Maurice J, of a claim by Warumungu, Warlmanpa, Warlpiri, Alyawarr and Kaytetye people to unalienated Crown Land in the Tennant Creek area of the Northern Territory, henceforth the 'Warumungu Land Claim'), researchers working for the claimants (including the author and another linguist) were issued with subpoenas for the production of all their field-notes relating to the claimants. The validity of the subpoenas was challenged, but with only partial success; and most of us had to produce some of our field-notes.

This was the first time that I and others learned that in Australia anthropologists or linguists could be required to hand over field-notes. Up till then, many researchers had, in good faith, promised the people they worked with to keep certain information confidential. Therefore, the decision in the Warumungu Land Claim has important consequences for ethnographers when they work with confidential data, and when they act as expert witnesses. Perhaps the single most important consequence is that in Australia *no researcher can guarantee confidentiality to the people they work with, unless they are prepared to break the law.*

Here, I shall examine the background to the issue of the subpoenas, the reasons for the failure to block production of the field-notes, and some of the consequences of the case for ethnographers.

BACKGROUND

The Warumungu land claim was lodged on 20 November 1978. The Northern Territory Government (henceforth the NT Government) strongly opposed the claim. There were many reasons for this. One was that the land under claim included land around the town of Tennant Creek, which was the constituency of an influential member of the NT Government. Of significance also was that the NT Government's supporters are mostly Euro-Australian, while the Aboriginal Australians tended to vote for the opposition party. (See Reyburn, 1990, for a forceful account of the role of the NT Government.)

The hearing of the claim started at Tennant Creek on 1 November 1982. For many of the Aboriginal claimants, this was the first time that they had the chance to explain their views on land ownership, what they felt about their country, and the indignities and injustice they had suffered from their dispossession. So, the claim started in an air of excitement. But, two days after the hearing started, the NT Government announced that it had already alienated some of the land under claim, and that therefore the Aboriginal Land Commissioner, Kearney J, did not have the jurisdiction to hear the claim to the alienated land. The Aboriginal Land Commissioner accepted this argument, and the hearing of the claim was halted, while this ruling was appealed.

The High Court ruled on 23 March 1984, that the alienation did not affect the Aboriginal Land Commissioner's jurisdiction. However, the NT Government's strategy succeeded in delaying the hearing of the claim for two and a half years. In those years, several senior claimants died, and were thus denied the chance to give evidence in support of their families' case.

On 4 March 1985, a second hearing of the claim started, under a new Aboriginal Land Commissioner, Maurice J. The claimants and objectors gave evidence in March, April and May. The NT Government continued to spare no expense in opposing the claim, employing Queen's Counsel, including Ian Barker, (who had gained a reputation from his role in the prosecution of Lindy and Michael Chamberlain for the alleged murder of their daughter Azaria). The expense sometimes seemed quite out of proportion to the potential benefits, for instance nearly a day was spent in discussing ownership of one small area, Whistleduck Waterhole, whose value was assessed by the Valuer-General to be about 60 Australian dollars (around US$50).

In previous land claims, the normal procedure had been for the claimants' evidence to be followed by oral evidence from the expert witnesses (anthropologists and linguists). This evidence was usually tested by cross-examination on the basis of the oral evidence, the transcript and published material. But in this hearing, the Aboriginal Land Commissioner indicated that he found this unsatisfactory. He felt that the researchers' proofs of evidence should have been given before the claimants' evidence was heard, so as to allow proper testing. Since this was no longer possible, he wanted written proofs of evidence to be tendered by the researchers.

In late April and early May, we prepared written proofs of evidence with great haste, in the midst of doing other work for the claim connected with the claimants' evidence. There were no models for what could be expected in written proofs of evidence, and there was no time to discuss what should go in, and what the consequences might be of including some things and leaving out others. The proofs were tendered, and, predictably, the NT Government objected to much of the content on the grounds that it was 'hearsay' evidence.

The claimants' evidence continued to be heard. Then came the bombshell. Most of the researchers and the Central Land Council were served by the NT Government with orders from the Aboriginal Land Commissioner requiring them to produce on 13 May 1985:

all files, reports, statements, letters, diaries, notebooks, memoranda, drafts, documents and writings and all maps, plans and sketches and

all photographs and tape recordings which were compiled, written, made, or taken, as the case may be, for the purposes of:
(a) research into Warumungu land tenure

The scope of this request was extraordinary, and could best be described as a 'fishing expedition'. The researchers and the Central Land Council spent several days preparing affidavits and lists of documents, a time-consuming and sometimes difficult task.

Legal advice obtained by the Central Land Council suggested that the orders were not valid. However, we knew that challenging the orders would result in yet more delays in the hearing of the case, and consequently in the return of land to the claimants. The Central Land Council took instructions from the claimants, and the researchers thought seriously about handing over all the material requested to the Aboriginal Land Commissioner. In our view, the information in the notes would in many instances have given useful supporting evidence for the claimants' case, and, at worst, would have shown only minor discrepancies.

But two issues of principle arose. First, we did not wish to set a precedent for courts to force ethnographers to disclose their material.

Secondly, it seemed to us (based on field experience, discussion with claimants, and on reports from other ethnographers), that much of the information contained in the field-notes has a status in Aboriginal societies which is different from that which it has in the Australian legal system. This information[1] is capable of being 'owned', and is owned by the Aboriginal people who entrusted it to the researchers (see also Walsh, this volume, on 'knowledge economy'). It is a form of intellectual property, just as trade secrets are intellectual property in our society, and patents and copyright protect other kinds of intellectual property. Furthermore, intellectual property is, for many Aborigines, the most important property which they own. It is bought, sold, inherited and bestowed. However, rights can be maintained. When an Aboriginal person passes on information to someone, she/he does not necessarily thereby stop owning that information. If the information is kept in a small group of people, the exclusiveness of the group maintains the value of the property. However, making information public to a wide audience can devalue it. Unfortunately, older, non-literate Aborigines are not always aware of the many ways in which information can now be broadcast and thus lose its property value.

Hence, we were unwilling to disclose material without the informed consent of the people who had given it to us. We felt that they were being put in an untenable position – either give consent to disclosure of material (and thus risk losing their property, depending on how widely publicised the material then was), or delay still further the hearing of the claim.

Both the researchers and the Central Land Council felt it was necessary to resist the orders for production. And so, on 28 May 1985 and the following days, there was argument before the Aboriginal Land Commissioner about the notices. The point was taken that the notices were too broad in scope. They were withdrawn, and new notices were issued. These relied heavily on the written proofs of evidence tendered by the researchers, and ordered production of documents mentioned in these proofs, or whose existence could be inferred from the proofs. The scope was still wide-ranging; thus I was ordered to produce on 1 July, among other material:

3. draft genealogies;
7. notes made on field trips;
8. notes made at ceremonies of 28.4.85;
9. all copies of the above.

The Aboriginal Land Commissioner's desire for written proofs of evidence made it much easier for the NT Government to prepare valid notices, ones that were not subject to accusations of 'fishing'.

From the arguments before the Aboriginal Land Commissioner it became clear that the NT Government was asking to see at least three categories of material:

1. material prepared specifically for the Warumungu Land Claim;
2. material which had been used by the researchers, but which had not been prepared for the land claim, but rather for a body with a duty of confidentiality towards Aborigines, the Aboriginal Sacred Sites Protection Authority;
3. material prepared by the researchers as part of their own ethnographic research.

Each of these categories was, arguably, subject to a different type of 'privilege', that is, immune from production in court.

Category 1 material was, so the Central Land Council argued, subject to 'legal professional privilege'. This privilege belongs to the client. It normally covers the letters and conversations, etc., between a lawyer and her/his client about the client's case. Such material must be prepared solely for the purpose of the case (Grant v Downs (1976) 135 CLR 674, High Court of Australia).

An unusual feature of land claim hearings is that they involve several legal systems, that of Australia, and those of the Aborigines. Consequently, ethnographers play a much greater part than usual in assisting to prepare the case. In effect, they act as go-betweens for the experts of different legal systems (senior Aboriginal people and lawyers). The need for such mediators in land claim hearings has been recognised from the start (Neate 1989: 248).

Australian law, however, treats the material produced by the lawyers, and the material produced by the ethnographers differently. Technically, a lawyer receives instructions from her/his clients, and what she/he says about those instructions is not evidence. In practice, in land claims and no doubt in many other cases, the lawyer does gather material, which he/she may draw out in examination of the client, or may add to the material being compiled by his/her researchers. If a genealogy is prepared by a lawyer representing the claimants, it is covered by legal professional privilege. If an identical genealogy is prepared by an ethnographer at the lawyer's request, it is probably, but not necessarily covered by legal professional privilege. It must be argued that the ethnographer is employed by the claimants, acting as the lawyer's agent, and has prepared the genealogy for the sole purpose of carrying out the lawyer's instructions. A crucial difference between the status of the two genealogies concerns 'waiver'. If the lawyer refers to the genealogy in her/his submissions as instructions from her/his clients, the genealogy is still considered privileged. Other parties cannot obtain an order to look at it. But if the claimants call the ethnographer as an expert witness in support of their case, and if the ethnographer talks about that genealogy, then the claimants have waived their privilege with respect to that genealogy. The other parties can now ask for it to be produced. (Byrne and Heydon 1991: 668.)

Category 2 material was, so the Aboriginal Sacred Sites Protection Authority argued, subject to 'public interest immunity'. That is, judges can decide that they will not look at some material because it is not in the public interest that they should do so. They have to weigh up the harm done by not looking at the material, against the harm done by making the material public. Factors that they may take into consideration include:

1. Was the material made by people who thought it was confidential?
2. Can the relationship between the person who provided the material and the person who received it continue if they cannot promise confidentiality?
3. If the relationship cannot continue without confidentiality, does the public think this relationship is important enough to warrant keeping confidentiality?

Category 3 material appears not to be covered by any recognised privilege, just as personal diaries are not covered, and a person may be required to produce personal diaries in court. In another society, Category 3 material might be covered by 'professional privilege'. In states with specific legislation, this covers a few relationships, such as doctor–patient and priest–penitent. It does not include anthropologists, linguists or social scientists. States would have to adopt specific new legislation for such a 'researcher–consultant' professional privilege to be available. As far as I know, no state in the world grants professional privilege to the researcher–consultant relationship, although the US First Amendment gives limited protection.

So, in the Warumungu Land Claim hearing, the researchers argued instead that it is not in the public interest for the relation of confidence between researcher and Aboriginal to be destroyed. This position received strong support at the Annual General Meeting of the Australian Linguistics Society in 1985 (Nash 1987), as well as from individual linguists and anthropologists who prepared affidavits and publicised the issues (Bell 1985; McKeown 1985; Mewett 1985), and some of whom acted as witnesses in the arguments about these issues.

Arguments about these issues were heard by the Aboriginal Land Commissioner in mid-July. On 1 October 1985 the Aboriginal Land Commissioner handed down his judgment allowing limited disclosure of some material. The main reason for production was 'fairness to opponents of the claim'. No one should be able to offer evidence based on privileged material, and expect to retain that privilege. If a researcher gives evidence, and says that he/she holds an opinion based on his/her research, then the Court (and the opponents) have the right to ask to see the evidence on which the opinion is based.

This doctrine of fairness is seen as fundamental to the Court procedure of presenting evidence. Euro-Australians in the main accept the right of Courts to see material gained in any way, except that deriving from a lawyer–client relation, and, to a lesser extent, a doctor–patient or priest–penitent relation, and trade secrets. The difficulty comes when people from another culture with widely differing attitudes towards 'the right to know' are exposed to our Courts. It could be argued that, by accepting the legitimacy of the Court as a way of getting what they want, they have accepted the doctrine of fairness with respect to disclosing material. Unfortunately, very often such people do not know how much is expected of them, how much they will be expected to disclose, or even that they will be expected to accept disclosure of material they thought they had given in confidence. Herein lies the difficulty with the doctrine of fairness.

In the case of the Warumungu Land Claim, the claimants, by having ethnographers act as expert witnesses, had thereby waived any privilege in the material they had given to the ethnographers. Hence the ethnographers had to produce Category 3 material that they had relied on in the course of giving their evidence. Some material falling under the Category 1 heading was also ordered for production, although the Aboriginal Land Commissioner accepted the claim of legal professional privilege for some documents, notably those prepared when lawyers were present. Thus, if an ethnographer talked to a claimant about the claim with the claimants' lawyer present, legal professional privilege would hold, whereas the same information collected in the absence of a lawyer and with the same intent was less likely to be deemed privileged. The Aboriginal Land Commissioner rejected the Aboriginal Sacred Sites Protection Authority's claim for public interest immunity over Category 2 material. On 25 October the Aboriginal Sacred Sites Protection Authority appealed against this decision.

A great success of the appeal was that the Aboriginal Land Commissioner recognised that the material was confidential and imposed fairly strict protective measures when sensitive field material was produced for inspection under the order. The researchers and lawyers worked out detailed protective measures.

For example, sensitive documents were not removed from the researchers' presence, no photocopying was allowed, and protective measures applied in turn to any notes the lawyers made about the field-notes. The issue of compliance was discussed with some of the Aborigines who had provided the material. I went through that material which seemed to me likely to be most sensitive with the people who had given it, and worked out which sections they did, or did not want, to be made public. The few lines which they were not happy with were covered over, and marked as such.

On 28 October 1985, lawyers for the NT Government and opposing parties started to inspect in a desultory way some of the documents in our presence, subject to these protective measures. But on 29 October 1985, in the midst of this disclosure, the NT Government appealed to the Federal Court for less restricted revelation of field material. The appeal was dismissed by the Federal Court. The NT Government then took the appeal on to the High Court. On 16 December 1986, the High Court dismissed the appeal with costs. Again, at great public expense, another delay in the hearing had been achieved.

In April 1987 some documents (including field-notes) of researchers were inspected by the Northern Territory Government in accordance with the protective measures. Cross-examination of three of the researchers who had had to produce material followed. Substantial use was made of the material of only one of the researchers, but this failed to reveal anything damaging to the Aborigines' claim. However, during the cross-examination, when a number of claimants were sitting in the public gallery, a lawyer read out a field-note from a researcher's notebook. The note attributed to one Aboriginal a remark about others which could be construed as slighting. Fortunately, discussion was not pursued, but the incident showed the way in which a lawyer could create conflict by revealing the sorts of comments to be found in field-notes. At the end of cross-examination in April, the other parties handed over to the researchers the photocopies of subpoenaed material that they had made.

The Aboriginal Land Commissioner's findings on the claimants' arguments for the land was handed down in 1988. He found that the claimants included the traditional owners (within the meaning of the Act) for a large part of the area claimed. The claimants received title to the land recommended for grants in stages between 1991 and 1992.

CONCLUSIONS

1. No researcher can guarantee confidentiality to the people they work with. A judge of a court can order the material to be produced. It seems that no country has legislation granting a 'researcher–consultant' professional privilege. A court can order production of material irrespective of what guarantees the researcher has given to the people who provide the information, on the grounds of fairness to the opponents. If the question of confidentiality is important, researchers must explain this to the people they work with. We cannot guarantee confidentiality without being prepared to break the law. This does not apply only to Australia. For example, Milroy (1980) in her work in working-class areas of Belfast probably recorded discussion of terrorist activity. She was in the community in a position of trust, yet it is clear now that she could have been placed under a legal constraint to betray that trust.

Furthermore, researchers and lawyers working in cases involving traditional law should discuss with their clients the possibility that the doctrine of fairness will require the clients themselves to disclose information which they may feel they should not reveal. In Australia, there is some hope of improving the situation with respect to Aboriginal material because there is some legal recognition (by Woodward J in particular) of the need to keep the confidentiality of secret Aboriginal and Islander religious and ceremonial material. Moreover, in 1986, the Australian Law Reform Commission proposed, in the context of recognising Aboriginal customary laws, that there should be a provision allowing courts to protect confidential material (including field-notes and tapes) relating to customary laws provided by Aboriginal people (Australian Law Reform Commission, 1986, Draft Aboriginal Customary Laws (Recognition) Bills ALRC 31 para. 661 cl.30). But again, the judgment as to what must be disclosed belongs to the court and not to the aboriginal people or to the ethnographer.

Maurice J's acceptance of the need for stringent protective

measures when sensitive documents are produced provides an important safeguard against wholesale abuse of confidential material, and represents the major success of the appeal against production of documents in the Warumungu Land claim.

2.   Anyone preparing to act as an expert witness should work out beforehand what material they are prepared to disclose.

There is a tension between the need for an expert witness to document their evidence and the need to preserve confidentiality. If an expert witness can document their statements or assertions, they are of more use to the client of the lawyer who is calling them to testify. The nearer the documentation to the time of the reported events, the more credible that documentation. Thus field-notes made at the time of the event are usually given more credence than a report made on the following day. However, once material is known to contribute to the basis of evidence in a hearing, it is at risk of disclosure. An expert witness may be required to show any material in her/his possession to the court, and this material may be distributed to the parties to the case, subject only to restrictions that the court places on it. It may be shown to the client, and the client may be cross-examined on it.

3.   Researchers and litigants who wish to challenge production of material must be aware of the lengthy delays in the hearing that will probably result.

The tactics of the NT Government in obtaining orders for the production of the field-notes were unsuccessful in that no evidence damaging to the claimants' case was found. However, it was a bitter victory. By resisting the NT Government's attempt to damage the relationship between ethnographer and Aboriginal, and to make public the intellectual property of Aboriginal people, the researchers had helped the NT Government delay the hearing of the claim by nearly two years. In that time more claimants died. Not only were they thus denied justice, and the pleasure of seeing their land returned to them, but their deaths have had great effects on the maintenance and development of knowledge of the land among younger people. Without secure title to land, the traditional owners have little authority under Australian law to control developments on their traditional land, and have little chance of establishing viable communities living on that land. If they live away from the land, it is also hard for knowledge of the country to be passed on to their children. Delaying the return of land to Aboriginal people means that we are returning to them land which we have in part emptied of what gives it meaning – the knowledge and history and songs of the people who knew and know it best.

ACKNOWLEDGEMENT

I thank Neil Andrews, Ross Howie, David Nash and Bruce Reyburn for commenting on earlier drafts.

NOTE

1. While there are a variety of views among researchers, and the Aboriginal people they work with, it seems to be commonly believed that field-notes contain intellectual property over which three separate people or bodies have rights, namely, the person providing the material, the person who records the material, and the body or people sponsoring the recorder. Intellectual property must be distinguished from physical property which would be the notebooks and tapes in which the material is recorded. These usually belong to the recorder or to the people or body sponsoring the recorder.

NINETEEN

Lawyer's response to forensic linguistics

Dyson Heydon

To a lawyer, the interest of this section of the book lies in two main areas. The first is the problem of voice identification. The second is the linguistic analysis of prose in order to demonstrate or disprove its authorship or indicate the mode of its composition.

Voice identification raises difficult questions, as Nolan and Jones explain, because speakers are normally more concerned to communicate meanings, emotions and attitudes than they are to indicate who is speaking: the identity of the speaker is normally communicated by visual inspection or by inference from context, and if the person whose voice is being used to identify him is heard using it in the context of preparing for or committing a crime, he will usually be abstaining from permitting his identity to be detected by inspection or inference, let alone from asserting it. In these circumstances the risk of mistake grows.

It has been natural for lawyers dealing with voice identification to look to the legal principles governing visual identification. Visual identification raises tricky problems with which the law has been struggling for a century. As Jones points out, it is considered normal to recognise a face after a single meeting; faces differ from one another in innumerable ways, and it is regarded as inefficient and discourteous not to recognise the many people with whom a non-reclusive citizen chooses, or feels obliged, or is even paid, to deal. For these reasons, people experience, or assert, dogmatic confidence about their own powers of facial and other visual recognition, even when the opportunities for this, or for avoiding errors in recollection and narration, may be inherently defective. Daily life affords instances enough of false recognition, but it took the occurrences of miscarriages of justice caused by errors of recognition – arising quite independently of any bad faith or carelessness in police work – in various *causes célèbres* to generate the modern legal rules. From wrong identification by a mother of the Tichborne claimant as her son, to the cases of Beck and Slater early this century, to their present-day equivalents, a visceral confidence in visual identification evidence has gradually been disturbed. More recently, scientific and other experimental evidence has confirmed that unease. So there now exist rules, largely judge-made, encouraging the use of properly organised identification parades, providing for the use of detailed warnings as to the frailty of uncorroborated identification evidence, excluding evidence of identification for police photographs, heavily restricting the use of identification of the accused in court, and permitting the discretionary exclusion of certain types of identification evidence.

Given that these rules were developed because of the danger in trusting the evidence of one's own eyes, is the evidence of one's own ears any better? From a lawyer's point of view the question can be approached from two directions – first, searching for rules applying to informal voice recognition, and, second, considering the admissibility of expert evidence of voice identification.

So far as informal voice recognition is concerned, there is a division between the New South Wales and the Victorian courts. The Victorian courts seek to apply to voice identification the rules as to visual identification with modifications: R v. *Harris (No. 3)* [1990] VR 310. These modifications will probably come to be extensive in practice, because of the difference between faces and voices. While physical appearance lends itself to some extent to objective description, this is less true of a voice. While faces can be recorded by photographs and identikit techniques, only audio-tapes made in good conditions can record a voice reliably. There is no real equivalent for voices to identification parades: voices can be changed much more readily than appearances, and the goal of ensuring that the suspect uses his voice on the 'parade' in the same way as during the alleged crime may be an unachievable one. For reasons of this kind the New South Wales courts have rules for voice identification which are stricter than for visual identification. It must be shown either that the identifying witness was very familiar with the voice identified before the crime alleged or that the voice identified is very distinctive (in which case it need not have been first heard by the identifying witness before the crime alleged): R v. E. J. *Smith*

[1984] 1 NSWLR 462; (1986) 7 NSWLR 444; *R* v. *Brownlowe* (1987) 7 NSWLR 461. That additional requirement has not been imposed in Victoria: *R* v. *Hentschel* [1988] VR 362; *R* v. *Harris (No. 3)* [1990] VR 310. In view of the difficulties of informal voice recognition revealed by Nolan and Jones, as a matter of prudence the New South Wales approach is to be preferred, even though it offends legal purism by treating matters going to the weight of evidence as factors relevant to its admissibility.

Does expert evidence on voice recognition afford any comfort that the accuracy of identification is increased? The contribution of experts appears most useful where there is available a sample, e.g. by means of a taped telephone call, of a voice associated with a criminal, which can be compared to samples provided by the accused. The analysis and comparison of this material, whether it turns on comparing measurements of fundamental frequency or on spectrographic analysis, is a type of analysis producing probability figures on the likelihood of similarity or difference. It runs into an unresolved controversy in, or on the fringes of, the law as to the utility of that general type of evidence. It also runs into an emotion which is often experienced though less rarely spoken about by lawyers, and which has intensified since the success of the Chamberlains in their campaign against their convictions: a distrust of expert forensic evidence in fields which are not very familiar. However, the courts have received the evidence: e.g. *R* v. *Gilmore* [1977] 2 NSWLR 935; *R* v. *McHardie* [1983] 2 NSWLR 733. They will probably continue to do so unless there is a demonstrated risk of error in the particular case.

The other main activity described in this section of the book – linguistic analysis to prove authorship – encounters a similar caution. The courts, particularly those operating trials by jury, are troubled by the length of time the reception and leading of expert evidence takes; and they are troubled by the risk of an unjustified aura of special trustworthiness surrounding a relatively young and untried science, particularly when a standard of proof beyond reasonable doubt has to be met. The moderate scepticism of Smith would reinforce those fears. The difficulty appears to be that, as Eagleson and Coulthard demonstrate, linguistic analysis can point towards particular possible authors as against others; whether it does so with a sufficient degree of decisiveness and intelligibility for lay triers of fact to use it as an aid to rational thinking is more doubtful.

Bibliography

Abrahams, R. (1976) *Talking Black* Rowley, A, Mass: Newbury House.

Adelsward, V., Aronsson, K., Jonsson, L. and Linell, P. (1987) The unequal distribution of interactional space: dominance and control in courtroom interaction. *Text*, 7, 4, 313–46.

Adelsward, V. (1989) Defendants' interpretations of encouragements in court. *Journal of Pragmatics*, 13, 741–9.

Advisory Committee Notes, 80 F.R.D. 323, 337 (1979).

Advisory Committee Notes, 48 F.R.D. 509, 514 (1970).

Agar, Michael (1985) Institutional discourse. *Text*, 5, 3, 147–68.

Agar, Michael (1990) Language scenes and political schemas. *Journal of Pragmatics*, 14, 25–38.

Akinnaso, F. N. (1982a) On the difference between spoken and written language. *Language and Speech*, 25, 2, 97–125.

Akinnaso, F. N. (1982b) The literate writes and the nonliterate chants: written language and ritual communication in sociolinguistic perspective. In W. Frawley (ed.) *Linguistics and Literacy*. New York, NY: Plenum Press, pp. 7–36.

Akinnaso, F. N. (1985) On the similarities between spoken and written language. *Language and Speech*, 28, 4, 323–59.

Allen, J. R. (1974) Methods of author identification through stylistic analysis. *The French Review*, XLVII, 904–16.

Allot, A. N., Epstein, A. L. and Gluckman, M. (1969) Introduction. In M. Gluckman (ed.) *Ideas and Procedures in African Customary Law*. Oxford: Oxford University Press, pp. 1–96.

Andersen, P. (1985) Nonverbal immediacy in interpersonal communication. In A. Siegman and S. Feldstein (eds) *Multichannel integrations of non-verbal behavior*. Hillsdale, NJ: L. Erlbaum Associates, pp. 1–36.

Anderson, J. T. (1985) The Woolworths' extortion. *Australian Police Journal*, 39, 2, 51–75.

Anderson-Hsieh, J. and Koehler, K. (1988) The effect of foreign accent and speaking rate on native speaker comprehension. *Language Learning*, 38, 561–92.

Apple, W., Streeter, L. and Krauss, R. (1979) Effects of pitch and speech rate on personal attributions. *Journal of Personality and Social Psychology*, 37, 715–27.

Ariz. R. Civ. P. 30(c).

Aron, R., Fast, J. and Klein, R. (1986) *Trial Communication Skills*. New York, NY: McGraw-Hill.

Atkinson, J. and Drew, P. (1979) *Order in Court: The Organisation of Verbal Interaction in Judicial Settings*. London: Macmillan.

Austin, J. (1956) A plea for excuses. *Proceedings of the Aristotelian Society*, 57, 1–30.

Austin, J. L. (1962) *How to Do Things with Words*. Oxford: Oxford University Press.

Austin, J. L. (1970) *Philosophical Papers*. Oxford: Oxford University Press.

Australia (1985) Subpoena of field-notes in the Warumungu Land Claim. *Language in Central Australia*, 3, 15–19.

Australia (1986) Attorney-General for the Northern Territory v. Maurice in the Matter of the Warumungu Land Claim. *Australian Law Reports*, 65, 247.

Australia. Aboriginal Land Commissioner (1989) Kenbi Land Claim. Transcript of Proceedings. Darwin: Office of the Aboriginal Land Commissioner.

Australia. Aboriginal Land Commissioner (1990) Kenbi Land Claim. Transcript of Proceedings. Darwin: Office of the Aboriginal Land Commissioner.

Australian Law Reform Commission (ALRC) (1986) *Report 31: The Recognition of Aboriginal Customary Laws*. Canberra: Australian Government Publishing Service.

Australian Law Reform Commission (1987) *Report No. 38: Evidence*, Canberra: Australian Government Publishing Service.

Bailey, R. W. (1979) Authorship attribution in a forensic setting. In D. E. Ager, F. E. Knowles and Joan Smith (eds) *Advances in Computer-Aided Literary and Linguistic Research, Proceedings of the Fifth International Symposium on Computers in Literary and Linguistic Research*. Birmingham, pp. 1–15.

Bain, M. (1979) At the interface: the implications of opposing views of reality. Unpublished MA thesis. Monash University.

Baines, J. (1983) Literacy and ancient Egyptian society. *Man*, 18, 572–99.

Bakhtin, M. (1981) *Dialogic Imagination*. Austin, Texas: University of Texas Press.

Baldwin, J. (1977) The forensic application of phonetics, *Police Review*, 1609.

Baldwin, J. (1979) Phonetics and speaker identification, *Medicine, Science and the Law*, 19, 231–2.

Baldwin, J. and French, P. (1990) *Forensic Phonetics*. London: Pinter.

Bandler, R. and Grinder, J. (1979) *Frogs into Princes: Neuro-linguistic Programming*. Moab, UT: Real People Press.

Barber, C. L. (1962) Some measurable characteristics of modern scientific prose. In Behre, F. (ed.) *Contributions to English Syntax and Philology*, Götesburg: Almqvist and Wiksell, pp. 21–43.

Barfield, O. (1962) Poetic diction and legal fiction. In M. Black (ed.) *The Importance of Language*. Englewood Cliffs, NJ: Prentice-Hall.

Barnes, J. A. (1979) *Who Should Know What? Social Science, Privacy and Ethics*. Harmondsworth: Penguin.

Barnett, T. E. (1973) Law and Justice Melanesian style. In A. C. Ross and J. Langmore (eds) *Alternative Strategies for Papua New Guinea*. Melbourne: Oxford University Press, pp. 59–85.

Basso, K. (1970) 'To give up on words': silence in Western Apache culture. *Southwestern Journal of Anthropology*, 26, 213–30.

Bateson, G. (1972) *Steps to an Ecology of Mind*. London: Intertext.

Baugh, J. (1983) *Black Street Speech*. Austin, TX: University of Texas Press.

Baüml, Franz H. (1980) Varieties and consequences of medieval literacy and illiteracy. *Speculum*, 55, 237–365.

Beard v. *Mitchell* 604 F. 2d 485, 503 (7th Cir. 1979).

Bell, D. (1985) Have anthropologists had their day in court? *Australian Anthropological Society Newsletter*, 28 (September), 18–27.

Bell, D. (1986) In the case of lawyers and anthropologists. *Legal Service Bulletin*, 11, 202.

Belli, M. (1982) Videotaped deposition: a new frontier of advocacy. In M. Belli (ed.) *Modern Trials*. St Paul, MN: West Publishing, pp. 376–430.

Bennett, W. L. and Feldman, M. S. (1981) *Reconstructing Reality in the Courtroom*. New Brunswick, NJ: Rutgers University Press.

Berk-Seligson, S. (1988) The impact of politeness in witness testimony: the influence of the court interpreter. *Multilingua*, 7, 441.

Berk-Seligson, S. (1990) *The Bilingual Courtroom Court Interpreters in the Judicial Process*. Chicago, IL: University of Chicago Press.

Berliner, L. and Barbieri, M. K. (1984) The testimony of the child victim of sexual assault. *Journal of Social Issues*, 40, 2, 125–37.

Bernard, J. R. (1967) Measurements of Sounds in Australian English. Unpublished PhD thesis, University of Sydney.

Best, C. T., Morrongiello, B. and Robson, R. (1981) Perceptual equivalence of acoustic cues in speech and nonspeech perception. *Perception and Psychophysics*, 29, 191–211.

Bhatia, V. K. (1982) An Investigation into Formal and Functional Characteristics of Qualifications in Legislative Writing and its Application to English for Academic Legal Purposes. PhD thesis, University of Aston in Birmingham, UK.

Bhatia, V. K. (1983) *Applied Discourse Analysis of English Legislative Writing*. A Language Studies Unit Research Report. Birmingham: University of Aston in Birmingham.

Bhatia, V. K. (1984) Syntactic discontinuity in legislative writing and its implications for academic legal purposes. In A. K. Pugh and J. M. Ulijn (eds) *Reading for Professional Purposes – Studies and Practices in Native and Foreign Languages*. London: Heinemann, pp. 90–6.

Bhatia, V. K. (1987a) Language of the Law. *Language Teaching*, 20, 4, 227–34.

Bhatia, V. K. (1987b) Textual-mapping in British legislative writing. *World Englishes*, 6, 1, 1–10.

Bhatia, V. K. (1991) Pragmatics of the use of nominals in academic and professional genres. A paper delivered at the Fifth Annual International Conference on Pragmatics and Language Learning University of Illinois at Urbana-Champaign, Urbana.

Biber, D. (1985) Spoken and written textual dimensions in English: resolving the contradictory findings, *Language*, 62, 2, 384–414.

Biber, D. (1988) *Variation Across Speech and Writing*. Cambridge: Cambridge University Press.

Bird, G. (1987) Fieldwork in South Australia. In K. Hazlehurst (ed.) *Ivory Scales: Black Australia and the Law*. Sydney: New South Wales University Press.

Birdwhistell, R. L. (1970) *Kinesics and Context: Essays on Body Motion Communication*. Philadelphia, PA: University of Pennsylvania Press.

Blake, N. F. (1977) *The English Language in Medieval Literature*. London: Dent.

Blom-Cooper, L. and Drewry, G. (1972) *Final Appeal*. Oxford: Clarendon Press.

Bohannan, P. (1969) Ethnography and comparison in legal anthropology. In L. Nader (ed.) *Law in Culture and Society*. Chicago, IL: Aldine, pp. 401–18.

Bowden, R. (1987) Sorcery, illness and social control in Kwoma society. In M. Stephen (ed.) *Sorcerer and Witch in Melanesia*. Victoria: Melbourne University Press, pp. 183–208.

Bowers, F. (1985) Judicial systemics: function and structure in statutory interpretation. In J. D. Benson and W. S. Greaves (eds) *Systematic Perspectives on Discourse Volume 2: Selected Theoretical Papers from the 9th International Systemic Workshop*. Norwood, NJ: Ablex, pp. 39–48.

Bowers, F. (1990) *Linguistic Aspects of Legislative Expression*. Vancouver: University of British Columbia Press.

Brandl, M. M. and Walsh, M. (1981) Speakers of many tongues: towards understanding multilingualism among Aboriginal Australians. *International Journal of the Sociology of Language*, 36, 71–81.

Brennan, M. and Brennan, R. E. (1988) *Strange language – child victims under cross examination*. Wagga Wagga, New South Wales, Australia: Charles Sturt University.

Burgoon, J. (1985) Nonverbal signals. In M. Knapp and G. Miller (eds) *Handbook of Interpersonal Communication*. Beverly Hills, CA: Sage Publications, pp. 344–90.

Burke, K. (1969) *A Rhetoric of Motives*. Berkeley, CA: University of California Press.

Bülow-Møller, A. M. (1991) Trial evidence: overt and covert communication in court. *International Journal of Applied Linguistics*, 1, 1, 38–60.

Bülow-Møller, A. M. (in press) The notion of coercion in courtroom questioning. *Proceedings from Nordfest Conference*, 1990, Abo Academy Finland.

Byrne, D. and Heydon, J. D. (1991) *Cross on Evidence*. Sydney: Butterworths.

Candlin, C. N. (1981) Discoursal patterning and the equalising of interpretive opportunity. In L. Smith (ed.) *English for Cross-cultural Communication*. London: Macmillan.

Cardozo, B. N. (1931) *Law and Literature and other Essays*. New York, NY: Harcourt Brace.

Carlson, R., Fant, G. and Granström, B. (1975) Two-formant models, pitch and vowel perception. In G. Fant and M. A. A. Tatham (eds) *Auditory Analysis and Perception of Speech*. London: Academic Press.

Carlton, C. (1970) *Descriptive Syntax and the Old English Charters*. The Hague: Mouton.

Carranza, M. (1982) Attitudinal research on Hispanic language varieties. In E. Ryan and H. Giles (eds) *Attitudes Towards Language Variation*. London: Edward Arnold, pp. 63–83.

Cashmore, J. and Horsky, M. (1987) Child sexual assault: the court response. Sydney: NSW Bureau of Crime Statistics and Research, Attorney General's Department.

Catford, J. C. (1988) *A Practical Introduction to Phonetics*. Oxford: Clarendon.

Certoma, G. L. (1990) Law in a multicultural society: the Australian case. Paper presented at the One-day Conference on Multiculturalism and the Law, Federation of Ethnic Communities Councils, July, Sydney.

Chafe, W. (1985) Linguistic differences produced by differences between speaking and writing. In D. L. Olson, W. Torrance and A. Hildgard (eds) *Literacy, Language and Learning*. Cambridge: Cambridge University Press, pp. 105–23.

Chafe, W. and Tannen, D. (1987) The relation between written and spoken language. *Annual Review of Anthropology*, 16, 383–409.

Charrow, R. and Charrow, V. (1979) Making legal language understandable: A psycholinguistic study of jury instructions. *Columbia Law Review*, 79, 1306.

Child Sexual Assault Task Force (1985) Report to the Hon. Neville Wran QC MP, Premier of New South Wales. Sydney: New South Wales Government.

Chowning, A. (1987) Sorcery and the social order in Kove. In M. Stephen (ed.) *Sorcerer and Witch in Melanesia*. Victoria: Melbourne University Press, pp. 149–82.

Christie, M. (1984) The classroom world of the Aboriginal child. Unpublished PhD thesis. University of Queensland.

Clanchy, M. T. (1979) *From Memory to Written Record: England, 1066–1307*. Cambridge, MA: Harvard University Press.

Cohen, D. (1990) You did it, didn't you? *New Scientist*, 27, 39–41.

Cohen, M. (ed.) (1984) *Ronald Dworkin and Contemporary Jurisprudence*. London: Duckworth.

Cohen, P. (1970) The tensing and raising of short (a) in the metropolitan area of New York City. Master's degree essay, Columbia University.

Coldrey, J. (1987) Aboriginals and the criminal courts. In Hazlehurst, K. (ed.) *Ivory Scales: Black Australia and the Law*. Sydney: New South Wales University Press.

Coldrey, J. and Vincent, F. (1980) Tales from the frontier: white laws – black people. *Legal Service Bulletin*, 5, 5, 221–4.

Comrie, B. (1978) Ergativity. In W. P. Lehmann (ed.) *Syntactic typology: Studies in the Phenomenology of Language*. Austin, TX: University of Texas Press, pp. 329–94.

Conley, J., O'Barr, W. and Lind, E. (1978) The power of language: presentational style in the courtroom. *Duke Law Review*, 78, 1375–99.

Conley, J. M. and O'Barr, W. M. (1990) Rules versus relationships in small claims disputes. In A. D. Grimshaw (ed.) *Conflict Talk*. Cambridge: Cambridge University Press.

Coode, G. (1852) Legislative expression, or the language of the written law. In S. Robinson (ed.) *Drafting* (1973). Sydney: Butterworth, pp. 335–98.

Coode, G. (1848) On legislative expression or the language of written law. Appeared as Introduction a digest of the Poor Laws, appendixed to the 1843 Report of the Poor Law Commission. Reprinted in E. A. Driedger (1957) *The Composition of Legislation*. Ottawa: Queen's Printer.

Coulthard, R. M. (ed.) (1986) *Talking about Text*. Birmingham: English Language Research, University of Birmingham.

Craies on Statute Law (1971) 7th edn. Edited by S. G. Edgar. London: Sweet & Maxwell.

Crouch, A. (1979) Barriers to understanding in the legal situation, *Law Institute Journal*, 53, 505.

Crouch, A. (1985) The way, the truth and the right to interpreters in court, *Law Institute Journal*, 59, 687.

Crystal, D. and Davy, D. (1969) *Investigating English Style*. London: Longman.

Danet, B. (1980a) Language in the legal process. *Law and Society Review*, 14, 3, 445–564.

Danet, B. (1980b) 'Baby' or 'fetus': language and the construction of reality in a manslaughter trial. *Semiotica*, 32, 187–219.

Danet, B. (1985) Legal discourse. In T. Van Dijk (ed.) *Handbook of Discourse Analysis*, Vol. 1. London: Academic Press, pp. 273–91.

Danet, B. (1990) Language and law: an overview of fifteen years of research. In Howard Giles and W. Peter Robinson (eds) *Handbook of Language and Social Psychology*. Chichester: Wiley, pp. 537–59.

Danet, B. and Bogoch, B. (1980) Fixed fight or free-for-all? An empirical study of combativeness in the adversary system of justice. *British Journal of Law and Society*, 7, 36–60.

Danet, B. and Bogoch, B. (1992) 'Whosoever alters this, may God turn His face from him on the day of judgment': Curses in Anglo-Saxon legal documents. *Journal of American Folklore*, 105, 416, 132–65.

Danet, B. and Bogoch, B. (in press) From oral law to literate law: orality, literacy and formulaicity in Anglo-Saxon wills. In Bernard S. Jackson (ed.) *The Semiotics and Sociology of Law*. Papers from the Onati Workshop on the Semiotics and Sociology of Law, July. Onati, Spain: The Onati International Institute for the Sociology of Law.

Davis, T. (1986) Forensic handwriting analysis. In R. M. Coulthard (ed.) *Talking about Text*. Birmingham: English Language Research, University of Birmingham.

Den Boer, M. (1990) A linguistic analysis of narrative coherence in the courtroom. In P. Herhot (ed.) *Law, Interpretation and Reality*. Dordrecht: Kluwer Academic Publisher, pp. 346–78.

Denning, The Rt Hon Lord (1980) *The Due Process of Law*. London: Butterworths.

Devlin, P. (1979) *The Judge*. Oxford: Oxford University Press.

Diamond, A. S. (1951) *The Evolution of Law and Order*. London: Watts & Co.

Dickerson, R. (1975) *The Interpretation and Application of Statutes*. Toronto: Little, Brown.

Dixon, R. M. W. (1979) Ergativity. *Language*, 55, 1, 59–138.

Drew, P. (1985) Analysing the use of language in courtroom interaction.

In T. Van Dijk (ed.) *Handbook of Discourse Analysis, Vol. 3, Discourse and Dialogue*. London: Academic Press.

Druckman, D., Rozelle, L. and Baxter, J. (1982) *Nonverbal Communication: Survey, Theory and Research*. Beverly Hills: Sage Publications.

Dundas, C. (1915) The organisation and laws of some Bantu tribes in E. Africa, *Journal of the Royal Anthropological Institute*, 45, 234–64.

Dunstan, R. (1980) Context for coercion: analysing properties of courtroom 'questions', *British Journal of Law and Society*, 7, 61–7.

Dueñas Gonzalez, R. (1977) The design and validation of an evaluative procedure to diagnose the English aural-oral competency of a Spanish-speaking person in the justice system, University of Arizona: Unpublished doctoral dissertation.

Dworkin, R. (1977) *Taking Rights Seriously*. Cambridge, MA: Harvard University Press.

Dworkin, R. (1986) *Law's Empire*. London: Fontana.

Eades, D. (1982) You gotta know how to talk . . . Information seeking in Southeast Queensland Aboriginal society. *Australian Journal of Linguistics*, 2, 1, 61–82. Reprinted in J. Pride (ed.) (1988) *Cross Cultural Encounters: Communication and Miscommunication*. Melbourne: River Seine Publications.

Eades, D. (1984) Misunderstanding Aboriginal English: the role of sociocultural context. In G. McKay and B. Sommer (eds) *Applications of Linguistics to Australian Aboriginal Contexts*. Applied Linguistics Association of Australia, Occasional Papers No. 8, 24–33.

Eades, D. (1988) They don't speak an Aboriginal language or do they? In I. Keen (ed.) *Being Black. Aboriginal Cultures in 'Settled' Australia*. Canberra: Aboriginal Studies Press, pp. 97–116.

Eades, D. (1991) Communicative strategies in Aboriginal English. In S. Romaine (ed.) *Language in Australia*. Cambridge: Cambridge University Press, pp. 84–93.

Eades, D. (1992) *Aboriginal English and the law: Communicating with Aboriginal English speaking clients: A handbook for legal practitioners*. Brisbane: Queensland Law Society.

Eades, D. (1993) The case for Condren: Aboriginal English, pragmatics and the law, *Journal of Pragmatics*, 20, 2, 141–62.

Eades, D. (in press) Language and the law: White Australia vs Nancy. In M. Walsh and C. Yallop (eds) *Language and Culture in Aboriginal Australia*. Canberra: Aboriginal Studies Press, pp. 181–90.

Eagleson, R. D. (1985) The plain English debate in Australia. In J. E. Clark (ed.) *The Cultivated Australian: Festschrift fur Arthur Delbridge*. Hamburg: Helmut Buske Verlag, pp. 143–50.

Eagleson, R. D. (1991) The plain English movement in Australia and the United Kingdom. In E. T. Steinberg (ed.) *Plain Language – Principles and Practice*. Detroit: Wayne State University Press.

Eagleton, T. (1991) *Ideology: an Introduction*. London: Verso.

Earle, J. A. (ed.) (1888) *A Handbook to the Land Charters and Other Saxonic Documents*. Oxford: Clarendon Press.

Eckermann, A-K. (1988) Culture vacuum or cultural vitality? *Australian Aboriginal Studies*, 1, 31–9.

Eggleston, E. (1976) *Fear, Favour or Affection: Aborigines and the Criminal Law in Victoria, South Australia and Western Australia*. Canberra: Australian National University Press.

Ekman, P. (1982) *Emotion in the Human Face*. Cambridge: Cambridge University Press.

Ekman, P. and Friesen, W. (1969) Nonverbal leakage and clues to deception. *Psychiatry*, 32, 88–106.

Ekman, P., Friesen, W. and Scherer, K. (1976) Body movement and voice pitch in deceptive interaction. *Semiotica*, 16, 23–7.

Elias, T. O. (1956) *The nature of African customary law*. Manchester: Manchester University Press.

Elkin, A. P. (1947) Aboriginal evidence and justice in North Australia. *Oceania*, 17, 173–210.

Ellegård, A. (1962) *A Statistical Method for Determining Authorship: the Junius Letters, 1769–1772*. Gottenburg: Gottenburg Studies in English.

Enright, C. (1983) *Studying Law*. Sydney: Branxton Press.

Epstein, A. L. (1967) Injury and liability: legal ideas and implicit assumptions. *Mankind*, 6, 9, 376–83.

Epstein, A. L. (1973) The reasonable man revisited. *Law and Society Review*, 6, 643–66.

Evans-Pritchard, E. E. (1937) *Witchcraft, Oracles and Magic among the Azande*. Oxford: Clarendon Press.

Everitt, B. S. (1977) *The Analysis of Contingency Tables*. London: Chapman and Hall.

Fagan, D. (1990) Uncertainty and judicial discretion in commercial law, *Policy*, 6, 4, Centre for Independent Studies, Sydney.

Fairclough, N. (1985) Critical and descriptive goals in discourse analysis, *Journal of Pragmatics*, 9, 93–137.

Fairclough, N. (1989) *Language and Power*. London: Longman.

Fairclough, N. (ed.) (1992) *Critical Language Awareness*. London: Longman.

Farmer, L., Williams, G., Cundick, B., Howell, R., Lee, R. and Rooker, C. K. (1976) The effect of the method of presenting testimony on juror decisional process. In B. Sales (ed.) *Psychology in the Legal Process*. New York, NY: Spectrum, pp. 77–86.

Fed. R. Civ. P. 30(b)(4) (1970) (amended 1980), 85 F.R.D. 521, 52 (1980).

Fed. R. Civ. P. 30(b) (4), 48 F.R.D. 509, 510 (1970).

Fed. R. 30(c) Civ. P.

Fed. R. Civ. P. 52.

Finnegan, R. (1988) *Literacy and Orality: Studies in the Technology of Communication*. Oxford: Blackwell.

Fisher, S. and Todd, A. (1986) *Discourse and Institutional Authority: Medicine, Education and Law*. Norwood, NJ: Ablex.

Fitzgerald, G. (1989) Report of a Commission of Inquiry Pursuant to Orders in Council. Brisbane: Government Printer.

Foley, M. (1984) Aborigines and the police. In P. Hanks and B. Keon-Cohen (eds) *Aborigines and the Law*. Sydney: George Allen & Unwin, pp. 160–90.

Fowler, R. (1991) *Language in the News: Discourse and Ideology in the Press*. London: Routledge.

Frank, J. (1963) *Law and the Modern World*. New York, NY: Russell Sage Foundation.

Freckelton, I. (1987) *Trial of the Expert: a Study of Expert Evidence and Forensic Experts*. Melbourne: Oxford University Press.

Friedlund, A., Ekman, P. and Oster, H. (1987) Facial expressions of emotion. In A. Siegman and S. Feldstein (eds) *Nonverbal Behavior and Communication*. Hillsdale, NJ: L. Erlbaum Associates, pp. 143–224.

Friedman, L. (1964) Law and its language. *George Washington Law Review*, 33, 563–79.

Friedman, L. (1975) *The Legal System*. New York, NY: Russell Sage Foundation.

Fry, D. B. (1979) *The Physics of Speech*. Cambridge: Cambridge University Press.

Fugita, S., Hogrebe, M. and Wexley, K. (1980) Perceptions of deception: perceived expertise in detecting deception, successfulness of deception and nonverbal cues. *Personality and Social Psychology Bulletin*, 6, 637–43.

Fuller, L. (1967) *Legal Fictions*. Stanford, CA: California University Press.

Galbraith, V. R. (1935) The literacy of medieval English kings. Raleigh Lecture on History, July.

Gaur, A. (1984) *A History of Writing*. London: British Library.

Gibbons, J. (1986) Courtroom application of Second Language Acquisition Research. *Australian Review of Applied Linguistics*, Series S, No. 3, 131–3.

Gibbons, J. (1990) Applied Linguistics in Court. *Applied Linguistics*, 11, 3, 229–37.

Giles, H. and Coupland, N. (1991) *Language: Contexts and Consequences*. Buckingham: Open University Press.

Givón, T. (1975) Cause and control: On the semantics of interpersonal manipulation. In J. Kimball (ed.) *Syntax and Semantics, Vol. IV*. New York, NY: Academic Press, pp. 58–89.

Glasse, R. M. (1968) *Huli of Papua: A Cognatic Descent System*. Paris: Mouton.

Gluckman, M. (1955) *The Judicial Process Among the Barotse of Northern Rhodesia*. Manchester: Manchester University Press.

Gluckman, M. (1963) *Order and Rebellion in Tribal Africa*. London: Cohen and West.

Gluckman, M. (1965) *The Ideas of Barotse Jurisprudence*. New Haven, CT: Yale University Press.

Gluckman, M. (1966) Reasonableness and responsibility in the law of segmentary societies. In L. and H. Kuper (eds) *African Law: Adaptation and Development*. Los Angeles, CA: University of California Press, pp. 120–46.

Gluckman, M. (1970) The logic of African science and witchcraft. In M. Marwick (ed.) *Witchcraft and Sorcery*. Harmondsworth: Penguin, pp. 321–31.

Goffman, E. (1959) *The Presentation of Self in Everyday Life*. Garden City, NY: Doubleday Anchor Books.

Goffman, E. (1981) *Forms of Talk*. London: Basil Blackwell.

Goldman, L. R. (1983) *Talk Never Dies: the Language of Huli Disputes*. London: Tavistock.

Goldman, L. R. (1986a) The presentational style of women in Huli disputes. *Pacific Linguistics*, 24, 213–89.

Goldman, L. R. (1986b) A case of 'questions' and a question of 'case'. *Text*, 6, 4, 345–92.

Goldman, L. R. (1986c) Anatomical terms in Huli: names and games. *Mankind*, 16, 3, 190–208.

Goldman, L. R. (1988) Premarital sex cases among the Huli. *Oceania Monographs*, No. 34, University of Sydney.

Goldman, L. R. (1993) *The Culture of Coincidence: Accident and Absolute Liability in Huli*. Oxford: Oxford University Press.

Goodrich, P. (1984) The role of linguistics in legal analysis, *Modern Law Review*, 47, 523–34.

Goodrich, P. (1987) *Legal Discourse*. London: Macmillan.

Goodrich, P. (1988) Modalities of annunciation: an introduction to courtroom speech. In R. Kevelson (ed.) *Law and Semiotics Vol. 2*. New York, NY: Plenum Press.

Goody, J. (1986) *The Logic of Writing and the Organization of Society*. Cambridge: Cambridge University Press.

Goody, J. (1987) *The Interface Between the Written and the Oral*. Cambridge: Cambridge University Press.

Gordon, R. J. and Meggitt, M. J. (1985) *Law and Order in the New Guinea Highlands*. Hanover: University Press of New England.

Graff, H. J. (1987a) *The Legacies of Literacy: Continuities and Contradictions in Western Culture and Society*. Bloomington, IN: Indiana University Press.

Graff, H. J. (1987b) *The Labyrinths of Literacy: Reflections on Past and Present*. London: Falmer Press.

Grice, P. (1975) Logic and conversation. In P. Cole and M. Morgan (eds) *Syntax and Semantics: Speech Acts*. New York, NY: Academic Press.

Gudjonsson, G. H. and Haward, L. R. C. (1983) Psychological analysis of confession statements, *Journal of the Forensic Science Society*, 23, 113–20.

Gunn, J. S. (1963) The influence of background on the speech of Teachers' College students. *Forum of Education*, 22, 1.

Gunnarsson, Britt-Louise (1984) Functional comprehensibility of legislative texts: experiments with a Swedish act of parliament. *Text*, 4, 1–3, 71–105.

Gustafsson, M. (1975) *Some Syntactic Properties of English Law Language*. Publication No. 4. Department of English, University of Turku, Turku, Finland.

Gustafsson, M. (1984) The syntactic features of binomial expressions in legal English. *Text*, 4, 1–3, 123–41.

Halberstadt, A. (1985) Race, socioeconomic status and nonverbal behavior. In A. Siegman and S. Feldstein (eds) *Multichannell Integrations of Nonverbal Behavior*. Hillsdale, NJ: L. Erlbaum Associates, pp. 227–66.

Hall, E. (1959) *The Silent Language*. Garden City, NY: Doubleday.

Hall, J. (1978) Gender effects in decoding nonverbal cues. *Psychological Bulletin*, 85, 845–57.

Halliday, M. A. K. (1978) *Language as Social Semiotic*. London: Edward Arnold.

Halliday, M. A. K. (1985a) *Introduction to Functional Grammar*. London: Edward Arnold.

Halliday, M. A. K. (1985b) *Spoken and Written Language*. Geelong, Victoria: Deakin University Press.

Halliday, M. A. K. and Hasan, R. (1976) *Cohesion in English*. London: Longman.

Hamilton, A. (1981) *Nature and Nurture: Aboriginal Child-rearing in North-Central Arnhem Land*. Canberra: Australian Institute of Aboriginal Studies.

Hanks, P. and Keon-Cohen, B. (eds) (1984) *Aborigines and the Law*. Sydney: George Allen and Unwin.

Hardcastle, R. A. (1993) Forensic Linguistics: and assessment of the CUSUM method for the determination of authorship. Journal of the *Forensic Science Society*, 33, 95–106.

Harmer, F. E. (ed.) (1914) *Select English Historical Documents of the Ninth and Tenth Centuries*. Cambridge: Cambridge University Press.

Harmer, F. E. (ed.) (1952) *Anglo-Saxon Writs*. Manchester: Manchester University Press.

Harris, S. (1984a) Questions as a mode of control in magistrates' courts. *International Journal of the Sociology of Language*, 49, 5–28.

Harris, S. (1984b) The form and function of threats in court, *Language and Communication*, 4, 4, 247–72.

Harris, S. (1988) Court discourse as genre. In R. P. Fawcett and D. J. Young (eds) *New Developments in Systemic Linguistics, Vol. 2: Theory and Application*. London: Frances Pinter, pp. 94–115.

Harris, S. (1989) Defendant resistance to power and control in court. In H. Coleman (ed.) *Working with Language: A Multi-Disciplinary Consideration of Language Use in Work Contexts*. The Hague: Mouton.

Harris, William V. (1989) *Ancient Literacy*. Cambridge, MA: Harvard University Press.

Harrison, Kenneth (1973) The beginning of the year in England, *c*. 500–900. In P. Clemoes, et al. (ed.) *Anglo-Saxon England, Vol. 2*. Cambridge: Cambridge University Press, pp. 51–70.

Harrison, R. (1974) *Beyond Words*. Englewood-Cliffs, NJ: Prentice-Hall.

Hart, H. L. A. (1949) The ascription of responsibility and rights. *Proceedings of the Aristotelian Society*, 49, 171–94.

Hart, H. L. A. (1961) *The Concept of Law*. Oxford: Oxford University Press.

Hartley, J. and Montgomery, M. (1985) Representations and relations: ideology and power in press and T.V. news. In Teun van Dijk (ed.) *Discourse and Communication: new approach to the analysis of mass media discourse and communication*. Walter de Gruyter: Berlin, 233–69.

Hasan, R. (1984) The Nursey Tale as Genre. In *Nottingham Linguistic Circular*, 13.

Hasan, R. (in press a) Situation and the definition of genres. In A. D. Grimshaw (ed.) *Perspectives on Discourse: Multi-Disciplinary Study of a Naturally Occurring Conversation* (tentative title). Norwood, NJ: Ablex.

Hasan, R. (in press b) Questions as a mode of learning in everyday talk. In M. McCausland and Thao Lee (eds) *Proceedings of the Second International Conference of Language Education: Interaction and Development*, Ho Chi Minh City, Vietnam 30 March–1 April 1991. To be published by the University of Tasmania at Launceston.

Hayano, D. (1980) Communication competency among poker players. *Journal of Communication*, 30, 113–20.

Hayes, J. (1981) Lesbians, gay men and their 'languages'. In Chesebro, J. (ed.) *Gayspeak: Gay Male and Lesbian Communication*. New York, NY: Pilgrim Press.

Hazeltine, H. D. (1986) [1930]. General Preface. *Anglo-Saxon Wills*. D. Whitelock (ed.). Holmes Beach, Florida: William W. Gaunt & Sons (Originally published 1930, Cambridge University Press.)

Hazlehurst, K. (ed.) (1987) *Ivory Scales: Black Australia and the Law*. Sydney: New South Wales University Press.

Henley, N. M. (1977) *Body Politics: Power, Sex and Nonverbal Communication*. New York, NY: Simon & Schuster.

Herden, G. (1965) [A contribution to a] Discussion on the Paper by Mr Morton. *Journal of the Royal Statistical Society*, Ser. A, 128, 229–31.

Herrnstein-Smith, B. (1968) *Poetic Closure: a Study of How Poems End*. Chicago: University of Chicago Press.

Hetzron, R. (1976) On the Hungarian causative verb and its syntax. In M. Shibatani (ed.) *The Grammar of Causative Constructions. Syntax and Semantics Vol. 6*. New York: Academic Press, pp. 371–98.

Hill, R. (1957) The theory and practice of excommunication in medieval England. *History*, 42, 1–11.

Hill vs. O'Bannon. 554 F. Sup. 190 (E.D. Pa. 1982). St Paul, MN: West Publishing Co.

Hilton, M. L. and Holmes, D. I. (1993) An assessment of cumulative sum charts for authorship attribution. *Literary and Linguistic Computing*, 8, 73–80.

Hjelmquist, E. (1984) Memory for conversations, *Discourse Processes*, 7, 321–36.

Hocking, J. D. (1976) Detecting deceptive communication from verbal, visual, and parlinguistic cues: an exploratory experiment. Unpublished PhD, Michigan State University, E. Lansing.

Hodge, R. and Kress, G. (1988) *Social Semiotics*. Oxford: Polity Press.

Hollien, H. (1990) *The Acoustics of Crime*. London: Plenum.

Horton, R. (1967) African traditional thought and western science. *Africa*, 37, 50–71, 155–87.

Houts, M. (1981) Presenting medical evidence. *Personal Injury Annals*, 368–84.

Howell, P. P. (1954) *A Manual of Nuer Law*. Oxford: Oxford University Press.

Human Rights and Equal Opportunity Commission (1991) *Racist Violence: Report of the National Inquiry into Racist Violence in Australia*. Canberra: Australian Government Publishing Service.

Hurford, J. and Heasley, B. (1983) *Semantics: a Coursebook*. Cambridge: Cambridge University Press.

Hurst, W. (1982) *Dealing with Statutes*. New York, NY: Columbia University Press.

Ibik, J. O. (1969) The customary law of wrongs and injuries in Malawi. In M. Gluckman (ed.) *Ideas and Procedures in African Customary Law*. Oxford: Oxford University Press, pp. 305–17.

ICAC (1990) *Report on Investigation into Harassing Telephone Calls Made to Edgar Azzopardi*. Sydney: Independent Commission Against Corruption.

Jackson, B. (1988a) Narrative models in legal proof. *International Journal for the Semiotics of Law*, 1, 3, 226–46.

Jackson, B. (1988b) *Law, Fact and Narrative Coherence*. Roby, UK: Deborah Charles Publications.

Jackson, B. S. (1985) *Semiotics and Legal Theory*. London: Routledge & Kegan Paul.

Johnson, P. F. (1974) The use of statistics in the analysis of the characteristics of Pauline writing. *New Testament Studies*, 20, 92–100.

Just, P. (1990) Dead goats and broken betrothals: liability and equity in Dou Donggo law, *American Ethnologist*, 17, 1, 75–90.

Kaldor, S. and Malcolm, I. (1982) Aboriginal English in country and remote areas: A Western Australian perspective. In R. Eagleson, S. Kaldor and I. Malcolm (eds) *English and the Aboriginal Child*. Canberra: Curriculum Development Centre, pp. 75–162.

Kaldor, S. and Malcolm, I. (1991) Aboriginal English – an overview. In S. Romaine (ed.) *Language in Australia*. Cambridge: Cambridge University Press, pp. 67–83.

Kaufman, M. (1983) Video in the courtroom. *California Lawyer*, October, 42, 41–43.

Keen, I. (1978) One ceremony, one song: an economy of religious knowledge among the Yolngu of North-East Arnhem land. Unpublished PhD thesis, Australian National University.

Keen, I. (ed.) (1988) *Being Black: Aboriginal Cultures in 'Settled' Australia*. Canberra: Aboriginal Studies Press.

Kelman, M. (1987) *A Guide to Critical Legal Studies*. Cambridge, MA: Harvard University Press.

Kelsen, H. (1945) *General Theory of Law and the State*. New York, NY: Russell and Russell.

Kenny, A. (1986) *A Stylometric Study of the New Testament*. Oxford University Press.

Key, M. R. (1975) *Paralanguage and Kinesics*. Metuchen, NJ: Scarecrow Press.

Keynes, S. (1980) *The Diplomas of King Æthelred 'The Unready', 978–1016: A Study in Their Use as Historical Evidence*. Cambridge: Cambridge University Press.

Keynes, S. and M. Lapidge (eds) (1987) *Alfred the Great: Asser's Life of King Alfred and Other Contemporary Sources*. Harmondsworth: Penguin.

Kieckhefer, R. (1990) *Magic in the Middle Ages*. Cambridge. Cambridge University Press.

Kiralfy, A. K. R. (ed.) (1958) *Potter's Historical Introduction to English Law*. 4th edn. London: Sweet & Maxwell.

Kitto, F. (1975) 'Why Write Judgments?' *Judicial Essays*. Sydney and Melbourne: Law Foundation of New South Wales and Victorian Law Foundation.

Knapp, M. K. (1980) *Essentials of Nonverbal Communication*. New York, NY: Holt, Rinehart & Winston.

Knapp, M., Hart, S. and Dennis, H. (1975) An exploration of deception as a communication construct. *Human Communication Research*, 1, 15–29.

Knerr, C. What to do before and after a subpoena of data arrives. In J. E. Sieber (ed.) *The Ethics of Social Research*. New York, NY: Springer-Verlag.

Koch, H. (1985) Nonstandard English in an Aboriginal land claim. In J. B. Pride (ed.) *Cross-cultural Encounters: Communication and Miscommunication*. Melbourne: River Seine, pp. 176–95.

Koch, H. (1991) Language and communication in Aboriginal land claim hearings. In S. Romaine (ed.) *Language in Australia*. Cambridge: Cambridge University Press, 94–103.

Koch, K. F. (1974) *War and Peace in Jalémo*. Cambridge, Mass.: Harvard University Press.

Koch, K. F. (1984) Liability and social structure. In D. Black (ed.) *Toward a General Theory of Social Control, Vol. 1: Fundamentals*. Orlando: Academic Press, pp. 95–129.

Kochman, T. (1981) *Black and White Styles in Conflict*. Chicago, IL: The University of Chicago Press.

Koskenniemi, I. (1968) *Repetitive Word Pairs in Old and Early Middle English Prose*. Turku: Turun Yliopisto.

Kramer, S. N. (1956) *From the Tablets of Sumer: Twenty-five Firsts in Man's Recorded History*. Indian Springs, CO: The Falcon's Wing Press.

Kress, G. (1985) Ideological structures in discourse. In T. Van Dijk (ed.) *Handbook of Discourse Analysis, Vol. 4*. London: Academic Press, pp. 27–42.

Kress, G. and Hodge, R. (1979) *Language as Ideology*. London: Routledge & Kegan Paul.

Kriewaldt, Justice M. (1960) The application of criminal law to the Aborigines of the Northern Territory of Australia. *University of Western Australia Law Review*, 5, 1–50.

Kroch, A. (1972) Lexical and inferred meanings for some time adverbs. *Quarterly progress report of the Research Laboratory of Electronics of MIT*, 104, 19, 19–23.

Kroch, A. (1979) *The Semantics of Scope in English*. New York, NY: Garland.

Kurath, H., Kurath, R. and McDavid, I. (1961) *The Pronunciation of English in the Atlantic States*. Ann Arbor, Mich.: University of Michigan Press.

Kurzon, D. (1984) Themes, hyperthemes and the discourse structure of British legal texts. *Text*, 4, 1–3, 31–56.

Kurzon, D. (1986) *It is Hereby Performed: Explorations in Legal Speech Acts*. Philadelphia, PA: John Benjamins.

Kurzon, D. (1985) How lawyers tell their tales: narrative aspects of a lawyer's brief. *Poetics*, 14, 467–81.

Kurzon, D. (1990) Silence in the legal process. Paper delivered at the Onati Workshop on the Semiotics and Sociology of Law, Onati, Spain.

Labov, W. (1972) *Sociolinguistic Patterns*. Philadelphia, PA: University of Pennsylvania Press.

Labov, W. (1988) The judicial testing of linguistic theory. In Deborah Tannen (ed.) *Linguistics in Context: Connecting Observation and Understanding*. Norwood, NJ: Ablex, 159–182.

Labov, W. (forthcoming) The three dialects of English. In P. Eckert (ed.) *Quantitative Analyses of Sound Change*. New York, NY: Academic Press.

Labov, W. and Fanshel, D. (1977) *Therapeutic Discourse*. New York, NY: Academic Press.

Ladefoged, P. (1982) *A Course in Phonetics*. New York, NY: Harcourt Brace Jovanovich.

Lake, D. J. (1975) *The Canon of Thomas Middleton's Plays*. London: Cambridge University Press.

Landtman, G. (1927) *The Kiwai Papuans*. London: Macmillan.

Langton, M. (1988) Medicine square. In I. Keen (1988) pp. 210–26.

Laster, K. (1990) Legal interpreters: conduits to social justice. *Journal of Intercultural Studies*, 11, 2, 15–32.

Laver, J. (1980) *The Phonetic Description of Voice Quality*. Cambridge: Cambridge University Press.

Law Reform Commission of Victoria (1987) *Plain English and the Law. Report No. 9*. Melbourne: F. D. Atkinson Government Printer.

Lester, J. (1973) *Aborigines and the Courts*. Alice Springs: Institute for Aboriginal Development.

Levi, E. (1949) *An Introduction to Legal Reasoning*. Chicago, IL: University of Chicago Press.

Lévy-Bruhl, L. (1923) *Primitive Mentality*, L. A. Clare (trans). London: George Allen & Unwin.

Lewis, B. and Pucelik, F. (1982) *Magic Demystified*. Lake Oswego, OR: Metamorphous Press.

Liberman, K. (1978) Problems of communication in Western Desert courtrooms. *Legal Service Bulletin*, 3, 94–6.

Liberman, K. (1981) Understanding Aborigines in Australian courts of law, *Human Organization*, 40, 247–55.

Liberman, K. (1985) *Understanding Interaction in Central Australia: An Ethnomethodological Study of Australian Aboriginal People*. Boston: Routledge & Kegan Paul.

Light, R. Y., Richard, D. P. and Bell, P. (1978) Development of children's attitudes towards speakers of standard and non-standard English. *Child Study Journal*, 8, 253–65.

Linn, M. C., de Benedictis, T., Delucchi, K., Harris, A. and Stage, E. (1987) Gender differences in national assessment of educational progress science items: what does 'I don't know' really mean, *Journal of Research in Science Teaching*, 24, 3, 267–78.

Logan, F. D. (1984) Excommunication. In J. R. Strayer (ed.) *Dictionary of the Middle Ages, Vol. 4*. New York, NY: Scribners, pp. 536–38.

Lyons, G. (1984) Aboriginal legal services. In P. Hanks and B. Keon-Cohen (eds) *Aborigines and the Law*. Sydney: George Allen and Unwin, pp. 137–59.

Lyons, J. (1977) *Semantics*. London: Cambridge University Press.

MacCormick, N. (1990) Reconstruction after deconstruction: a response to critical legal studies, *Oxford Journal of Legal Studies*, 10, 4, 539–58.

Maher, F. K. H., Waller, P. L. and Derham, D. P. (1971) *Cases and Materials on the Legal Process*. Sydney: Law Book Company.

Maine, H. [1861] (1972) *Ancient Law*. London: Everyman.

Maley, Y. (1985a) The semantic field of homicide. In J. Benson and W. Greaves (eds) *Advances in Discourse Processes XVI*. New Jersey: Ablex, pp. 152–68.

Maley, Y. (1985b) Judicial discourse: the case of the legal judgment. In J. E. Clark (ed.) *The Cultivated Australian: Festschrift for Arthur Delbridge*. Hamburg: Helmut Buske Verlag, pp. 159–73.

Maley, Y. (1987) The language of legislation. *Language and Society*, 16, 25–48.

Maley, Y. (1989) Interpersonal meanings in judicial discourse. In *Occasional Papers in Systemic Linguistics, Vol. 3*. Nottingham: University of Nottingham, pp. 69–89.

Maley, Y. and Fahey, R. (1991) Presenting the evidence: constructions of reality in court. *International Journal for the Semiotics of Law*, IV, 10.

Mann, V. A. and Repp, B. H. (1980) Influence of vocalic context on perception of the [ʃ]-[s] distinction. *Perception and Psychophysics*, 28, 213–28.

Marlboro Products Corp. v. *North Amer. Phillips Corp.*, 55 FRD 487, 488 (SDNY 1972).

Martin, J. R. (1992) *English Text: System and Structure*. Amsterdam: John Benjamins.

Martin, J. R. (1986) Grammaticalising ecology: the politics of baby seals and kangaroos. In Threadgold, T., Grosz, E. A., Kress, G. and Halliday, M. A. K. (eds) *Semiotics, Ideology, Language*. Sydney: Sydney Association for Studies in Society and Culture.

Matthews, R. (1993) Harsh words for verbal fingerprints. The Sunday Telegraph, July 4.

Matisoff, J. A. (1976) Lahu causative constructions. In M. Shibatani (ed.) *The Grammar of Causative Constructions. Syntax and Semantics, Vol. 6* . New York, NY: Academic Press, pp. 413–42.

Matlon, R. (1988) *Communication in the Legal Process*. New York, NY: Holt, Rinehart & Winston.

Maurice, Justice M. (1988) *Warumungu Land Claim. Report by the Aboriginal Land Commissioner*. Darwin: Office of the Aboriginal Land Commissioner.

Maynard, D. (1984) *Inside Plea Bargaining: the Language of Negotiation*. New York: Plenum.

McClintock, C. and Hunt, R. (1975) Nonverbal indicators of affect and deception in an interview setting. *Journal of Applied Social Psychology*, 5, 54–67.

McCorquodale, J. (1987) Judicial racism in Australia: Aboriginals in civil and criminal cases. In K. Hazlehurst (ed.) *Ivory Scales: Black Australia and the Law*. Sydney: New South Wales University Press, 30–59.

McElhaney, J. (1988) Presenting depositions: how to make transcripts and videos come alive. *American Bar Association Journal*, July, 84–5.

McFarlane, K., Waterman, J., Conerley, S., Damon, L., Durfee, M. and Long, S. (1986) *Sexual Abuse of Young Children*. New York, NY: Guildford Press.

McGeehee, F. (1937) The reliability of the identification of the human voice. *Journal of General Psychology*, 17, 249–71.

McGeehee, F. (1944) An experimental study of voice recognition. *Journal of General Psychology*, 31, 53–65.

McKay, G. (1985) Language issues in training programs for Northern Territory police: a linguist's view. *Australian Review of Applied Linguistics*, Series S, no. 2, 32–43.

McKeown, F. (1985) Anthropology, ethics and the law: a recent development. *Australian Anthropological Society Newsletter*, 27 June, 6–7.

McKitterick, R. (1989) *The Carolingians and the Written Word*. Cambridge: Cambridge University Press.

Mehrabian, A. (1972) *Nonverbal Communication*. Chicago, IL: Aldine.

Mehrabian, A. (1971) *Silent Messages*. Belmont, CA: Wadsworth.

Mellinkoff, D. (1963) *The Language of the Law*. Boston, MA: Little, Brown.

Mewett, P. (1985) Professional privilege, a matter of concern to all anthropologists. *Australian Anthropological Society Newsletter*, 27 8–10.

Michaels, E. (1985) Constraints on knowledge in an economy of oral information. *Current Anthropology*, 26, 4, 505–10.

Michaelson, S., Morton, A. Q. and Hamilton-Smith, N. (1978a) *To Couple is the Custom*. Edinburgh: Department of Computer Science, University of Edinburgh.

Michaelson, S., Morton, A. Q. and Hamilton-Smith, N. (1978b) *Justice for Helander*. Edinburgh: Department of Computer Science, University of Edinburgh.

Miller, G. and Boster, F. (1977) Three images of the trial: their implication for psychological research. In B. Sales (ed.) *Psychology in the Legal Process*. New York, NY: Spectrum, pp. 19–38.

Miller, G. and Burgoon, M. (1982) Factors affecting assessments of witness credibility. In N. Kerr and R. Bray (eds) *The Psychology of the Courtroom*. New York, NY: Academic Press.

Miller, G. and Fontes, N. (1978) Real versus reel: What's the verdict? The effects of videotaped court materials on juror response. NSF Report. Department of Communication, Michigan State University.

Millett, T. (1989) Rules of interpretation of E.E.C. legislation, *Statute Law Review*, 10, 3, 163–82.

Milroy, L. (1980) *Language and Social Networks*. Oxford: Basil Blackwell.

Mitchell, A. G. and Delbridge, A. (1965) *The Speech of Australian Adolescents*. Sydney: Angus & Robertson.

Mitchell, J. C. (1966) The meaning of misfortune for urban Africans. In M. Fortes and G. Dieterlen (eds) *African Systems of Thought*. Oxford: Oxford University Press, pp. 192–302.

Moore, S. F. (1969) Introduction. In L. Nader (ed.) *Law in Culture and Society*. Chicago, IL: Aldine, pp. 337–48.

Moore, S. F. (1972) Legal liability and evolutionary interpretation: some aspects of strict liability, self-help and collective responsibility. In M. Gluckman (ed.) *The Allocation of Responsibility*. Manchester: Manchester University Press, pp. 51–107.

Morris, D. (1977) *Manwatching: A Field Guide to Human Behavior*. New York, NY: H. N. Abrams.

Morris, H. (1973) Legal responsibility. In P. Wiener (ed.) *Dictionary of the History of Ideas, Vol. 3*. New York, NY: Scribner's, pp. 33–6.

Morton, A. Q. (1978) *Literary Detection – How to Prove Authorship and Fraud in Literature*. New York, NY: Scribner's.

Morton, A. Q. (1986) Once. A test of authorship based on words which are not repeated in the sample. *Literary and Linguistic Computing*, 1, 1–8.

Morton, A. Q. (1991) The scientific testing of utterances: cumulative sum analysis. *Journal of the Law Society of Scotland*, 357–9.

Morton, A. Q. and Michaelson, S. (1984) The nature of stylometry. Technical report prepared for 'Stylometrics '84': Department of Computer Science, Edinburgh University.

Mosteller, F. and Wallace, D. L. (1964) *Inference and Disputed Authorship: the Federalist*. Reading, MA: Addison-Wesley.

Mugerwa, P. J. N. (1969) Status, responsibility and liability: a comparative study of two types of society in Uganda. In M. Gluckman (ed.) *Ideas and Procedures in African Customary Law*. Oxford: Oxford University Press, pp. 279–91.

Mullin, C. (1990) *Error of Judgement* 3rd edn. London: Chatto and Windus.

Napier, A. S. and Stevenson, W. H. (1894) *The Crawford Collection of Early Charters and Documents. Anecdotia Oxoniensia.* Medieval and Modern Series No. 7. Oxford: Oxford University Press.

Nash, D. (1979) Foreigners in their own land. *Legal Service Bulletin*, 4, 105–7.

Nash, D. (1984) Linguistics and land rights in the Northern Territory. In G. R. McKay and B. A. Sommer (eds) *Further Applications of Linguistics to Australian Aboriginal Contexts.* Melbourne: Applied Linguistics Association of Australia. Occasional Papers, No. 8, pp. 34–46.

Nash, D. (1987) Warumungu land claim: subpoena of field notes. *The Australian Linguistics Society Newsletter*, 87, 2, 5.

Neate, G. (1981) Legal language across cultures: finding the traditional Aboriginal owners of land. *Federal Law Review*, 12, 187–211.

Neate, G. (1989) *Aboriginal Land Rights Law in the Northern Territory.* Chippendale, NSW: Alternative Publishing Co-operative.

Negev, Eilat (1990) Now video wills. *Yediot Ahronot*, January 12, pp. 30–31 (Hebrew).

Nolan, F. (1983) *The Phonetic Bases of Speaker Recognition.* Cambridge: Cambridge University Press.

Nolan, F. (1990) The limitations of auditory-phonetic speaker identification. In H. Kniffka (ed.) *Texte zu Theorie und Praxis forensischer Linguistik.* Tübingen: Niemeyer.

Nolan, F. (1991) Forensic phonetics. *Journal of Linguistics* 27, 483–93.

O'Barr, W. M. (1982) *Linguistic Evidence: Language, Power and Strategy in the Courtroom.* New York, NY: Academic Press.

O'Brien, D. P. and Darnell, A. C. (1982) *Authorship Puzzles in the History of Economics: A Statistical Approach.* London: Macmillan.

Ochs, E. (1988) *Culture and Language Development.* New York, NY: Cambridge University Press.

O'Connor, J. D. (1973) *Phonetics.* Harmondsworth: Penguin.

Ong, W. J. (1971) Oral Residue in Tudor Prose Style. *PMLA* 80: 145–54.

Ong, W. J. (1982) *Orality and Literacy: the Technologizing of the Word.* London: Methuen.

Ordway, D. P. (1983) Reforming judicial procedures for handling parent child incest – A special report. *Child Welfare*, LXII, 1, 69–75.

Parise, F. (ed.) (1982) *The Book of Calendars.* New York: Facts on File.

Parker, D. (1987) The administration of justice and its penal consequences. In K. Hazlehurst (ed.) *Ivory Scales: Black Australia and the Law.* Sydney: New South Wales University Press, pp. 136–52.

Payne, A. (1980) Factors controlling the acquisition of the Philadelphia dialect by out-of-state children. In W. Labov (ed.) *Locating Language in Time and Space.* New York, NY: Academic Press, pp. 143–78.

Pearce, D. C. (1974) *Statutory Interpretation in Australia.* Sydney: Butterworths.

Penman, R. (1987) Discourse in courts: cooperation, coercion and coherence. *Discourse Processes*, 10, 201–18.

Penman, R. (in press) Goals, games and moral orders: A paradoxical case in court? In K. Tracey (ed.) *Goals and Discourse*. Hillsdale, NJ: Lawrence Erlbaum.

Philips, S. U. (1976) Some sources of cultural variability in the regulation of talk. *Language in Society*, 5, 81–95.

Philips, S. U. (1984) The social organisation of questions and answers in courtroom discourse, *Text*, 4, 1–3, 228–48.

Philips, S. U. (1985) Strategies of clarification in judges' use of language: from the written to the spoken. *Discourse Processes*, 8, 421–36.

Piaget, J. (1926) *The Language and Thought of the Child*. London: Routledge & Kegan Paul.

Piaget, J. (1932) *The Moral Judgement of the Child*. London: Routledge & Kegan Paul.

Plank, F. (1979) Ergativity, syntactic typology and universal grammar: some past and present viewpoints. In F. Plank (ed.) *Ergativity*. New York, NY: Academic Press, pp. 3–36.

Pollock, F. (1969) Fiction theory of corporations. In *Essays in the Law*. Hamden, CT: Archon Books.

Quirk, R., Greenbaum, Sidney, Leech, G. and Svartvik, J. (1972) *A Grammar of Contemporary English*. London: Longman.

Rao, M. and Bashir, E. (1985) On the semantics and pragmatics of Telegu causatives. In W. H. Eilfort, P. D. Kroeber and K. L. Peterson (eds) *Causatives and Agentivity*. Papers from the parasession on causatives and agentivity, Vol. 21, Part 2. Chicago, IL: Chicago Linguistic Society, pp. 228–40.

Rasmussen, S. (1989) Accounting for belief: causation, misfortune and evil in Tuareg systems of thought. *Man*, 24, 124–44.

Redish, J. C. (1985) The Plain Language Movement. In S. Greenbaum (ed.) *The English Language Today: Public Attitudes toward the English Language*, 125–38. New York: Pergamon.

Renton, D. (1975) *The Preparation of Legislation: Report of a Committee Appointed by the Lord President of Council*. London: HMSO.

Repp, B. (1982) Phonetic trading relations and context effects: new experimental evidence for a speech mode of perception. *Psychological Bulletin*, 92, 81–110.

Reyburn, B. (1990) A message to the leaders of our profession. Poster session at the Australian Anthropological Society meeting, 1990. Unpublished ms, Tennant Creek.

Roberts, M. (1987) *Trial Psychology: Communication and Persuasion in the Courtroom*. Austin, TX: Butterworth Legal Publishers.

Robertson, A. J. (ed.) (1956) *Anglo-Saxon Charters*. Cambridge: Cambridge University Press. Original edition, 1939.

Roberts-Smith, L. W. (1989) Communication breakdown. *Law Society Bulletin*, 14, 2.

Rosen, L. (1977) The anthropologist as expert witness. *American Anthropologist*, 79, 3, 555–78.

Ross, A. (1968) *Directives and Norms*. London: Routledge & Kegan Paul.

Rouse, R. H. and Rouse, M. A. (1989) Wax Tablets. *Language and Communication*, 9, 2/3: 175–91.

Roxburghe Club (1968) *The Will of Æthelgifu: a Tenth Century Anglo-Saxon Manuscript*, (trans., ed.) Dorothy Whitelock. Oxford: Roxburghe Club.

Royal Commission into Aboriginal Deaths in Custody (RCADC) (1988) *Interim Report*. Canberra: Australian Government Publishing Service.

Royal Commission into Aboriginal Deaths in Custody (1991) *National Report*. Canberra: Australian Government Publishing Service.

Ryan, D. (1961) *Gift Exchange in the Mendi Valley*. Unpublished PhD Thesis, University of Sydney.

Ryle, G. (1949) *The Concept of Mind*. Harmondsworth: Penguin.

Rypinski, I. (1982) Videotaping depositions. *Hawaii Bar Journal*, 17, 67–76.

Sambur, M. R. (1976) Speaker recognition using orthogonal linear prediction. *IEEE Transactions on Acoustics Speech and Signal Processing*, 24, 4, 283–9.

Sansom, B. (1980) *The Camp at Wallaby Cross: Aboriginal Fringe-dwellers in Darwin*. Canberra: Australian Institute of Aboriginal Studies.

Schapera, I. (1970) *A Handbook of Tswana Law and Custom*. London: Frank Cass.

Schieffelin, B. (1990) *The Give and Take of Everyday Life. Language Socialisation of Kaluli Children*. New York, NY: Cambridge University Press.

Schieffelin, E. L. (1976) *The Sorrow of the Lonely and the Burning of the Dancers*. St Lucia: Queensland University Press.

Scollon, R. and Scollon, S. (1981) *Narrative, Literacy and Face in Interethnic Communication*. Norwood, NJ: Ablex.

Searle, J. R. (1969) *Speech Acts: An Essay in the Philosophy of Language*. Cambridge: Cambridge University Press.

Searle, J. R. (1979) *Expression and Meaning*. Cambridge: Cambridge University Press.

Sebastian, R. J. and Ryan, E. B. (1985) Speech cues and social evaluation: Markers of ethnicity, social class and age. In H. Giles and R. N. St Clair (eds) *Recent Advances in Language, Communication, and Social Psychology*. London: L. Erlbaum.

Shavell, S. (1987) *Economic Analysis of Accident Law*. Cambridge, MA: Harvard University Press.

Sheehan, M. M. (1963) *The Will in Medieval England*. Rome: Pontifical Institute of Mediaeval Studies.

Shibatani, M. (1976) The grammar of causative constructions: a conspectus. In M. Shibatani (ed.) *The Grammar of Causative Constructions. Syntax and Semantics Vol. 6.* New York, NY: Academic Press, pp. 1–40.

Shibatani, M. (1973) The semantics of Japanese causativisation, *Foundations of Language*, 9, 327–73.

Shirt, M. (1984) An auditory speaker recognition experiment, *Proceedings of the Institute of Acoustics*, 6, 1, 101–4.

Shuy, R. (1986) Language and the law. In *Annual Review of Applied Linguistics*. Cambridge: Cambridge University Press, pp. 50–63.

Sillitoe, P. (1979) *Give and Take: Exchange in Wola Society*. Canberra: Australian National University Press.

Sillitoe, P. (1981) Some more on war: a Wola perspective. In R. Scaglion (ed.) *Homicide Compensation in New Guinea*, Papua New Guinea Law Reform Commission: Monograph No. 1, pp. 70–81.

Simonds, A. P. (1989) Ideological domination and the political information market. *Theory and Society*, 18, 2, 181–211.

Simpson, J. and Nash, D. (1987) Warumungu land claim. *The Australian Linguistics Society Newsletter*, 87, 3, 6.

Smith, L. and Malandro, L. (1985) *Courtroom Communication Strategies*. New York, NY: Kluwer Law.

Smith, M. W. A. (1982a) A stylometric analysis of *Hero and Leander*. *The Bard*, 3, 105–32.

Smith, M. W. A. (1982b) The authorship of *Pericles*: an initial investigation. *The Bard*, 3, 143–76.

Smith, M. W. A. (1983a) The authorship of *Pericles*: collocations investigated again. *The Bard*, 4, 15–21.

Smith, M. W. A. (1983b) Stylometry: the detection of literary authorship, *Computer Bulletin*, ser. II, 35, 8–9, 11.

Smith, M. W. A. (1984) Critical reflections on the determination of authorship by statistics (Parts I and II). *The Shakespeare Newsletter*, 34, (1984).

Smith, M. W. A. (1985) An investigation of the basis of Morton's method for the determination of authorship. *Style*, 19, 341–68.

Smith, M. W. A. (1987a) *The Revenger's Tragedy*: the derivation and interpretation of statistical results for resolving disputed authorship. *Computers and the Humanities*, 21, 1, 21–55 and 267.

Smith, M. W. A. (1987b) Hapax legomena in prescribed positions: an investigation of recent proposals to resolve problems of authorship. *Literary and Linguistic Computing*, 2, 145–52.

Smith, M. W. A. (1989a) Forensic stylometry: a theoretical basis for further developments of practical methods. *Journal of the Forensic Science Society*, 29, 15–33.

Smith, M. W. A. (1989b) A procedure to determine authorship using pairs of consecutive words: more evidence for Wilkins' participation in *Pericles*. *Computers and the Humanities*, 23, 113–29.

Smith, M. W. A. (1991) The authorship of *Timon of Athens*. *Text: Transactions of the Society for Textual Scholarship* (USA), 5, 195–240.

Stiger, S. M. (1983) Review of *Authorship Puzzles*, *Journal of Economic History*, 43, 547–50.

Stock, B. (1983) *The Implications of Literacy*. Princeton: Cambridge University Press.

Stone, J. (1968) *Legal Systems and Lawyers' Reasonings*. Sydney: Maitland Publications.

Strathern, M. (1979) The self in self-decoration. *Oceania*, XLIX, 4, 241–57.

Street, C. (1987) *An Introduction to the Language and Culture of the Murrinh-Patha*. Darwin: Summer Institute of Linguistics.

Street, R. and Hopper, R. (1982) A model of speech style evaluation. In E. Ryan and H. Giles (eds) *Attitudes Towards Language Variation*. London: Edward Arnold, pp. 175–88.

Strehlow, T. G. (1936) Notes on native evidence and its value. *Oceania*, 6, 323–35.

von Sturmer, J. (1981) Talking with Aborigines, *Australian Institute of Aboriginal Studies Newsletter*, 15, 13–30.

von Sturmer, J. (1987) *Warumungu Land Claim. Report to the Aboriginal Land Commissioner by the Anthropological Consultant. (Exhibit 286)*. Darwin: Office of the Aboriginal Land Commissioner.

Summit, R. and Kryso, J. (1978) Sexual abuse of children: a clinical spectrum, *American Journal of Orthopsychiatry*, 48, 2, 237–51.

Sumner, C. (1979) *Reading Ideologies: an Investigation into Marxist Theory of Ideology and Law*. London: Academic Press.

Suplee, D. and Donaldson, D. (1988) *The Deposition Handbook: Strategies, Tactics and Mechanics*. Eau Claire, Wis: Professional Education Systems.

Svartvik, J. (1968) *The Evans Statement: a Case for Forensic Linguistics*. Gottenburg: Gottenburg Studies in English.

Swales, J. M. (1981a) *Aspects of Article Introductions*. Aston ESP Research Report No. 1. Birmingham: University of Aston in Birmingham.

Swales, J. M. (1981b) Definitions in science and law – evidence for subject-specific course component, *Fachsprache*, 3, 4.

Swales, J. M. and Bhatia, V. K. (1983) An approach to the linguistic study of legal documents. *Fachsprache*, 5, 3, 98–108.

Swanson, R. N. (1989) *Church and Society in Late Medieval England*. Oxford: Basil Blackwell.

Tabuteau, E. Z. (1988) *Transfers of Property in Eleventh-Century Norman Law*. Chapel Hill and London: University of North Carolina Press.

Tannen, D. (ed.) (1982) *Spoken and Written Language: Exploring Orality and Literacy*. Norwood, NJ: Ablex.

Taylor, K., Buchanan, R. and Strawn, D. (1984) *Communication Strategies for Trial Attorneys*. Glenview, IL: Scott, Foresman.

Thomas, K. (1971) *Religion and the Decline of Magic: Studies in Popular Beliefs in Sixteenth and Seventeenth Century England*. London: Weidenfeld and Nicholson.

Thomas, R. (1989) *Oral Tradition and Written Record in Classical Athens*. Cambridge: Cambridge University Press.

Thompson, John B. (1984) *Studies in the Theory of Ideology*. Oxford: Polity Press.

Tosi, O. (1979) *Voice Identification: Theory and Legal Applications*. Baltimore, MD: University Park Press.

Totty, R. N., Hardcastle, R. A. and Pearson, J. (1987) Forensic linguistics: the determination of authorship from habits of style. *Journal of the Forensic Science Society*, 27, 13–28.

Trew, T. (1979) 'What the papers say': linguistic variation and ideological difference. In R. Fowler, R. Hodge, G. Kress and T. Trew *Language and Control*. London: Routledge & Kegan Paul, pp. 117–56.

Turner, V. W. (1964) Lunda medicine and the treatment of disease. *Rhodes Livingstone Occasional Paper*, No. 15. Lusaka: Government Printer.

Valdes, G. (1986) Analysing the demands that courtroom interaction makes upon speakers of ordinary English: toward the development of a coherent descriptive framework, *Discourse Processes*, 9, 269–303.

Van den Broek, J. (1977) Class differences in syntactic complexity in the Flemish town of Maaseik, *Language in Society*, 6, 149–82.

Van Dijk, T. (ed.) (1985) *Discourse and Communication*. Berlin: Walter de Gruyter.

Van Dijk, T. (1977) *Text and Context*. London: Longman.

Victoria Police and Australian Bicentennial Multicultural Foundation (1991) *Police Services in a Multicultural Australia*, Conference Report. Melbourne: Unpublished manuscript.

Vodola, E. (1986) *Excommunication in the Middle Ages*. Berkeley: University of California Press.

Walsh, M. (1991) Conversational styles and intercultural communication: an example from Northern Australia, *Australian Journal of Communication*, 18, 1, 1–12.

Walsh, M. (forthcoming) Language socialization at Wadeye. In J. Williams (ed.) *Ethnographic Approaches to Language Contact*. Cambridge: Cambridge University Press.

Wetter, J. G. (1960) *The Styles of Appellate Judicial Opinions: A Case Study in Comparative Law*. Leyden: A. W. Sythoff.

White, J. B. (1985) *Heracles Bow. Essays on the Rhetoric and Poetics of the Law*. Wisconsin: University of Wisconsin Press.

Whitelock, D. (ed.) (1979) *English Historical Documents, Vol. 1*. London: Oxford University Press, pp. 500–1042.

Whitelock, D. (ed.) (1986) *Anglo-Saxon Wills*. Holmes Beach, FL: William Gaunt & Sons. (Originally published by Cambridge University Press, 1930.)

Whitney, T. (1988) Seeing is believing: the advent of video, *Maricopa County Lawyer*, July, 7.

Wiegman, A. (1985) Expressive correlates of affective states and traits. In A. Siegman and S. Feldstein (eds) *Multichannel Integrations of Nonverbal Behavior*. Hillsdale, NJ: L. Erlbaum Associates, pp. 37–68.

Winfield, P. H. (1926) The myth of absolute liability. *Law Quarterly Review*, clxv, 37–51.

Wodak, R. (1985) The interaction between judge and defendant. In Teun A. Van Dijk (ed.) *Handbook of Discourse Analysis Vol. 4*. London: Academic Press, pp. 181–92.

Wodak, R. (1989) *Language, Power and Ideology*. Amsterdam: John Benjamins.

Wodak-Engel, R. (1984) Determination of guilt: discourse in the courtroom. In C. Kramarae, M. Schulz and W. O'Barr (eds) *Language and Power*. Beverley Hills, CA: Sage.

Woodbury, H. (1984) The strategic use of questions in court, *Semiotica*, 48, 3, 4, 197–228.

Woolley, L. (1963) *The Beginnings of Civilization, Vol. 1, Part 2. History of Mankind: Cultural and Scientific Development*. London:

Wrenn, C. L. (1967) *A Study of Old English Literature*. London: Harrap.

von Wright, G. H. (1963) *Norm and Action*. London: Routledge & Kegan Paul.

Zerubavel, E. (1981) *Hidden Rhythms: Schedules and Calendars in Social Life*. Berkeley, CA: University of California Press.

Zuckerman, M. and Driver, R. (1985) Telling lies: verbal and nonverbal correlates of deception. In A. Siegman and S. Feldstein (eds) *Multichannel Integrations of Non-verbal Behavior*. Hillsdale, NJ: L. Erlbaum Associates, pp. 129–47.

Zunin, L. and Zunin, N. (1972) *Contact: The First Four Minutes*. New York, NY: Ballantine Books.

Index

story, forensic disputation as,
34–5, 37–41, 47, 81–2
stylometry, 321–2, 324, Ch. 16
swearing, *see* obscenities
syntax, 237, 281–2, 319, 320, 368
causatives, 87–90
discontinuities in, 147–9, 209
of legislative provisions, 140–9
systemic linguistics, 7, Ch. 1
passim, Ch. 5 *passim*

tape recordings, 287–99, 324
Teitelbaum, Judge H., 279, 282, 286
television, closed circuit, 307
termination notice, 267–77
testing
for bias, 284–6
for compensation, 196, 197,
200–5, 266–87
third party (in interviews and
examination), 251, 310
Thornfare Case, 266–77
time, *see also* dating
adverbials, 282–6
reference, 247–8, 282–6
tort, 23, Ch. 2
trading relations, 342
training, *see* education
trauma, psychological, 197
turn taking, 226, 236

uncertainty, 206–8
unclear expression, *see* clarity
US Steel Case, 277–87

verballing, 246, 364
video, 131–3, 135, Ch. 6, 258,
264 n8
visual identification/recognition,
440–1
vocabulary, 5, 6, 12, 22, 28, 41, 164,
167–8, 189–90, 214, 231, 319,
320
voice
identification/recognition,
109–12, 162, 190–1, Ch. 13–14,
440–2
print, 288, 290, 293, 321–2, 335–6,
350, 357–8, 442
quality, 331–2
voicing, phonetic, 342
volume of information, 209

Wadeye, Ch. 8 *passim*
waiver, 278–87, 433
Waramungu Land Claim, Ch. 18
wills, 5, 16, Ch. 3
witchcraft, 62–3
witnesses, 113–14, 175–6
women and the law, 197, 277–8, *see
also* gender
Woodward, Justice J., 437
word pairs, 377, 389–94

yes-no questions, 37, 199, 200,
206–8, 243, 246, 323

Ziff, Donald, 287